T0379277

A CRITICAL ASSESSMENT OF THE INTERGOVERNMENTAL PANEL ON CLIMATE CHANGE

The Intergovernmental Panel on Climate Change (IPCC) has become a hugely influential institution. It is the authoritative voice on the science on climate change, and an exemplar of an intergovernmental science–policy interface. This book introduces the IPCC as an institution, covering its origins, history, processes, participants, products and influence. Discussing its internal workings and operating principles, it shows how IPCC assessments are produced and how consensus is reached between scientific and policy experts from different institutions, countries and social groups. A variety of practices and discourses – epistemic, diplomatic, procedural, communicative – that make the institution function are critically assessed, allowing the reader to learn from its successes and failures. This volume is the go-to reference for researchers studying or active within the IPCC, as well as invaluable for students concerned with global environmental problems and climate governance. This title is also available as Open Access via Cambridge Core.

KARI DE PRYCK is a lecturer at the University of Geneva. She is interested in knowledge production on global environmental problems and has been studying the IPCC's internal workings since 2013.

MIKE HULME is a professor of human geography at the University of Cambridge. He has spent his career studying climate change. In 2007 he received a personal certificate from the Nobel Committee marking his 'significant contribution' to the work of the IPCC, which received a joint award of the Nobel Peace Prize that year. He is the author of *Why We Disagree About Climate Change* (Cambridge University Press, 2009).

A CRITICAL ASSESSMENT OF THE INTERGOVERNMENTAL PANEL ON CLIMATE CHANGE

Edited by

KARI DE PRYCK
University of Geneva

MIKE HULME
University of Cambridge

CAMBRIDGE
UNIVERSITY PRESS

Shaftesbury Road, Cambridge CB2 8EA, United Kingdom

One Liberty Plaza, 20th Floor, New York, NY 10006, USA

477 Williamstown Road, Port Melbourne, VIC 3207, Australia

314–321, 3rd Floor, Plot 3, Splendor Forum, Jasola District Centre, New Delhi – 110025, India

103 Penang Road, #05-06/07, Visioncrest Commercial, Singapore 238467

Cambridge University Press is part of Cambridge University Press & Assessment,
a department of the University of Cambridge.

We share the University's mission to contribute to society through the pursuit of
education, learning and research at the highest international levels of excellence.

www.cambridge.org
Information on this title: www.cambridge.org/9781316514276

DOI: 10.1017/9781009082099

First published 2023

A catalogue record for this publication is available from the British Library.

Library of Congress Cataloging-in-Publication Data
Names: Pryck, Kari de, 1988- editor. | Hulme, Mike, 1960- editor.
Title: A critical assessment of the Intergovernmental Panel on Climate Change / edited by Kari De Pryck, Mike Hulme.
Description: Cambridge, United Kingdom ; New York, NY : Cambridge University Press, 2022. |
Includes bibliographical references and index.
Identifiers: LCCN 2022022838 (print) | LCCN 2022022839 (ebook) | ISBN 9781316514276 (hardback) |
ISBN 9781009082099 (epub)
Subjects: LCSH: Intergovernmental Panel on Climate Change–Evaluation. | Environmental policy–International
cooperation. | Climate change mitigation–International cooperation. | Climatic changes–Government policy.
Classification: LCC JZ5009.5.U555 C75 2022 (print) | LCC JZ5009.5.U555 (ebook) | DDC 363.7/0526–dc23/eng/
20220701
LC record available at https://lccn.loc.gov/2022022838
LC ebook record available at https://lccn.loc.gov/2022022839

ISBN 978-1-316-51427-6 Hardback

Contents

Figures

Tables

Boxes

Contributors

Shinichiro Asayama is a senior researcher at the National Institute for Environmental Studies, Tsukuba, Japan. His research focuses on understanding the role of discourses, framings and narratives in shaping the public debates around climate change, especially about carbon removal and solar geoengineering technologies.

Silke Beck is Professor of Sociology of Science at the Technical University München, Germany. Her research focuses on the role of expertise in environmental politics. She is an internationally recognised expert in the field of global environmental assessments as well as evidence-based policymaking on climate change, biodiversity and sustainability. She is the co-leader of the Helmholtz Centre for Environmental Research (UFZ) Science-Policy Expert Group, which has contributed to a variety of practical attempts to integrate research insights into recent assessment activities, including the IPCC and IPBES.

Béatrice Cointe is a researcher in STS at the Centre for Sociology of Innovation (Mines Paris, PSL University, CNRS) in Paris, France. Her work explores the relations between knowledge, environmental concerns and the organisation of the economy. She is currently investigating the making of climate and energy scenarios, especially by Integrated Assessment Models, and how their use of economics frames the climate challenge.

Kari De Pryck is a lecturer at the Institute for Environmental Sciences, University of Geneva (UNIGE), Switzerland. Before joining the UNIGE, she worked at the University of Cambridge, the Institute for Advanced Sustainability Studies (IASS) in Potsdam and the Université Grenoble Alpes. She is interested in the production of international expert knowledge and has been studying the IPCC since 2013.

Dalee Sambo Dorough (Inuit-Alaska) is the International Chair of the Inuit Circumpolar Council, a non-governmental organisation that represents approximately 180,000 Inuit from Chukotka (Russia), Alaska, Canada and Greenland. She holds a PhD from the University of British Columbia, Faculty of Law (2002), and a Master of Arts in Law & Diplomacy from the Fletcher School at Tufts University (1991). She is also a senior scholar and special advisor on Arctic Indigenous Peoples at the University of Alaska Anchorage and presently the Arctic Region representative to the Facilitative Working Group, the newest constitutive body of the UNFCCC.

Navroz K. Dubash is a professor at the Centre for Policy Research, New Delhi, India, and an adjunct senior research fellow at the Lee Kuan Yew School of Public Policy, National University of Singapore. He has been actively engaged in global and national debates on climate change, air quality, energy and water as a researcher, policy advisor and activist for over 25 years. Dubash is a Coordinating Lead Author for the Sixth Assessment Report of the IPCC, the editor of *India in a Warming World* (Oxford University Press), 2019 and has worked to inform and advise Indian government policymaking on climate change, energy, and air and water policy over the last decade. In the early 1990s, he helped establish the global Climate Action Network as its first international coordinator.

Paul N. Edwards is Director of the Program in Science, Technology & Society at Stanford University and Professor of Information and History (Emeritus) at the University of Michigan, USA. His research centres on the history and politics of climate knowledge. He is the author of *A Vast Machine: Computer Models, Climate Data, and the Politics of Global Warming* (MIT Press, 2010); co-editor (with Clark Miller) of *Changing the Atmosphere: Expert Knowledge and Environmental Governance* (MIT Press, 2001); and academic editor (with Janet Vertesi) of the MIT Press book series *Infrastructures*.

Hélène Guillemot is a researcher at the Centre Alexandre Koyré (CNRS, EHESS) in Paris, France. Trained as a physicist, she worked as a scientific journalist before receiving a PhD with a thesis on the history of climate modelling in France. Her current research interests include, from an STS perspective, climate sciences, modelling practices, climate change expertise and the relation between climate science and politics.

Karin M. Gustafsson is an associate professor of sociology at the Environmental Sociology Section, School of Humanities, Educational and Social Sciences, Örebro University, Sweden. Her research is situated in the field of environmental sociology and STS. She is currently studying science's role in international environmental governance and the socialisation of early career researchers as experts in IPCC and IPBES.

Jordan Harold is a lecturer in psychology at the University of East Anglia, UK. Drawing on cognitive science, he researches how people interpret scientific evidence to help inform improved communication between scientists and society. He has worked in collaboration with the IPCC, authors and policymakers on the co-production of data visuals to several SPMs of the IPCC sixth assessment cycle.

Friederike Hartz is a PhD candidate in Geography at the University of Cambridge, UK, studying the IPCC and notions of responsibility at the science–policy interface. She has an interdisciplinary background in Political Science, International Relations and Environmental Sustainability Studies.

Hannah Hughes is a senior lecturer in international politics and climate change at the Department of International Politics, Aberystwyth University, Wales. Her work explores the relationship between knowledge, power and social order in the response to climate change and global environmental degradation.

Mike Hulme is a professor of human geography in the Department of Geography at the University of Cambridge, UK. His work sits at the intersection of climate, history and culture, studying how knowledge about climate and its changes is made, represented and used in public discourse around the world. He was awarded a personal certificate from the Nobel Committee for his 'significant contribution' to the work of the IPCC, which received the joint award of the 2007 Nobel Peace Prize. He is the author of ten books on climate change, including *Why We Disagree About Climate Change* (Cambridge, 2009).

Bård Lahn is a researcher at CICERO Centre for International Climate Research, Oslo, Norway, and a doctoral candidate in STS at the University of Oslo's TIK Centre for Technology, Innovation and Culture. His work focuses on the role of scientific knowledge in climate politics, in particular in controversies about North–South justice and fossil fuel extraction.

Olivier Leclerc is a CNRS senior researcher at the Centre de Théorie et Analyse du Droit (UMR 7074 CTAD), CNRS, Université Paris Nanterre, Ecole normale supérieure (France). His primary area of research involves studying the production, diffusion and use of scientific and technical knowledge in public and private decision-making. His research interests include expertise, evidence, whistleblowing and scientific work.

Rolf Lidskog is Professor of Sociology at the Environmental Sociology Section, School of Humanities, Educational and Social Sciences, Örebro University, Sweden. His research concerns the epistemic and social conditions for expertise and its role in international environmental governance.

August Lindemer is a PhD candidate of sociology in the Department of Sociological Studies at the University of Sheffield and the Grantham Centre for Sustainable Futures, UK. His research concerns the constructions of climate change within the medical professions, with a particular interest in medical professional climate activism and advocacy. He has a background in environmental science with a focus on natural resource management and communication.

Jasmine E. Livingston is a researcher at the Copernicus Institute of Sustainable Development at Utrecht University, the Netherlands. Previously, she was also a postdoctoral researcher at the Centre for Environmental and Climate Science, Lund University, Sweden and a visiting researcher at Wageningen University, the Netherlands. She is interested in the science–policy dynamics of climate targets and the production of scientific knowledge for global policy. Her PhD examined the IPCC's role in and around the Paris Agreement.

Irene Lorenzoni is associate professor at the School of Environmental Sciences at the University of East Anglia, UK. As an environmental social scientist, she researches the relationships between perceptions and understandings of climate change and responses. Her interests encompass climate change communication; during the IPCC's sixth assessment cycle, she contributed to the co-design of visuals in some of the SPM reports.

Martin Mahony is a lecturer in human geography in the School of Environmental Sciences, University of East Anglia, UK. He works on the histories and geographies of science and technology, with a particular interest in the science–policy interface within the governance of climate change. He has a long-standing interest in the work of the IPCC and in the roles of models, scenarios and visualisations in shaping political imaginations of environmental futures. He is the co-editor of *Cultures of Prediction in Atmospheric and Climate Science* (with Gabriele Gramelsberger and Matthias Heymann; Routledge, 2017) and of *Weather, Climate, and the Geographical Imagination* (with Samuel Randalls; University of Pittsburgh Press), 2020.

Jean Carlos Hochsprung Miguel is a researcher at the Federal University of Sao Paulo, Brazil. He teaches sociology at the Federal Institute of Education, Science and Technology of Mato Grosso do Sul, Brazil. His work explores how climate knowledge infrastructures constitute forms of governmentality, and he is currently researching climate services for the energy sector and energy transitions in Brazil.

Clark Miller is the Director of the Center for Energy and Society and a professor in the School for the Future of Innovation in Society at Arizona State University, USA. His research explores the ontological construction of climate change as a global threat and how human societies are reconfiguring themselves to know and respond to that threat. He is especially engaged in how societies can leverage this transformation to create more just human futures.

Marko Monteiro is currently an associate professor at the Science and Technology Policy Department, University of Campinas, Brazil. His research interests lie in STS and Anthropology of Science and Technology. His research focuses on sociotechnical controversies and governance, ethnographies of interdisciplinary scientific practice and science–policy interfaces.

Jessica O'Reilly, associate professor of International Studies at Indiana University Bloomington, USA, is an anthropologist who studies the science and politics of climate change, in Antarctica and among climate experts internationally. She is the author of *The Technocratic Antarctic: An Ethnography of Scientific Expertise and Environmental Governance* (2017, Cornell University Press), and a co-author of *Discerning Experts: Understanding Scientific Assessments for Public Policy* (2019, Chicago University Press).

Warren Pearce is a senior lecturer at iHuman and the Department of Sociological Studies, University of Sheffield, UK. He researches the social life of climate change using STS and digital methods, with a focus on how science is used in political debate and how climate change knowledge circulates online. He was a contributing author for the IPCC's Sixth Assessment Report.

Arthur C. Petersen is Professor of Science, Technology and Public Policy at University College London (UCL), UK. Before he joined UCL in 2014, he was Chief Scientist of the PBL, the Netherlands Environmental Assessment Agency. From 2001 until 2014 he served as Dutch government delegate to the IPCC.

Joanna Petrasek MacDonald is the lead on the climate change file for the Inuit Circumpolar Council (ICC) and coordinates the ICC's work at the UNFCCC and at the IPCC. She holds a Masters of Arts from McGill University. Her academic published work has focused on Arctic climate change adaptation and spanned issues of food security, mental health and well-being, and participatory research methods with Inuit youth. She has worked on climate change adaptation at local, regional, national and international levels, including for the Government of Nunavut and the UNFCCC.

Bernd Siebenhüner is Professor of Ecological Economics at the Carl von Ossietzky University of Oldenburg, Germany. In his research, he studies social learning, international organisations, global environmental governance, climate adaptation, biodiversity governance, and the role of science in global environmental governance.

Tora Skodvin is a professor of political science at the University of Oslo, Norway. Her research concerns science–policy relations in the early phases of the IPCC process. She also studies domestic sources of international politics with a particular focus on climate policy in the United States.

Adam Standring is a Marie Sklodowska Curie Actions Individual Fellow in the Centre for Urban Research on Austerity at De Montfort University, UK. Prior to this, he was a postdoctoral researcher in Environmental Sociology at Örebro University, Sweden. His research concerns the political sociology of expertise and knowledge production, the relationship between facts and values in politics and public policy, and the diversity of expertise necessary for transformative social change. He is currently researching the construction and practice of expertise in the IPCC.

Göran Sundqvist is a professor of STS at the Department of Sociology and Work Science, University of Gothenburg, Sweden, and a professor II at CICERO Center for International Climate Research, Oslo, Norway. His research is on the interplay between science and policy, with a special focus on the role of expert knowledge in climate transition.

Renzo Taddei teaches anthropology and science and technology studies at the Federal University of Sao Paulo, Brazil. His research addresses the interactions between scientific and traditional knowledge about the atmosphere in the Global South. He leads one of the National Science and Technology Institute for Climate Change clusters in Brazil and integrates a standing committee of the WMO.

Bianca van Bavel is a postdoctoral research fellow in climate change and health with the Priestley International Centre for Climate at the University of Leeds, UK. Her work considers the equity and justice of responses to climate change and determinants of health. Her experience conducting place-based research, evidence syntheses and global assessments has sparked critical reflection about what is included and excluded as evidence and knowledge, as well as the responsibility and necessity to engage with multiple distinct knowledge systems.

Mark Vardy teaches sociological understandings of crime, deviance and justice in the Criminology Department of Kwantlen Polytechnic University, Canada. He is currently studying knowledge production in the IPCC. Past projects include ethnographic studies of the near-real-time visualisation of Arctic sea ice at the US National Snow and Ice Data Center, and how residents in Houston Texas experience their relation to home after being flooded in Hurricane Harvey.

Yulia Yamineva is a senior researcher at the Centre for Climate Change, Energy and Environmental Law, Law School, University of Eastern Finland, and a docent in Climate Law and Policy. Her research concerns the international law and governance of climate change and air pollution as well as science–policy interfaces. Previously, she worked for the UN Climate Change Convention Secretariat and International Institute for Sustainable Development Reporting Services.

Foreword

The Intergovernmental Panel on Climate Change (IPCC) project is simultaneously indispensable and near impossible. Established over 30 years ago by governments to assess policy relevant knowledge, the IPCC is an essential bridge from science to policymaking. It is built on three emergent principles: holding the line between policy relevance and prescription, enlisting geographically diverse participants, and evolving a thicket of procedures to guard scientific credibility. Over three decades, its carefully calibrated and synthetic statements have provided the moorings for intergovernmental action.

Yet, in many ways, this is an impossible project and getting increasingly so. Three decades and counting into global climate change deliberations, the balance of global attention – and therefore the IPCC's role – has shifted. Instead of nailing down scientific certainty – is climate change real and how do we know? – the IPCC is now charged with informing concrete policy actions in diverse national contexts – how do we act, who acts and how fast? Yet, with its current construct, the IPCC project faces challenges in answering this call.

Tasked with informing fraught global negotiations, seemingly simple data tasks like presenting greenhouse gas emission trends are freighted with political meaning. Should emissions be sliced by regions, as conventionally done, or by income categories that shine a spotlight on political negotiation categories like 'developed' and 'developing' countries? Does it matter that a ton of emissions contributes far more to human welfare in poorer rather than richer countries, and how can this be represented in scientific assessments? These questions very nearly derailed an 'approval plenary' I was privileged to participate in as an author.

North–South politics also inflect the knowledge industry that underpins the IPCC. Research funds, editorial control of journals and subliminal signals of research authority disproportionately rest in North America and Western Europe. When not only the robustness of the answer matters, but also the way in which the question is framed, this imbalance threatens the perceived credibility of the IPCC.

Not least, the recognition that local policy and political context matters for how knowledge is authorised becomes a serious challenge for the IPCC's clipped synthesis-driven style of formulating and communicating knowledge. Informing policymaking for polities that have domestic consensus on the existential nature of the climate crisis is very different from finding ways to smuggle policies through politically divided contexts, or seeking 'co-benefits' where other concerns dominate. Advising well-functioning states on climate resilience is entirely different to informing those that already struggle to keep the lights on. The tried-and-tested high-level synthesis approach of the IPCC is ill-equipped to equally inform diverse national and local contexts. Yet, the global community cannot give up on trying to find a way through such challenges, and the IPCC remains our best chance of doing so.

For this reason, this new book – *A Critical Assessment of the Intergovernmental Panel on Climate Change* – is enormously important and, because of the IPCC's turn to solutions, extremely timely. Collectively, the chapters in this volume interrogate not only what the IPCC has achieved, but also how it has done so. This opens the door to exploring whether and how established IPCC objectives, norms and practices are up to the task of informing future policymaking. The 26 concise, yet substantive, chapters are organised around evocative keywords, grouped into five categories, which have been carefully chosen to cover both foundational IPCC ideas like 'peer review' and 'uncertainty', and probe emergent fault lines such as 'policy relevance and neutrality' and 'boundary objects'.

The editors bring both empirical and conceptual richness to this task. I have known Kari De Pryck through her meticulous work observing IPCC processes and interviewing authors as part of a pioneering multi-year research project. Through his work, Mike Hulme has unflinchingly shone a spotlight on how differing values and perspectives are central to *Why We Disagree About Climate Change?* – a book that has been foundational to my understanding of the topic. The contributing authors come from diverse disciplinary backgrounds, and draw on experience of either participating in or studying the IPCC. That the geographical mix of authors is perhaps a bit skewed to the Global North, mirroring the IPCC itself, is an indication of the deep structural nature of asymmetries in the knowledge economy.

At a moment when we still need the IPCC, but also need it to be better, this book delivers on its promise of a 'critical assessment'. And it does not pull its punches in doing so: diversity is described as a 'box-checking exercise' and the IPCC's response to past controversies is termed procedural and adaptive rather than reflexive and transformational.

But the book moves well beyond critique, to offer ideas that could help shake the existing cognitive lock-in on the role and functioning of this seminal knowledge institution. For example, prioritising relevance may require the IPCC to push the boundaries of its traditional emphasis on neutrality: the IPCC may need to seek rather than avoid hot potatoes. While the authors don't name these, good examples might be allocation of future carbon budgets and the treatment of fossil fuel subsidies. Even more ambitious, various authors suggest the IPCC should focus less on being a 'maker of facts', and instead embrace the diversity within its ranks to facilitate dialogue and generate shared meaning. These suggestions go beyond incremental shifts, and will require a reorientation of hallowed IPCC norms and procedures. They offer the prospect of updating the IPCC to meet the changing requirements of international cooperation and national and local policymaking.

The IPCC remains necessary and salient. But it also requires a critical perspective and the injection of fresh thinking. This book, ably edited by Kari De Pryck and Mike Hulme, offers both.

Navroz K. Dubash
Professor, Centre for Policy Research, New Delhi
February 2022

Acknowledgements

The idea for this book emerged through conversations between the two editors, during the period when Kari was a visiting scholar at the University of Cambridge in 2019/20. This stay was funded thanks to a postdoctoral fellowship from the Swiss National Science Foundation (SNSF), without which this book would not have been produced. We also acknowledge the financial support of the Department of Geography at the University of Cambridge. This support covered the book's open-access fee, enabled an author workshop held at Pembroke College, Cambridge, in December 2021 in the middle of the Omicron scare, and supported employment of a part-time editorial assistant. In this latter role, the editors are deeply indebted to the wonderful assistance provided by Maya Goel. Her organisational, literary and intellectual skills are many, and they were all put to excellent use through her liaison with editors and authors, with University and College officers, and with multiple Google Drive folders. At Cambridge University Press, we wish to thank Matt Lloyd for being enthusiastic about our proposal for this book and Sarah Lambert for her speedy and helpful answers to all of our many questions.

Martin Mahony would like to extend thanks to Conrad George for reading and commenting on an earlier draft of Chapter 21. Renzo Taddei would like to acknowledge support received from the São Paulo Research Foundation (project numbers 2014/50848-9 and 2015/50687-8). Irene Lorenzoni and Jordan Harold acknowledge their contribution to the Summaries for Policymakers (SPMs) of the IPCC Special Report on Global Warming of 1.5 °C, the IPCC Special Report on Climate Change and Land, and the IPCC AR6 WGI SPM (Harold as drafting author to the former two; Harold and Lorenzoni to the latter). Harold and Lorenzoni received funding from the IPCC Working Group III Technical Support Unit to support work on the Special Report on Climate Change and Land.

The views expressed in Chapter 25 are the authors' own and do not necessarily represent the views of the IPCC.

Finally, we thank the Earth Negotiations Bulletin from the International Institute for Sustainable Development, the IPCC and its AR6 Working Group I for permission to use their pictures.

Abbreviations

AGGG	Advisory Group on Greenhouse Gases
AMIP	Atmospheric Model Intercomparison Project
AR	IPCC Assessment Report
AR1 (or FAR)	First Assessment Report (1990)
AR2 (or SAR)	Second Assessment Report (1996)
AR3 (or TAR)	Third Assessment Report (2001)
AR4	Fourth Assessment Report (2007)
AR5	Fifth Assessment Report (2013/14)
AR6	Sixth Assessment Report (2021/22)
BECCS	bioenergy with carbon capture and storage
BMPC	Brazilian Panel on Climate Change
BOG	Breakout Group
CBD	[United Nations] Convention on Biological Diversity
CLA	Coordinating Lead Author
CMIP	Coupled Model Intercomparison Project
COP	Conference of the Parties (to the UNFCCC)
DAI	dangerous anthropogenic interference
ECR	Early Career Researcher
ECS	equilibrium climate sensitivity
eLAM	electronic [virtual] Lead Author Meeting
EMIC	Earth System Model of Intermediate Complexity
EPA	Environmental Protection Agency
ESM	Earth System Model
EU	European Union
FAQ	frequently asked questions
FGD	Final Government Distribution
FOD	First Order Draft

GARP	Global Atmospheric Research Programme
GCC	Global Climate Coalition
GCM	General Circulation Model/Global Climate Model
GEA	global environmental assessment
GEO	Global Environmental Outlook
GHG	greenhouse gas
GWP	global warming potential
IAC	InterAcademy Council
IAM	Integrated Assessment Model(ling)
IAMC	Integrated Assessment Modelling Consortium
ICC	Inuit Circumpolar Council
ICSU	International Council for Science (was International Council of Scientific Unions)
IEA	International Energy Agency
IGY	International Geophysical Year
IIASA	International Institute for Applied Systems Analysis
IIPFCC	International Indigenous Peoples Forum on Climate Change
IISD	International Institute for Sustainable Development
IK	Indigenous knowledge
ILO	International Labour Organisation
IMAGE	Integrated Model for Assessing the Greenhouse Effect
INC	Intergovernmental Negotiating Committee
IPBES	Intergovernmental Science-Policy Platform on Biodiversity and Ecosystem Services
IP	Indigenous Peoples
IPO	Indigenous Peoples' Organisation
IS92	IPCC Scenarios 1992
IUCN	International Union for the Conservation of Nature
LA	Lead Author
LAM	Lead Author Meeting
LCIPP	Local Communities and Indigenous Peoples Platform
LTGG	long-term global goal
MEA	Millennium Ecosystem Assessment
MIPs	Model Intercomparison Projects
NDCs	Nationally Determined Contributions
NETs	negative emission technologies
NFP	national focal point
NL	Netherlands
OAS	Organisation of American States

OECD	Organisation for Economic Cooperation and Development
OO	observer organisation
PBL	Netherlands Environmental Assessment Agency
PRSQs	policy-relevant scientific questions
RCP	Representative Concentration Pathway
RE	Review Editor
RIVM	Rijksinstituut voor Volksgezondheid en Milieu (Dutch National institute for public health and the environment)
SBSTA	Subsidiary Body for Science and Technology Advice
SED	Structured Expert Dialogue
SLR	sea-level rise
SOA	solutions-oriented assessment
SOD	Second Order Draft
SPM	Summary for Policymakers
SR	(IPCC) Special Report
SR15	Special Report on Global Warming of 1.5 C (2018)
SRCCL	Special Report on Climate Change and Land (2019)
SRES	Special Report on Emission Scenarios (2000)
SREX	Special Report on Managing the Risks of Extreme Events and Disasters to Advance Climate Change Adaptation (2012)
SRLULUCF	Special Report on Land Use, Land Use Change and Forestry (2000)
SROCC	Special Report on the Ocean and Cryosphere in a Changing Climate (2019)
SSP	Shared Socioeconomic Pathway
STS	science and technology studies
SYR	Synthesis Report
TFI	Task Force on National Greenhouse Gas Inventories
TG-Data	Task Group on Data Support for Climate Change Assessments
TGICA	Task Group on Data and Scenario Support for Impacts and Climate Analysis
TS	Technical Summary
TSU	Technical Support Unit (for a Working Group, WG)
UNEP	UN Environment Programme
UNFCCC	UN Framework Convention on Climate Change
UNPFII	UN Permanent Forum on Indigenous Issues
VOSL	value of statistical life
WCRP	World Climate Research Programme
WG	(IPCC) Working Group

WGI	Working Group I (of the IPCC)
WGII	Working Group II (of the IPCC)
WGIII	Working Group III (of the IPCC)
WHO	World Health Organisation
WMO	World Meteorological Organisation
ZOD	Zero Order Draft

1

Why the Need for This Book?

MIKE HULME AND KARI DE PRYCK

Overview

This chapter introduces the aims, scope, framing, intended readership and organisation of the book. We explain why a book offering a critical assessment of the Intergovernmental Panel on Climate Change (IPCC) is necessary and we situate this justification in the context of other global environmental assessments. We point out the intended readership of the book and why it is of importance and relevance for these readers. We conclude by explaining how the book is structured around five parts.

1.1 Why a Book About the IPCC

This is a book about the Intergovernmental Panel on Climate Change, more widely known and referred to as 'the IPCC'. It is a book about the IPCC as *a knowledge institution*; that is, an organisation with the responsibility – mandated by the world's governments – to assess and synthesise scientific and social scientific knowledge about the phenomenon of climate change. As an institution, the IPCC also formalises a set of rules and norms about *how* to assess and synthesise such knowledge. And it is a book that *critically assesses* the IPCC as a knowledge institution, that is, this book evaluates and synthesises social scientific knowledge about the nature of the institution and how it works.

The IPCC was formally constituted through a Special Resolution of the 70th Plenary Meeting of the United Nations General Assembly in New York, passed on 6 December 1988, and established under the auspices of the UN Environment Programme (UNEP) and World Meteorological Organization (WMO). In its 34-year history, the IPCC has become the most prominent and influential of the various global environmental assessments (GEAs) that emerged in the 1980s and beyond – such as those for stratospheric ozone depletion, biodiversity loss, land degradation and so on. It has also been the GEA most frequently studied by social scientists who are motivated to understand what science and technology studies (STS) scholar Sheila Jasanoff (2005) refers to as its 'knowledge ways'. Knowledge ways are sets of knowledge practices – ways of making and dealing with knowledge and expertise – that become stabilised within particular institutional settings. Already in the years following the publication in 1990 of the IPCC's First Assessment Report, social scientists had been interested to learn how the institution works, what forms of knowledge it produces and how this knowledge is produced (e.g. Boehmer-Christiansen, 1994a,b; Moss, 1995; Shackley & Skodvin, 1995). Social scientists had also been studying what influence the IPCC has on broader scientific, political and public life.

For more than 30 years, institutions like the IPCC, and other GEAs, have become ubiquitous actors of international environmental policy regimes, playing a key role in the construction of global environmental problems and their solutions. Well-known examples include the IPCC, the Millennium Ecosystem Assessment (MEA), the Global Environment Outlook (GEO) and the Intergovernmental Science-Policy Platform on Biodiversity and Ecosystem Services (IPBES). Yet, the knowledge these GEAs produce and make public is still too often taken at face value – or else ignored, misunderstood or downright denied.

With respect to climate change, for example, political actors hold varying views about the status or adequacy of the IPCC's Assessment Reports (ARs). Some environmental activists claim that the IPCC produces assessments of knowledge that are too cautious and conservative; some public critics claim that the IPCC's assessment of climate science has become too politicised; some political leaders may argue that the IPCC's reports are authoritative and reliable, while others that they are only provisional or compromised by conflicts of interests. There is no unanimity within or between countries about the epistemic status or the political role of the IPCC's reports in public life and policymaking. And yet most world leaders agree that with respect to climate change and its geopolitics, the IPCC matters. It is an important institution that cannot be ignored.

A Critical Assessment of the Intergovernmental Panel on Climate Change introduces its readers to the governance, products, participants, knowledge-making practices and influence of the institution. The book demonstrates the importance of social science research for illuminating the social and political processes that enable authoritative intergovernmental knowledge about climate change to be made. *How* this happens, and how this changes *over time*, needs careful investigation and evaluation. It is certainly not the case that such authoritative knowledge is made easily. More generally, the book highlights the role that the social sciences – and especially STS – can play in understanding transnational knowledge institutions like the IPCC. Our critical assessment of the IPCC has value not just for understanding *this particular* GEA, but it offers a model for understanding other GEAs as well.

There is as yet no *comprehensive* book about the IPCC that critically assesses the variety of practices and discourses – epistemic, diplomatic, procedural, communicative – that make the institution function. Nor is there a single volume that explains the different conceptual approaches and methods that have been applied to study such practices. The IPCC has been discussed in a steadily growing number of articles and book chapters, but it has not yet been the primary subject of a dedicated book. The objective of *A Critical Assessment of the Intergovernmental Panel on Climate Change* is therefore twofold. First, it offers a systematic introduction to a field of social enquiry that – after more than 30 years of multidisciplinary research into the institution – can now be called 'IPCC studies'. Second, based on this field of study, it offers a critical assessment of the epistemic, cultural, social, ethical and political norms and practices guiding the IPCC and its transnational processes of climate knowledge production. In other words, the book explains how the IPCC makes 'global kinds of climate knowledge' (Hulme, 2010).

The IPCC is an important institution to study for several reasons. To start, there is the authoritative status and role of the IPCC in the global climate regime. For over 30 years the IPCC has had significant influence on climate change knowledge, on public discourse about climate change, and on climate policy development. The IPCC has also gained increasing visibility in public forums as the authoritative voice of climate change knowledge – 'the privileged speaker and discursive leader' – a visibility enhanced in 2007 through it being awarded, jointly, the Nobel Peace Prize. The 'boundary work' between science and policy that the IPCC performs has also legitimised the scientific vocabulary that governments, campaigners, businesses and NGOs have been able to deploy in public speech.

Second, there is no doubt that – amongst the various GEAs – the IPCC has generated the largest research literature within the social science and humanities disciplines. In a review article published in 2010, Mike Hulme and Martin Mahony evaluated over 100 research articles that had by then been published studying the institution of the IPCC (Hulme & Mahony, 2010). During the subsequent decade we estimate this number has increased by a factor of about four; now, on average, at least one new research article specifically about the IPCC is published each week. And although a growing number of PhD theses have also been written about the IPCC, surprisingly only two books specifically about the institution have been published. One of these was a rather idiosyncratic – if interesting – reflection on the science and politics of climate change from the IPCC's first chairman, Bert Bolin (Bolin, 2007). The other was the result of Tora Skodvin's PhD thesis on the scientific diplomacy of climate change using the IPCC as a case study (Skodvin, 2000b).

A third reason for a book that critically assesses the IPCC is that this institution has been seen by many actors as a role model for organising policy-relevant knowledge for other global problems. For example, IPBES, established in 2012, is often called 'the IPCC for biodiversity' and calls are regularly made to establish IPCC-like institutions for fields such as antimicrobial resistance, migration and asylum, desertification, food systems, and chemical pollution and waste. For example, in an essay calling for a global science–policy body on chemicals and waste, Wang et al. (2021: 776) point to the IPCC as demonstrating that 'the successful integration of natural scientific data, insights from social sciences, and local knowledge forms a strong basis for producing policy-relevant and usable information'. Similarly, an editorial in *Nature* in July 2021 focused on recent calls to develop a new science-to-policy process for food systems. The editorial pointed out the importance of learning from the IPCC with respect to structure and governance and 'how to navigate topics that, like food systems, are both deeply political, and must take into account the voices of industry, non-governmental organisations, farmers, Indigenous people and others' (Anon, 2021: 332).

In the context of the 30 years of existence of the IPCC – celebrated by the institution in 2018 – and of the newly published Sixth Assessment Report (AR6), *A Critical Assessment of the Intergovernmental Panel on Climate Change* offers a unique opportunity to reflect on the achievements, limitations and future challenges of the IPCC. As many scholars have argued, the challenge of communicating the science of climate change is not only about getting the facts right – in other words, 'the message' – and presenting them to a wide range of audiences. It is also increasingly about understanding *how* this message was constructed, *who* the 'messenger' is and how it can be trusted. The IPCC has operated under the rubric of being 'policy relevant but not policy prescriptive'. On the other hand, as Beck and Mahony (2018a) have argued, the IPCC is facing new challenges to its value-free and policy-neutral stance, since it is increasingly called upon to offer 'solutions' to climate change in the post-Paris context. This changing expectation of the role of the IPCC is something that the AR6 cycle has begun to navigate, but there remain many challenges for the organisation, some of which we highlight in our concluding Chapter 28.

A Critical Assessment of the Intergovernmental Panel on Climate Change applies a number of STS concepts that help understand the IPCC as a knowledge institution. Rather than presenting results from a new empirical study of the IPCC, the book offers a structured and coherent series of critical mini-assessments of different aspects of the knowledge-making practices of the IPCC. These chapters draw upon published literature about the IPCC, and in this sense we mimic the IPCC itself – just as the IPCC assesses published knowledge about climate change, so we synthesise and critically evaluate published knowledge about the IPCC.

On the other hand, many of our contributors have been active within the IPCC or have been closely researching the IPCC themselves over many years. Their critical assessments and observations therefore reflect their own judgements about the achievements of the institution and the challenges ahead.

1.2 Readership

A Critical Assessment of the Intergovernmental Panel on Climate Change is intended for a wide audience: for undergraduate and postgraduate students, research scholars, scientists, and policy actors, advisors and advocates. It will be useful for students and scholars interested in better understanding the institution of the IPCC and how it produces global kinds of environmental knowledge. In a context in which academic publications have both significantly increased in volume, but also become more fragmented and dispersed, the book reflects in a coherent and systematic manner on the multifaceted dimensions of the IPCC as a knowledge-making and policy-influencing institution. The book synthesises material from across the social science disciplines, in particular science and technology studies, sociology, human geography, anthropology, political science, and law.

A Critical Assessment of the Intergovernmental Panel on Climate Change is offered as a reference text for courses in a wide range of disciplines – in both the natural and the social sciences – that have a general interest in global environmental problems and their governance, and in climate change in particular. For example, it would be very relevant as a textbook for courses in the disciplines and topics of climate change, science and technology studies, global environmental politics, climate governance, international relations, anthropocene studies, environmental science, and policy. The book is also intended as a reference for both younger and senior scholars interested in understanding the IPCC as a social and political actor and who are looking for an introduction to how the critical social sciences can study such an institution. Finally, the book will be important for IPCC practitioners – administrators, government advisors, policymakers, authors and reviewers. The book is published in the 'lull' between the IPCC's Sixth and Seventh Assessment Reports, so it is timely for informing the process of reflection that the IPCC undergoes at the end of each assessment cycle.

1.3 How the Book Is Structured

A Critical Assessment of the Intergovernmental Panel on Climate Change is designed in a handbook-style format, with 26 short, but substantive chapters, together with introductory and concluding chapters. The book is organised to work systematically through important design features, participatory functions, knowledges, concepts, practices and communication features of the IPCC that are essential for understanding the nature of the institution (see Box 1.1 for a note on terminology). Each chapter is authored by one or more active researchers on the

---

Box 1.1
A word on problematic terminology

We should say something about the terminology used throughout the book, given that there is no harmonisation of some terms within the literature, nor between IPCC usage and the wider literature. For example, the 'expert authors' of the IPCC are frequently referred to generically as 'scientists', but many IPCC contributors come from disciplines that are not in the 'sciences' as generally understood – for example, human geography, sociology, political science, development studies, holders of Indigenous knowledge and so on. Without being overly pedantic, we will on occasions, as merited, refer specifically to scientists and/or social scientists, or researchers. There is a similar issue with respect to how the knowledge assessed and created by the IPCC is described. It is not simply 'science' in the usual anglophone sense of knowledge deriving from 'the natural or physical sciences'. So we either use the more generic term 'knowledge(s)'– cf. *Wissenschaft* in German – or may explicitly refer to different subsets of knowledge – for example, science, social science, humanities, Indigenous knowledge and so on. There can be similar imprecision about 'early career scientists' and so although this is how the IPCC describe them, we prefer the more general term 'Early Career Researchers' (see **Chapter 8**).

The IPCC has gone through six full assessment cycles and the terminology of the various reports emanating from these cycles has evolved. In 1990, before it was known what the future of the IPCC would turn out to be, the First Assessment Report became abbreviated as FAR. In similar fashion the Second and Third reports became SAR and TAR, but thereafter IPCC naming has been standardised as AR4, AR5 and AR6. For simplicity and continuity, we refer to the IPCC's six full assessment reports as AR1 to AR6 (see Table 5.1 for a comprehensive mapping of these report titles).

Finally, there is the thorny issue of how to refer to different groupings of the world's nations. From its inception, the IPCC differentiated between 'developed' and 'developing' nations and this nomenclature continues to be used by the IPCC to the present day, even though the world of 2022 is very different from that of 1988. Brazil and China, for example, both continue as 'developing' countries under this scheme. Other common differentiators are the shorthand Global North and Global South, or simply 'rich(er)' and 'poor(er)' countries. All three of these formulations are used in the book, but readers should be alert to the different meanings of these contested labels and note that we use 'developed' and 'developing' when referring specifically to their ongoing political usage within the IPCC.

IPCC and draws upon the main studies about the institution from the social science literature that have been published over the past three decades. The 34 contributing authors (see Contributing Author List on p. xi) originate from 13 different countries – Belgium, Brazil, Canada, Finland, France, Germany, Japan, Netherlands, Norway, Russia, Sweden, the United Kingdom and the United States – and comprise a mixture of early career, mid-career and well-established scholars. We acknowledge that the contributors are principally located in the Global North and hope that this book will encourage further research on the IPCC from a wider range of perspectives, including those emanating from the Global South.

Each chapter is designed to reflect these three central features:

- a presentation and discussion of the relevant social science literature, highlighting what is and what is not known about the IPCC;
- illustrated with specific examples taken from IPCC Reports and debates, some of them from the respective authors' own experience of the IPCC, either as participants or observers;
- a critical evaluation of the work of the institution and suggestions about some of its future challenges.

The chapters draw upon work published through to the end of 2021 and upon 34 years' work of the IPCC, including the preparation and publication of AR6.

The book is organised into five parts, with each part comprising five chapters (Part V has six chapters).

Part I on *Governance* covers the origins, governance, locations, outputs and learning processes of the IPCC. It offers an overview of the IPCC as an institution with its own status, practices and procedures; an organisation divided in several divisions – Working Groups, Secretariat, Bureau, Panel, Technical Support Units; a network of meetings organised all around the world; a space for deliberation and learning; and a series of differentiated reports (comprehensive, special and methodological).

Part II on *Participation* examines the different experts – individuals and organisations – who participate in the work of the IPCC, and their respective roles. It considers those experts who participate as authors – as Lead Authors, Coordinating Lead Authors, Review Editors, Early Career Researchers, Chapter Scientists – or as government representatives – from the Global North and South. It also considers the representatives of observer organisations – academic institutions, civil society organisations, private sector associations and so on – and also the much broader network of contributors who take part in the external review process.

Part III on *Knowledges* examines and evaluates the different knowledge inputs into the IPCC assessments, but also how the IPCC itself shapes knowledge products, and how and when these knowledges lead to controversies. It focuses on scientific knowledges – from the natural and social sciences – as well as on other forms of knowledge, in particular Indigenous knowledge systems. It discusses the central role of climate models and scenarios in IPCC assessments and the ways in which different scientific communities maintain their prominence within the IPCC.

Part IV on *Processes* deals with some of the most important internal processes by which the IPCC's assessments are crafted, including how scientific uncertainties are understood and operationalised, how the integration between disciplines, experts and concepts is organised, and how the Summaries for Policymakers (SPMs) are approved by governments. It also draws attention to some of the norms that guide these processes, in particular the striving for consensus, policy relevance and neutrality.

Part V on *Influence* explores the influence of the IPCC's work on different audiences. It examines how IPCC reports become relevant for international and domestic decision-making processes and how the knowledge contained in these reports is interpreted and communicated in different contexts. It also considers the particular role played by objects, concepts and visuals in enabling and structuring dialogues between science, policy and publics.

As editors, we draw together the conclusions of the various chapters of the book in Chapter 28. Here, we evaluate the overall history, operation and nature of the IPCC as an institution and, building on the various chapter contributions, we highlight its achievements, limitations and challenges. We offer some thoughts about the possible roles for the IPCC in the years ahead, and what these might mean for the institution's future development.

Part I

Governance

This part sets the stage understanding the nature of the organisation. **Tora Skodvin** (Chapter 2) places the establishment of the Intergovernmental Panel on Climate Change (IPCC) in the context of the epistemic and political construction of global climate change as a problem in the second half of the twentieth century. This chapter gives particular attention to the *intergovernmental* nature of the IPCC and the historical reasons for that design choice. **Olivier Leclerc** (Chapter 3) reviews the function of IPCC procedures in the assessments and their role in striking a balance between scientific robustness and policy relevance. It also examines several procedural reforms the IPCC has gone through. **Friederike Hartz** and **Kari De Pryck** (Chapter 4) survey the places that host plenary sessions of the IPCC Panel and Lead Author Meetings, including the recent move online, and discuss the important function of meetings and venues in the assessment process. **Jasmine E. Livingston** (Chapter 5) reviews the design, role and function of the various reports produced by the IPCC (Assessment Report, Special Reports, Methodology Reports) and the influence of scientific and policy contexts on their commissioning and compilation. Finally in this part, **Silke Beck** and **Bernd Siebenhüner** (Chapter 6) assess whether the IPCC is a 'learning' institution by considering its responses to various internal and external controversies. Both Chapter 5 and Chapter 6 consider the new expectations placed on the IPCC and its Working Groups (WGs) arising from the post-Paris world and the 'solution turn'.

2

Origin and Design

TORA SKODVIN

Overview

This chapter discusses the precursors and origin of the Intergovernmental Panel on Climate Change (IPCC), with a particular focus on the developments that led to the panel's intergovernmental design. When the IPCC was established in 1988 as an intergovernmental body, the design choice was both novel and risky and came to have significant consequences for the panel's subsequent operation and impact. The chapter summarises some prominent events from the early scientific discovery of a possible human influence on global climate to the various international science–policy initiatives of the 1970s and 1980s that preceded the IPCC's establishment. It then draws attention to a set of factors that can explain the decision to deliberately establish the IPCC as an inter*governmental* body.

2.1 Introduction

When the IPCC was established in 1988 as an intergovernmental body, this design choice had significant consequences for the panel's operation and impact (see, for instance Agrawala, 1998a,b). On the one hand, the IPCC's intergovernmental status gave policymakers a direct channel of influence on its work, thus potentially undermining the panel's scientific authority (Agrawala, 1998a; Bolin, 2007). On the other hand, this design also provided a direct and powerful channel of communication between governments and the scientific community. In a conversation with Agrawala, Jean Ripert, chairman of the Intergovernmental Negotiating Committee (INC), stated that 'the intergovernmental nature of the IPCC was in large part responsible for educating many government bureaucrats about the problem which made them more willing to come to the negotiating table' (Agrawala, 1998a: 611). In 2022, moreover, it is possible to speculate that this design feature has also been a contributing factor to the IPCC's subsequent success in keeping the climate issue on the international political agenda and in maintaining its relevance in the climate policy debate.

It was not obvious that an intergovernmental design would be appropriate for a scientific assessment body such as the IPCC. First, there was no precedence for this level of policy involvement in the large-scale scientific assessment processes that preceded the IPCC. Second, while controversial (then and now), it is a commonly held belief that science and politics are and should be separated (see, inter alia, Jasanoff, 1987; Skodvin, 2000b; Oppenheimer et al., 2019; also see **Chapter 22**). Thus, for example, Haas and Stevens (2011: 131) have argued that 'the more autonomous and independent science is from policy, the greater its potential influence'. So why was an intergovernmental design chosen for the IPCC?

This chapter discusses the origin of the IPCC with a particular focus on the developments that led to the panel's intergovernmental design. After a very brief history of scientific assessments presented in Section 2.2, Section 2.3 explores pathways to the IPCC's establishment. Focusing on the nature of science–policy interactions, the section summarises some of the prominent events from the early discovery of a possible human-induced climate change to the various climate initiatives of the 1970s and 1980s that preceded the IPCC's establishment. Section 2.4 then directs attention more specifically to a set of key factors that can contribute to explaining the decision to establish the IPCC as an intergovernmental body.

2.2 A Very Brief History of Scientific Assessments

Scientific assessments are not a new phenomenon. With the growth of science as a professional activity, Oppenheimer et al. (2019: 3) trace 'early forms of the modern scientific assessment' to the nineteenth century. Interestingly, vaccination was 'a major domain of expert assessment' during this period (Oppenheimer et al., 2019:4). In the United States, scientific assessments were particularly associated with an 'increased alignment of the focus of scientific investigations with the goals of the national security state' after 1945 (Oppenheimer et al., 2019: 9). The aim of early scientific assessments, however, was not very different from modern assessments. This is understood by Oppenheimer et al. (2019: 3) to be 'any attempt to review the state of expert knowledge in relation to a specific question or problem, judge the quality of the available evidence, and offer findings relevant to the solution of the problem'. As assessments became increasingly institutionalised, they also grew in size. Thus by the late twentieth century, when environmental assessments became increasingly common, 'large-scale, organised, and formalised assessments of the state of scientific knowledge had become a feature of the scientific landscape' (Oppenheimer et al., 2019: 9).

Environmental assessments were closely associated with the emergence of environmental multilateralism in the early 1970s (Jabbour & Flachsland, 2017). Jabbour and Flachsland note that an increasing awareness of large-scale environmental phenomena and 'the imperative to comprehend the potential consequences and threats to human well-being' contributed to increased recognition of international scientific cooperation (Jabbour & Flachsland, 2017: 195). Another contributing factor to this development was the establishment of the United Nations Environment Programme (UNEP) in 1972, which was given the explicit mandate 'to facilitate the monitoring, reporting and ongoing assessment of the state of the global environment' (Jabbour & Flachsland, 2017: 195).

International assessments – often referred to as Global Environmental Assessments (GEAs) – became dominant during the late twentieth century. GEAs are 'global' in the sense of possessing at least one, and often all, of three key features: 'they may address environmental problems caused by actors in more than one country; they may address problems that have implications for decision makers in more than one country; or they may simply involve participants from more than one country' (Clark et al., 2006: 4). GEAs include 'iconic examples' such as climate change, stratospheric ozone depletion and biodiversity loss (Jabbour & Flachsland, 2017: 193).

The institutionalisation of scientific assessments from the 1970s and onwards was accompanied by an increasing focus on scientific consensus, which 'appears to provide a way of signalling the agreement of experts about what knowledge is important enough and sufficiently settled to inform policy-making' (Oppenheimer et al., 2019: 11). The notion of consensus as a demarcation criterion between established knowledge and contested knowledge claims is subject to a continuing discussion among science philosophers and students of science and technology studies.[1] One incentive for adopting a consensus approach in environmental assessments is suggested to be that 'expert disagreement, or even the appearance of it, can undermine public confidence in those experts and the science they are trying to communicate' (Oppenheimer et al., 2019: 17). An equally important motivation may be that policymakers and other actors called upon to abate environmental degradation may see lack of consensus as a warrant for delaying action (see **Chapter 19**).

Sometimes the IPCC is erroneously referred to as the *International* Panel on Climate Change (see, for instance, Boehmer-Christiansen, 1995), but the distinction between 'international' and 'intergovernmental' is important. Whereas an *international* (or 'global') scientific assessment usually refers to a process that includes an international group of scientists, an *intergovernmental* design indicates that the members are states, not individual scientists. While scientific participation in an intergovernmental assessment process is often based on scientists' individual scientific merit, this choice is left to the discretion of the states that nominate them and implies that scientific merit is not necessarily the key selection criterion used (see **Chapter 7**).

2.3 Pathways to the IPCC Establishment

The discovery of a potential human-induced greenhouse effect is often attributed to the Swedish scientist Svante Arrhenius in 1896 (Agrawala, 1998a; Bolin, 2007). Arrhenius' discovery 'was discussed for a few years, but there was not enough data to tell whether he was right or wrong' (Bolin, 2007: 7; Weart, 2008). Even though climate-related research during the next 50 years consisted of curiosity-driven side projects, important scientific discoveries were made in this period, including Charles Keeling's method and measurement of atmospheric carbon dioxide in 1957 and Roger Revelle's and Hans Suess' conclusion the same year that 'human beings are now carrying out a large scale geophysical experiment' (cited in Weart, 2008: 29).

Within the nascent field of post-World War II climate science,[2] two important modes of science–policy interaction should be mentioned. First, with military funding and support, meteorology was transformed from a subjective undertaking, where forecast weather maps were 'created completely by hand based on the forecaster's best judgement', to '[mathematically computed] prognostic weather maps which predicted large-scale atmospheric motion' (Harper, 2003: 667). Numerical weather prediction techniques are precursors of the more advanced Global Climate Models (GCMs) that have played a key role for our understanding of the climate system since the 1960s (Harper, 2003; Weart, 2008).

Second, an important framework for science–policy interaction in the immediate post-war era was science's role as a vehicle for 'peaceful internationalism', when 'fostering transnational scientific links became an explicit policy of the world's leading democracies' (Weart, 2008: 30–31). In the United States, policymakers reportedly used 'the political neutrality of science and technology as an instrument in the construction of liberal international organizations' (Miller, 2001a: 170). Intergovernmental harmonisation and international cooperation in scientific research were two key modes of interaction that were pursued (Miller, 2001a). The latter was particularly important within geophysics, which is interdisciplinary and international by nature, and which by the early 1950s had become 'intolerably fragmented' (paraphrasing Weart, 2008: 33). As a result of coordinated efforts by a group of prominent scholars, the International Geophysical Year (IGY) of 1957–1958 was launched. Miller describes the IGY 1957–1958 as 'the first large-scale example of intergovernmental cooperation in scientific research and a model for numerous subsequent efforts to address global issues' (Miller, 2001a: 199).

During the 1950s and 1960s there was an increasing awareness that scientific discoveries could be associated with a risk to public health[3] (Jasanoff, 1987; Weart, 2008). The 1972 UN Conference on the Human Environment in Stockholm seems to have been particularly instrumental in bringing about a shift in perceptions of what was at stake with regard to climate change. Bolin notes that the authors of that conference report 'felt that human global interdependence was beginning to require a new capacity for global decisions and attention and that coordinated efforts for overview and research were required' (Bolin, 2007: 28).

In this period, science–policy interactions on climate change were intensified and developed within a context with a distinct intergovernmental component (see, for instance, Agrawala, 1998a; Hulme & Mahony, 2010). In 1961 and 1962, the UN General Assembly agreed to use satellites for weather observations and called on the intergovernmental World Meteorological Organisation (WMO) and the non-governmental International Council of Scientific Unions (ICSU)[4] to collaborate in the further development of the scientific opportunities that had emerged (Bolin, 2007; Zillman, 2009). In November 1967 the Global Atmospheric Research Programme (GARP) was launched with a Joint Organising Committee (JOC) whose members were appointed by the two parent organisations, WMO and ICSU. In 1974, the UN General Assembly called on the WMO 'to undertake a study of climate change', resulting in an expert report issued in 1977 where the 'general scientific expectation of greenhouse warming' was reaffirmed, 'trigger [ing] the WMO decision to convene a World Climate Conference in 1979' (Zillman, 2009: 143). This was swiftly followed by the establishment of the World Climate Programme.

The 1985 Villach conference convened by UNEP, WMO and ICSU has been referred to as a 'historic turning point' (Weart, 2021) in which the forthcoming ICSU assessment by the Scientific Committee on Problems of the Environment (SCOPE 29), edited by Bert Bolin, served as a 'basis for the much-quoted conclusions regarding the prospects of climate change reached by scientists and politicians' in Villach in 1985 (Rodhe, 2013: 3). Following the Villach meeting, UNEP, WMO and the ICSU decided to set up the Advisory Group on Greenhouse Gases (AGGG) in 1986, to which each organisation nominated two experts (Agrawala, 1998a; Bolin, 2007). While the AGGG did important work during the 1980s, key actors such as UNEP, WMO and the United States did not consider the AGGG 'to have the status and composition that would be required in view of the major issues that were emerging' (Bolin, 2007: 47). With the strong support and influence of the United States, the IPCC was established by a resolution of the WMO Executive Council in May 1987, which 'requested the Secretary General of the WMO, "in coordination with the Executive Director of UNEP to establish an *intergovernmental* mechanism to carry out internationally coordinated scientific

assessment of the magnitude, impact and potential timing of climate change"'
(Agrawala, 1998a: 611, emphasis in original).[5]

2.4 Factors Contributing to the IPCC's Intergovernmental Design

In a conversation with Bert Bolin in the mid-1980s, Stephen Schneider expressed
scepticism that (yet another) scientific assessment would be worth the toll it would
take on the scientists providing it. Bolin reportedly responded that 'right now,
many countries, especially developing countries, simply don't trust assessments in
which their scientists and policymakers have not participated ... Don't you think
global credibility demands global representation?' (Schneider, 1991: 25).
Agrawala makes a similar observation with regard to the legitimacy of the
AGGG, whose six members reportedly were compared by a close observer,
unfavourably, to 'a group of private consultants to the *heads* of WMO, UNEP and
ICSU' (Agrawala, 1998a: 613, emphasis in original).

An important motivation for establishing an *international* scientific assessment
process on climate change in the late 1980s was thus to ensure the credibility of the
conclusions and the legitimacy of the process. However, to fully understand the
choice of an *intergovernmental* design for the IPCC we need to take into account
the role of the United States (Hecht & Tirpak, 1995; Agrawala, 1998a).

Numerous national scientific assessments had been undertaken by several US
governmental bodies and agencies since the mid-1970s (for an overview, see
Agrawala, 1998a). As the country with most 'cumulative expertise both in climate
change research and in assessments', the United States played an important role in
the establishment and design of the IPCC (Agrawala, 1998a: 608). However, the
positions on climate change among US agencies and assessment bodies varied
significantly with regard to the emphasis given to scientific uncertainty and the
need for regulatory policies to respond to the climate threat (Hecht & Tirpak,
1995). There were a number of factors influencing the US position – internal
disagreement among US agencies, UNEP activism urging the US to take policy
action to address climate change, lack of trust in the AGGG's ability to provide
adequate and balanced scientific assessments, and the US Department of Energy's
rejection of the Villach report because 'it was not prepared by government
officials' (Hecht & Tirpak, 1995: 381). The compromise solution to these tensions
was for the US to recommend that 'an *"intergovernmental mechanism"* be set up to
conduct scientific assessment of climate change' (Agrawala, 1998a: 611, emphasis
in original).

One likely motivation for the United States' promotion of an intergovernmental
design for the IPCC was to acquire a stronger degree of control of the process,
specifically with regard to potential decisions on governmental action to abate

climate change (Haas & McCabe, 2001). In 1988, there was no strictly political body to which negotiations on this question could be channelled. The United States' involvement in the IPCC's establishment and design ensured it retained a firm grip on this discussion within the IPCC framework (Agrawala, 1998a; Haas & McCabe, 2001). During the first two years of its operation, the IPCC's WGIII was set up to assess 'Response Strategies' under US chairmanship and 'was charged with considering "legal" issues as part of its broader agenda' (Haas & McCabe, 2001: 332). The United States reportedly used this position 'to demonstrate the efficacy of US domestic efforts and the absence of any urgency for further action' (Haas & McCabe, 2001: 332–323). WGI and WGII were in charge of providing the scientific and impacts assessments, respectively.

While the United States contributed to bringing the deeply political issue of climate policy action to the IPCC, this feature may not have been altogether negative for the scientific integrity of the assessment. The old (AR1) WGIII served as an arena for pre-negotiations for the 1991 INC and thus ensured important political deliberations during a period when no such arena existed elsewhere. In this sense, the old WGIII may have served a 'buffer function' during a time when the IPCC process was particularly vulnerable to undue political influence (see Skodvin, 2000b).

2.5 Achievements and Challenges

Scientific assessments have been traced back to the nineteenth century, but international environmental assessments emerged with increasing multilateralism in the 1970s. The intergovernmental design was both novel and risky when it was adopted for the IPCC in 1988. There was no precedent for this design choice in large-scale environmental assessments that preceded the IPCC and it also ran counter to the controversial, but common view (then and now) that science and politics are and should be separate. Politics in the United States seem to have been a decisive factor in the intergovernmental design choice for the IPCC.

With the increasing politicisation of the climate issue during the 1980s, as governmental and economic actors increasingly started to comprehend the potential costs associated with major policy measures to abate climate change, it could be argued that the establishment of the IPCC can be seen as a major achievement in itself. The panel's intergovernmental status provided a direct and powerful channel of communication between governments and the scientific community. This has been important for the panel's work and its continued relevance for international climate policies. The panel's intergovernmental status, however, has also been associated with increased vulnerability to undue political influence – or at least vulnerable to *charges* of such influence. An important tool for meeting this challenge has been to introduce increasingly specific and detailed rules of procedure (see **Chapter 3**), which have in turn led to the development of an increasingly complicated and time-consuming assessment process. Nevertheless, the IPCC has succeeded in providing six full Assessment Reports and numerous Special Reports on specific topics. It has contributed to keeping the climate change issue on the international political agenda throughout its 34-year existence.

Notes

1 For an account of the various positions in this debate, see for instance Skodvin, 2000b: pp. 29ff; for a discussion of the role of consensus in the IPCC, see Hulme, 2013; for an account of how consensus is developed in the IPCC, see De Pryck, 2021a.
2 Climate science did not exist in the vocabulary at this time. Rather, this research was the aggregate, and often uncoordinated, outcome of activities within distinct disciplines like geophysics, oceanography, meteorology, climatology etc. In fact, the IPCC establishment itself was instrumental in the development of climate science as a more unified academic field (Weart, 2008). For simplicity, however, here I use the term climate science in reference to these activities.
3 An illustrative example is the 1952 London 'killer smog' episode, when 'visibility was so impaired ... that pedestrians were unable to see their own feet' (Martinez, 2020) and an estimated 12,000 people died from the incident (Bell et al., 2004).
4 In 1998, the International Council of Scientific Unions changed its name to the International Council for Science, but it retained its original acronym.
5 See also IPCC History, retrieved 11 January 2022 from IPCC – Intergovernmental Panel on Climate Change, www.ipcc.ch/about/history/

Three Key Readings

Agrawala, S. (1998). Context and early origins of the Intergovernmental Panel on Climate Change. *Climatic Change*, 39: 605–620. http://doi.org/10.1023/A:1005315532386
Agrawala, S. (1998). Structural and process history of the Intergovernmental Panel on Climate Change. *Climatic Change*, 39: 621–642. http://doi.org/10.1023/A:1005312331477

These two articles – although written more than 20 years ago – still provide a very good overview of the establishment of the IPCC and the first decade of its operation.

Jasanoff, S. (1987). Contested boundaries in policy-relevant science. *Social Studies of Science*, 17: 195–230. http://doi.org/10.1177/030631287017002001

Sheila Jasanoff is a pioneer in advancing understanding of complex science–policy relations in national and international decision-making. While not explicitly about the IPCC, this article presents a perspective that helps to understand some of the mechanisms at work in the IPCC process.

3

Procedures

OLIVIER LECLERC

Overview

Since its creation in 1988, the Intergovernmental Panel on Climate Change (IPCC) has taken increasing care to formalise its procedures. IPCC procedures define the creation and role of the IPCC Bureau, Task Forces and Working Groups (WGs), as well as the steps that must be taken by experts when preparing reports, and by administrators for overseeing the institution's funding. Increasingly detailed over time and now running over several dozen pages, the IPCC procedures are not a boring part of IPCC studies. They are key observation points of the main issues that the IPCC has had to address over time. They reflect the compromises it has made in its efforts to give the greatest political efficiency to its reports, while ensuring that their scientific robustness remains irreproachable. The procedures therefore constitute a site from which many of the issues addressed in this book can be read. However, they should not be taken as descriptions of *actual* practices: their implementation is open to interpretation and thereby to debate. The drafting and amendment of procedures therefore remains an open process.

3.1 Introduction

At the first session of the IPCC, held at the joint initiative of the World Meteorological Organisation (WMO) and UN Environment Programme (UNEP) in Vienna in November 1988, the participants agreed on the tasks entrusted to the newly formed body – the constitution of three WGs, the governance of the Panel and its WGs, and the importance of letting experts from other international organisations attend as observers. These issues were addressed without much detail in the minutes of the session or in the 'Terms of reference for the working groups' annexed to it. In 1991, the Panel adopted the *Principles governing IPCC work*, a relatively brief text composed of 12 points, to be reviewed annually.

The *Principles governing IPCC work* are still the main procedural framework for the work of the IPCC. Over the years, they have been continuously developed and refined (Agrawala, 1998b; Siebenhüner, 2002; Bolin, 2007; Provost, 2019). The current version of the *Principles governing IPCC work* was adopted in 1998 and it has been amended several times since then. They now include three appendices, which may themselves include annexes, devoted respectively to *Procedures for the preparation, review, acceptance, adoption, approval and publication of IPCC reports* (Appendix A), *Financial procedures for the IPCC* (Appendix B) and *Procedures for the Election of the IPCC Bureau and any Task Force Bureau* (Appendix C). In addition, the Panel adopted an *IPCC policy and process for admitting observer organisations* (2006), an *IPCC Conflict of interest policy* (2011), an *IPCC Communication strategy* (2011), and an *IPCC Gender Policy and Implementation Plan* (2020). Occasionally, IPCC procedures also refer to UNEP and WMO procedures (e.g. the participation in the IPCC is determined with reference to WMO and UN membership).

The IPCC is not an international organisation with legal personality and so the formal procedures do not legally constitute international treaties (Ghaleigh, 2016: 59). Moreover, they coexist with a multitude of informal and unwritten procedures and 'ways of doing things' (Farrell et al., 2001) which often differ from one WG to another according to the disciplinary cultures of their members. These 'ways of doing things' have sometimes been incorporated in the formal procedures and at other times have been resisted. The decision to formalise a procedure has strategic implications. Although it reduces the authors' room for manoeuvre, the formalisation of procedures is a central lever for the IPCC to ensure its legitimacy and the credibility of its reports (Sundqvist et al., 2015). Procedures are one of the main ways by which the IPCC has been institutionalised and has established itself as a central player in global climate governance. All IPCC procedures are available on its website. The IPCC gradually recognised that it is not only important to follow procedures, but also to publicise them. IPCC procedures have served two main functions over time, which this chapter describes successively. On the one hand, they have been a crucial channel through which the IPCC has sought to establish a balance, always subject to discussion, between science and politics (see **Chapter 21**). On the other hand, the procedures have been pivotal in strengthening the IPCC's legitimacy and credibility when both are challenged.

3.2 Balancing Science and Politics in the IPCC

IPCC procedures reveal which matters and methods the Panel and governments have found necessary to establish and formalise. First of all, the procedures state the mandate of the IPCC: 'the role of the IPCC is to assess on a comprehensive, objective, open and transparent basis the scientific, technical and socio-economic information relevant to understanding the scientific basis of risk of human-induced climate change, its potential impacts and options for adaptation and mitigation' (*Principles governing IPCC work*, §2). Sometimes referred to as a 'boundary organisation' (Agrawala et al., 2001; Miller, 2001b; Sundqvist et al., 2015), the IPCC is always seeking a balance between the scientific robustness of the assessments carried out under its aegis and the relevance of its reports for governments policies, the international negotiations on climate change, and the wider public. As the *Principles governing IPCC work* state, 'IPCC reports should be neutral with respect to policy, although they may need to deal objectively with scientific, technical and socio-economic factors relevant to the application of particular policies'.

The balance between science and politics that is inherent to the IPCC's mandate has been intensely debated (Skodvin, 2000b; Siebenhüner, 2003; Miller, 2004; Beck, 2011b; De Pryck, 2018). The procedures are indicative of where the Panel places the cursor, both in establishing the IPCC organs and in determining their prerogatives and working methods. Members involved in its governance (Bureau, WGs Bureaux, Bureau of the Task Force), and the experts involved in the preparation of its reports (Lead Authors, Coordinating Lead Authors, Review Editors, Contributing Authors), are in general chosen for their scientific competence. The *Principles governing IPCC work* nevertheless reconcile this imperative with maintaining a role for states: while the appointment of experts is decided by the Bureaux of the WGs, states are responsible for proposing the names of competent persons through their Government Focal Point. Similarly, the *Principles governing IPCC work* specify that the experts must reflect a range of scientific, technical and socio-economic views and expertise; geographical representation (ensuring appropriate representation of experts from developing and developed countries and countries with economies in transition); a mixture of experts with and without previous experience in IPCC; and gender balance (see **Chapter 7**). With regard to the elaboration of IPCC assessment reports, the *Principles governing IPCC work* establish a complex procedure involving experts as authors in the crafting of draft reports, followed by a first external review by experts and a second review by both governments and experts (see Figure 3.1).

Eventually, the report must be endorsed by the countries represented in the Panel. Depending on the nature of the report in hand (see **Chapter 5**), this entails a more or less thorough examination ranging from 'acceptance' (the material as a whole presents a comprehensive, objective and balanced view of the subject matter), 'adoption' (the material is discussed and endorsed section by section by the Panel) to 'approval' (the material is discussed and agreed to line by line).

By specifying the role of the different actors involved in the IPCC's work – scientists, states, non-governmental actors – and by organising its working

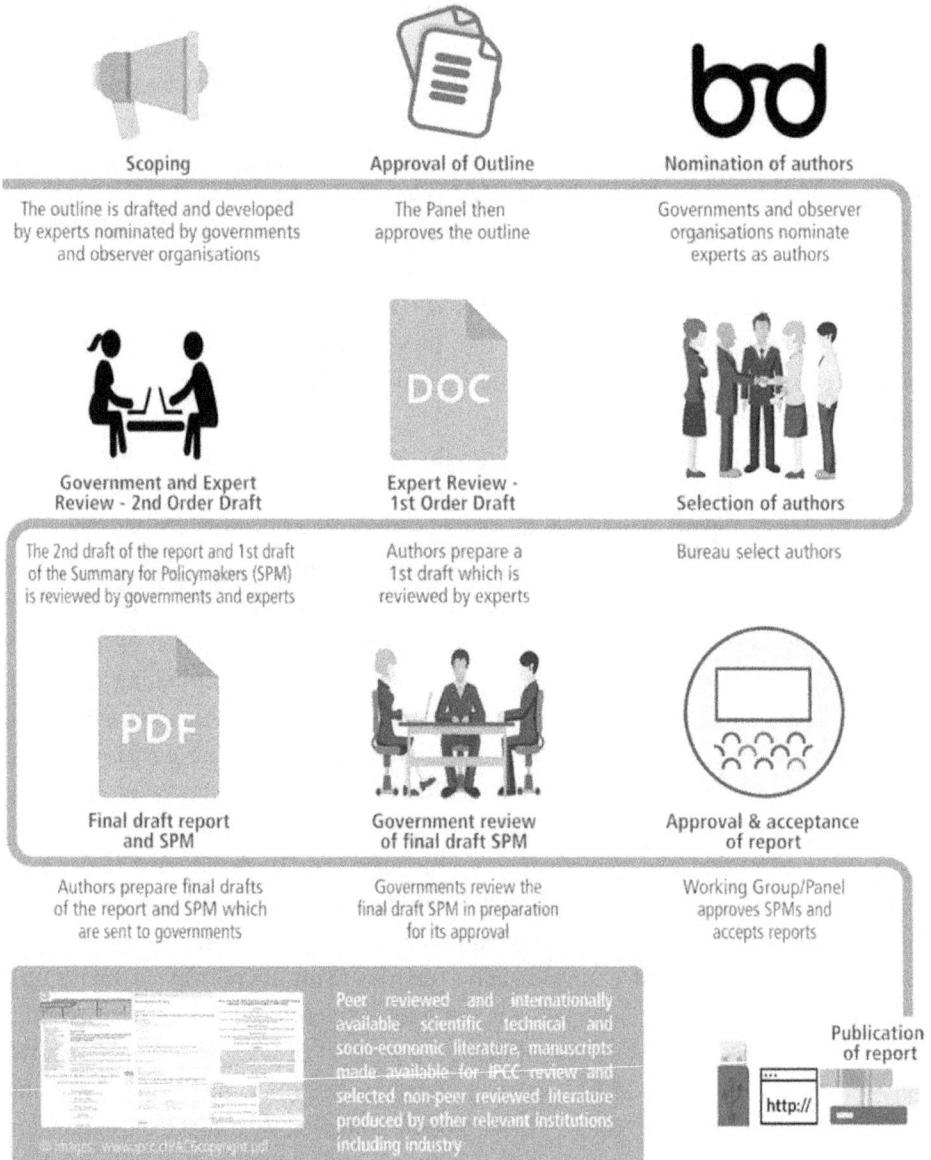

Figure 3.1 A schematic illustration of the preparation of IPCC reports.
Source: IPCC 2021 [www.ipcc.ch/about/preparingreports/]

methods, the procedures have served as a constitution for the IPCC. They have established the identity of the IPCC and have made it a unique body of expertise at the interface of science and politics. The working procedures established by the Panel depart from the classical representation of a 'linear model of expertise' (Leclerc, 2009; Beck, 2011a) in which a knowledge phase precedes a decision phase. Instead, the procedures organise an iterative process linking scientific assessment to political questions and international negotiations on climate change.

3.3 Strengthening the Legitimacy of the IPCC

IPCC procedures have been the target of constant discussion, criticism and suggestions for change (Farrell et al., 2001; Boehmer-Christianson & Kellow, 2002; Hulme et al., 2010). Few plenary sessions of the Panel do not include a review of its formal procedures. The criticism to which the IPCC is regularly subjected has been a powerful driving force for the development or modification of its procedures. Very early in the IPCC's existence, its legitimacy and credibility were contested by some economic and governmental actors concerned with limiting international climate action. The institutional response of the Panel to these concerns was not only to demonstrate the accuracy of the information contained in its reports, but rather also to strengthen its procedures. The increasing proceduralisation of the assessment process therefore appears to be a prime means of responding to the criticisms levelled at the IPCC.

This procedural rather than substantive response by the IPCC to criticisms has not always been easily adopted however. The scientific background of the Panel's Bureau officers and experts meant that their training and instincts would have led them to engage in discussion and argumentation about scientific substance, not about procedures. This is all the more true because a number of criticisms of the IPCC were made by actors who were clearly interested in manufacturing doubt and countering the adoption by states of measures limiting greenhouse gas emissions (Dunlap & McCright, 2011). Nevertheless, the Panel could not afford to ignore criticisms widely reported in the media; otherwise they would risk being accused of 'tribalism' (Beck, 2011b). Agreeing to undergo procedural strengthening, rather than defending the institution solely on the basis of science, therefore reflects a cultural shift for many IPCC officers (see **Chapter 6**). On a subject as politically important as climate change, expert assessment of knowledge could not remain governed by the informal rules of the scientific community.

Criticism of the IPCC has led to a significant proceduralisation of new areas of IPCC work. The areas in which the Panel has formalised or strengthened the procedures are indicative of the fundamental difficulties it has encountered. These difficulties are undoubtedly familiar to most expert bodies working in areas of public controversy (Social Learning Group, 2001; Oppenheimer et al., 2019), but because of the high political stakes involved in international climate negotiations they have been acute in the case of the IPCC. Two episodes had a particularly significant impact on the IPCC's procedures (see **Chapters 11** and **16**). The first occurred in 1996 during the adoption of the IPCC's Second Assessment Report

(AR2). Strong criticism was raised by several American scientists, and relayed by pressure groups such as the Global Climate Coalition (GCC), claiming that some IPCC Lead Authors had not respected the Panel's procedures and had deliberately undermined sceptical views on the anthropogenic origin of climate change (Skodvin, 2000b: 215; Miller & Edwards, 2001; Oreskes & Conway, 2010: 201). In response, the IPCC created the new function of 'Review Editors' charged, for each chapter, to 'assist the WG/Task Force Bureaux in identifying reviewers for the expert review process, ensure that all substantive expert and government review comments are afforded appropriate consideration, advise lead authors on how to handle contentious/controversial issues, and ensure genuine controversies are reflected adequately in the text of the Report' (*Principles governing IPCC work*, Appendix A, Annex 1, §5).

The second and more significant episode was triggered late in 2009. Emails of scientists at the University of East Anglia were made public which critics believed revealed a willingness by some of them – who were also IPCC Lead Authors – to 'hide' data or to present it in a way that would support the view that global warming is primarily caused by human activities. Around the same time, the Chair of the IPCC, Rajendra Pachauri, was accused of a conflict of interest, since he was the director of a research centre – The Energy and Resource Institute in India – which provided consultancy to companies interested in reducing greenhouse gas emissions. And finally early in 2010, a gross error in AR4, published more than two years earlier, was made public. This concerned the melting rate of Himalayan glaciers. Some of these criticisms were found, after investigation, to be unsubstantiated (House of Commons, 2010; PBL, 2010). Nevertheless, after a delay in responding to the critique (Beck, 2011b), the IPCC commissioned the InterAcademy Council (IAC) to evaluate its procedures and make recommendations (Paglia & Parker, 2021).

In its report, released in October 2010, the IAC first encouraged the IPCC to make better use of the procedures already adopted at its Panel sessions or in its WGs. For example, with regard to the review of draft reports, 'the IPCC should encourage Review Editors to fully exercise their authority to ensure that reviewers' comments are adequately considered by the authors' (IAC, 2010: 3). The IAC also reaffirmed the need to unify the wording used by IPCC WGs to describe the levels of uncertainty affecting the statements, in accordance with the guidelines already adopted in 2005 (IPCC, *Guidance Notes for Lead Authors of the IPCC Fourth Assessment Report on Addressing Uncertainties*, 2005; see **Chapter 17**). The IAC report also suggested that the Panel strengthen the procedures it had previously designed for using 'grey-literature' (*Principles governing IPCC work*, Appendix A, Annex 2, *Procedure for using unpublished/non-peer-reviewed sources in IPCC*, 2003). Other IAC recommendations called on the Panel to adopt new procedures – the creation of an executive committee to take decisions between Panel sessions; the election of an executive director to head the secretariat; improved communication; and the adoption of 'a rigorous conflict of interest policy that applies to all persons directly involved in the preparation of IPCC reports' (IAC, 2010: 46).

The assessment made by the IAC was welcomed and acknowledged by the Panel. Many of its recommendations were immediately implemented at the 32nd Session of the IPCC in 2010, or else at subsequent plenary sessions of the Panel following the publication of the reports of the IPCC Task Groups on Procedures, Governance and Management, Conflict of Interest Policy and Communication Strategy – task groups set up by the Panel to further implement the IAC's recommendations (see also **Chapter 6**).

3.4 Achievements and Challenges

The IPCC's procedures describe in detail the different functions of the IPCC and the work processes to be followed. Whether to learn from difficulties in its operation or to respond to criticism, the Panel has refined and expanded the IPCC's procedures considerably, covering an ever-widening range of issues. The procedures have thus played a key role in making the IPCC a major player in global environmental governance. IPCC procedures also emerge as a model for 'governance by scientific assessment' (Biermann, 2011). They served as a reference for the drafting of the Intergovernmental Science-Policy Platform on Biodiversity and Ecosystem Services (IPBES) *Rules of procedure for the plenary of the platform* (2012) (Futhazar, 2016). The procedural convergence between the IPCC and the IPBES has greatly facilitated their joint assessment on the relationship between climate change and biodiversity loss (Pörtner et al., 2021).

However, IPCC procedures are not immune from criticism. It is interesting that the procedures established for the IPBES – although clearly modelled on those of the IPCC – have departed from them on certain points. For example, the IPBES allows for the possibility of using a fast-track procedure for carrying out expert assessments, which gives it a responsiveness that the IPCC lacks. The strengthening of IPCC procedures has sometimes resulted in extremely complex decision schemes, as illustrated by the *IPCC Protocol for Addressing Possible Errors in IPCC Assessment Reports, Synthesis Reports, Special Reports or Methodology Reports* (*Principles governing IPCC work*, Appendix A, Annex 3). To help users navigate the many steps in the process, the IPCC had to prepare explanatory diagrams in decision-tree form. The necessary caution with regard to claims that authors have made a mistake, and the no less legitimate concern to involve them in the implementation of the error protocol, may ultimately be detrimental to the effectiveness of the process.

Similarly, the IPCC deviates from most expert bodies in deciding that the Conflict of Interest Disclosure Form filled in by experts remains confidential. They limit the form to three broadly formulated questions relating to professional activities, significant and relevant financial interests, and 'anything else that could affect [the] objectivity or independence [of the experts]' (*IPCC Conflict of interest policy*). Greater transparency would have demanded that the forms be more detailed and accessible. Nevertheless, the Panel must take into account that experts involved in the IPCC's assessments volunteer their time without financial compensation. Procedural requirements that are considered too stringent could discourage participation. This concern is explicit in the *Conflict of interest policy*: 'The Panel recognizes the commitment and dedication of those who participate in IPCC activities. The policy should maintain the balance between the need to minimise the reporting burden, and to ensure the integrity of the IPCC process'.

The IPCC's procedures are constantly being re-assessed in the academic literature, by the IPCC and in the media. The underlying idea is that the right procedural configuration must be found to ensure the IPCC's continuing legitimacy. In addition to the fact that opinions differ on what the ideal procedural configuration should be, it is questionable whether the procedures can fully meet the expectations placed on them. Indeed, procedures are references and do not describe actual social practices. Moreover, they need to be implemented to produce an effect. It is notable that the IAC review in 2010 emphasised the need for the IPCC to better implement the procedures that already exist. However, the implementation of the procedures leaves some room for interpretation by the actors, and can be challenged by others. The balance achieved by the procedures at any given time can therefore only be temporary and fragile. The drafting of the IPCC procedures is bound to remain an open-ended process.

Three Key Readings

Agrawala, S. (1998). Structural and process history of the Intergovernmental Panel on Climate Change. *Climatic Change*, 39: 621–642. http://doi.org/10.1023/A:1005312331477

This article provides an early overview of how the IPCC procedures were constructed.

InterAcademy Council (2010). *Climate Change Assessments. Review of the Processes and Procedures of the IPCC*. Amsterdam, Netherlands: IAC. Available at: https://archive.ipcc.ch/pdf/IAC_report/IAC%20Report.pdf

In this report issued in 2010, the IAC thoroughly appraised the IPCC procedures and suggested a range of modifications.

Hulme, M., Zorita, E., Stocker, T. F., Price, J. and Christy, J. R. (2010). IPCC: cherish it, tweak it or scrap it? *Nature*, (463): 730–732. http://doi.org/10.1038/463730a

This article proposed a wide range of alternative institutional and procedural arrangements for the IPCC and illustrates the variety of views on what these procedures could be.

4

Venues

FRIEDERIKE HARTZ AND KARI DE PRYCK

Overview

By highlighting the importance of venues and meetings for the work of the Intergovernmental Panel on Climate Change (IPCC), this chapter offers a novel angle from which to study the institution. Thinking of the IPCC as a 'travelling village' and a 'system of meetings', we discuss the various functions of venues and meetings in organising and maintaining the IPCC's assessment process. We argue that because of the global and networked nature of its activities and institutional arrangements, participating in the IPCC means making the world one's workplace. The chapter also shows how established IPCC meeting practices have been tested by the COVID-19 pandemic and sheds light on some of the implications of the shift from in-person to virtual meetings.

4.1 Introduction

The IPCC describes itself as a 'huge and yet very small organization' (IPCC, n.d. (a)). The dozen staff members of its Secretariat are hosted by the World Meteorological Organisation (WMO) in Geneva, but most of the scientists and government representatives who carry out the bulk of its activities are scattered worldwide across many institutions. In order to function as a network organisation (Venturini et al., 2022) and carry out its work, the IPCC relies on a complex 'system of meetings' (Brown & Green, 2017: 46) organised in various places around the world. Unlike other practices, actors, institutions and objects that make up the IPCC, the Panel's venues and meetings have so far received little attention. This is somewhat surprising since these venues and meetings play a key role in the coordination of the assessment work and contribute to building consensus in the IPCC. They also serve as a 'visible stage' (Craggs & Mahony, 2014: 415; see also Death, 2011) from which the authority of the organisation is projected.

This chapter is based on ethnographic experience with IPCC meetings since 2014. Studying the IPCC means travelling to many countries, and going into different venues and meeting rooms to observe global climate assessments in the making – although, amid the global pandemic, meetings have been held virtually since spring 2020. The chapter is structured as follows. Sections 4.2 and 4.3 explore the spatial and material nature of IPCC venues. Section 4.4 explores the orchestration of meetings and their various functions in the work of the IPCC. It also discusses some of the repercussions of the COVID-19 pandemic on its meeting practices (see Box 4.1).

4.2 All Over the Place? Locating the IPCC Assessment Process

In science and technology studies (STS), the role of places and venues in knowledge production has been acknowledged since the 1970s (Shapin, 1998; Livingstone, 2003). Against the commonplace assumption that scientific knowledge is universal, scholars have shown that places shape the production of knowledge (Latour & Woolgar, 1979; Knorr Cetina, 1999). All forms of knowledge are situated and reflect the particular conditions of their production (Haraway, 1988). Places are 'a way of understanding' (Cresswell, 2004: 11) because they make it possible to 'see attachments and connections between people and place [. . . and] see worlds of meaning and experience'. STS scholars have also shown that the aesthetic features of the environment in which scientific knowledge is produced and presented are crucial for underpinning the authority of science. Some places can even act as 'truth-spots' (Gieryn, 2018: 172) that provide 'believability and authority to claims or assertions associated with that spot'.

The assessment work of the IPCC is bound to multiple and specific locations. For example, the location of the Secretariat at the WMO in Geneva – 'a United Nations city' – provides the IPCC with solid institutional and scientific credibility and contributes to its authoritative status. As the Panel describes it, 'Geneva is a perfect example of an international and multicultural city' (IPCC, 2019a), which succeeded in attracting numerous international and non-profit organisations and turned into a UN ecosystem (Dairon & Badache, 2021).

The other 'parts' of the organisation are spread across the globe. IPCC authors who write the reports are based in their home institutions, as are the representatives of the member states who review and accept them. Authors meet at least three to four times at so-called Lead Author Meetings (LAMs), to coordinate and write their collective report. IPCC member states meet at least once a year in Panel/

Plenary sessions and take major decisions regarding the mandate of the three Working Groups (WGs), the budget of the organisation and outreach activities. These plenaries are also attended by observer organisations (see **Chapter 10**). LAMs and Panel sessions take place worldwide and the organisation relies on the willingness and resources of its member states to offer venues. The IPCC may thus be characterised as a 'travelling village' (to take a metaphor used by one participant) whose thousands of scientific experts and delegates regularly leave their home institutions to meet in various locations.

Since 1988, the IPCC has organised hundreds of gatherings in over 57 countries (see Figure 4.1). Such widespread spatial organisation projects the image of a truly global endeavour. It also reflects the way in which the IPCC derives its authority from its 'convening power', much like its parent organisation, the UN Environment Programme (UNEP), which seeks to bring 'the world together to protect the environment, support sustainable development and ensure the health of the planet for future generations' (UNEP, 2021).

Figure 4.1 shows that, overall, IPCC activities have taken place in some regions more than in others. As the top panel illustrates, Switzerland (Geneva, 11 sessions), Kenya (Nairobi, 6), Canada (Montreal, 5) and France (Paris, 4) have hosted the most IPCC Panel sessions. This is not surprising since these four cities host UN institutions that offer adequate plenary venues. Interestingly, the United States only hosted one session in 1990 in Washington (IPCC-3). No Panel session so far has been held in Oceania. The middle panel shows that countries that hosted the most LAMs for regular assessment as well as special reports are Switzerland (16), the USA (12), Australia (12), the UK (9) and Norway (9). It is worth highlighting that only a few LAMs were held in the Middle East, Africa and Central Asia. These numbers illustrate the centrality of the Global North, in particular Switzerland, in hosting both Panel sessions and WG meetings.

Finally, a less visible component of the IPCC, the Technical Support Units (TSUs), deserve attention, as depicted in the bottom panel of Figure 4.1. TSUs, generally a dozen people, support the work of the WGs and the Task Force on National Greenhouse Gas Inventories (TFI) and play a key role in the coordination of the assessment activities. Each TSU is jointly chaired by two co-chairs, one from a 'developed country' and one from a 'developing country', but is generally hosted and funded by the developed country. The co-chair whose country funds a TSU thus has a particularly strong voice in running the WG (IAC, 2010). As the map shows, only a handful of countries have supported the establishment of TSUs: the UK and USA have together financed 8 out of 18 of the WG TSUs, while Japan has been in charge of the TFI since 1999.

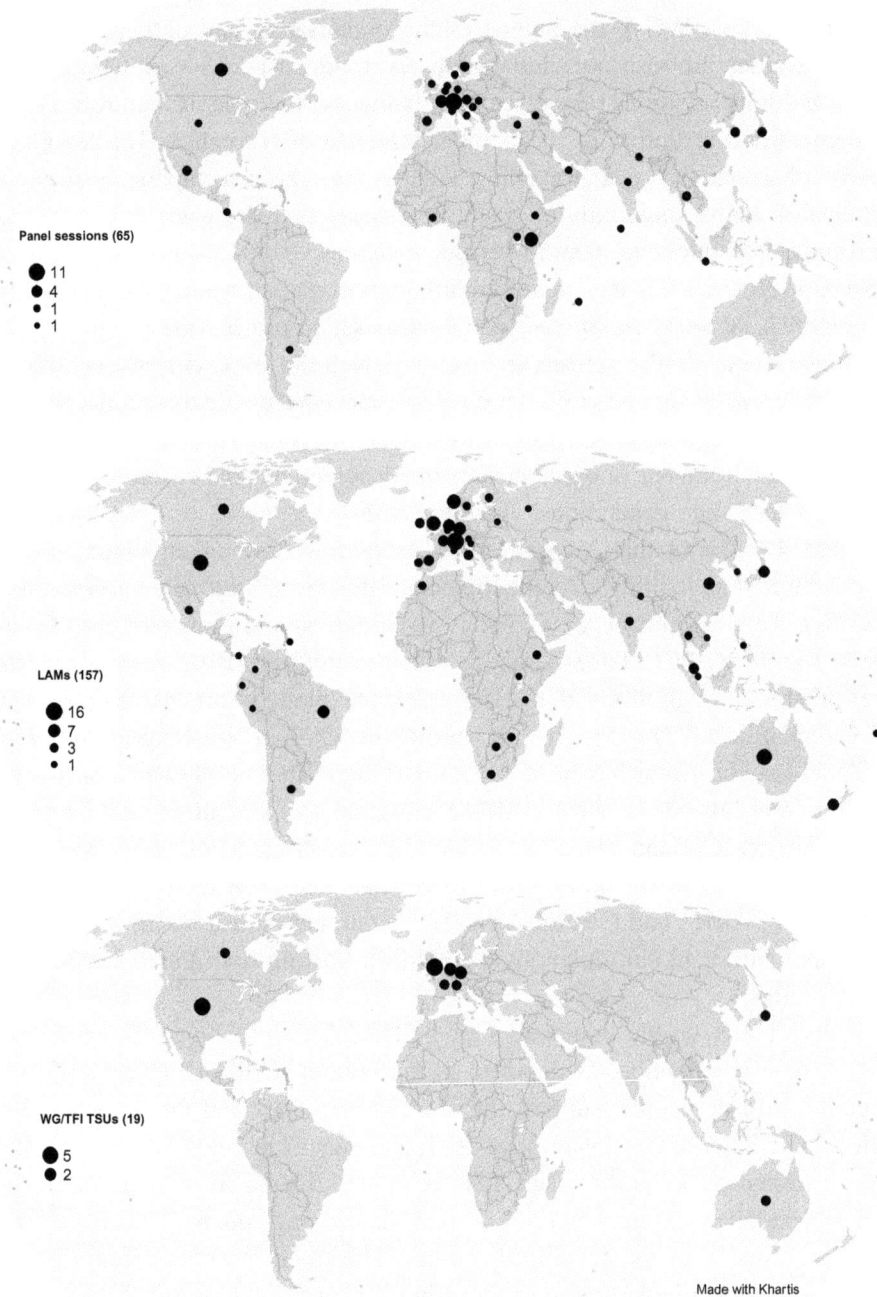

Figure 4.1 The global distribution of IPCC gatherings (1988–2020).
The top panel displays the distribution of the plenary sessions of the Panel. The middle panel shows where LAMs took place. The bottom panel presents the locations of the TSUs of the WGs and of the TFI. The locations were found in meeting documents available on the IPCC website. A few locations, from the early days of the IPCC, could not be found in the available documentation.

4.3 IPCC Venues, Enclosing Climate?

Examining the venues, and more specifically the buildings and rooms that have hosted IPCC meetings, draws attention to the materiality of the spaces that underpins the Panel's work. Venues and their distinct spatial features, including their locality and architecture, have an impact on how science and policy are (co-)produced. As McConnell (2019: 47) has argued, places can carry with them distinct 'affective atmospheres', relating, *inter alia*, to the way in which official buildings convey a sense of neutrality and universality through their function and design. The WMO building (Figure 4.2), for example, carries a clear symbolic meaning. According to WMO (2021), its main building is 'at once pragmatic and emblematic – a hi-tech response to geography from the creativity of science and a symbol of the commitment of WMO to the protection of the environment and the rational and economical use of energy'. Originally, the 'Chic Planète project', submitted by the architects Rino Brodbeck and Jacques Roulet in 1993, sought to accommodate budget constraints, the geography of the site (a narrow strip bound by roads, a railway and existing buildings) and care for the environment. Its interior design is a

Figure 4.2 The WMO headquarters in Geneva, Switzerland.
Source: WMO (CC BY-NC-ND 2.0 https://creativecommons.org/licenses/by-nc-nd/2.0/)

perfect illustration of the desire of humans to control their climate, as the 'natural process of heat transfer [put in place by the architects] maintains the building at a constant optimal temperature, between 20 and 26°C' (WMO, 2021).

The buildings that accommodate IPCC Panel sessions and LAMs also have distinctive features from which the organisation can draw credibility and legitimacy. These meetings usually take place in universities, resort hotels, conference centres or UN buildings – places that, for different reasons, strive for neutrality, conventionality and universality (cf. Augé, 1995). These buildings are meant not only to 'keep the weather out' (Gieryn, 2002: 35) but also to accommodate the daily flow and gathering of hundreds of people, thereby ensuring the smooth and efficient proceedings of meetings and events. IPCC venues have a particular ordering function in which they 'arrange in space things and people, building-in strict patterns of movement and interpersonal contacts that are sequenced by entrances, passages, barriers, and exits' (Gieryn, 2018: 174). Over the years, the layout of the rooms for LAMs and Panel sessions has come to look alike and the steady flow of movement in and between plenary and adjacent rooms, interrupted by regular breaks, has become routinised. As Figure 4.3 shows, IPCC venues generally consist of one main conference room, where the plenary meetings take place, and several smaller breakout rooms to host contact groups and chapter meetings. Corridors also play a key role in facilitating informal gatherings of participants.

As for most UN bodies, such venue configurations are also meant to create a strict separation between participants and the rest of society. Such separation becomes visible through the badges worn by participants and observers – the fruits of a long process of accreditation and registration started several months before the meetings – which allow them to enter rooms that are often guarded and not open to other users of the building and the public.

4.4 Meetings within Meetings

Places and venues can also shape the practices that prevail at a science–policy interface (Mahony, 2013; see also Palmer et al., 2019). When the IPCC meets in a certain place (e.g. a conference centre, university or hotel), it temporarily creates an 'IPCC space'. Such 'boundary spaces' (Mahony, 2013: 31) can be instrumental in bringing science and politics into closer relation (Mahony, 2013: 37). They support and constrain 'individual performances and in doing so shap[e] the narratives and knowledges produced' (Craggs & Mahony, 2014: 415).

The activities of the IPCC are organised through a complex system of large-scale and small-scale meetings, in constant dialogue with one another. Each of these gatherings has specific functions aimed at ensuring that the assessment reports will be published according to the approved timeline and based on the latest published literature. Meetings are also a vehicle to order the process and

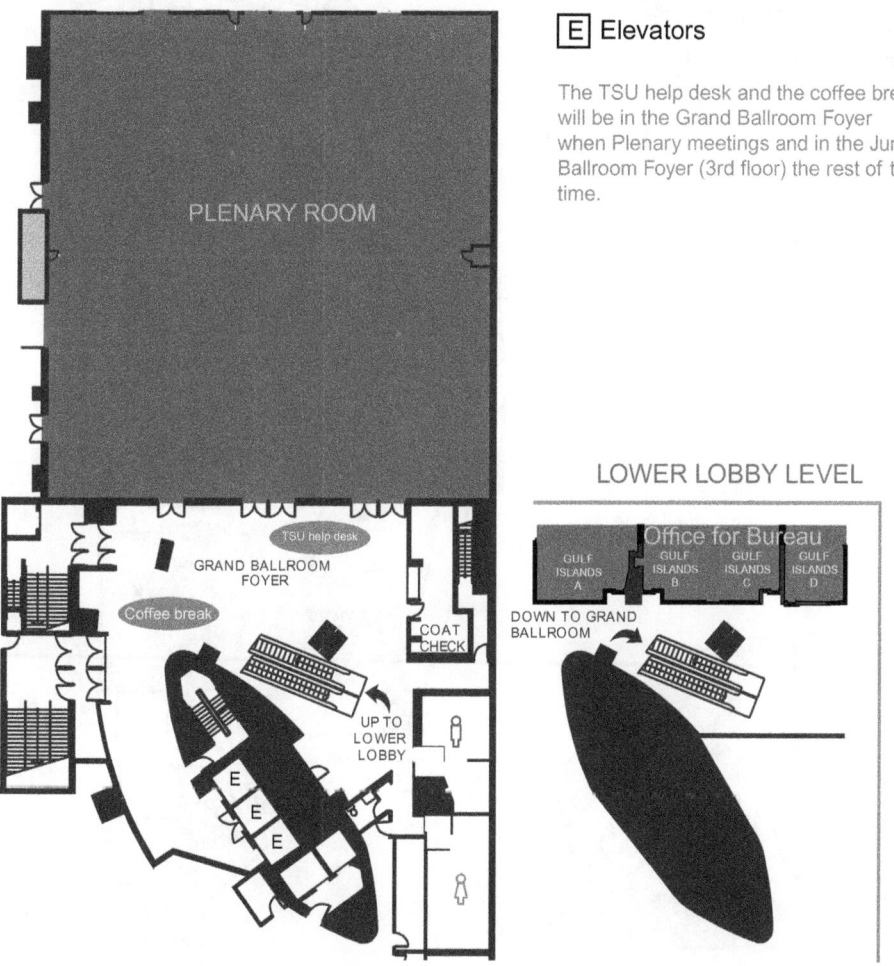

Figure 4.3 Example of the layout of a Lead Author Meeting.
Source: IPCC, 2019a

make sure that the otherwise geographically and institutionally scattered assessment cycles follow the rules of procedures that underpin the credibility and legitimacy of the IPCC (see **Chapter 3**). Each meeting is therefore bound to a strict agenda and to the achievement of predefined tasks and milestones within the assessment process – agreeing on the outline of a report, answering reviewers' comments, approving the Summaries for Policymakers (SPMs) and so forth.

Each meeting is also bound to specific norms and codes. WG LAMs closely resemble large academic gatherings and abide by largely informal deliberative

NORTH TOWER

FOURTH FLOOR

STAIRS AND ELEVATOR DOWN TO N'T LOBBY

PORT ALBERNI Chap.1

PORT HARDY

FOYER

P'RT McNEIL Chap.9

SOUTH TOWER

FOURTH FLOOR

GRANVILLE BOGs
BURRARD
COLUMBIA
FRASER
FOYER
HUDSON
VANCOUVER
GALIANO BOGs

THIRD FLOOR

AZURE FOYER
DOWN TO LOBBY
AZURE Chap.5
CRACKED ICE LOUNGE

E Elevators

The TSU help desk and the coffee breaks will be in the Grand Ballroom Foyer when Plenary meetings and in the Junior Ballroom Foyer (3rd floor) the rest of the time.

DOWN TO LOBBY AND GRAND BALLROOM

TSU help d

UP TO 4TH FLOOR

Coffee break

JUNIOR BALLROOM FOYER

JUNIOR Chap.2
JUNIOR B Chap.3
Chap.8
JUNIOR C
JUNIOR D CLAM

JUNIOR BALLROOM FOYER

HEALTH CLUB STAIRS

CHARTROOM

COAT CHECK

PARKSVILLE Chap.4

Reception

PAVILION BALLROOM FOYER

PAVILION A Chap.6
PAVILION B Chap.10
Chap.11
PAVILION C
Chap.12
PAVILION D

PAVILION BALLROOM FOYER

DOWN TO HEALTH CLUB

COAT CHECK

B TOWER

BLUE WHALE

LINK SHERATON BUSINESS CENTRE

THIRD FLOOR CONCOURSE

BELLIGA

FINBACK Chap.7

ORCA Atlas

Figure 4.3 (cont.)

34

practices. Discussions are mainly held in English, making it more challenging for non-native speakers. The domination of certain individuals is also sometimes difficult to avoid. In contrast, IPCC Panel sessions are more akin to UN meetings (with a ceremonial opening session, the presence of interpreters, the names of countries displayed on tables, the use of diplomatic courtesy and formalities, etc.). At the same time, because of the scientific aura of the IPCC, government representatives need to adapt their interventions to the register of science (e.g. political interventions can be dismissed on the grounds of being 'too political').

Brown et al. (2017: 14) define meetings as 'spaces for the alignment and negotiation of distinct perspectives [...] constituted through the contextual interplay of similarity and difference'. As an essential tool of collective deliberation, meetings – and meetings within meetings (chapter meetings, Bureau meetings, Breakout Groups (BOGs), SPM meetings, contract groups, huddles and so on; see Figure 4.4) – lie at the heart of the IPCC consensus-building strategy (see **Chapter 19**). Meetings allow participants to deliberate on specific issues, to identify agreements and disagreements, and to formulate informed assessments and decisions. Meetings are considered the 'locus and embodiment of ideas of appropriate, transparent decision-making' (Brown et al., 2017: 11), and the numerous guiding documents that are issued by the IPCC are expected to support and legitimise such processes.

Meetings also have an important socialising function as they offer moments of interaction and opportunities for relationship building. As 'a series of situated relationships between people, places, tools, and documents' (Yarrow, 2017: 97), meetings bring together IPCC participants and familiarise them with the norms and practices of the organisation. They help develop connections with other participants by creating a sense of community, shared identity and trust in the 'IPCC family'.

The Panel's system of meetings is also in constant dialogue with events happening outside the IPCC context. Smaller-scale in-person or virtual meetings between distinct expert communities aim to organise, orchestrate and align the activities of these communities with IPCC assessment cycles to ensure that their outputs are published in time to be included in IPCC reports (see **Chapter 18**). IPCC meetings are also part of even larger orchestration efforts that take place in other international institutions and fora (UN Framework Convention on Climate Change (UNFCCC), UNEP, WMO, Intergovernmental Science-Policy Platform on Biodiversity and Ecosystem Services (IPBES), etc.) (Campbell et al., 2014: 3). These events are connected by the individuals who circulate between them and who weave together ideas, practices and objects to build the global governance of the environment.

IPCC AR6 WGI LAM2 - Overview

Sunday Day 0	Monday	Tuesday	Wednesday	Thursday	Friday
	07:45-08:30 Registration	8:00 CLAM / CS* / MD**	8:00 CLAM / MD**	8:00 CLAM / MD**	8:00 CLAM / Bureau
	8:30 Opening Plenary	9:15 Chapter Meetings	9:15 Plenary 2	9:15 BOGs / Chap. Meetings	9:15 Chap. Meetings
	10:30 - break	10:30 - break	10:30 - break	10:30 - break	10:30 - break
	11:00 Plenary 1	11:00 Chapter Meetings	11:00 X-Chapter Meetings	11:00 BOGs / Chap. Meetings	11:00 Chapter Meetings
	Group Photo				
	12:45 - LUNCH	12:30 - LUNCH	12:30 - LUNCH	12:30 - LUNCH	12:30 - LUNCH
		13:00 FAQs / Glossary	13:30 Informal Q&A	13:30 Informal Q&A	
	14:00 Chapter Meetings	14:00 BOGs	14:00 X-Chapter Meetings	14:00 Chapter Meetings	13:30 Plenary 3
14:00-16:00 CLA welcome & training	15:30 - break	15:30 - break	15:30 - break	15:30 - break	15:30 - break
15:00-16:00 Bureau Meeting	16:00-18:15 Chapter Meetings	16:00 BOGs	16:00 Chapter Free Time	16:00 Chapter Meetings	16:00 Optional Chapter Meetings
16:15-17:15 CLAM	18:00 Bureau	18:00 Bureau / CLA mtg	16:00 Bureau meeting	18:00 Bureau / CLA mtg	
16:00-19:00 Early Registration	18:30-19:30 RECEPTION	18:30-20:00 Comms Mini-Workshop	18:30-20:30 Outreach Event	18:00-19:00 Chapter Scientist mtg	

*Chapter Scientists

** Mini-dialogues on participatory practices, collaboration and inclusive group-dynamics

Figure 4.4 Types of meetings scheduled during a Lead Author Meeting.
Source: IPCC, 2019a

Box 4.1
From in-person to virtual meetings

From April 2020, as a result of the global pandemic, LAMs and Panel sessions were moved online. The move to virtual meetings brought IPCC deliberations into the intimacy of the homes of authors, delegates, staff and observers. This required significant changes to the carefully orchestrated IPCC system of meetings. It meant, for instance, setting up a very complex schedule to ensure hospitable meeting times for participants across different time zones. The length of the meetings was also adapted. Author meetings were more frequent (WGIII for instance organised two 'Light Touch Stocktake' meetings) and virtual approval sessions lasted twice as long as in-person ones (i.e. two weeks).

Adapting the format of the meetings impacted participation both positively and negatively. Some participants welcomed, for example, the possibility to attend meetings which they otherwise could not have attended because of other commitments, limited resources or visa issues. Others appreciated the opportunity to save money and reduce their ecological footprint by avoiding air travel. WGIII for instance saved 368 tonnes of CO_2 emissions and about $1 million in travel costs (IPCC, 2020b). While both eLAMs and virtual Panel sessions recorded high attendance rates, challenges remained. For example, connectivity issues and limited internet access were a barrier for effective participation in some regions and some participants had to work through the night, as in Oceania and the Pacific Islands.

Deliberations were both facilitated and hindered by the process of moving online. For instance, through a well-balanced sequencing of the SPM sections, WGI succeeded in having most issues resolved on time. Instead of following the order of the SPM text as would be the case for in-person meetings, WGI moved the discussion of some of the trickiest statements to the first days of the approval, thus allowing more time for their resolution. In the eLAMs, the use of the Zoom chat function prompted reactions and comments that could easily be recorded by the authors and the TSUs and taken into account in following discussions. At the same time, the spontaneity, intensity and proximity of face-to-face meetings were often lost, and group dynamics were impacted. Virtual meetings reduced the possibility of moving between tables and rooms to meet other participants, of organising informal meetings, and of socialising in the corridors and during breaks. For instance, during the WGI approval session, some participants found it much harder to reach consensus online. Especially during heated debates, the difficulty to see other participants, their facial and bodily expressions, made deliberations more challenging. The WGIII TSU (IPCC, 2020b) also noted that meetings were sometimes dominated by more vocal and Zoom-savvy participants.

Virtual meetings are certainly no perfect substitute for in-person meetings, but they did open a space for considering new deliberation formats. It also allowed the organisation to publish the WGI report in time for the UN Climate Change Conference (COP26), thus providing a timely 'reality check' for the UNFCCC negotiations.

4.5 Achievements and Challenges

This chapter has shown why the IPCC is both large – in relation to the number of contributors who participate in its activities and the assessment function it provides – and small – in relation to its material reality and physical footprint. It functions through a carefully orchestrated and structurally embedded system of meetings spread throughout the world (although more occur in the Global North than in the Global South). Through this system of meetings, the IPCC has succeeded in bringing together scientific experts from all over the world to produce probably the most sophisticated global environmental assessment. It has also managed to socialise policymakers from all countries to the issue of climate change. However, building and maintaining such spaces in which researchers and government representatives can deliberate undisturbed comes at the cost of separating the organisation from the rest of society and organising its meetings behind closed doors.

As a result of the pandemic, and its subsequent restrictions on international travel and gatherings, in 2020 all IPCC meetings were moved online. The IPCC became a laboratory in which to experiment with new forms of participation and deliberation (Box 4.1). Notwithstanding the challenges of the global pandemic, the perceived success of eLAMs and virtual WG approval sessions proved the adaptive capacity of the IPCC's system of meetings. It also provided important lessons to be learned for the future of the organisation, notably suggesting the possibility of organising hybrid events, or alternating virtual and in-person meetings, to retain some of the advantages of eLAMs in terms of inclusivity and a lower carbon footprint.

Three Key Readings

Brown, H., Reed, A. and Yarrow, T. (2017). Introduction: towards an ethnography of meeting. *Journal of the Royal Anthropological Institute*, 23(S1): 10–26. http://doi .org/10.1111/1467-9655.12591

This article demonstrates the relevance of meetings as objects of study.

Craggs, R. and Mahony, M. (2014). The geographies of the conference: knowledge, performance and protest. *Geography Compass*, 8(6): 414–430. http://doi.wiley .com/10.1111/gec3.12137

This article draws attention to the role of conferences as an important part of political and academic life.

Gieryn, T. F. (2018). *Truth-Spots: How Places Make People Believe*. Chicago: University of Chicago Press. http://doi.org/10.7208/chicago/9780226562001.001.0001

This book shows how truth and place are inextricably linked and examines those places that lend credibility to beliefs and claims.

5

Reports

JASMINE E. LIVINGSTON

Overview

This chapter outlines the process of the report writing of the Intergovernmental Panel on Climate Change (IPCC) and discusses, through specific examples, how these reports are produced within, and shaped by, political and scientific contexts. The IPCC produces Assessment Reports, Special Reports, and Methodological Reports, which are central to the institution's operations and perceived impact. There are also sub-elements of these reports – Summary for Policymakers and Technical Summary – which fulfil important stand-alone roles. The process of writing these reports is well-institutionalised and involves maintaining a balance between scientific credibility and policy relevance. The reports produced are therefore accountable to, and co-produced with, scientific *and* policy communities. The chapter shows how the framing of IPCC reports has changed over time and continues to evolve. This also raises questions about the future of IPCC reports in relation to IPCC processes and in response to diversifying audiences and new media.

5.1 Introduction

At its inception in 1988, the IPCC was tasked with providing regular, comprehensive scientific assessments on climate change. The production of these reports is the central purpose and mandate of the IPCC (Agrawala, 1998b). Since then, the IPCC has produced 6 full Assessment Reports, as well as 14 Special Reports, and 6 Methodology Reports (see Table 5.1 for a list of all reports produced to date).[1]

IPCC reports are produced within a well-institutionalised architecture and through processes that aim to maintain scientific integrity and policy relevance. The effort to be 'neutral, policy-relevant but not policy-prescriptive' (IPCC, 2021b) guides their production, organisation and reception. In other words, through their connection to

Table 5.1. *List of all IPCC Assessment, Special and Methodology Reports to 2023*

Year of publication	Assessment Reports, Special Reports, Methodology Reports

First assessment cycle (1988–1990)

1990   First Assessment Report, known as FAR or (AR1)
 – WGI Scientific Assessment of Climate Change (approved May 1990)
 – WGII Impacts Assessment of Climate Change (July 1990)
 – WGIII The IPCC Response Strategies (October 1990)

Second assessment cycle (1990–1995)

1992   Supplementary Reports
1994   Special Report on Radiative Forcing of Climate Change and An Evaluation of the IPCC IS92 Emission Scenarios
1994   IPCC Guidelines for National Greenhouse Gas Inventories
1994   IPCC Technical Guidelines for Assessing Climate Change Impacts and Adaptations
1995   Second Assessment Report, known as SAR (or AR2)
 – WGI The Science of Climate Change (November 1995)
 – WGII Impacts, Adaptations and Mitigation of Climate Change: Scientific-Technical Analyses (October 1995)
 – WGIII Economic and Social Dimensions of Climate Change (October 1995)
 – Synthesis Report (December 1995)

Third assessment cycle (1995–2001)

1996   Revised 1996 IPCC Guidelines for National Greenhouse Gas Inventories
1997   Special Report on The Regional Impacts of Climate Change: An Assessment of Vulnerability
1999   Special Report on Aviation and the Global Atmosphere
2000   Special Report on Emissions Scenarios, known as SRES
2000   Special Report on Methodological and Technological Issues in Technology Transfer, known as SRTT
2000   Special Report on Land Use, Land-Use Change, and Forestry, known as SRLULUCF
2001   Third Assessment Report, known as TAR (or AR3)
 – WGI The Physical Science Basis (January 2001)
 – WGII Impacts, Adaptation and Vulnerability (February 2001)
 – WGIII Mitigation (March 2001)
 – Synthesis Report (September 2001)

Fourth assessment cycle (2001–2007)

2005   Special Report on Carbon Dioxide Capture and Storage, known as SRCCS
2005   Special Report on Safeguarding the Ozone Layer and the Global Climate System, known as SROC
2006   IPCC Guidelines for National Greenhouse Gas Inventories
2007   Fourth Assessment Report, known as AR4
 – WGI The Physical Science Basis (February 2007)
 – WGII Impacts, Adaptation and Vulnerability (April 2007)
 – WGIII Mitigation of Climate Change (May 2007)
 – Synthesis Report (November 2007)

Table 5.1. (*cont.*)

Year of publication	Assessment Reports, Special Reports, Methodology Reports
Fifth assessment cycle (2007–2014)	
2011	Special Report on Renewable Energy Sources and Climate Change Mitigation, known as SRREN
2012	Special Report on Managing the Risks of Extreme Events and Disasters to Advance Climate Change Adaptation, known as SREX
2014	Fifth Assessment Report, known as AR5 – WGI The Physical Science Basis (September 2013) – WGII Impacts, Adaptation and Vulnerability (March 2014) – WGIII Mitigation of Climate Change (April 2014) – Synthesis Report (October 2014)
Sixth assessment cycle (2014–2023)	
2018	Special Report on Global Warming of 1.5 °C, known as SR15
2019	Refinement to the 2006 IPCC Guidelines for National Greenhouse Gas Inventories
2019	Special Report on Climate Change and Land, known as SRCCL
2019	Special Report on The Ocean and Cryosphere in a Changing Climate, known as SROCC
2020	Methodology Report on Short Lived Climate Forcers
2021–23	Sixth Assessment Report, known as AR6 – WGI The Physical Science Basis (August 2021) – WGII Impacts, Adaptation and Vulnerability (February 2022) – WGIII Mitigation of Climate Change (March 2022) – Synthesis Report March (2023)

The dates indicated relate to official IPCC approval.

scientific and policy worlds, IPCC reports are accountable to both. This chapter outlines the processes of commissioning and designing different IPCC report styles, and their roles and functions. It expands on how the IPCC's unique situation between science and policy has led to its reports evolving in line with changing policy expectations and developments in scientific knowledge. It shows that IPCC reports have a broad audience and that the challenges to keeping them relevant comes from both political and scientific arenas.

5.2 Types and Styles of Reports

The periodic IPCC assessments are made up of four reports: individual reports for Working Group (WG) I – The Physical Science Basis; WGII – Impacts, Adaptation, and Vulnerability; and WGIII – Mitigation of Climate Change; and a

Synthesis Report. With an increasing body of published literature to draw upon, the size of Assessment Reports has grown. Thus the WGI report in the First Assessment Report (AR1) in 1990 was around 400 pages in length compared to over 1500 pages for WGI in AR6 in 2021. Since AR2, the three WGs are brought together in a shorter Synthesis Report, which aims to highlight the most important cross-cutting aspects (IPCC, 2013a). These reports are comprehensive updates of knowledge on climate change, each with a different set of authors and a different literature base.

The IPCC has also produced 14 Special Reports to date. Special Reports are led by either one WG or else by a combination of WGs. Although the context for these Special Reports differs, their collective role is to provide more detailed information, in between the Assessment Reports, on specific topics deemed particularly relevant by its member governments (Fogel, 2005, and see **Chapter 20**). All IPCC reports include a Summary for Policymakers (SPM) – a shorter summary of the main policy-relevant findings (around 30 pages), and a Technical Summary (TS) – a longer and more detailed summary with technical detail that cannot be included in the SPM. The IPCC also produces Methodological Reports in the form of practical guidelines. Most recently in this category has been the Methodology Report on Short-lived Climate Forcers, and updated IPCC Guidelines on National Greenhouse Gas Inventories.

The production of IPCC reports is a well-documented process (see Hughes, 2012; IPCC, 2013a; Livingston et al., 2018; De Pryck, 2021a). The process of report preparation is generally the same for all Assessment, Special, and Methodological Reports (see Figure 3.1 in **Chapter 3**). Reports are scoped and their draft outline determined. The outline is approved by the Panel in Plenary, a process that is important because agreement on the outline is considered to increase the likelihood that the final report will be accepted (Hughes, 2012). Following approval of the outline by the Panel, Coordinating Lead Authors, Lead Authors, and Review Editors are nominated and selected. Authors then start to prepare the report based on the scoping outline and an assessment of the relevant underlying literature. The draft report undergoes two external review rounds following the First Order Draft (FOD) by experts and following the Second Order Draft (SOD) by both governments and experts. At the time of the SOD, the summary sections of the report (the SPM for Assessment and Special Reports, or the Overview Section of Methodology Reports) are prepared and circulated for review (see **Chapter 11**). Based on these expert and government reviews the Final Draft is prepared. The summary sections of the report are sent out for one final government review (the Final Government Distribution) in advance of the final Approval/Acceptance Plenary (see **Chapter 20**).

Reports are presented at the final plenary for approval by governments. In the case of the WG and Synthesis reports this takes place at the WG and Panel Plenary

Sessions, respectively (see IPCC, 2013a). The SPM undergoes line-by-line 'approval' – meaning that it is subject to in-depth discussion, and agreed upon between the Panel and the report's authors. The underlying report is 'accepted' – which means it has not been subject to as detailed scrutiny as the SPM, but still presents what is deemed to be 'a comprehensive, objective and balanced view of the subject matter' (IPCC, 2013a). The longer Synthesis Report has the special status of being 'adopted' section by section. The TS is prepared by the authors alone, but is an integrated part of the full report, and thus accepted alongside the full report. The different methods of approval may also have an effect on how a report is read, as well as who the audience is deemed to be. For example, policymakers may refer mainly to the SPM for top level messaging, the language of which has been agreed upon in plenary. However, more technical information on specific topics may be found in the TS or in the underlying chapters.

A core aspect of IPCC reports is that they are co-produced between governments, IPCC authors and other experts partaking in the review process. In doing this, the IPCC both entrenches and performs its mandate to be 'policy relevant, but never policy prescriptive' and produces a report which is accountable to, and yet also an outcome of, scientific *and* policy worlds. The next section outlines and provides some examples of how the IPCC's connections to both science and policy have also had tangible impacts on the framing and outcome of products.

5.3 Framing Products in Changing Contexts

The climate change policy landscape has changed considerably since the IPCC was founded in 1988. The exact nature of the connection between the IPCC and its policy context is much commented on and debated both within critical social science circles and the IPCC itself (e.g. Haas & Stevens, 2011; Lidskog & Sundqvist, 2015). Yet the products of the IPCC have undoubtedly been shaped by this context. An example of this would be the early reorganisation of the WG structure (see Agrawala, 1998b; Skodvin, 2000b). In AR1, published in 1990, the job of assessing possible Response Strategies lay with WGIII. But with the establishment in 1991 of the Intergovernmental Negotiating Committee (INC) – the precursor to the UN Framework Convention on Climate Change (UNFCCC) – the task of dealing with policy responses was passed to this new political body. As Skodvin (2000b: 121) notes, 'the establishment of a negotiating committee enabled the IPCC to reorganise itself, withdraw from the (explicit) advisory function and reformulate its task to a provision of assessments for all WGs'.

Following the Paris Agreement in 2015 and the end of the 5th Assessment Cycle (AR5), the IPCC was again subject to discussion over its future and the structure of its products. The bottom-up nature of the Paris Agreement based on Nationally Determined Contributions (NDCs), in comparison to the top-down nature of the Kyoto Protocol, was identified as a reason for the need to reassess the nature of the IPCC's products to better suit this new climate politics (Provost, 2019). Many critical scholars argue that broad global assessments of climate are no longer politically relevant, and provide suggestions about how IPCC reports might evolve. These suggestions include dividing reports up into several diverse assessments (e.g. Beck et al., 2014), producing shorter, more focused reports on specific topics and geographical contexts (Devès et al., 2017), or engaging in more ex-post assessment of policies (Carraro et al., 2015). Related to this, calls have been made for a 'solutions turn' in environmental assessments – assessments which, through collaborative processes, can evaluate the potential associated with different policy alternatives and their consequences (Kowarsch et al., 2017; see **Chapter 21**). This sentiment has also been recognised by the current IPCC Chairman, Hoesung Lee (see De Pryck & Wanneau, 2017).

It is not always easy to assess the ways in which changes in policy expectations and in broader policy context shape the framing of IPCC reports. The periodic Assessment Reports provide comprehensive updates on the state of the science of climate change and of knowledge about socio-economic impacts, adaptation processes and mitigation options. Other reports, for example Methodological and Special Reports, are more closely connected to the policy discourse and focus on specific topics identified by the countries in Plenary.

Fogel (2005) outlines how the commissioning by the Subsidiary Body for Science and Technology Advice (SBSTA) and preparation of the Special Report on Land Use, Land Use Change, and Forestry in 2000 were directly linked to political debates on the provisions of biotic carbon sequestration in the Kyoto Protocol. This was a highly policy-relevant and politically sensitive report because its approval was in some ways used to help resolve a political debate over what different countries wanted to include in the Kyoto Protocol (see Box 16.2 in **Chapter 16**). Another more recent example is that of the Special Report on Global Warming of 1.5 °C (SR15), requested in conjunction with the approval of the Paris Agreement in 2015 and published in 2018. The framing of SR15 around a specific temperature target, itself the result of protracted political discussions, revealed the complicated science–policy dynamics surrounding the preparation of IPCC reports, and Special Reports in particular (see Box 5.1 for more details). Methodology Reports are also key to the development and framing of NDCs, and are central to debates in current climate politics surrounding emissions inventories (see Dahan-Dalmedico, 2008; Yona et al., 2022).

These examples illustrate the tight connections IPCC reports maintain with the political realm and, in particular, with the UNFCCC. In addition, the IPCC also

---

Box 5.1
The Special Report on Global Warming of 1.5 °C (SR15)

The need to limit 'dangerous anthropogenic interference' in the climate system has been a part of Article 2 of the UNFCCC from its inception in 1992. Discussions about what is deemed dangerous climate change has been a point of political contention, and the IPCC – in its role as scientific assessment body – has at times been asked to weigh into this discussion. During the preparation and approval of the IPCC AR5 SYR in 2014, there was a protracted discussion about the inclusion in the SPM of a box addressing Article 2 (Livingston et al., 2018). However, it was ultimately decided that there was not enough scientific information available to provide a robust evidence base.

Limiting global warming to 2 °C as a long-term global goal (LTGG) had been widely discussed in political circles prior to 2015, and had been used in scenario modelling in the scientific community. Yet the voices supporting a lower figure of 1.5 °C – initially small island states and NGOs – grew louder in the run up to the Paris Conference of the Parties (COP) in 2015. This was supported by the Structured Expert Dialogue (SED) which was held under the UNFCCC between 2013 and 2015 with the goal of promoting discussion around the state of knowledge on both the adequacy and progress towards the LTGG. The IPCC partook in this process as an expert body providing evidence from the AR5 cycle. The main conclusion from IPCC speakers was still often that there was not enough information to be able to make comparisons, particularly on impacts, between 1.5 °C and 2 °C. Despite this uncertainty in the scientific evidence, the Paris Agreement in 2015 enshrined 1.5 °C into the text as a target to aspire to, and the COP asked the IPCC to produce a Special Report on 1.5 °C. Discussions with IPCC authors involved in the preparation of SR15 showed how this unexpectedly specific and ambitious request took scientists by surprise (see Livingston & Rummukainen, 2020).

Following its acceptance of the request from the UNFCCC to produce the report, the IPCC put out a series of calls to the research community for new studies to be undertaken with the specific goal of being included in SR15 (see Livingston & Rummukainen, 2020). A cut-off date for publishing this new research was set by the IPCC. Nevertheless, during the review process of SR15, it became apparent that the lack of available literature, alongside the specific mandate to focus on 1.5 °C of warming, limited the framing of the report (see Hansson et al., 2021), and the technological pathways to achieve this goal that the report identified. The example of SR15 illustrates the tight connection the IPCC has with the scientific and social scientific communities upon whose work it bases its assessments (see also **Chapter 12**).

SR15 is an interesting case of an IPCC report that addresses a politically contentious topic, deemed either not scientifically interesting or 'too policy relevant' in previous AR cycles (see Livingston & Rummukainen, 2020). It had the effect of challenging

Continued

> ### Box 5.1 (cont.)
>
> the norms of detachedness and value-free science on which the IPCC bases its assessment practices. In turn, through requests for new scientific evidence on which to base its assessment – calls for papers, new scenarios, and accelerated research on 1.5 °C of warming – the IPCC had a role in shaping new interdisciplinary communities of researchers working on this policy relevant, although still politically contentious, topic that has increasingly gained traction in recent years.

maintains its position as an authoritative body of climate change expertise through its connection to the scientific evidence base (van der Hel & Biermann, 2017). As debates surrounding the preparation of the Special Reports discussed previously show, this is not always a straightforward task. Fogel (2005) outlines how discussions over the need to focus on 'scientific and technical' data over more cultural and socio-economic concerns in the Land Use Report from 2000 also influenced the types of literature assessed and the authors involved in the report preparation. Ultimately, this meant that the focus of the report was more on the technical definition of carbon sinks and involved experts with primarily physical science backgrounds. The SR15 report however is in line with calls for the IPCC to adopt a more solutions-orientated approach (Hulme, 2016). This has led to a reordering of the types of questions and framings within the IPCC itself (for example connecting the work of all three WGs), and the types of knowledge on which the assessment was based (see also **Chapter 18**).

The type of literature assessed for different IPCC reports to a large degree determines their nature. This is a question that has increasingly occupied IPCC discussions in more recent years in debates about representation between scientific disciplines. The IPCC bases its assessment on syntheses primarily of peer-reviewed literature published in academic journals (although it has in more recent years attempted to open up to a broader evidence base – see **Chapter 13**). Reliance on the underlying literature means that the IPCC is shaped by what literature is available at the time of writing, and by its framing and language. The structuring and sequencing of IPCC Assessment Reports – moving from WGI to WGIII – reflects a particular problem-solution framing which is largely based on the logic of natural science and a linear model of science to policy (see Beck, 2011a).

In a study of AR3, Bjurström and Polk (2011) found a strong bias towards natural scientific and economic literature. This had implications for how the IPCC frames climate change, for example by placing humans outside nature. In a more recent study undertaken on AR5, Fløttum et al. (2016) suggested that the language of the IPCC reports, while often chosen to ensure policy neutrality, did not successfully communicate the meaning of climate change to people and communities. One way to deal with these issues related to framing, suggested by many commentators, is for the IPCC to draw from a broader range of expertise and, in particular, to pay attention to the interpretative social sciences and humanities disciplines that have historically been absent from IPCC assessments (Carey et al., 2014). The reordering of expertise and of the kinds of questions being asked within research communities following the Paris Agreement may indeed herald a change in the way the IPCC assesses knowledge in the coming years.

5.4 Achievements and Challenges

The IPCC has been a highly productive institution during its 34-year history, and its reports are referenced in contexts as broad as the Fridays for Future movement, and in recent cases of climate litigation. This suggests that the 'relevance' of its reports extends far beyond the audiences envisaged by the IPCC itself. In addition, considerable media coverage surrounds their publication (O'Neill et al., 2015; see **Chapter 26**). The sheer number and reach of its publications can therefore be seen as a fundamental achievement. The so-called IPCC style of scientific assessment and process, which is tightly tied up with the production of reports, has been used as a model for other kinds of global environmental assessment, such as Intergovernmental Science-Policy Platform on Biodiversity and Ecosystem Services (IPBES).

However, the IPCC faces new challenges alongside the changing policy and scientific contexts within which it operates. Diversifying audiences and new social media suggest that new products, alongside the traditional IPCC report, may assume larger significance. These currently include IPCC FAQs and its Interactive Atlas (Lynn & Peeva, 2021). This chapter has illustrated how the IPCC's aim of producing reports that are policy relevant but never policy prescriptive forms a key part of both the preparation of reports, and their positioning in relation to broader political and scientific practice. Within the current political climate, continued strict adherence to the value-free ideal of science could limit the IPCC's reach because growing numbers of voices call for more direct policy recommendations and messaging (Lynn & Peeva, 2021). The IPCC's reports have forged an authoritative role in today's society, but to maintain this authority will require diversification and flexibility in the design of future IPCC reports and products.

Note

1 The IPCC has also produced a series of Technical Papers, based on material already existing in IPCC reports, the last of which was 'Climate Change and Water', published in 2008 (see Afsen & Skodvin, 1998).

Three Key Readings

Fløttum, K., Gasper, D. and St Clair, A. L. (2016). Synthesizing a policy-relevant perspective from the three IPCC "Worlds" – A comparison of topics and frames in the SPMs of the Fifth Assessment Report. *Global Environmental Change*, 38: 118–129. http://doi.org/10.1016/j.gloenvcha.2016.03.007

This article provides an interesting analysis of the language used in different WG Reports.

Livingston, J. E. and Rummukainen, M. (2020). Taking science by surprise: the knowledge politics of the IPCC Special Report on 1.5 degrees. *Environmental Science & Policy*, 112: 10–16. http://doi.org/10.1016/j.envsci.2020.05.020

This article provides detail on the science–policy context and preparation of the Special Report on 1.5 °C, a valuable case study of the changing nature of IPCC reports.

De Pryck, K. (2021a). Intergovernmental expert consensus in the making: the case of the Summary for Policy Makers of the IPCC 2014 Synthesis Report. *Global Environmental Politics*, 21(1): 108–129. http://doi.org/10.1162/glep_a_00574

This article provides insights into how IPCC reports are written, in particular the SPMs.

6

Learning

SILKE BECK AND BERND SIEBENHÜNER

Overview

This chapter discusses the performance of the Intergovernmental Panel on Climate Change (IPCC) as a 'learning' organisation. The Panel has responded to novel challenges by adjusting its governance structure and its underlying objectives and principles. Building on a heuristic of organisational learning, we reconstruct and map these past learning processes. We find that most of these challenges resulted in the IPCC adopting an *adaptive mode of learning* by incrementally adjusting procedures. There were only a few moments of *reflexive learning*. Against this backdrop, the chapter discusses future challenges for the IPCC emerging from the Paris Agreement and the call for a 'solution-oriented assessment'. The IPCC has faced demands in the past for greater political relevance, geopolitical representation, scientific integrity, transparency and accountability. In the post-Paris world, the Panel has to cope with its role in the polycentric architecture of the climate regime and its role as 'mapmaker' in the assessment of pathways to achieve the Paris ambition. We conclude by discussing how the IPCC can best use its learning capacities in responding to these challenges.

6.1 Introduction

Since the IPCC's inception in 1988, the magnitude, scale and complexity of climate change research have grown significantly. This is true also of the IPCC's assessment tasks and the public expectations of these assessments. In this chapter, we explore how the IPCC as an organisation learned to tackle the challenges of accommodating advances in scientific understanding and meeting the evolving needs of policymakers. We argue that the performance of the IPCC stands and falls according to its learning capacity. By this we mean its ability to evaluate its governance structures, to apply lessons learned from one assessment to the next, and to adjust its processes to address new needs (IAC, 2010). In order to reconstruct forms of organisational learning, we focus on the Panel's governance and institutional arrangements which consist of its decision-making structures, principles, procedures and work programme. The chapter applies the concept of *organisational learning* in order to analyse past learning processes within the organisation. We assess whether the IPCC is fit to address novel challenges and to perform new assessment tasks. Against this historical backdrop, the chapter then discusses the challenges for the IPCC arising after the Paris Agreement, which prompts the question of whether the IPCC is still fit for function.

6.2 Forms of Organisational Learning

In this section we develop a heuristic for reconstructing different forms of organisational learning (Siebenhüner, 2002) in order to distinguish between two forms of learning (see also Table 6.1):

Adaptive learning responds to changes in the environment of an organisation and its externally determined functions. This form of learning leads to incremental adjustments and partial improvements, but it does not transform the organisation's objectives, its conceptual frames and values, or its main practices. It allows for the optimisation and promotion of performance in a given target structure (Fiol & Lyles, 1985; Schön & Argyris, 1996).

Reflexive learning, by contrast, fundamentally changes the objectives, conceptual frames and value systems of an organisation. Wynne (1993) and Beck et al. (1994) draw upon the notion of 'institutional reflexivity', which they define as the organisation's capacities and processes to continually evaluate the impacts of its objectives and actions in relation to their changing contexts, to critically examine (and thus render open to change) their own basic assumptions, and then to adjust them in the light of this newly acquired knowledge. In these so-called 'constitutional moments' (Jasanoff, 2011a), key design choices of how to govern an assessment are revisited and institutional arrangements reconfigured. These choices refer to questions such as who counts as a credible expert, what counts as relevant expertise and on what ground, and who is entitled to speak for the organisation (Beck, 2012; Pallett & Chilvers, 2013; Borie et al., 2020). Reflexive learning includes responses to both internal and external developments in the socio-political context, reflecting the institution's own role in the wider politics of global environmental change (Beck & Mahony, 2018a).

In order to evaluate the IPCC's learning processes, we need to consider its nature as a hybrid organisation. The Panel performs both scientific and political tasks,

Table 6.1. *Types of organisational learning*

Types of learning	Moments of unsettlement	Ways of learning	Consequences	Criteria / goals
Adaptive	Critical	Loop between expectations and con-sequences	Incremental change/ Adjustment of procedures	Political salience/ authority
Reflexive	Constitutional	Loop between expectations, consequences and objectives	Transformative change: recon-figuration of targets, values and practices	Responsiveness, openness, flexibility, accountability

Source: Authors.

includes rather different communities in science, politics and civil society, and needs to maintain credibility, trust and legitimacy to all. Situated at the interface between international science and politics, the IPCC has to maintain political relevance as well as scientific integrity in the face of intense political pressures (internal and external), tight deadlines and a continually evolving, multi-disciplinary scientific landscape. It has to reconcile political demands – salience, legitimacy, geopolitical representation – with the need for expert decision-making, such as integrity and the relative autonomy of scientific self-organisation. The hybrid nature of the Panel suggests that there is neither a single, exclusive criterion – such as political relevance – nor a single, linear path to evaluate its performance and learning capacity. Different forms of learning serve different functions/purposes and may have trade-offs and unintended consequences. Adaptive learning serves to maintain its political salience and robustness, while reflexive learning can be considered as a means to enact the organisation's responsiveness, openness, innovation, transparency and accountability.

6.3 A Track Record of Adaptive Learning

A prominent site to observe organisational learning in action is the Plenary of the Panel, where governance structures and rules of procedures are adopted by the member states of the IPCC (see **Chapter 3**). There are plenary sessions that take place at the beginning and end of an assessment cycle in order to draw lessons from existing processes and incorporate these lessons into the new phase of assessment (Beck, 2012; see **Chapter 2**). Figure 6.1 depicts the major events and significant changes in the history of the IPCC.

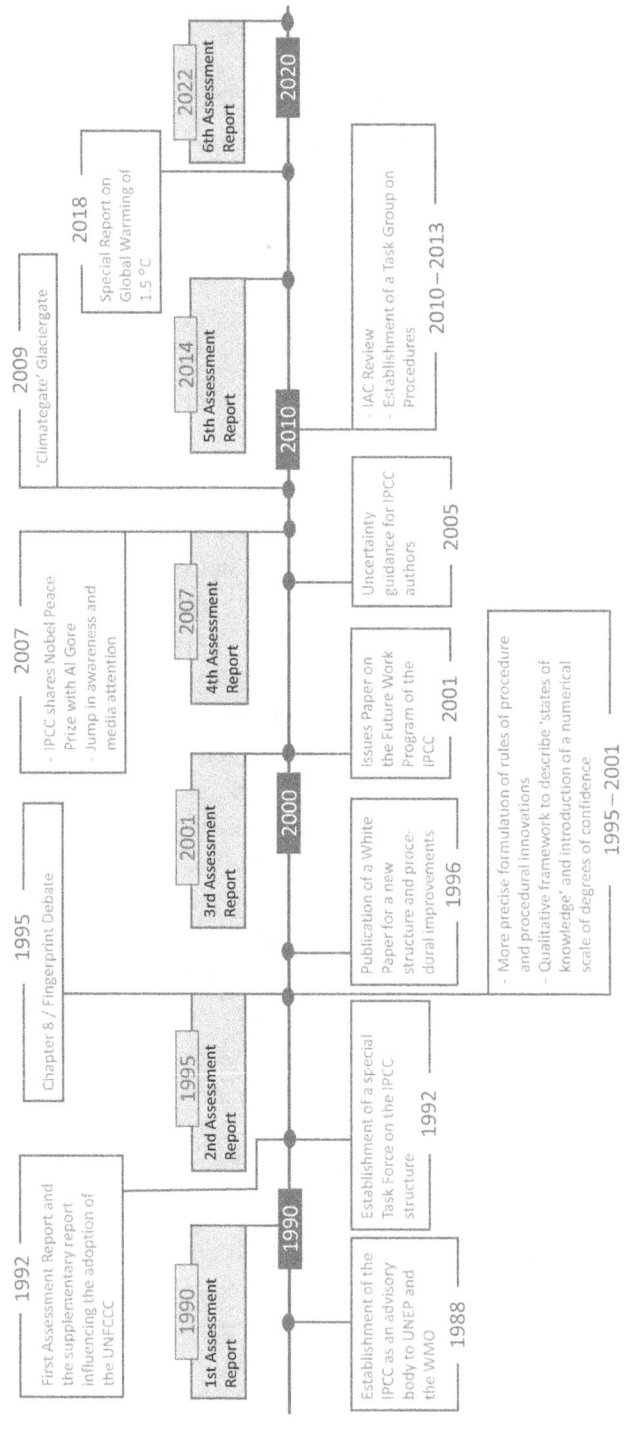

Figure 6.1 Major events and changes in the IPCC structure and processes.
Source: Authors

As several case studies indicate (Siebenhüner, 2002, 2014; Beck, 2012), the IPCC effectively improved its procedures to enhance its political salience and legitimacy, while maintaining its scientific standards. Over the period of its existence, the Panel has substantially revised procedures at least three times – in 1993, 1999 and 2010. Almost all the changes shown in Figure 6.1 qualify as adaptive learning, resulting in incremental changes, adjustments of the conceptual frames, and stepwise improvements of procedures. Examples include the establishment of an iterative review process for the draft assessment reports, embracing uncertainties by a system of levels of confidence, and the inclusion of cross-cutting themes such as costing methodologies and equity.

In response to the so-called 'Chapter-8 debate' in 1995 (see also **Chapter 11**), the Panel introduced radically new ways of addressing external criticisms, which differed remarkably from former forms of adaptive learning. The Chapter-8 debate indicated 'a constitutional moment', which resulted in a form of reflexive learning. In this debate, the IPCC faced a massive attack launched by some U.S. scientists alongside antagonistic media coverage. IPCC authors were accused of deliberately circumventing scientific review procedures and falsifying scientific results for political reasons. In contrast to former criticism, the charges focused on procedural aspects rather than on scientific findings themselves, questioning the legitimacy of the processes by which the report – and in particular the WGI Chapter 8 – had been produced.

In response to such attacks, in 1999 the IPCC began to revise and formalise its scientific quality-control procedures. These revisions indicated a constitutional moment because the IPCC turned, by itself, from a scientific to a legal mode of governance standardising its rules and procedures (Lahsen, 1999; Edwards & Schneider, 2001). Henceforth, the IPCC faced the challenge of reconciling forms of scientific self-organisation with these newly formalised legal modes of coordination. Although the formalising of procedures contributed towards greater coherence of governance structures – and therefore increased the political robustness of the organisation – these efforts constrained the flexibility of scientific processes, which form the backbone of the IPCC (Edwards & Schneider, 2001).

6.4 The Review by the InterAcademy Council (IAC)

The Panel's public recognition increased significantly after it released its Fourth Assessment Report (AR4) in 2007 and in the same it year received a share of the Nobel Peace Prize. But early in 2010, errors were discovered in the AR4 Report. Media coverage focused on the WGII analysis of the potential impacts of global warming, including a controversial statement that Himalayan glaciers might disappear by 2035. The revelation of these errors came shortly after another highly publicised controversy involving the unauthorised release of email exchanges between prominent climate scientists, many of whom had contributed to IPCC assessments (IAC, 2010: 59; Beck, 2012).

Since its inception, the IPCC has evaluated its own management structure, scope, and the mandate of its Working Groups (WGs). This internal evaluation, conducted during the Panel's plenary sessions, is a key part of its scoping process at the beginning of a new assessment cycle. In response to this vociferous public criticism in the early months of 2010, IPCC procedures were reviewed externally, however, by national and international agencies. In particular, the InterAcademy Council (IAC), an alliance of national scientific academies, published a prominent review in August 2010 focusing on the IPCC's procedures and management structure (IAC, 2010). It identified shortcomings in terms of transparency surrounding the selection of authors, reviewers, and scientific and technical information for assessment reports, a general reluctance to make data publicly available, and the absence of a comprehensive communication strategy. The IAC final report rejected the accusation of deliberate manipulation by authors and highlighted that all of the most prominent statements contained in the IPCC reports were correct. It also noted that there was a mismatch between the growing complexity of the tasks facing the IPCC and its available capacities and management structures. The IAC concluded that the Panel was no longer able to cope adequately with the challenges it faced (IAC, 2010: 6), and fundamental changes to the process and management structure were essential to ensure its continued success (IAC, 2010: 63; Tollefson, 2010).

In October 2010, the IPCC initiated steps to implement the IAC recommendations; however, the organisation remained in an adaptive-learning mode. The negotiations over IPCC reform focused on adjusting specific procedures, from the selection of authors and review procedures to the way errors were dealt with in published assessment reports. The resulting revisions of rules of procedures were adopted by the Plenary of the Panel in 2011 (IPCC, 2011). The IPCC's responses showed that the same mechanisms that served to maintain its political authority (such as its intergovernmental status, the governmental approval mechanism and consensus-based procedures) contributed to closing down the range of reform options. This finally resulted in a 'lowest common denominator' acceptable to all parties involved. This incremental reform solely targeted scientific quality by rendering procedures more transparent for the scientists and nation state representatives already involved (IPCC, 2011). At the same time, the IPCC did not address demands for public transparency and accountability (IAC, 2010), for example by opening up the assessment processes in its WGs to broader audiences, such as the UN, IPCC observer organisations, non-governmental organisations or the wider public, and it did not introduce a public disclosure mechanism. The reform efforts thus merely focused on incremental revisions and contributed to stabilising its core principles and arrangements and consolidated its fit within the wider climate regime. Even invited by the IAC to rethink its process and management structure and fundamentally change them, the IPCC adapted in an incremental way and missed this opportunity for catalysing reflexive learning.

6.5 The Demand for Solutions: Calls for Reflexive Learning

The Paris Agreement in 2015 represented a major change in the climate regime. Climate politics were no longer about raising awareness about global warming, but about shaping the solutions to achieve politically adopted temperature targets. National governments in countries such as Germany and Sweden were additionally held accountable by social movements such as the Fridays for Future, which drew substantial strength from its reading of IPCC reports. More recently, government initiatives have been launched, such as the European Union Green New Deal and the Biden administration's climate plan. This changing political context raises novel challenges for the IPCC.

First, the IPCC has to adapt to the polycentric political architecture of the Paris Agreement and become more responsive to the needs of state and non-state actors at different levels of decision-making (Beck & Mahony, 2018a). There are broader questions to be asked: Should the 'audience' and 'owners' of IPCC assessments continue to just be nation-state parties? Should the IPCC be more directly accountable to a broader set of actors, such as local and regional authorities, civil-society groups and private companies? It also raises questions about the spatial scale at which a solution-oriented global assessment fits local decision-makers' needs on the ground.

Second, there is a growing political demand for the IPCC to assess solutions for meeting the ambition of the Paris Agreement. The IPCC WGIII responded by developing a 'mapmaker strategy' (Edenhofer & Kowarsch, 2015; IPCC, 2015a). Following the mapmaker metaphor, the WG provided a comprehensive assessment of pathways to achieve politically adopted temperature goals. It is an open and contested question whether a solution-oriented assessment is consistent with the IPCC's mandate to be policy neutral, or whether this mandate needs updating (see **Chapter 21**).

Third, for achieving politically adopted temperature targets the Integrated Assessment Modelling (IAM) community, which provides input to the IPCC, introduced 'negative emissions technologies' (NETs) as a backstop strategy to meet temperature targets. IPCC reports have presented large-scale use of NETs as necessary or inevitable for reaching the goals formulated in the Paris Agreement (IPCC, 2018a). Policy options based on behavioural change and societal transformations, rather than on technologies, are left out of IPCC assessments because they cannot be easily scaled up and aggregated into the IAMs to the level required to meet the temperature targets (see **Chapter 15**). As a consequence, the IPCC tends to narrow the climate solution space to technological pathways that are deemed feasible by economic models designed to optimise global economic growth. The large-scale deployment of NETs has become a fully-fledged policy option under consideration by powerful actors, even if these technologies are not available in the real world at the scale or scope projected by the IAMs.

The influential role of IAMs with respect to IPCC assessment and policy processes has drawn attention and scrutiny to the practices of this modelling community (Pielke, 2018). As a response to this scrutiny, the modelling community and the IPCC have taken steps to open up the black box of IAMs (Skea et al., 2021), but only in an incremental way. Critics, however, point to the lack of public transparency and accountability, from early energy models in the 1990s through to the most recent generation of IAMs and the pathways assessed by the IPCC (Wynne, 1984; Anderson, 2015). As a consequence, key methodological decisions – addressing issues such as emission pathway characteristics, temperature overshoot, the balance of mitigation action in the near-and long-term, remaining carbon budgets, the role of carbon dioxide removal, and the choice of discount rates applied to future technologies – have not been treated as legitimate objects of political debate or public scrutiny despite having major governance implications (Robertson, 2021).

These novel challenges emerging in the post-Paris context indicate that the relationship between climate science and policy can be seen as undergoing a fundamental transformation (see **Chapter 21**). The challenges call for reflecting on and rethinking the Panel's mandate and its embeddedness in the climate regime if future expectations for the IPCC are to be met. This constitutes an opportunity – and, we would state, a necessity – for reflexive learning leading to substantial changes in the IPCC's governance and procedures.

6.6 Achievements and Challenges

One of the major achievements of the IPCC is that it has already made significant progress in organisational learning. To its credit, the IPCC has shown that it is a flexible and adaptive organisation. Our reconstruction presented in this chapter indicates that the IPCC has mainly learned in an adaptive mode; there are only a few moments where it has chosen reflexive forms of learning. In the past, the Panel responded to novel challenges by incrementally adjusting its internal management structure, as well as its assessment and review processes. Since the IPCC's inception, however, its governance structure has remained remarkably stable.

The IPCC's incremental learning efforts contributed to maintaining and stabilising its institutional arrangements, rather than making it open to change.

External evaluations – such as the IAC report in 2010 – encouraged the IPCC to explore structural transformations in order to address the increasingly multi-disciplinary nature of climate change research and new demands for increased transparency and accountability. The external evaluation by the IAC, for example, can be seen as a constitutional moment where the assessment frameworks, the Panel's mandate, as well as its internal institutional arrangements, were critically evaluated and opened to the possibility of change. The IPCC, however, missed this opportunity. It decided in favour of forms of adaptive learning in order to maintain its political authority. These forms have been, in several cases, counterproductive to other goals of the organisation, by making it more legalistic in its processes. This has made it harder for the IPCC to manoeuvre and be as innovative and responsive as some other large-scale international science assessments.

The NETs example, illustrates one of the consequences of pursuing only adaptive learning, namely the IPCC's lack of public transparency and accountability. The IPCC assessed a set of unproven carbon dioxide removal technologies as technically feasible, based on a narrow set of criteria and linear, techno-optimistic assumptions about technological change and economic growth. Even though these technologies deployed at a large-scale, as recommended by the IPCC, would have major governance implications, they have not been treated as a matter of political choice and public scrutiny.

Our findings give reason to question whether the path of adaptive learning taken in the past will be adequate to cope with future challenges. It is fair to assume that the IPCC's future performance will depend on how the Panel adjusts its management structure to meet demands for relevance, transparency and accountability regarding those peoples most affected by climate policies. This would require forms of reflexive learning. However, reflexive forms of learning challenge – and potentially change – core elements of the Panel's governance, which partly explains why they face resistance and are hard to implement. The response to the IAC review in 2010 illustrates that the decision-making authority of nation states in the Plenary – along with consensus-based procedures – contributed to closing down the range of reform options. It excluded consideration of alternatives to the IPCC's institutionalised governance structure and procedures, alternatives that could have enabled greater public transparency and accountability (IAC, 2010; Robertson, 2021).

The turn towards assessing solutions comes with challenges to cope with a diversity of problem and solution frames and the involvement of a broader range of experts and forms of knowledge (Castree et al., 2021). These novel challenges require rethinking the mandate of the IPCC. But they also call for rethinking the

Panel's role and responsibility in the climate regime and respective broader questions of scale, representation and subsidiarity. This novel situation into which the IPCC is moving represents a stress test for the IPCC's capacities to learn. In order to address these challenges – and to seize new opportunities – modes of reflexive learning will be even more necessary. Yet in the current structure they will be harder to implement.

Three Key Readings

Siebenhüner, B. (2014). Changing demands at the science-policy interface: organisational learning in the IPCC. Chapter 7 in: Ambrus, M., Arts, K., Hey, E. and Raulus, H., (eds.), *The Role of 'Experts' in International and European Decision-Making Processes. Advisors, Decision Makers or Irrelevant Actors?* Cambridge: Cambridge University Press. pp. 126–147. http://doi.org/10.1017/CBO978113987 1365.009

This book chapter analyses several sequences of the IPCC's learning processes in the first 25 years of its existence.

Beck, S. and Mahony, M. (2018). The IPCC and the new map of science and politics. *Wiley Interdisciplinary Reviews: Climate Change*, 9(6): e547. http://doi.org/10.1002/wcc .547

This paper analyses the challenges emerging from the post-Paris polycentric governance regime and the new culture of 'post-truth' politics.

Robertson, S. (2021). Transparency, trust, and integrated assessment models: an ethical consideration for the Intergovernmental Panel on Climate Change. *Wiley Interdisciplinary Reviews: Climate Change*, 12(1): e679. http://doi.org/10.1002/wcc .679

This commentary, written by a former IPCC Lead Author, illustrates how and why transparency and accountability matter when it comes to modelling and assessing future pathways to climate targets.

Part II

Participation

This part examines the different actors involved in the work of the Intergovernmental Panel on Climate Change (IPCC) and their respective roles. **Adam Standring** (Chapter 7) reviews the changing diversity profile of IPCC authors, considering their expertise, gender, language and geographical origin. This chapter examines how the IPCC has sought to increase the diversity of its pool of authors, but also the challenges it has faced to support an active, inclusive and meaningful participation for all. **Karin M. Gustafsson** (Chapter 8) assesses how the IPCC has engaged early career researchers and sought to indirectly build capacity through the IPCC's Scholarship Programme and the role of Chapter Scientists. **Hannah Hughes** (Chapter 9) reviews the participation and role of governments in the various stages and processes of the IPCC and, similarly to Chapter 7, assesses the factors that limit participation in the IPCC, especially for developing country representatives. **Yulia Yamineva** (Chapter 10) explains the role of observers in the IPCC, and in particular of non-governmental organisations, and their capacity to influence the IPCC's assessment and approval process. Finally, **Paul N. Edwards** (Chapter 11) gives an account of the evolving role of internal and external peer review in the construction of the authority of the IPCC and discusses this role in the context of scientific peer review practices more generally.

7

Participant Diversity

ADAM STANDRING

Overview

Diversity has become increasingly important as an analytic concept and organising principle in the general scientific community. Advancing diversity is seen to be even more essential in a global science–policy interface such as the Intergovernmental Panel on Climate Change (IPCC). Being able to claim to speak *from* a broad perspective of geographies, genders and experiences is considered to be important if the IPCC is to produce legitimate and authoritative climate knowledge *for* policy. This chapter applies a critical lens to examine the IPCC's procedures and practices in selecting its authors with respect to securing a diverse base of expertise across gender, geography and experience. It then considers *how* diversity is important, identifying different logics – substantive and instrumental – that have guided the IPCC's efforts to date. The chapter concludes by considering *why* diversity should matter and what possibilities are opened for global climate knowledge-making through enhanced capacity building.

7.1 Introduction

The IPCC has expressed a strong commitment to ensuring that the authors selected to contribute to the assessment reports reflect a 'range of scientific, technical and socio-economic views and backgrounds', and also 'a balance of men and women, as well as between those experienced with working on IPCC reports and those new to the process, including younger scientists' (IPCC, 2018b). This commitment is reflected in the formal procedures for selecting authors. These explicitly direct that gender, geography, experience and expertise be taken into account when selecting author teams (IPCC, 2019b). Ongoing debates within the research community at large (Medin & Lee, 2012; Anon, 2018) have also argued for the critical importance of diversity, in terms of both the substantive validity and the external legitimacy of science. These questions are important for research practice in a broad sense, but are vital for science–policy interfaces such as the IPCC whose authority is derived from both the substantive legitimacy of its expertise and the representational legitimacy to speak for multiple voices, as well as from the means through which it negotiates between the two (Cash et al., 2002; Beck & Mahony, 2018a; see also Chapter 20).

Despite the IPCC's stated commitment to diversity, numerous scholars have highlighted the significant cultural, social and institutional barriers that many underrepresented groups face – particularly women, those from the Global South[1] and non-native English speakers. These barriers are twofold – first, in being represented within the IPCC and, second, in being able to actively participate in the assessment process. Women already face a number of significant barriers to participation in scientific work, including unequal access to funding and training, lower wages, fewer role models and greater family responsibilities (Liverman et al., 2022). It is not enough to simply be selected to participate. It is also a question of having the resources to attend meetings – including communication infrastructures for digital meetings – and then being given opportunities and a voice within the meetings (Gay-Antaki & Liverman, 2018; IPCC, 2019b). A number of scholars have also focused on the difficulties facing the IPCC to advance epistemic – including the recognition of indigenous knowledge systems – disciplinary and viewpoint diversity (Ford et al. 2016; Corbera et al., 2016, see also Chapters 12 and 13). A smaller body of critical literature has recognized the improvements made by the IPCC in diversifying author demographics, whilst also emphasising the still unequal representation within the IPCC's authors and what needs to improve (Standring & Lidskog, 2021).

This chapter comprises three main sections. The first provides a detailed outline of the selection process for contributors to assessment reports, accounting for formal and informal practices. It asks whether these attempts to create a more diverse authorship have worked. The second section develops a critical account of diversity within the IPCC, asking in what ways diversity is important to the organisation in the first place. What are the prevailing logics and justifications used to support increased diversity in the IPCC in relation to broader discussions on diversity in science/knowledge production? The third main section adopts a critical perspective on the implications of diversity for both the epistemic legitimacy of the IPCC and its continued policy relevance. It offers capacity building – a process of developing the expertise and experience of both the individual and the organisation – as an important alternative to the prevailing substantive and institutional logics of the IPCC.

7.2 Participant Selection

The institutional process of nominating and selecting experts across all author categories is elaborated in Appendix A, S.4.3 of the IPCC's *Principles for Governing IPCC Work* (IPCC, 2013a). Once the scoping of a new assessment report has been completed and the outline and structure decided, the IPCC Secretariat sends an open call for experts to all IPCC national focal points (NFP) and observer organisations (OO). NFP are national bodies that are responsible for disseminating the call among appropriate research networks. Interested experts then provide their motivation and curricula vitae to their respective NFP or OO who then – compliant with their own specific procedures – transmit the applications to the appropriate Working Groups (WGs)/Technical Support Units (TSUs). The extent to which NFPs conduct their own national selection, or transmit all applications directly to the IPCC, varies from country to country. This can be a site of political conflict. For example, different national institutions may lay claims to possessing authoritative climate expertise (private/public, energy/ environment, university/government institute, and so on). In some cases questions may also arise about whether national experts are likely to align or not with government policy (Gustafsson & Lidskog, 2018a, discuss this process in the context of Intergovernmental Science-Policy Platform on Biodiversity and Ecosystem Services (IPBES), but the principle remains the same).

The co-chairs of each Working Group, with the TSU's support, then select authors to fill the chapter writing teams. These include Coordinating Lead Authors (CLAs) with responsibility for managing contributions, Lead Authors (LAs) who draft contributions, and Review Editors (REs) who assess the quality of the process, ensuring inclusivity and appropriate responses to all review comments. The first criteria for selection are substantive and epistemic – appropriately knowledgeable experts must be identified to cover the topics required, ranging, for example, from 'the Changing State of the Climate System' to 'Climate Resilient Development Pathways'. Each WG co-chair and TSU has their own way of identifying experts, but each must consider the criteria laid out in the Principles. These aim to reflect:

- the range of scientific, technical and socio-economic views and expertise;
- geographical representation (ensuring appropriate representation of experts from developing and developed countries and countries with economies in transition); there should be at least one, and normally two or more, from developing countries;
- a mixture of experts with and without previous experience in IPCC;
- gender balance.

Recent studies have helped to shed light on the active role that TSUs and OOs play in 'filling in gaps' within chapter teams with experts from groups – typically

women and experts from the Global South (Standring & Lidskog, 2021: 9–11) –
who might otherwise be marginalised or underrepresented in a competitive assessment process. The IPCC reports that, for the Fifth Assessment Report (AR5), a
total of 831 experts were selected from 3,598 national and observer nominations
(a 23 per cent success rate); for AR6, the figures were 721 experts from 2,858
(a 25 per cent success rate). The availability of these statistics is welcome.
Nevertheless, a significant opacity remains in the IPCC's selection processes. It
is difficult to understand the significance of the interplay between the formal
institutional procedures for expert selection – including the leeway that they allow –
and the informal practices – including the impact of national pre-selection procedures – that contribute to the final author teams.

Recent scholarship has shown that the diversity of chapter writing teams has
improved over time across the dimensions of gender (IPCC, 2019b) and
geographic distribution (Standring & Lidskog, 2021). But some significant caveats
must be added to this assessment for a more accurate picture to emerge. The
following discussion focuses exclusively on the issues of gender and geographical
distribution; Chapter 8 focuses in more detail on questions relating to previous
experience in IPCC, and Chapter 12 on disciplinary contributions.

Trends towards securing more diverse author groups started from an extremely
low baseline, with AR1 (1990) overwhelmingly dominated by male authors from
North America and Western Europe. While there have been improvements in
female representation, women remain a minority within author groups – as well
as within categories of authors with more responsibilities within chapters
(Standring & Lidskog, 2021). This situation looks even worse when it is
considered how and where different categories intersect. Barriers to representation for women from the Global South, or for those for whom English is not a
native language, are higher still. Their participation in the IPCC is even more
difficult (Gay-Antaki & Liverman, 2018; Gay-Antaki, 2021).

Second, as seen both in Figure 7.1 and in previous research (Ho-Lem et al.,
2011; Corbera et al., 2016; Standring & Lidskog, 2021), the involvement of
authors from the Global South – representing three quarters of the world's
population – account for a little over a third of the authors selected to contribute
to IPCC assessment reports (El-Hinnawi, 2011). The proportion has improved
since the first assessment cycle, which can be attributed to a number of factors.
These include a more active geopolitical lobbying for representation from
countries such as Brazil, China and India,[2] as well as the rapid development of
scientific infrastructures, not least aided by the IPCC's own capacity-building
efforts (Chapter 8). In the broadest terms, the proportion of participants from
developing countries has increased, but the gains are more modest when looking
at the poorest countries alone. Those countries designated by the World Bank as

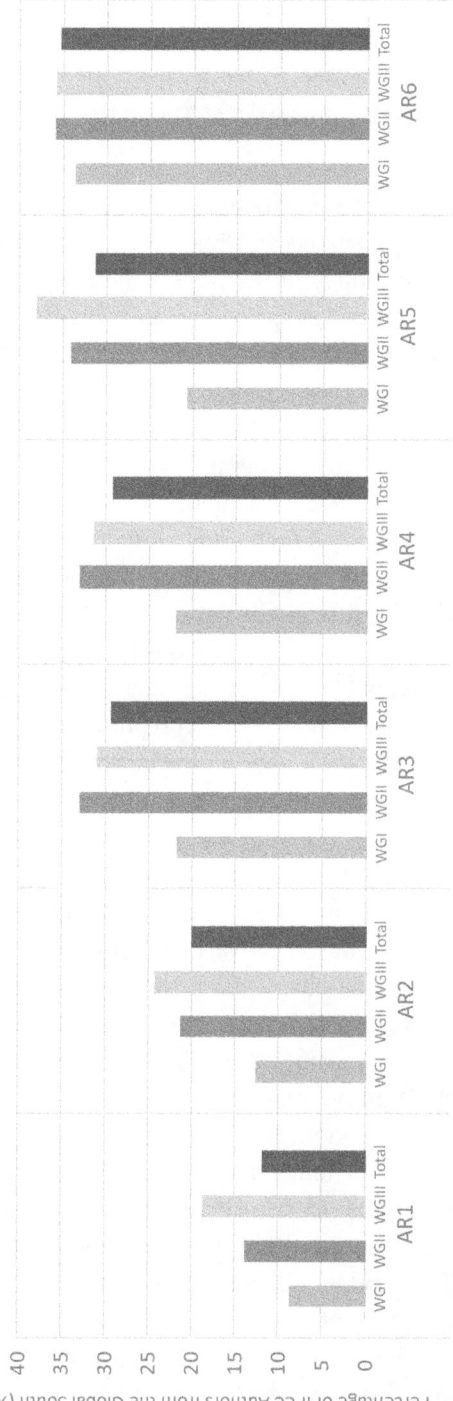

Figure 7.1 Proportion of IPCC authors from Global South countries, across the six assessment cycles (AR1 to AR6) and according to different Working Groups.

Source: data from Kari De Pryck (cf. Venturini et al., 2022) and the author's own

low or lower-middle income economies account for only 14 per cent of authors in the most recent assessment cycle.

7.3 The Importance of Diversity

The IPCC's approach to diversity and expertise emerges from an organisational structure and role that is geared towards providing a comprehensive knowledge base for international negotiations, agreements and treaties. Valuing epistemic neutrality/objectivity ('policy relevant not policy prescriptive') and consensus, the IPCC has been described on multiple occasions as 'providing the view from nowhere' (Borie et al., 2021). This 'science-driven' perspective of climate knowledge gives pre-eminence to universalistic perspectives on the nature of climate problems. Within such an epistemic framework, questions of diversity – of representation, experience and voice – are relegated as secondary concerns. Within the IPCC, this philosophy is most prominently visible in the way that, until recently, WGI has lagged well behind WGII and WGIII in terms of the representation of a range of identities (see Figure 7.1; also IPCC, 2019b; Standring & Lidskog, 2021). This is also the case with regards to the integration of different disciplinary and epistemic contributions (Ford et al., 2012; Stern & Dietz, 2015). A blindness, or strategic ignorance, to questions of identity and diversity helps to reproduce dominant attitudes and assumptions about how science is produced and who produces it. Recently, Miriam Gay-Antaki (2021: 4) has asked, 'what does a climate scientist look like?' On the IPCC's author database, for example, the placeholder avatar (Figure 7.2) for authors who have not provided a photograph is a greyed out yet clearly indicative image of how experts are typically perceived – male and white.

Debates within the wider research community have challenged the strong separation between independent and objective facts on the one hand, and values and subjective interpretation on the other – both for pure science and for science for decision-making (e.g. Funtowicz & Ravetz, 1993; Jasanoff, 2005). In this case, diversity is not simply to be considered an additional concern, intended to complement substantive or cognitive expertise. Rather, the argument is that '[a] more representative workforce is more likely to pursue questions and problems that go beyond the narrow slice of humanity that much of science ... is currently set up to serve' (Anon, 2018). With an issue such as climate change, in which the effects are likely to be severe but unevenly distributed both within and between countries (Hulme et al., 2020), and in which existing power structures are likely to obscure this unevenness, diversity of expertise is all the more necessary.

The IPCC is not a purely scientific organisation. As a science–policy interface it inhabits (and constructs) the boundary between the spheres of science and policy (Beck & Mahony, 2018a). On the international policy stage, representation is

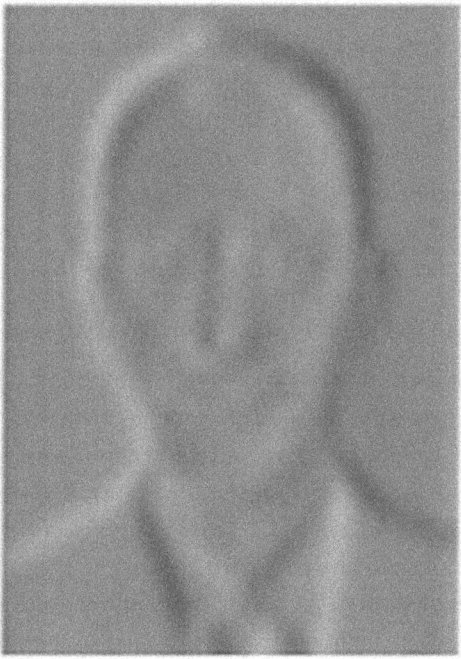

Figure 7.2 Placeholder avatar from the IPCC author database.
Source: IPCC website

extremely important for organisational legitimacy and to evade a critique of imposing a particular Western/Global North vision of science, knowledge and climate problems – a view expressed by a number of Global South participants (Biermann, 2001; Lahsen, 2009). In a telling quote (reported in Standring & Lidskog, 2021), one contributor to the IPCC concludes

if you want a good well written report on any aspect of climate change you could get half a dozen white European men to write it ... It would have a fraction of the impact that an IPCC report does because it just wouldn't be seen as being representative of the global body scientific or relevant to the body politic.

The legitimacy and authority of the IPCC's outputs and its impact on global policy should therefore be considered as much a consequence of the acceptance of the reports by national governments (see **Chapter 20**) as it is because of the accuracy and quality of the knowledge that is synthesised and communicated. At least part of the willingness to accept the report is the belief that a range of views, particularly those of the Global South, are being represented within the body of expertise making up the IPCC.

Two particular logics of diversity within the IPCC emerge from this picture. On the one hand, the substantive view of expertise acknowledges the contextual nature of scientific and social scientific knowledge. It understands that by adding a more diverse set of perspectives, experience and values, new and innovative ways of both viewing problems and developing solutions may emerge. On the other hand, an instrumental or strategic view of expertise focuses instead on the internal or external legitimacy that diversity bestows on both the institution and the products it produces. In this respect, diversity is primarily viewed as a goal for increasing institutional credibility (Standring & Lidskog, 2021).

7.4 Consequences of Diversity

When instrumental logics of diversity become institutionalised at an organisational level, the quest for diversity risks becoming an exercise in box-ticking. The measures of diversity – parity for marginalised group identities – become simply a target, divorced from broader social, cultural or epistemic concerns that diversity addresses (Ahmed, 2012). As shown in the previous sections, the IPCC's formal selection criteria comprise features such as gender, geographical location and experience, which can be easily operationalised and measured. But as Corbera and colleagues (2016) show in their analysis of WGIII authorship patterns, such an exercise leads to a reductive view of diversity as well as to practices of 'gaming the system'. Authors ostensibly from the Global South are frequently products of academic and professional networks firmly grounded in the Global North, limiting true representation.

Box-ticking exercises can also limit or obscure the importance of addressing aspects of diversity that are less easy to measure, such as epistemic or viewpoint diversity. Ongoing debates about the disciplinary breadth of the IPCC (Stern & Dietz, 2015) have helped draw attention to the necessity and the value of inputs from a range of social scientific academic disciplines such as sociology, human geography, urban studies and economics (Corbera et al., 2016; see **Chapter 12**). Yet these studies often fail to address questions about the extent to which those participating in the IPCC share similar ontological or epistemological approaches to the climate issue – for example, the unity/divisibility of the human and natural is one such issue – let alone questions of methodological approaches such as quantitative versus qualitative research methods. Additionally, the extent to which critical voices within the IPCC – critical of the range of expertise that 'counts', as well as critical of the formal role of the organisation as a non-prescriptive intergovernmental body – are given space to raise their concerns remains limited. The communication of expert consensus remains a priority (Pearce et al., 2017a; see **Chapter 26**). These are organisational critiques that have been absorbed to some extent by subsequent science–policy interfaces, such as IPBES, which integrate expert diversity and disagreement more openly within their practices (Borie et al., 2021).

One means of transcending the binary logics of diversity in the IPCC – and even using the informal/formal processes to subvert them – is to situate diversity of expertise within the concept of capacity building. Diversity of experience, viewpoint and voice strengthens the institution and empowers the individual. For this reason, co-chairs and members of the TSU have pointed to the ways in which they use the selection of IPCC authors to develop the networks and capacity of experts from more marginalised groups. As one of them reports (Standring & Lidskog, 2021: 12), 'even if people don't start out with the highest scientific qualifications or publications record it may help them to bring them into the process by doing it. So, I think the capacity building element of it shouldn't be ignored'. This process of building networks, peer support and development, and introducing a more diverse group of expertise, is something that occurs regularly, but outside of the formal rules and procedures of the IPCC (Gay-Antaki & Liverman, 2018). This capacity building constitutes a particularly gendered form of labour – falling disproportionately on already marginalised groups who must use resources for self-organisation – that goes unrecognised and unrewarded at the organisational level despite offering significant institutional benefits.

7.5 Achievements and Challenges

Diversity of expertise within the IPCC has improved remarkably since AR1 was published in 1990, reflecting broader changes in societal norms and expectations. The question of diversity has been written into the formal processes of the IPCC, which now seek to ensure that a representative and balanced range of authors are selected according to gender, geographical distribution and experience. In practice, however, authors from countries in the Global South and female authors are still in a minority and the dominance of a few countries – and relatively few institutions within those countries – remains strong. Equally difficult to ensure is that a diverse set of disciplines, epistemic positions and viewpoints are represented and that they are provided with the skills and space with which to make a contribution. The 2019 Report from the IPCC Gender Task Force makes a number of concrete suggestions to improve diversity. These include regular monitoring and reporting, increasing the share of women in leadership roles, providing training on inclusive practices, and increased sensitivity to the barriers that travel imposes (Liverman et al., 2022).

The legitimacy and authority of the IPCC rests not solely on its capacity to produce relevant knowledge in the area of climate change. It rests also on its ability to do so in a way that makes all signatory countries feel represented by the published outcomes. This is indicative of a tension that emerges in all processes of knowledge production, but which are especially evident within those bodies, such as the IPCC, that bridge the science–policy interface: how are calls for objective, reliable and reproducible scientific knowledge integrated with a demand for greater diversity and representation? In practice, the commitment to diversity is often reduced to a box-ticking exercise in which the benefits of diversity are left unreflected upon in favour of numerical targets or quotas.

One way to transcend this problem is to recognize that these goals are not necessarily mutually contradictory but are, rather, a product of particular social demands for 'relevant knowledge'. As has been increasingly acknowledged, the global framing of climate change is no longer sufficient to understand the uneven and divergent responsibilities, impacts and capacities to respond to climate risks. Diversity of experience and voice – including those with different disciplinary, epistemic and value commitments – is more necessary than ever to understand climate change. The IPCC faces the challenge of responding to this need.

Notes

1 The terms Global North/South are not unproblematic or uncontested within social science. They serve here as a blunt shorthand for what the United Nations Grouping of 77 (UN-77) has previously referred to as developed/developing countries.
2 The proportion of Brazil+China+India authors doubles between AR1 and AR6, up from 5.9 to 12.1 per cent of all authors.

Three Key Readings

Corbera, E., Calvet-Mir, L., Hughes, H. and Paterson, M. (2016). Patterns of authorship in the IPCC Working Group III report. *Nature: Climate Change*, 6: 94–99. http://doi.org/10.1038/nclimate2782

This study provides a detailed analysis of the diversity of authors within a single IPCC Working Group, analysing the CVs of hundreds of experts.

Gay-Antaki, M. and Liverman, D. (2018). Climate for women in climate science: women scientists and the Intergovernmental Panel on Climate Change. *Proceedings of the National Academy of Sciences of the United States of America*, 115(9): 2060–2065. http://doi.org/10.1073/pnas.1710271115

One of the most important accounts of women's access to and participation in the IPCC.

Standring, A. and Lidskog, R. (2021). (How) Does diversity still matter for the IPCC? Instrumental, substantive and co-productive logics of diversity in Global Environmental Assessments. *Climate*, 9(6): 99. http://doi.org/10.3390/cli9060099

This study attempts to compare diversity across multiple assessment cycles while providing a framework for analysis of why diversity is, and should be, important to the IPCC.

8

Early Career Researchers

KARIN M. GUSTAFSSON

Overview

This chapter argues that Early Career Researchers (ECRs) can contribute to the Intergovernmental Panel on Climate Change (IPCC) in two major ways. First, ECRs can contribute unique skills and competences to the assessment process. Second, ECRs can share the workload with senior researchers and thus enhance the quality of the assessment. By reviewing the IPCC's Scholarship Programme and the role of Chapter Scientists, this chapter explores the potentials and challenges of introducing ECRs into the IPCC, and for the Panel to engage in capacity-building to enhance the quality of the assessment. The review shows how the organisational set-up of the Scholarship Programme and the Chapter Scientist role allows the IPCC to informally engage in capacity-building without diverting from its mandate that does not include capacity-building. Even so, ECRs remains an untapped source of expertise that, through active and strategic work, can contribute to the future development of the IPCC.

8.1 Introduction

A key strategy the IPCC uses to ensure its credibility is to enrol world-leading researchers to assess the current state of knowledge about climate change (Hoppe, 1999; Beck, 2011a; IPCC, 2021b). To become relevant and legitimate, when selecting those who are to work on its assessments, the IPCC has complemented its requirement for credentialled experts with additional criteria that encourage diversity with respect to disciplines, gender, ethnicity, language and geographical representation (see **Chapter 7**). Even without engaging in a discussion about the extent to which this move has been successful, these strategies come across as having a rather short-term focus on how to make IPCC assessments credible, relevant and legitimate *here and now*. To continue to develop as an institution,

71

however, the IPCC also needs to consider longer-term strategies, including capacity-building and succession planning for future IPCC assessments. Although the selection criteria 'to create a mixture of experts with and without previous experience in the IPCC' could be seen as a plan to create continuity between assessments, capacity-building remains outside the IPCC's formal mandate. Even so, this chapter will show how the IPCC indirectly engages in capacity-building by supporting ECRs and introducing them to the assessment process. Such a move prepares the IPCC to become an expert organisation for both the present *and* the future (Chan et al., 2016; Gustafsson & Berg, 2020; Gustafsson, 2021).

The chapter reviews the potential, and the limitations and challenges, of engaging ECRs in the IPCC to enhance the quality of the assessments and to bring new perspectives to the assessment process. This will be done by looking at the IPCC's Scholarship Programme, which supports ECRs from developing countries through their academic studies, and by exploring how and why ECRs are enrolled as Chapter Scientists in IPCC assessments. Previous research on ECRs in the IPCC is, with a few exceptions, still rather sparse. Thus, this chapter will combine a review of existing studies on the topic with an empirical survey of where to find ECRs in IPCC.

8.2 Defining and Finding ECR in IPCC

The concept *Early Career Researcher* (ECR) refers, as the phrase implies, to a researcher at the beginning of their career. The concept lacks a universal definition and is instead defined through the empirical context in which it is used: for example, through guidelines of eligibility to fellowship programmes, jobs, and calls for research funding. ECR could refer to anyone from postgraduate research students up to researchers 7 or even 10 years post-PhD (e.g. Bazeley, 2003; Gustafsson, 2018; ERC, 2021).

Since 2009, the IPCC has supported ECRs through its Scholarship Programme in which ECRs are identified as postgraduate students and postdoctoral researchers (IPCC, 2009a). Since the 6th Assessment cycle, ECRs have also officially been invited by the IPCC to participate in the assessments as 'Chapter Scientists' (see later for a description of this role). The open calls for Chapter Scientists have identified ECRs as researchers with a Master's degree or PhD, but who are still in the early stages of their academic career. Someone who passes this early career stage is referred to as one who is 'overqualified' and experienced (Gustafsson & Berg, 2020). Before these two opportunities existed – the Scholarship Programme and Chapter Scientists – ECRs did not have a formally assigned position in the IPCC. Instead, prior to 2009, to be able to participate in the IPCC, ECRs had to compete for a position as Lead Author on the same terms as senior researchers, but with less academic work-life experience. Thus, participating in the IPCC as an ECR has been and still is very difficult, although not impossible or unheard of (Casado et al., 2019; Gulizia et al., 2019; Søgaard Jørgensen et al., 2019). Similarly, the literature also offers only a few examples where ECRs – in these cases defined as Master's students or early-stage PhD researchers – through special calls and invitations have participated in the IPCC review process, but generally with positive results (van der Veer et al., 2014; Casado et al., 2019).

Previous studies raise two general arguments as to why ECRs have a contribution to make in organisations such as the IPCC. First, ECRs contribute unique skills and competence to the assessment process (Lim et al., 2017). The fact that these researchers are early in their careers results in them bringing unique knowledge and experiences of great value to the process (Packalen & Bhattacharya, 2015; Gustafsson et al., 2019). This allows the ECR to approach issues with new ideas on how to collaborate successfully across disciplines, cultures and languages, as well as offer new perspectives on how to answer challenging questions (Kowarsch et al., 2016; Gustafsson & Berg, 2020). Second, ECRs are an overlooked group of competent researchers that, if included, could share the workload with the senior researchers and enhance the quality of the assessment (Gustafsson et al., 2020). Successfully contributing to global knowledge assessments requires skills and competencies to match the requirements and protocols of the assessment process. This needs to be learned by all new Lead Authors, regardless of their career stage. Studies have shown that, with appropriate guidance, ECRs can contribute to the assessment at the same level and quality as senior researchers (van der Veer et al., 2014; Gustafsson 2018; Casado et al., 2019; Gustafsson, 2021).

In the following two sections, I take a closer look at the IPCC's Scholarship Programme and the role of Chapter Scientist, to explore the potential of engaging ECRs in the IPCC to enhance the quality of its assessments.

8.3 IPCC's Scholarship Programme

The IPCC's need to build capacity among ECRs intersects with other issues that also affect its credibility, relevance and legitimacy (Gustafsson et al., 2019). One such issue, which the IPCC has struggled with since its inception, is the representational bias favouring industrialised countries of the Global North (Agrawala, 1998b; Ho-Lem et al., 2011; Hughes & Paterson, 2017; Standring & Lidskog, 2021; see **Chapter 7**). After being awarded a share of the 2007 Nobel Peace Prize, the IPCC decided to address these intersecting challenges by creating a Scholarship Programme Trust Fund to support young postgraduate students and postdoctoral researchers in climate change sciences from 'developing countries', especially 'least developed countries' (IPCC, 2009a). Although directed by the IPCC, the Scholarship Programme is organised outside of the IPCC's mandate and runs in parallel to the assessment process. Although capacity-building is not in the IPCC's mandate, the Scholarship Programme allows the IPCC to address the problem of geographical bias.

The Scholarship Fund is governed by a Science Board and a Board of Trustees. The Science Board is responsible for the Scholarship Programme's selection process and for deciding which scientific knowledge gaps and capacity-building needs are to be prioritised in each round of the program. The Board of Trustees carries the responsibility for the affairs of the Scholarship Programme Trust Fund. The Board of Trustees also holds the responsibility to create further economic support to the Fund and to develop collaborations on the Scholarship Programme. Since its establishment, the Scholarship Fund has received several monetary gifts and the Scholarship Programme has created a long-lasting collaboration with the Prince Albert II of Monaco Foundation, the Cuomo Foundation and, most recently, with the AXA Research Fund.

The IPCC's Scholarship Programme was launched in 2009 as a two-year program and has since had six admission rounds. These rounds have differed slightly with regard to the academic age and research interest with which ECRs are eligible to apply to the program. Still, all six calls have been aimed towards postgraduate students, and sometimes postdoctoral researchers, working on 'research that advances the understanding of the scientific basis of risk of human induced climate change, its potential impacts, and options for adaptation and mitigation' (IPCC, 2009a: 3).

In total, 90 ECRs have been accepted onto the IPCC's Scholarship Programme (IPCC, 2021c). Of this total, 33 were accepted in the sixth round. Fifty-five ECRs have participated in the Scholarship Programme supported by the Prince Albert II of Monaco Foundation, 25 by the Cuomo Foundation, 6 by the AXA Research Fund, and 4 by funds from the IPCC's Scholarship Programme Trust Fund. One contributing factor to the low number of IPCC-supported scholars is that the Board of Trustees was inactive for almost three years after the first Board of Trustees' mandate expired in 2016 and before a new Board was appointed in October 2018 (IPCC, 2018c). An additional challenge for the development of the Scholarship Programme has been administrative limitations within the IPCC's secretariat to manage a larger programme (e.g. IPCC, 2012a; 2015b; 2016a). Despite strong appreciation, validation and support of the Scholarship Programme from the IPCC, the Programme's organisation and management has therefore made it difficult – if not prohibited – to increase numbers of ECRs and to develop in other respects.

Three comments have recurred in the Panel's discussions on how to develop the programme (e.g. IPCC, 2012a; 2016a; 2018d). First, is the desire to generate additional funds and collaborations. Second, is to follow up on the progress of the ECRs in the programme and explore the need of making the Scholarship longer to ensure that the students can finish their studies. Third, is to work on ways to connect the ECRs in the programme more closely with the IPCC's work. However, it is not evident that these questions have resulted in any changes to or developments of the program up until 2018. In 2018, as part of the discussion on how to make closer ties between ECRs and the IPCC, the Panel reviewed whether funds from the Scholarship Programme Trust Fund could be used to cover travel costs and honoraria for Chapter Scientists from 'developing countries' (IPCC, 2018d). In subsequent discussions about this proposal, concerns were raised about potential negative consequences on the Scholarship Programme Trust Fund's capacity to contribute economic support to graduate and postgraduate studies. The outcome of these extended discussions was that the Panel decided, in May 2019, that the IPCC's Scholarship Programme Trust Fund *could* be used to support 'developing country' Chapter Scientists, but only if such use did not negatively impact the running of the Scholarship Programme (IPCC, 2019c).

When discussing the options of how the Scholarship Programme could be developed, an interesting comparison can be made with the Fellowship Programme in the Intergovernmental Science-Policy Platform on Biodiversity and Ecosystem Services (IPBES) (Gustafsson, 2021). In comparison to the IPCC, capacity-building *is* included in IPBES's mandate and this has led to the development of a Fellowship Programme that allows ECRs to participate in IPBES's assessment process in a role that equals that of a Lead Author. The IPBES Fellowship Programme also provides a mentorship structure and an annual capacity-building workshop that addresses both formal and informal skills that are needed in an assessment process like the ones of IPBES and IPCC (Gustafsson, 2018; Gustafsson et al., 2019, 2020).

8.4 Chapter Scientists

During the assessment process for the IPCC's AR5 Report, which was presented in 2014, the role of Chapter Scientist was officially introduced by the IPCC for the first time (Schulte-Uebbing et al., 2015). The Chapter Scientists' task is to aid and support the Coordinating Lead Authors (CLA) and Lead Authors (LA) throughout the assessment process to ease their workload. The introduction of Chapter Scientists was suggested and implemented as one of many measures that aimed to strengthen the IPCC's quality control in the aftermath of the critique of AR4 (see Chapter 6). During the assessment cycle of AR6, the position of Chapter Scientist has been formalised by the IPCC Panel and decisions have been made to offer economic support to Chapter Scientists from 'developing countries', as discussed earlier (IPCC, 2019c, d). Before the introduction of Chapter Scientists, ECRs were recruited as research assistants outside of the IPCC's formal structure by individual CLAs with financial means to do so. To some extent, these personal and informal initiatives by CLAs continue in parallel to the formal work of the Chapter Scientists to create additional administrative support.

Despite being a formal designation within the IPCC, the role of Chapter Scientist has not yet been standardised in the same way as the role of CLAs and LAs (Gustafsson & Berg, 2020). Chapter Scientists are not nominated by IPCC member states and so their recruitment, and working conditions, have varied greatly between and within the three Working Groups (WGs). In WGI and WGII, Chapter Scientists have been recruited and employed by individual CLAs in a similar fashion as in the previous informal recruitment process of research assistants. This has often resulted in the engagement of locally known ECRs who come to work in the same institution as a CLA in a 'developed country'. WGIII, on the other hand, has engaged ECRs from 'developing countries' as Chapter Scientists through a general call administered by WGIII's Technical Support Unit (TSU). The assignment has been performed on a voluntary basis and the ECRs have been expected to be able to work for up to 30 per cent of their time in the role. Thus, the Chapter Scientists in WGIII have not been known to the CLA in advance and they have not come to work in the same institution. Until 2019, when the IPCC decided to offer economic support to cover travel expenses for Chapter Scientists from 'developing countries' (see earlier discussion), WGIII made use of external donations to cover such costs for their Chapter Scientists.

Chapter Scientists contribute to the organisation in two main ways: by contributing to IPCC's work on quality-control of current assessments in an assisting function; and by informally building capacity for future assessments as the ECRs gain inside experience of what it means to be an author in the IPCC. In addition to the value of Chapter Scientists' administrative support to current assessments, it is also important to recognise that many of the Chapter Scientists have come to contribute to the assessments in more substantive ways. Taking the Special Report on Global Warming of 1.5 °C (SR15) as an example, all Chapter Scientists ended up contributing qualitatively to the assessment in ways that enabled them to become recognized as Contributing Authors. Thus, in line with previous research discussed earlier, this example shows ECRs competence as an untapped pool of expertise that is relevant to the IPCC's assessments (Gustafsson & Berg, 2020).

To work as a Chapter Scientist offers ECRs a unique stepping stone towards future IPCC engagement. This is by having the possibility to gain state-of-the-art knowledge in the field, unique insights into the IPCC assessment process, and to develop networks that could help future career development. In this respect, the IPCC contributes to informal capacity-building. However, due to the variations in working conditions and tasks among the Chapter Scientists (see Box 8.1), the

---

Box 8.1
The tasks of Chapter Scientists

Chapter Scientists' tasks vary greatly and are determined in collaboration between the Chapter Scientists and the CLAs they support. An indicative list of potential tasks for Chapter Scientists across WGs include responsibilities such as (IPCC, 2019d):

- Identifying, compiling and keeping control of references.
- Assisting the author team in compiling, revising and organising chapter contributions.
- Assisting in the design and development of figures and tables.
- Assisting with traceability checking.
- Technical editing.
- Monitoring overlaps or inconsistencies across chapters.
- Keeping records of review responses up to date.
- Assisting CLAs during online meetings and at LAMs, for example note-taking, correspondence and so on.
- Assisting with quality control in relation to the style guide, chapter formatting and glossary.

---

capacity-building process that takes place through the role of the Chapter Scientist is very much an ad hoc process without promises of designated capacity-building goals and outcomes. Important to note is that the ad hoc character of this process, in combination with the hierarchical organisation of the IPCC, also makes the role of Chapter Scientist a potentially insecure position. The informal ways in which work is assigned to the Chapter Scientist by the CLA creates a situation in which the ECR, due to differences in power dynamics, risks being exploited and overworked with limited resources to object to or change their situation.

8.5 Achievements and Challenges

The IPCC Scholarship Programme has been running for more than ten years, supporting 90 ECRs. This is a significant achievement. However, the lack of attention paid to the Programme's development raises questions about how it could be further enhanced through more active management. The Scholarship Programme has the potential to transform itself from being a passive activity that awards financial scholarships to ECRs to something more active. For example, taking inspiration from the IPBES Fellowship Programme, the IPCC Scholarship Programme could ensure closer and more regular contact between ECRs and the IPCC while the ECR completes their studies, allowing the ECR to contribute to the development of the IPCC. Such an extension of the Scholarship Programme would require more administrative and economic resources.

The chapter has also shown how the role of Chapter Scientist has been introduced as a first attempt to formally make use of ECR's capacities in current IPCC assessments. The role of Chapter Scientist offers a unique formal opportunity for ECRs to gain an insight into the IPCC's assessment process, enhance their knowledge in the field of climate change research, and develop important professional networks. The role allows for informal capacity-building for the individual ECR, as well as enhancing the quality of current assessments. However, shaping the role of Chapter Scientist so as to be beneficial to both the IPCC and the ECR has been neither standardised nor monitored by the IPCC at an institutional level. The responsibility has been left with individual CLAs and ECRs, and becoming an IPCC Chapter Scientist therefore comes with potential challenges for the individual ECR.

This chapter has shown how ECRs are an untapped resource of expertise and competence that could contribute to the future development of the IPCC. However, unlocking this resource is not something that will happen by itself. Developing the IPCC's inclusion of ECRs' expertise to enhance their capacity – as well as that of the IPCC – will require active and strategic work. First, would be to create new entry points to the assessment process for ECRs. Second, would be to offer more guidance on the execution of tasks in the assessment assigned to ERCs. And third, would be to change the mandate of the IPCC's assessment process to allow for capacity-building of ECRs; this would welcome and acknowledge their contribution to the IPCC of ECRs' knowledge, ideas and perspectives.

Three Key Readings

Schulte-Uebbing, L., Hansen, G., Macaspac Hernández, A. and Winter, M. (2015). Chapter Scientists in the IPCC AR5 – experiences and lessons learned. *Current Opinion Environmental Sustainability*, 14: 250–256. http://doi.org/10.1016/j.cosust.2015.06.012

This article provides an insightful description of the introduction of Chapter Scientists, accomplished by surveying experiences from IPCC's first cohort of Chapter Scientists in AR5.

Gustafsson, K. M. and Berg, M. (2020). Early-career scientists in the Intergovernmental Panel on Climate Change. A moderate or radical path towards a deliberative future? *Environmental Sociology*, 6(3): 242–253. http://doi.org/10.1080/23251042.2020.1750094

This article provides important knowledge on how the role of Chapter Scientist shapes the conditions for ECR's socialisation and capacity-building within IPCC.

Casado, M., Gremion, G., Rosenbaum, P., et al. (2019). The benefits to climate science of including Early Career Scientists as reviewers. *Geoscience Communication*, 3: 89–97. http://doi.org/10.5194/gc-2019-20

This article provides revealing knowledge of the untapped competence among ECRs, accomplished by problematising the outcomes of a group peer-review of the First Order Draft of the IPCC Special Report on Ocean and Cryosphere in a Changing Climate.

9

Governments

HANNAH HUGHES

Overview

This chapter explores the role of governments in the Intergovernmental Panel on Climate Change (IPCC), how this is theorised, and how government participation in the organisation has changed over time. One of the most distinctive features of the IPCC is its intergovernmental character. While some scholars criticise government membership of the IPCC, many IPCC actors see this as key to ensuring the political relevance of the assessment. But what does government membership mean? What do member governments do in the organisation? And who are IPCC delegates and focal points? This chapter addresses these questions and identifies how member governments have deepened their involvement in the IPCC over time as their knowledge has grown and as the stakes in climate politics have risen. However, participation between countries remains uneven and the chapter explores how concerns about developing countries' capacity to contribute has shaped the IPCC and assessments of climate change.

9.1 Introduction

The IPCC is composed of member governments that meet once or twice a year in plenary session. Membership to the Panel is open to all member countries of the World Meteorological Organisation (WMO) and the UN Environment Programme (UNEP) and there are currently 195 member countries. However, of this number, only half regularly send representatives to plenary and about one quarter could be described as active participants (IPCC, 2009b). The Panel is involved at every stage of the IPCC's assessment practice, which enables governments to have considerable influence over the organisation and its work. Although member governments are not directly involved in authoring the reports, they approve the report outline, nominate authors, elect the Bureau review draft reports, and accept and approve the final products, including the Summaries for Policymakers (SPM) (see **Chapter 20**). Financially, the IPCC is dependent on donations from governments, and all IPCC expenditure is agreed upon by the Panel, which gives governments the final decision over the organisation's continuation, its assessment activities, and the expert meetings and workshops that inform these.

In this chapter, I explore how the role of governments in the IPCC is understood and theorised, and how government participation in the organisation and its assessment activities has changed over time. One of the distinctive features of the IPCC as a global environmental knowledge body is its intergovernmental character (Agrawala, 1998a). While some scholars have been critical of government membership of the IPCC (Haas, 2004), many actors within the organisation see this as a key feature for ensuring the policy relevance of the reports produced and their impact on government action. As a result, this model has been emulated in newly established global environmental assessment bodies, such as the *Intergovernmental* Science-Policy Platform on Biodiversity and Ecosystem Services (IPBES). I use the lenses of the 'epistemic community' model and the 'boundary organisation' (BO) concept to unpack how science and policy are intertwined in the IPCC. This approach illuminates the avenues member governments have open to them to influence the organisation and its assessment process. The chapter identifies how governments have deepened their involvement in the assessment practice of the IPCC, as their confidence in the organisation and its process has grown and as the stakes in climate politics have increased. I also highlight how asymmetries between 'developed' and 'developing' country participation persist.

9.2 From Epistemic Community to Boundary Organisation

Two main perspectives informing the study of governments and the relationship between science and politics in the IPCC are the epistemic community model and the boundary organisation concept (Hughes, 2015; Lidskog & Sundqvist, 2015; Hughes & Paterson, 2017). An epistemic community is defined as 'a network of professionals with recognized expertise and competence in a particular domain and an authoritative claim to policy relevant knowledge within that domain or issue-area' (Haas, 1992: 3). These transnational communities of scientists and other experts are said to play a critical role in helping states to identify their interests in complex and uncertain issue areas, framing them for collective debate, proposing specific policies and identifying salient points for negotiation (Haas, 1992). This approach has been influential in exploring the establishment of the IPCC (Lunde, 1991; Boehmer-Christiansen, 1994a,b; Paterson, 1996; Bernstein, 2001; Newell, 2006). Matthew Paterson (1996: 144), for example, concluded that 'the international development of climate as a political issue ... can plausibly be interpreted in terms of the effect of the development of an epistemic community on the subject' and that 'in the IPCC we can see the epistemic community at its most organised' (Paterson, 1996: 146).

Although the epistemic community model has been used to explain the origins of the IPCC and the politicisation of climate change, Peter Haas (2004) is sceptical of its applicability to the IPCC. He has been critical of the intergovernmental nature of the Panel, suggesting that it stifles the epistemic community's ability to function as theorised. In fact, Haas considers the IPCC an attempt by governments to gain control *over* the scientists and the diplomatic process, which had ascended too quickly up the political agenda in the 1980s under the epistemic community's influence (Haas & McCabe, 2001; Haas, 2004). From this theoretical approach, science and politics are, and should remain, separate realms (Lidskog & Sundqvist, 2015).

The boundary organisation approach, on the other hand, takes the organised intertwining of science and politics in the production of scientific knowledge for political action as its starting point (Guston, 2001). A BO is identified by its location between the distinct social worlds of politics and science, by the participation of actors from both sides, and by the distinct lines of accountability to each (Guston, 2001: 399–400). From this perspective, relevant knowledge emerges from the productive collaboration between the institutions of science and politics. Empirical studies informed by the BO concept highlight the importance of maintaining a distinction or a 'boundary' between science and politics during the production of assessments. They illuminate how this is achieved in practice through IPCC activities (Skodvin, 2000b; Fogel, 2005; Gustafsson & Lidskog, 2018b) (see also **Chapter 24** for the related idea of boundary objects). As the study of the IPCC has matured, 'boundary organisation' has emerged as the most important concept for characteris-ing the nature of the IPCC, with the IPCC identified as 'the preeminent boundary organisation on climate change' (Adler & Hirsch Hadorn, 2014: 663; O'Neill et al., 2015: 380). From this perspective, the IPCC reflects in equal measure the scientisation of politics and the politicisation of science (Hoppe et al., 2013), but it is not considered tainted by its intergovernmental nature.

However, when the role of governments is explained, and their deepening involvement in the work of the IPCC and its assessment practice are documented, Haas' criticism of government interference cannot be completely dismissed. Maintaining the distinctiveness and boundary between science and politics within the IPCC, either discursively or in knowledge products, has become increasingly difficult as the stakes in climate politics have risen (Beck & Mahony, 2018a; Livingston et al., 2018; Livingston & Rummukainen, 2020; De Pryck, 2021a). The potential effect of IPCC reports on climate negotiations within the UN Framework

Convention on Climate Change (UNFCCC) means that governments invest at every stage of the assessment to control the potential 'weight' or effect of IPCC knowledge on global climate policymaking. This is most observable during the approval of the report's key findings in the SPM (Hughes & Vadrot, 2019; see also **Chapter 20**). Furthermore, sometimes overlooked in this focus on the relationship between science and politics, is the asymmetries in participation between developed and developing countries. These asymmetries shape both the intergovernmental character of the organisation and assessment authorship. While there is a growing body of literature documenting the effects of this on the assessment reports (Hulme & Mahony, 2010; Ho-lem et al., 2011; Corbera et al., 2016; Hughes & Paterson, 2017), it is less well studied within member government relations (see Siebenhüner, 2003; Hughes, 2015; Yamineva, 2017).

9.3 Governments as Panel Members and Focal Points

Member governments effectively have two roles within the IPCC: the first, inward facing, as members of the Panel, and the second, nationally facing, as national focal points. Returning to the establishment of the IPCC allows us to examine how government participation in these roles has evolved and how the issue of developing country involvement has been addressed. The IPCC's establishment in 1988 was led by a relatively small group of individuals identified as representatives of government, the parent organisations (WMO and UNEP), and prominent members of the international climate science community (see **Chapter 2**). The First Assessment Report (AR1) was originally envisioned as an exercise for a small group of core members, and although all WMO and UNEP members were invited to the IPCC's first Panel session, only 30 countries sent delegates (IPCC, 1988).

However, the organisational leadership quickly realised it would need to increase developing country participation if the assessments were going to be recognised and accepted as *global* assessments of climate knowledge. As acknowledged by the first IPCC chair, Bert Bolin, in the oft-cited quote: 'Right now, many countries, especially developing countries, simply do not trust assessments in which their scientists and policymakers have not participated. Don't you think global credibility demands global representation?' (Schneider, 1991: 25). To address this, a Trust Fund was established to financially support one representative from each of the developing countries and countries with economies in transition to attend plenary meetings of the Panel and for appointed experts to attend author meetings (Agrawala, 1998b). The issue over developing country involvement, however, was not solved with the establishment of this fund. It would become a defining feature of the IPCC's work in the years ahead and an issue that remains on the organisational agenda today for reasons explored later.

The organisational distinction between government members of the Panel and scientific experts on the Bureau was also blurred in the early years of the IPCC. This is reflected, for example, in the principle that 'to provide for the best possible coordination, the Chairmen and vice-Chairmen of the Working Groups (WGs) should be, where possible, Principal Delegates of their respective countries in [the] IPCC' (IPCC, 1988: 6). From the perspective of some of the founding members, this blurring between Bureau and Panel actors was a unique feature of the IPCC and one that enabled 'the harmonious resolution of difficult situations which arose in the work of the panel' (Zillman, 2007: 877). Today, however, the Bureau and the Panel have more distinct memberships and tensions exist between Panel member governments and Bureau members. One of the most publicised incidents of this was the Bureau election in 2002, when incumbent IPCC chairman, Dr Robert Watson, was not re-elected for a second term in an election process that divided opinion within the Panel (Lawler, 2002; Zillman, 2007: 875).

This was the first time in the IPCC's history that it was necessary for the Panel to take a vote on the position of chair. The two most cited reasons for this struggle highlight how political dynamics and developing country participation shape the organisation and its work. The first was that the USA – under the George W Bush administration – opposed Watson's re-election because of his advocacy on climate action (McRight & Dunlap, 2010: 120), and the second, was that it was necessary for the chairmanship to be held by a developing country member, after it had been held by two developed country experts for three assessment cycles (Bolin, 2007: 185–187). However, this struggle over Bureau elections also indicates how important Bureau membership is to governments, as evidenced by the pre-election manoeuvring that was revealed during AR5 by Wikileaks (Guardian, 2010a,b,c). Bureau membership can offer an important source of information to government delegates in position-taking on issues concerning the Panel. Countries with Bureau members may also attend Bureau meetings, which gives them further knowledge and insight into IPCC processes and may help them make authoritative interventions during decision-making and the approval of text.

In addition to being members of the Panel, government participants have an outward-facing role as national focal points. In this role, they act as conduits between the organisation, the national government and national scientific communities. The appointed focal point alerts the relevant community of scientists at the start of a report process, nominates authors, and coordinates national review processes for draft reports and input into other relevant IPCC documents and assessment activities (see **Chapters 3** and **9**). Governments' capacities to invest and fulfil these activities, and thereby actively participate in and shape the process, provides further insight into the asymmetries between developed and developing country involvement and its effects.

9.4 Why Are Levels of Participation between Governments Unequal?

One of the reasons that the Trust Fund was unable to 'solve' the issue of developing country participation is because attending an IPCC panel meeting is not the same as being able to meaningfully participate (see Box 9.1). The differences between levels of involvement by governments in IPCC activities can be discerned by taking a closer look at what makes an authoritative Panel member. In order to be able to wield influence over the organisation and its assessment activities, it is essential to have knowledge of the process. This knowledge is attained over time and through investment and participation in the IPCC and through cultivating relations with the Bureau, Secretariat and other members of the Panel. This knowledge of the process translates into influence during plenary proceedings through informed interventions on the issue or text under discussion.

This investment in the IPCC is also a reflection of a government's interest in the climate issue. At a national level, this could be identified as *self*-interest, with both

---

Box 9.1
Why delegates' levels of participation vary

Why is the interest and investment in the IPCC by governments so uneven between countries? The dynamics around country participation are complex and multifaceted. Countries are identified as either 'developed' or 'developing' within the IPCC, but this classification can mask significant variation in the number of authors in the report and of government involvement in the Panel – for example when comparing Brazil, China or Saudi Arabia to Bolivia, the Maldives or Mali.

The following anecdote sheds light on some of the structural forces that shape participation for some developing countries, even for those at the 'more' developed end of the spectrum. In 2010, I attended the 32nd plenary of the Panel in Busan, South Korea. One of the things that I became aware of was that during proceedings the room was less than half-full and that interventions were dominated by a small group of countries highly immersed in the process (see Table 9.1). In contrast, several developing country delegates appeared disinterested and were entering and leaving in the middle of the proceedings. I asked one long-term observer why this was the case, and he responded that for some the trip to Busan was 'probably a political favour' and that they had 'come for the shopping'.

This response was similar to comments that widely circulate about developing country participation within the IPCC. But these comments often overlook the substantial human resources and economic investment that IPCC activities require and the historical order of intergovernmental relations that condition the availability of such.

Box 9.1 (cont.)

Table 9.1. *Top ten countries by frequency and total time of interventions at the 32nd Plenary Session of the Panel, hosted in South Korea, October 2010*

(Data collected by author; only interventions from the floor were counted, and not presentations by delegates or Bureau members chairing contact groups)

Top country by number of interventions	Number of Interventions	Top country by total time of interventions	Total Time (seconds)
1. US* (WGII)	50	1. Switzerland* (WGI)	4,849
2. Switzerland* (WGI)	43	2. US* (WGII)	4,240
3. Saudi Arabia*	33	3. Saudi Arabia*	3,218
4. Australia*	28	4. Australia*	2,854
5. UK*	25	5. UK*	1,960
6. Belgium*	24	6. Russia*	1,532
7. Germany* (WGIII)	24	7. Netherlands	1,288
8. Netherlands	23	8. Germany* (WGIII)	1,222
9. Austria	14	9. Austria	1,062
10. Sweden	12	10. Brazil*	942
Totals	276 (representing 64% of all interventions)		23,167 (representing 69% of total time)

WG designation indicates which country hosted the respective Technical Support Unit.
* signifies member countries with a Bureau member.

a scientific and political dimension. On the science side, many developed countries have well-established, well-funded natural and social science communities producing knowledge on climate change. Members of this community are well represented in the authorship of the reports and in the knowledge assessed (Corbera et al., 2016; Hughes & Paterson, 2017). Focal points mobilise these communities during author nomination and expert review processes to ensure national representation and input in the assessment. On the politics side, governments are increasingly aware of the potential influence that IPCC assessments have on UNFCCC negotiations. They actively participate in appointment, review and approval processes to keep abreast of this knowledge and its potential impact on future climate policymaking.

Interest in Panel activities is, in part, conditional on being able to participate meaningfully, which at a national level requires having the economic resources to invest in the IPCC and, relatedly, the human resources to undertake membership activities. Without the time and resources to invest in commenting on draft outlines, initiating a search for national expertise, and undertaking a government review of draft reports, member governments as delegates are effectively excluded, or at least limited in their capacity, to meaningfully participate in IPCC proceedings. This is evident in the approval of SPMs, where informed position-taking on the technical framing of climate change requires the expert knowledge generated through the review process and/or housed within the national delegation.

Nationally, this also requires recognition of the impact that IPCC assessment findings have on climate negotiations and coordinating IPCC participation accordingly. For example, the location of the focal point is important to ensure coordination between IPCC and UNFCCC participation and to enable cross-departmental input into the government review of reports. However, the focal point is more commonly within the meteorological service in developing countries than in dedicated environment and/or climate change departments as in developed countries (from list of focal points, IPCC, n.d.(b)). Furthermore, if a different delegate is sent to every meeting, the lack of continuity prevents knowledge of the process and procedures and the cultivation of good relations with other Panel, Bureau and Secretariat members. It requires personal time commitment, and national recognition and support, to enable the same delegate to attend every meeting, undertake focal point duties, initiate review processes and coordinate with the national UNFCCC delegation. While the Trust Fund has enabled a stronger developing country presence, the resources available are insufficient to enable the full participation of all countries. The effect of this is that the capacity to influence the Panel reflects broader global distributions of economic resources and the political order that are tied to colonial legacies and histories of dispossession.

9.5 Achievements and Challenges

Within IPCC scholarship, knowledge of member governments' role and participation within the organisation has been informed by the concepts of epistemic community and boundary organisation. The concept of boundary organisation illuminates the productive tensions between science and politics within the IPCC, which enables government members' interests in climate change to inform and shape knowledge products and ensure their relevance, at least for the active participants of the IPCC. Over time, governments have become more autonomous actors within the organisation, although still dependent on the Bureau for realising the assessment. Furthermore, as the stakes in the climate issue and negotiations have risen, so has member government investment in IPCC activities. This has led to increased tension at key moments when science and politics are brought together, such as during Bureau elections and the approval of report outlines and key findings in the SPM text (see **Chapter 20**). Here, it is the epistemic community model that enables the questioning of whether, within the IPCC, the level of government involvement is creating usable knowledge for political action – or whether the intergovernmental process is being used to facilitate political delay.

Both the epistemic community model and the boundary organisation concept focus on the relation between science and politics. This can mask the unequal governmental capacity to shape the organisation and the direction and content of the IPCC's assessment reports. While the establishment of the IPCC Trust Fund in the 1990s sought to facilitate developing country involvement, the economic and human resources required to conduct IPCC activities means that considerable asymmetries persist. Understanding these asymmetries, and reasons for their persistence, is an important area for future research.

Three Key Readings

Agrawala, S. (1998a). Context and early origins of the Intergovernmental Panel on Climate Change. *Climatic Change*, 39: 605–620. https://doi.org/10.1023/A:1005315532386

Agrawala, S. (1998b). Structural and process history of the Intergovernmental Panel on Climate Change. *Climatic Change*, 39: 621–642. https://doi.org/10.1023/A:1005312331477

These two papers provide an excellent account of the IPCC's establishment.

Bolin, B. (2007). *A History of the Science and Politics of Climate Change: The Role of the Intergovernmental Panel on Climate Change*. Cambridge: Cambridge University Press. https://doi.org/10.1017/CBO9780511721731

Bolin's book offers an interesting account of the organisation from the perspective of the first IPCC Chair.

Ho-Lem, C., Zerriffi, H. and Kandlikar, M. (2011) Who participates in the Intergovernmental Panel on Climate Change and why: a quantitative assessment of the national representation of authors in the Intergovernmental Panel on Climate Change. *Global Environmental Change*, 21: 1308–1317. https://doi.org/10.1016/j.gloenvcha.2011.05.007

This article presents a quantitative examination of developing country participation within the IPCC.

10

Observers

YULIA YAMINEVA

Overview

This chapter discusses the role of NGO observers in the Intergovernmental Panel on Climate Change (IPCC) and the extent to which they have access to and participate in the work of the Panel. Many UN institutions have arrangements for participation by NGOs and the IPCC is no exception. NGO observers include academic institutions, think tanks, civil society, indigenous peoples' organisations, and business associations. They take part in IPCC meetings and nominate their representatives to serve as authors and reviewers in the preparation of assessment reports. NGO observers' participation in the Panel is an important topic in light of the increasing emphasis on inclusiveness and diversity of views in science–policy interfaces and international institutions. The chapter also identifies related knowledge gaps and summarises the challenges and opportunities for enhanced NGO engagement in the IPCC.

10.1 Introduction

Recent international relations scholarship has shown that international institutions are transforming towards more open and inclusive participation by various stakeholders (Tallberg et al., 2013; Bäckstrand, 2015). The role of stakeholders has also been discussed in relation to global environmental assessments (GEAs). For example, scholars have suggested that GEAs should better accommodate a pluralism of views and perspectives because environmental governance is conducted not only through state-centric models, but also in a polycentric fashion with the participation of sub-national actors, cities, civil society and private sector entities (Maas et al., 2021). It has also been proposed that stakeholders' involvement in GEAs helps with the following: (i) seeking diversity of information and viewpoints; (ii) improving communication of assessment findings; (iii) fostering dialogue and enabling learning among all actors; and (iv) building a sense of ownership over assessment reports (Garard & Kowarsch, 2017: 235). Indeed, inclusive participation and a better integration of diverse views have become a commonly accepted expectation, and even a requirement, for the design of science–policy interfaces.

The IPCC has special provisions for the participation of observer organisations. According to IPCC rules, observer organisations include: (i) participating organisations that are other UN bodies and organisations; (ii) intergovernmental organisations, for example the European Union (EU) or the Organisation for Economic Co-operation and Development (OECD); and (iii) non-governmental organisations. This chapter discusses the third category of IPCC observer organisations, that is NGO observers. Over a hundred of them have been registered to date with the IPCC. Despite the importance of NGO participation, surprisingly little is known about which NGOs participate in the Panel, and why, nor how they influence the process, if at all. IPCC scholarship has reflected a great deal on who participates in the assessment process, but this has mostly been concerned with scientists and governments. Few papers have analysed the role of observers (Garard & Kowarsch, 2017; Yamineva, 2017).

This chapter briefly discusses the institutional arrangements for NGO access to the IPCC and the few research findings available on their participation in, and impact on, the IPCC's affairs and preparation of assessment reports. The chapter also identifies related knowledge gaps, and assesses institutional achievements, challenges and ways to increase NGO stakeholder participation in the Panel.

10.2 NGO Access and Participation in the IPCC

Like other UN institutions, the IPCC has special provisions for the access of observer organisations including NGOs. National and international organisations can acquire the status of NGO observers, but they have to fulfil two requirements in order to participate – they have to be non-profit and they must be 'qualified in matters covered by the IPCC' (IPCC, 2006a). The second requirement implies that their work should relate to the IPCC mandate, which is, conducting assessments of scientific, technical and socio-economic information on various aspects of climate change (IPCC, 2013a).

Whether NGOs meet these requirements is assessed during the accreditation process. The access of NGOs that have already observer status with the World Meteorological Organisation (WMO), the UN Environment Programme (UNEP) or the UN Framework Convention on Climate Change (UNFCCC) is simplified. As a general rule, applications for observer status are screened by the IPCC

ANT{

Table 10.1. *IPCC NGO observers*
This is based on the list of IPCC observer organisations as of 26 July 2021.

NGO type	Number of NGOs	Examples
Academic institutions	16	Imperial College London (UK), University of Nijmegen (Netherlands)
Think tanks	21	Center for International Forestry Research (CIFOR), Center for International Climate and Environmental Research (CICERO; Norway), Energy Research Austria
Civil society organisations	54	CARE International (Denmark), C40 Cities Climate Leadership, Germanwatch (Germany)
Private sector associations	24	The Alliance for Responsible Atmospheric Policy (USA), Campaign for a Hydrogen Economy (UK), International Aluminium Institute

The help provided by research assistant Raihanatul Jannat in preparing the table is greatly appreciated.

Secretariat and considered by the Bureau before being presented to the Panel. Governments have a validating role with respect to the access of non-governmental stakeholders (Yamineva, 2017), since the final decision on acceptance of an NGOs' observer status is made by the governmental plenary by consensus. In addition, applications from national organisations are 'brought to the attention' of the relevant Panel's member states (IPCC, 2006a). In principle, this implies that individual governments can block a national NGO accessing the IPCC, although so far this seems to have happened only once, when China conditioned accreditation of the Industrial Technology Research Institute from Taiwan on it being listed as from 'Taiwan, Province of China' (IPCC, 2009c).[1] As of July 2021, the Panel had 116 NGO observers of varying nature such as academic institutions, think tanks, civil society organisations and private sector associations (Table 10.1).

NGOs' access to IPCC meetings is limited to attendance of Panel and Working Group plenary meetings, but without the right to intervene or introduce proposals. With respect to interventions, the recent institutional practice has been to give observers an opportunity to take the floor, but only if no government delegation is asking for it. In making an intervention from the floor, observers cannot support a government's intervention. The right to attend IPCC meetings does not extend to informal consultations, Lead Author Meetings, workshops or expert meetings. Experts from NGOs may, however, be invited by the IPCC Secretariat to participate in expert meetings and workshops.

In addition to meeting attendance, NGOs can nominate their experts to participate in the assessment of the literature as IPCC Lead/Contributing Authors and as reviewers of draft reports. Providing comments at the review stage has been an important channel for observers to contribute to the preparation of reports, for example through highlighting the literature which may have fallen outside of Lead Authors' attention (Yamineva, 2017: 248). In all these cases, such experts act 'in their own right' (IPCC, 2006a) and not as representatives of their organisations. They are therefore deprived of the right to represent the perspectives and concerns of their constituencies. With such limited access, NGOs often turn to informal means of influencing the IPCC process, especially at the crucial stage of SPM approval, for example through informal interactions in the corridors of meeting venues (see **Chapter 4**). Some countries also include NGO representatives as members of their national delegations, providing them, indirectly, with expanded participation rights.

Observer organisations may also be invited to submit their views on general IPCC governance issues or matters related to the assessment process, such as the IPCC scoping meetings (see **Chapter 5**). In such cases, NGO engagement remains at the discretion of the IPCC management and is not mandated by the Panel's policies. Yet, in recent years, the institutional practice has been to seek input from observer organisations. For example, the task group on the future work of the Panel – which operated between 2018 and 2020 – worked on the basis of extended participation by observer organisations *with* the right to introduce proposals (IPCC, 2018e). That said, only two civil society organisations – Climate Action Network International and the Friends World Committee for Consultation – submitted their views to support the work of this task group (IPCC, 2019e).

10.3 Evaluating NGO Engagement in the IPCC

Literature has suggested distinguishing between access to, and participation in, international institutions. While *access* concerns formal rules and informal practices allowing for the participation of specific actors, *participation* is the realisation of those access rights, or actual contribution by those actors (Tallberg et al., 2013: 8). This distinction is helpful in assessing the de facto role of stakeholders in international arenas because inclusive access does not necessarily lead to participation (Yamineva, 2017). It is not certain how many of the accredited observer organisations contribute actively to the work of the IPCC: based on analysis of formal documentation, few of them seem to have taken part in the work concerning governance issues.

Access can also be analysed in terms of depth – level of involvement – and the range of actors – can *all* stakeholders participate or only some of them according to certain criteria? (Tallberg et al., 2013: 8). Accordingly, 'high' access means deep involvement of a broad spectrum of stakeholders on a permanent basis and is difficult to revoke. 'Low' access on the other hand implies shallow involvement extending to a narrow subset of stakeholders (Tallberg et al., 2013: 28). Low access is also temporary and can easily be revoked. From this perspective, access of observers to the IPCC can be assessed as 'low' because it is shallow, validated by governments, and extends only to a narrow group of stakeholders. The restricted access of non-governmental stakeholders to the IPCC can partly explain some of the challenges faced by the Panel. These would include the limited diversity of perspectives (see **Chapter 7**) and the exclusion of non-scientific insights from the assessment reports – for example those of local and indigenous knowledge holders (Ford et al., 2012: 81; Obermeister, 2017; see also **Chapter 13**) – and practitioner's expertise (Viner & Howarth, 2014).

The IPCC therefore follows a functionalist approach to the participation of NGOs. This approach – which is prevalent in the UN system – views NGO engagement from the perspective of whether they help advance institutional goals (von Bernstorff, 2021: 135–140). From this viewpoint, NGOs are to be involved in the IPCC assessment processes only to the extent that they can contribute relevant expertise for the provision of robust, scientifically credible assessment products. The functionalist approach stands in contrast to a model of NGO engagement viewed through the prism of democratising international institutions (von Bernstorff, 2021: 141–143). The idea of deliberative interest representation is reflected in the recent expansion of multi-stakeholder forums across international arenas and a stronger focus on the participation of communities who are negatively affected by international policy and rule-making, for example, small-scale farmers and indigenous peoples.

Overall, governments and scientists have been uneasy about NGO participation in the IPCC. In the early years, this was because of fears that climate sceptic organisations would disrupt the work of the Panel. Indeed, there are accounts of how the Global Climate Coalition (GCC) – a once prominent US-based industry lobbyist group with climate contrarian views – attempted to water down previous IPCC reports (Edwards & Schneider, 1997; Franz, 1998; Lahsen, 1999). The introduction of the IPCC *Policy and Process for Admitting Observer Organisations* in 2006 was partly due to the desire to shield the Panel from organisations which could undermine its work (e.g. Gutiérrez et al., 2007: 13).

Involvement of experts from the private sector and civil society organisations in the IPCC assessments remains controversial. The Panel was, for example, criticised for the participation of a Greenpeace employee as a Lead Author for the 2011 Special Report on Renewable Energy Sources and Climate Change Mitigation. In the view of critics, this led to the endorsement by the IPCC of a high renewables' deployment scenario, one that was also supported by Greenpeace

(Anon, 2011; Edenhofer, 2011; Lynas, 2011). In another example, the nomination of two senior employees from major oil companies – ExxonMobil and Saudi Aramco – as authors for the 2018 Special Report on Global Warming of 1.5 °C prompted wide criticism by civil society organisations and accusations of a conflict of interest (ETC Group, 2017).

The Panel's cautious sentiments towards NGOs remain today and some nations continue to warn the IPCC 'against elevating NGOs and special interest organisations to the same level as governments' (Gutiérrez et al., 2012: 8). As evidence of this, governments recently lacked enthusiasm to involve stakeholders in the AR6 pre-scoping activities (Allan et al., 2016). Expanding stakeholder engagement in government-led bodies is indeed problematic and not only in the IPCC – the same challenges have been reported for the Intergovernmental Science-Policy Platform on Biodiversity and Ecosystem Services (IPBES) (Beck et al., 2014). Such expansion does not only entail renegotiating the Panel's balance of power, but is also viewed by some governments – and by some scientists – as potentially decreasing the scientific robustness and credibility of assessment findings (Yamineva, 2017).

10.4 Knowledge Gaps

Studies of the participation of observers in the IPCC are somewhat lacking in the academic literature. Despite the number of admitted observer organisations, very few of these NGOs seem to actively contribute to the work of the IPCC. Contribution and impact of experts from NGOs in the preparation of assessment reports is also unclear. Further, NGO participation can be non-transparent and difficult to trace when it takes place informally in the corridors of meeting venues or when NGO representatives contribute to the process as members of national delegations.

Future work could shed light on the role of civil society and business associations in the IPCC, in particular the role of NGO-nominated experts in the assessment as Lead Authors and in review processes. Stepping outside of institutional boundaries, it would be interesting to know how NGOs engage with the IPCC assessment products and findings, helping in their communication and framing discourses around climate policy solutions. Similarly, NGOs sometimes exercise considerable influence in national contexts and may shape IPCC member states' attitudes towards the IPCC and its assessment findings (Franz, 1998; see **Chapter 23**).

10.5 Achievements and Challenges

NGO engagement in the IPCC has evolved towards a more structured input through the adoption of specific institutional policies and higher numbers of organisations admitted as observers. It is doubtful that the Panel would reform its institutional arrangements in the future to allow a significant expansion of NGO access to the assessment process, since this would likely face opposition by its member states. Many additional challenges to engaging non-governmental, non-scientific actors in GEAs are discussed in the literature. For instance, some scholars have pointed out that such a move would risk reducing the scientific credibility of IPCC reports (Garard & Kowarsch, 2017). Furthermore, NGO participation in international institutions is not necessarily unproblematic because of the dominance of the Global North NGOs and private sector lobbyism (von Bernstorff, 2021: 143–147; also Sénit et al., 2017). And there are also costs and other resource implications arising from significant reforms of the IPCC institutional design (Garard & Kowarsch, 2017).

At the same time, despite these challenges, the turn towards solutions in global climate policy discourse arguably suggests expanding the knowledge base of the IPCC assessments. Part of this could be reconsidering the role of NGO observers as potential holders of solutions-oriented knowledge(s). Expanding NGO participation might also address some of the challenges faced by the IPCC – as discussed in other chapters of the book – such as the legitimacy of IPCC findings (see **Chapter 6**), transparency and representativeness in modelling and scenario development (see **Chapter 15**), and inclusion of traditional forms of knowledge (see **Chapter 13**). What form such broadening of NGO participation should take is not self-evident – academic literature and policy practice does not provide straightforward answers. From the perspective of enhancing the democratic legitimacy of GEAs, some scholars have discussed creating a multi-stakeholder advisory body to coordinate stakeholder engagement and develop adaptive practices (Garard & Kowarsch, 2017). Other, more radical, suggestions include establishing 'deliberative mini-publics' consisting of randomly selected people from around the world to inform deliberations in GEAs (Maas et al., 2021). However, in the context of the IPCC, such ideas are unlikely to find support among governments and scientists. The experience of the IPBES also shows that striving for diversity and inclusiveness in science-for-policy institutions is challenging in the context of intergovernmentalism and consensus-seeking decision-making (Beck et al., 2014; Díaz-Reviriego et al., 2019).

A more realistic institutional format for expanding NGO participation in the IPCC would be establishing task groups composed of representatives of stakeholder constituencies – civil society, private sector and indigenous peoples (Yamineva, 2017; also Ford et al., 2016) – that would advise the IPCC Bureau. This would allow for a consolidated and more representative input by NGOs on a continuous basis, while at the same time maintaining an institutional boundary between the scientific assessment process and participation by NGO observers.

Establishing specific institutional arrangements for NGO contribution would also bring more transparency and accountability concerning their participation, as well as help the IPCC navigate the solutions-oriented knowledge landscape.

Note

1 China has also made attempts to keep critical NGOs out of the UN Economic and Social Council (von Bernstorff, 2021).

Three Key Readings

Franz, W. E. (1998). *Science, Sceptics and Non-state Actors in the Greenhouse.* ENRP Discussion Paper E-98-18, Kennedy School of Government, Harvard University. www.belfercenter.org/publication/science-skeptics-and-non-state-actors-greenhouse

This paper discusses the role of climate sceptics' and industry organisations, in particular the Global Climate Coalition, in the early years of the IPCC.

Garard, J. and Kowarsch, M. (2017). If at first you don't succeed: evaluating stakeholder engagement in global environmental assessments. *Environmental Science & Policy*, 77: 235–243. http://doi.org/10.1016/j.envsci.2017.02.007

This article assesses various modes of stakeholder engagement in GEAs, drawing on the examples of the IPCC and UNEP's Global Environmental Outlook.

Yamineva, Y. (2017). Lessons from the Intergovernmental Panel on Climate Change on inclusiveness across geographies and stakeholders. *Environmental Science & Policy*, 77: 244–251. http://doi.org/10.1016/j.envsci.2017.04.005

This article examines the involvement of developing countries and NGOs in the IPCC, building on the distinction between access and active participation.

11

Peer Review

PAUL N. EDWARDS

Overview

Despite many flaws, including variable quality and a lack of universal standards, peer review – the formal process of critically assessing knowledge claims prior to publication – remains a bedrock norm of science. It therefore also underlies the scientific authority of the Intergovernmental Panel on Climate (IPCC). Most literature used in IPCC assessments has already been peer reviewed by scientific journals. IPCC assessments are themselves reviewed at multiple stages of composition, first by Lead Authors (LAs), then by scientific experts and non-governmental organisations outside the IPCC, and finally by government representatives. Over time, assessment review has become increasingly inclusive and transparent: anyone who claims expertise may participate in review, and all comments and responses are published after the assessment cycle concludes. IPCC authors are required to respond to all comments. The IPCC review process is the most extensive, open and inclusive in the history of science. Challenges include how to manage a huge and ever-increasing number of review comments, and how to deal responsibly with review comments that dispute the fundamental framing of major issues.

11.1 Introduction

The IPCC's claim to scientific authority is heavily based on the multiple levels of peer review applied in its assessments. Peer review practices date to the 1730s, if not even earlier (Spier, 2002). They are a deeply entrenched norm, based in the fundamental scientific principles of communal knowledge production and methodological scepticism. When the IPCC was established in 1988, journal review systems had acquired a stable form, which remains prevalent today. Scientists submit articles to journals. Journal editors then locate referees, who write reviews detailing errors, methodological issues or other problems and recommend either rejection, revision or acceptance. The most common recommendation is to revise and resubmit. If the referees and editor agree that the revisions respond adequately to their comments, the paper is accepted.

Scholars have studied peer review systems for decades. Studies have unearthed problems ranging from failure to catch obvious mistakes to favouritism ('pal review') to outright fraud (Chubin & Hackett, 1990; Moran, 1998). It's a messy and imperfect process – and in practice there are few, if any, universal standards. Both referees and editors face time and expertise constraints, which lead to widely varying levels of investment in the process. Different journals require double-blind (neither referees nor authors know each other's names), single-blind (referees know the authors' names, but not vice versa), signed or optionally signed reviews. Many journals require referees to answer specific questions or fill out rating scales, but these are weak checks on an inherently qualitative process. In practice, reviews run the gamut from brief, pro forma recommendations to multi-page deep dives into methods, mathematics and supporting or conflicting literature.

A key weakness: unlike auditors in banking and corporate finance, peer reviewers rarely attempt to replicate or test any part of a study (McIntyre & McKitrick, 2005). They rely instead on their expert knowledge, and they assume the good faith and honesty of authors. This honour system has led to scandals in some fields when formal replication studies have disconfirmed results previously held as fundamental (Baker, 2015).

11.2 Who Counts as a Peer?

In journal review systems, 'peers' are generally understood to be experts in the same or closely related fields. Editors' choice of peers can influence publication decisions. Yet while the occasional arbitrary exercise of editorial power is real, a much more common issue is that finding arm's-length peers is not easy. Given the limits of their own knowledge, editors must sometimes (perhaps often) draw on lists of potential referees submitted by authors themselves, and they lack objective means to learn about authors' personal connections to those referees. Further, the best-qualified referees are often in high demand and unavailable. In such cases, editors may seek referees at some remove from the specific focus area, or rely on more-available junior scholars. In both cases, reviewers' expertise may be insufficient to detect key problems.

Starting in the 1990s, Internet-based publishing opened the door to new models of peer review, including much broader participation. Pre-print servers such as ArXiv (founded 1991) and the Social Science Research Network (SSRN, founded 1994) allowed authors to post draft articles, in part to seek informal commentary, but also to stake priority claims. In the 2000s, a sea change toward greater transparency across the sciences led to considerable revision of previous norms (Wilkinson et al., 2016). Some journals adopted more open or even fully public review processes, presenting articles online for comment by a larger scientific community, or by anyone at all, before publication. The IPCC has followed this trend.

11.3 What Is the Value of Peer Review?

In my own experience as an author, peer reviewer and editor, the process *usually* improves the quality of publication and weeds out many errors of fact, logic and calculation. Yet as suggested earlier, peer review is not a formal audit, its quality is highly variable, it cannot be standardised, it can reflect numerous biases, and it can miscarry, rejecting valuable contributions while accepting shoddy ones. Thus, although scientists hold the practice in high esteem, peer review is anything but a truth machine. So what are its benefits?

First, it operationalises crucial scientific norms. One of these is *methodological scepticism*: peer review invites an evidence-based, 'prove it to me' approach to knowledge claims – perhaps the most fundamental element of any scientific method. Reviewing others' work through this lens teaches reviewers how to think sceptically about their own work as well. Another is *communalism*. Science is organised community learning, a collective effort whose unique value stems from the care and attention of many individuals and the wide sharing of knowledge. Peer review also acts as a form of *expert certification*, similar to advanced academic degrees (reflecting training) and institutional affiliation (reflecting acceptance by other scientists).

Second, peer review serves a *gatekeeping* function. As already observed, this can be highly problematic. Yet it also benefits the scientific community in numerous ways. It reduces the likelihood of error and promotes collective attention to methodology. It also slows growth in the sheer number of scientific publications, a problem in its own right that is now especially acute in climate science (Haunschild et al., 2016). The gatekeeping function of journal review plays a critical role in IPCC assessments, by screening out material self-published by individuals, political interest groups, advocacy organisations, and others. The AR6 WGI report cited over 14,000 publications. Without the gatekeeping role of journal peer review, an almost unimaginable volume of dubious material from websites, self-published books and other 'alternative' publication venues might be submitted for formal assessment. This is not speculation: some reviewers of AR6 presented blogs, personal 'audits' and other self-published, unreviewed work for consideration in the assessment.

11.4 Review of IPCC Assessments

IPCC rules of procedure developed in tandem with the composition of its First Assessment Report (AR1) in 1990. Bert Bolin, the IPCC's first chairman, attached great importance to basing AR1 only on peer-reviewed publications (Bolin, 2007). Peer review of the assessments themselves was discussed at the first session of the IPCC Bureau in 1989, which took the decision to establish a review process that would include scientists from developing countries (Agrawala, 1998b). Importantly, review of science *assessments* differs substantially from journal peer review. Whereas journal reviewers have the power to recommend rejection, IPCC reviewers can only recommend revisions (including elimination of statements or entire topics). The focus of assessment review is therefore to ensure consideration of all relevant material and accurate characterisation of the full range of results (Oppenheimer et al., 2019). Box 11.1 summarises the different forms of peer review conducted by the IPCC, and these are elaborated in the following paragraphs.

Internal review. IPCC assessments begin with an onboarding meeting. There, each chapter team begins to fill in and expand the very brief chapter outline previously scoped out by IPCC leadership (see **Chapter 3**). In a few weeks, each chapter team rapidly composes a 'Zero Order Draft' (ZOD). The ZOD is incomplete and quite rough, with many elements existing only as placeholders. The purpose of this stage is to generate a skeleton structure, allow all LAs to get a sense of the entire report, and discover areas where additional content, expertise and cross-chapter interaction will be needed (see **Chapter 18**). LAs comment on the ZOD in a spreadsheet; once compiled, all comments are made available to all LAs. This internal peer review strongly guides early revision.

Expert review. Revision of the messy, incomplete ZOD results in the much more developed 'First Order Draft' (FOD), which is then opened to expert review.

Box 11.1

Types and stages of review/scrutiny in IPCC reports

Journal review. IPCC reports are based primarily on published, peer-reviewed scientific literature.

Internal review. IPCC Lead Authors review their own drafts at every stage.

Expert review. Review by scientists and self-declared experts outside the IPCC, starting with the first complete draft.

Government review. Representatives of IPCC member governments review middle- and end-stage drafts.

Approval. At a final meeting, government representatives approve the Summary for Policymakers (SPM) line by line.

Unlike journal peer review, where journal editors determine who qualifies as a 'peer', IPCC 'expert' review is open to essentially anyone: 'Because the aim of the expert review is to get the widest possible participation and broadest possible expertise, those who register are accepted unless they fail to demonstrate any relevant qualification' (IPCC, 2020a). Despite significant outreach by the IPCC, the majority of reviewers are male and most are from the developed world (see **Chapter 7**).

Most reviewers of the AR6 WGI FOD were climate scientists or others with genuine expertise. However, some very active reviewers listed no affiliation with any scientific organisation and had no publications other than blog posts or other self-published materials. Nonetheless, at least in my own experience, these unaffiliated reviewers occasionally flagged significant errors and contributed valuable revisions. A further observation is that because reviewers' names are attached to comments, those of senior scientists and experienced IPCC authors may be weighted more heavily by chapter teams. Thus prestige as well as expertise can affect responses to review comments; often there is no principled way to tell the difference. At this stage and beyond, chapter authors are required to respond to *all* comments. If they reject a comment, they must explain why. Typical reasons for rejection include out of scope (for example, promoting a policy, or unrelated to WGI purposes), not supported by published peer-reviewed literature, or no scientific evidence provided.

For authors new to the IPCC – as were about 30 per cent of the 234 LAs, including me, contributing to the AR6 WGI report – the scale of effort required by this review process comes as a very rude shock. It takes approximately four months for the IPCC's Technical Support Unit (TSU) to format and distribute the FOD for an eight-week comment period, and then compile the comments received. Meanwhile, revision of the draft continues at a rapid pace. This time lag means that chapter text has already been extensively changed and a great deal of new material added before LAs can even start to respond. As a result, responding to comments entails a tedious, confusing back-and-forth between the comment sheet, the formatted FOD and the active working draft.

Despite the warnings of experienced LAs, many of us underestimated the huge amount of time required to do this job well. Many comments cited publications we had not yet considered, requiring us to locate and read them on the fly, or to consult LAs from other chapters for help in interpreting what we learned. Notwithstanding its somewhat chaotic character, this review dramatically improved the draft and extended its evidence base.

Governmental and expert review. Revisions to the FOD result in the 'Second Order Draft' (SOD). This time, both experts and the 190+ United Nations member governments participate in the review. To avoid politicisation, government representatives cannot draft any part of the main report; they participate in review on the same basis as experts. At this point several Review Editors – senior scientists with previous IPCC experience – are assigned to each chapter, to provide external oversight of the final review stages. One Review Editor assigned to my own chapter was exceptionally diligent, while the other two were less so. For them as for us, the task of reviewing a 100,000-word, highly technical chapter and evaluating thousands of comments while also working a day job proved overwhelming.

Revision of the SOD leads to the 'Final Government Distribution' (FGD) of the Final Draft. At this stage the draft is essentially frozen; however, the TSU revisited comments on the FOD and SOD and required all chapters to respond to any comments they had previously missed or deferred for later action.

Approval. In the last 18 months or so of the assessment, each WG designates a subset of authors (Coordinating Lead Authors or LAs) to draft an SPM, typically around 30 pages in length. The SPM is first reviewed by experts and governments, then revised, then subjected to another round of government review. Once finalised, the SPM goes to a plenary approval session, where government representatives approve the SPM line by line.

The role of government representatives is problematic with respect to the concept of 'peer' review. While some are very well informed on the scientific issues, others are not, and all are by definition representing the interests of their own nations. The approval session includes both SPM authors (IPCC scientists) and government representatives. IPCC procedures codify that SPM approval 'signifies that it is consistent with the factual material contained in the full scientific, technical and socio-economic Assessment or Special Report accepted by the Working Group' (IPCC, 2013a). However, there are many ways to summarise any large, complex document, and seemingly minute changes in language can matter greatly to policymakers' reception of IPCC reports. As a result, during the approval process government representatives may propose alterations to SPM statements that suit their own purposes (De Pryck, 2021a). Still, the consensus requirement generally limits the power of any one nation in the approval process, and government acceptance greatly strengthens the political authority of the assessments (see **Chapter 20**).

11.5 Controversies Surrounding the IPCC Review Process

When AR2 was released in 1996, the IPCC's rules of procedure became the flashpoint of an intense public controversy. WGI's SPM and Chapter 8 both included the following sentences: 'Our ability to quantify the human influence on global climate is currently limited ... *Nevertheless, the balance of evidence suggests that there is a discernible human influence on global climate'* (IPCC, 1996: 5, italics added).

Here, the IPCC for the first time acknowledged a better-than-even likelihood of anthropogenic causes for observed global climate change. The sentence was introduced into Chapter 8 and the SPM by Chapter 8 Coordinating Lead Author Ben Santer following the final IPCC WGI plenary meeting at Madrid in November 1995. There, the exact wording of that sentence was intensely debated – with representatives of some oil-producing states, notably Saudi Arabia, seeking to soften its terms – before the final revision quoted above was approved (Houghton, 2008).

Following release of the revised text, physicist Frederick Seitz and others charged the IPCC with 'deception', saying it had 'corrupted the peer review process' and violated its own rules of procedure (Lahsen, 1999; Oreskes & Conway, 2010). These charges were demonstrably untrue; the changes were introduced by consensus among the participating governments. Nonetheless, the episode drew attention to IPCC rules, which lacked clear closure mechanisms for the review process (Agrawala, 1998b: 624; Edwards & Schneider, 2001). As a result, in 1999 the IPCC revised its rules of procedure and added the Review Editor oversight role described earlier (Skodvin, 2000a; Siebenhüner, 2002).

A second example resulted from controversy over errors found in AR4 (O'Reilly, 2015) and criticism of the IPCC resulting from the 2009 Climategate episode. In 2010, the UN Secretary-General and IPCC Chair jointly requested an independent review of IPCC rules and procedures – including its peer review practices – by the InterAcademy Council (IAC), which appointed a panel of distinguished scientists (see **Chapter 6**). Like many independent commentators (Jasanoff, 2010a; Beck, 2012), the IAC panel found that due to the social significance of climate change and the authority attached to the IPCC's conclusions, 'accountability and transparency must be considered a growing obligation' (IAC, 2010: viii).

The IAC review found the IPCC's existing peer review process essentially 'sound'. However, it noted that the number of review comments had more than doubled, to more than 90,000 for the entire AR4. Fourteen years later, some 78,000 comments were received on the AR6 WGI report *alone*. Adding the comments received by WGII (62,418) and WGIII (59,212), this makes a total of 199,630 comments! The IAC concluded that under time pressure, some review comments might not receive sufficient attention, which is consistent with my own experience.

11.6 Achievements and Challenges

The current IPCC review process is the most extensive, open and inclusive in the history of science – a landmark achievement by any measure. Further, the organisation has responded to ongoing critiques with ever greater transparency and accountability. Today's review process is essentially public, open to anyone (within limits: for example, the English language standard presents a significant hurdle for non-speakers). Since AR4 (2007), the IPCC has published the FOD and SOD of each report on its website, along with all comments and responses. This review process means that minority views and outlier results have been carefully considered by the climate science community at several points, from journal peer review through multiple rounds of assessment review. Nonetheless, no review process can eliminate all errors or guarantee the truth of conclusions.

One very difficult challenge is that comments that dispute the fundamental framing of particular issues may be dismissed, unless a significant constituency supports reframing them (O'Reilly et al., 2012). For example, during review of the IPCC Special Report on Global Warming of 1.5 °C (2018), many commentators expressed 'unease' about the report's presentation of bioenergy with carbon capture and storage (BECCS) as 'a viable carbon dioxide removal technology at grand scale' (Hansson et al., 2021: 1). Yet this misleading framing remained in the final report. Hansson et al. identified several 'boundary work' strategies successfully used by LAs to deflect reviewer critiques of BECCS's potential. For example, LAs claimed that the IPCC mandate restricted them from being 'policy prescriptive' (see **Chapter 21**) – a deflection I encountered and resisted, yet also sometimes used myself, in working on AR6 WGI.

Two further challenges lie in the inexorably growing numbers of relevant publications and review comments. Machine learning techniques have been proposed to augment human processing of scientific literature (Callaghan et al., 2021), but such methods may never be accepted as substitutes for expert judgement. The huge number of review comments already imposes an infelicitous trade-off on volunteer LAs, who must balance their time between careful evaluation of the scientific literature, composition of the report, and responding with care to peer review. Any attempt to restrict the openness of the review process – for example, by requiring reviewers to provide stronger evidence of expertise – could lead to backlash over transparency. Increasing the number of LAs and/or Review Editors might help, yet would also add complexity to an already elaborate report-writing process.

Three Key Readings

Oppenheimer, M., Oreskes, N., Jamieson, D., et al. (2019). *Discerning Experts: The Practices of Scientific Assessment for Environmental Policy*. Chicago: University of Chicago Press.

This book critically examines practices used by several science assessments, including the IPCC's peer review processes.

Hansson, A., Anshelm, J., Fridal, M., and Haikola, S. (2021). Boundary work and interpretations in the IPCC review process of the role of bioenergy with carbon capture and Storage (BECCS) in limiting global warming to 1.5°C. *Frontiers in Climate*, 3: 643224. http://doi.org/10.3389/fclim.2021.643224

This article is one of the few close studies of IPCC peer review of a particular issue.

InterAcademy Council (2010). *Climate Change Assessments: Review of the Processes and Procedures of the IPCC*. Amsterdam: InterAcademy Council. Available at: https://archive.ipcc.ch/pdf/IAC_report/IAC%20Report.pdf

The InterAcademy Council report closely examines all aspects of review in IPCC reports. The changes it recommended have been adopted.

Part III

Knowledges

This part tackles the different knowledge inputs into the assessments of the Intergovernmental Panel on Climate Change (IPCC), but also how the IPCC itself shapes knowledge products, and how and when these knowledges lead to controversy. **Arthur C. Petersen** (Chapter 12) assesses the disciplinary expert knowledges reflected in IPCC assessments, in particular those from the natural and social sciences, and shows how the IPCC's work streams end up structuring and impacting the production of scientific and social scientific research more generally. **Bianca van Bavel** and **colleagues** (Chapter 13) considers the climate knowledges that are poorly assessed in IPCC reports, in particular Indigenous knowledge systems. They discuss some of the processes through which these systems could be better integrated in the assessment process. **Hélène Guillemot** (Chapter 14) considers the central role that climate models play in IPCC assessments, and their evolution over the various IPCC assessment cycles, while **Béatrice Cointe** (Chapter 15) offers a parallel assessment of IPCC scenarios and the dependence of these influential scenarios upon Integrated Assessment Models. Both chapters discuss how international communities of modelers orchestrate their work around IPCC assessment cycles. Finally, **Shinichiro Asayama** and **colleagues** (Chapter 16) examine the nature of the scientific and political controversies that the IPCC has faced over time and the role of the organisation in triggering or absorbing them. All chapters in this part emphasise the positive feedback loops that exist between the IPCC and different scientific and policy communities.

12

Disciplines

ARTHUR C. PETERSEN

Overview

The knowledge that is used in the assessments of the Intergovernmental Panel on Climate Change (IPCC) predominantly stems from a wide variety of academic disciplines. Given the high scientific and political profile of the IPCC, the production of knowledge in disciplines is impacted by the existence and dynamics of the IPCC assessment process. In some cases, the dynamics between academic disciplines and the IPCC is characterised by the presence of positive feedback loops, where the production of knowledge is structured and programmed by the IPCC. The subsequent findings then receive a preeminent role in later IPCC assessments, and so the cycle continues. It is important to critically reflect on these dynamics, in order to determine whether visions of climate change's past, present, and future – for example, pathways for the climate change problem and its potential solutions, as far as they exist – have not been unduly constrained by the IPCC process. The IPCC runs the risk of unreflexively foregrounding some scientific and policy approaches at the expense of other approaches.

12.1 Introduction

Experts from different academic disciplines contribute to the IPCC via publications in the peer-reviewed literature and by being authors or reviewers in the IPCC assessment process. The IPCC reports' Lead Authors have a powerful authority to decide on which bodies of academic literature from different disciplines are most relevant for their chapters. And they have to weigh their reliance on disciplinary knowledge against the use of highly relevant, but non-disciplinary, expert knowledge – for example from practitioners, or Indigenous knowledge holders. The role of the review process is to ensure that author teams do not ignore relevant bodies of literature and expertise (see **Chapter 11**). This chapter critically analyses with which disciplines the IPCC engages and how it does this.

Within the IPCC, an epistemological hierarchy can be seen to be at play *between* and *within* different disciplines. In the IPCC, the physical sciences have typically been regarded as sitting at the top (the 'strongest' type of knowledge), with biological and ecological sciences, engineering, and economics being in the middle, and qualitative social sciences and humanities residing at the bottom (the 'weakest' type of knowledge). An example of an epistemological hierarchy *within* disciplines is that in Working Group I (WGI) – dealing with the physical science basis – estimates from process-based models have typically been awarded a higher status than other types of estimates (e.g. those based on past observations), as will be illustrated later. Furthermore, the IPCC process itself is having an impact on the practices of scientific research – that is, on the development of disciplines themselves. For example, visions of future 'solutions' to climate change are propagated by the IPCC and are impacting research agendas (see **Chapter 15**).

This chapter first reviews the extant literature on how the IPCC has engaged disciplines from both natural sciences and social sciences and humanities. Subsequently, the attention shifts to influences in the opposite direction – that is, the extent to which the IPCC has had an impact on the production of knowledge in disciplines.

12.2 Engagement with Natural Sciences

Climate (later Earth system) models have always been important within the IPCC (see **Chapter 14**). Bjuström and Polk (2011) have shown that the natural sciences, and in particular the earth sciences, have dominated the early assessment reports. In the 1990s, the use of complex climate models dominated the work of WGI (e.g. Petersen, 2000, [2006] 2012). For example, enacting an epistemological hierarchy, the IPCC modellers in WGI initially downplayed palaeoclimatological knowledge and studies on abrupt climate change in the past (Demeritt, 2001). It took until the Fourth Assessment Report (AR4) (2007) before there was a marked increase in the visibility and importance of palaeoclimate expertise within WGI assessments (Caseldine et al., 2010). But by that time the IPCC was still not ready to include expert judgements on rapid sea-level rise, which are partially based on palaeoclimatic expertise, instead preferring model-based assessments (see Box 12.1).

More generally, there has been a predominance within the IPCC of quantitative natural scientific knowledge. For example, 'attribution' studies have been very important, and increasingly so in recent assessment rounds. Initially, the attribution of global temperature change to human influences was the main focus; nowadays, attribution science has broadened to quantitatively attributing ecosystem and

Box 12.1
Expert judgement versus models on rapid sea-level rise

For decades, there have been palaeoclimatological studies of rapid sea-level rise in the distant past, including periods with several metres of sea-level rise in the timeframe of a century, which could provide useful information to assess future sea-level rise. But it has taken the IPCC six cycles of assessment, over 30 years, to integrate the results of these studies and provide – with the August 2021 release of the AR6 WGI report – a plausible upper estimate of sea-level rise in 2100 of 2 metres. (This is a much higher number than the 'likely' range, taking into account possible ice sheet instability.) More than 14 years earlier, in the IPCC WGI AR4 plenary session, I – as a Dutch government delegate – had not been able to convince the respective Lead Authors to provide their expert judgement, based on inputs from several disciplines including palaeoclimatology, as opposed to results from models with known limitations. This is evidenced by my diary entry, published shortly after the plenary:

> Early in the afternoon [of Wednesday 31 January 2007, acp] I have a conversation with two authors on the maximum height of the sea level rise in 2100. According to model projections the maximum sea level rise is 59 centimetres. This number does not include an estimate for the possible accelerated melting of Greenland and Antarctica. It seems that scientists really do not know what will happen with Greenland and Antarctica. But a possible accelerated meltdown could lead to a sea level rise of more than one metre. Should we mention that, without being able to say something about the probability? Or should we just say that we cannot identify an upper limit?

> The authors propose a text that now makes clear that we cannot give an upper limit. That is better than it was, but I still find it unsatisfactory. For readers it would be nice if we could give an indication of how much the sea level could maximally rise. But as IPCC we have a responsibility to say what is and is not known. The text on the ignorance regarding the upper limit appears acceptable to all delegations. Also to the Dutch – I do not push this further (Petersen, 2007: 21).

O'Reilly et al. (2012) later found that a (re-)organisation of chapters, assigning a central role to sea-level modellers, had made it harder to include an estimate for the upper limit of sea-level rise due to ice cap melting by 2100, in part because it did not consider information from palaeoclimatological studies. In a later publication, it was demonstrated how the difficulties of modelling accelerated meltdown of ice sheets had led to underestimates since the IPCC's beginnings (Oppenheimer et al., 2019). And due to an epistemological hierarchy that favoured process-based models over past observations it was hard to include palaeoclimatological evidence in the IPCC's expert judgement on the upper limit of sea-level rise.

human system changes (in WGII) and individual weather events (in WGI) to human-induced climate change.

12.3 Engagement with Social Sciences and Humanities

Social sciences and humanities scholarship has gradually been drawn in over the course of the different IPCC assessment cycles. Nevertheless, the relative autonomy of the separate WGs, combined with differences in their respective disciplinary mixes, has led social scientists to conclude that the interdisciplinary integration necessary for tackling climate change has been hindered by a 'unidisciplinary structure of work' (Godal, 2003). For example, in the context of designing greenhouse gas indices – which allow one to compare the warming effects of different greenhouse gases – the WG structure, with the exclusion of social science disciplines in WGI, made it harder to draw appropriately on existing interdisciplinary work to integrate damages and costs in greenhouse gas indices (on integration between WGs see **Chapter 18**). Another straightforward example of the lack of disciplinary interaction between different social scientific disciplines within the IPCC is that between the meta-policy domains of adaptation and mitigation, since these domains are covered by different WGs.

Epistemological hierarchies are evident both between WGs – with generally more authority being attributed to WGI – and within WGs. The Third Assessment Report (AR3) Report (2001) aimed to include a larger range of social sciences, but with mixed results (Rayner & Malone, 1998). AR4 (2007) was still weak on social science, which led to calls to the IPCC, as well as to the research community, to produce more studies on citizen participation, on culture, ethics and religion, and on the incorporation of more diverse actors (e.g. Hiramatsu et al., 2008). Economics has been predominant among the social sciences that have been mobilised by the IPCC (Yearley, 2009). It can certainly be argued that the IPCC engages less with social science disciplines than is possible or desirable. On the one hand, the IPCC is confronted with many questions that social science can address. On the other hand, it is also important to realise that some social science disciplines, such as political science, whilst important, do not address climate change as a central topic. More generally, because of ontological plurality in the social sciences, it can be harder to organise social-science knowledge compared to natural science (Victor, 2015). It also has not been easy to integrate the first philosophers into the IPCC process in the Fifth Assessment Report (AR5), as was evidenced by their different modes of working, both in the draft writing and in the plenaries. For example, their purview was typically not bound to assessing only the last few years of literature (Broome, 2020).

A major effect of the limited engagement with social science by the IPCC has been its poverty in terms of socio-technical visions. It has long been clear that the IPCC's integration of the topic of sustainable development has been limited (Najam et al., 2003) and that futures research has been only very modestly represented (Nordlund, 2008). The various sets of scenarios that have been constructed by, or for, the IPCC have also been constrained and focused on extreme 'business-as-usual' scenarios (Demeritt, 2001; Pielke & Ritchie, 2021). This critique parallels a growing prominence of integrated assessment modelling (IAM) analyses in subsequent IPCC reports (see **Chapter 15**). This has several causes, ranging from the particular features of these modelling approaches – including their flexibility, breadth, and hybridity – that allowed them an 'anchoring' function between WGs, to proactive behaviours by those involved in the discipline of IAM (van Beek et al., 2020a). This has had consequences. For example, Integrated Assessment Models do not pay much (if any) attention to the impacts of policies on land use, food security, human rights and investment costs, and the wider politics of developing new plantations and infrastructures. One consequence of this has been a large global reliance in the IPCC's projections of future development pathways – certainly since AR5 – on Bio-Energy Carbon Capture and Storage (BECCS) to stay below or return to global average temperature increases of 1.5 °C or 2 °C by 2100.

Note also that the IPCC does not only rely on knowledge deriving from academic disciplines but also – although until recently to a very limited extent – on knowledge that stems from elsewhere, for example various types of practitioners including legal experts or Indigenous knowledge holders. For example, Viner and Howarth (2014) argue that knowledge on climate adaptation from practitioners is relevant for IPCC reports and should be included centrally. And an answer is needed to the critique that expertise on Indigenous peoples has been brought in only obliquely and problematically through 'the narrative of pending catastrophe, the tropes of cultural loss and the urgent need for pan-global solutions' (Ford et al., 2016: 351; see **Chapter 13**).

12.4 Impact on Disciplines

Far from merely *assessing* existing published knowledge, the IPCC – directly or indirectly – shapes the types of questions research communities investigate and therefore has an active presence in determining what research gets funded. The IPCC's engagement with disciplines has an impact on their development. This becomes evident from the pervasiveness and dominance in the academic literature of a structural linearity of knowledge which moves from geoscience to impact, adaptation and mitigation, mirroring the IPCC WG structure (see, for example, the presentations at the Copenhagen Congress in 2009; O'Neill et al., 2010). IPCC reports are also regularly cited in the primary scientific literature, with a skewness towards geophysical sciences, although this skewness is gradually decreasing as the IPCC's assessments increasingly impact on the shaping of other disciplines (Vasileiadou et al., 2011).

Evolving policy needs, embodied in IPCC assessments, create selection mechanisms for climate science (Vasileiadou et al., 2011). The IPCC is regularly asked to treat subjects for which there is not yet a strong underlying research base (see **Chapter 5** on the reports process), especially in the social sciences. This has led to calls for bringing together descriptive and interpretive social science methods to usefully tackle questions on, for instance, vulnerability and adaptation (Malone & Rayner, 2001).

Early studies on the IPCC already observed that WGI anticipated reductions in scientific uncertainty about climate change that would come through particular national and international research programmes (Shackley & Wynne, 1996). This led to the introduction of new subjects in climate science research as a direct consequence of IPCC discussions (Shackley & Wynne, 1997). For example, funding for palaeoclimatological research has been framed in terms of its expected contribution to the testing of complex models necessary for IPCC assessments. In the 1990s, IPCC-influenced funding was also made available for reducing physical-science uncertainties, but not so much for studying uncertainties pertaining to the human dimensions of climate change, especially those that do not connect well to a natural science frame (Demeritt, 2001). Finally, in past decades, the main impetus behind climate modelling and model intercomparison projects (see **Chapter 14**) has come from the IPCC assessment process (Yearley, 2009). Funding opportunities for palaeoclimate research have increased more recently with the growing importance of palaeoclimate reconstructions within the IPCC (Caseldine et al., 2010).

A direct impact on knowledge generation of participation in the IPCC has been identified by social scientists, namely how IPCC authors flag gaps in the published literature and then pursue the called-for new research themselves in order to fill those gaps. For example, in the climate-mitigation field, individuals and institutions are organising their research, collaboration and publication strategies around the assessment of knowledge in IPCC reports. This makes climate-mitigation research, as a discipline, effectively dependent on the IPCC (Hughes & Paterson, 2017). The 2015 UNFCCC request to produce a special report on 1.5 °C signalled a shift from 'science-driven co-production' to 'policy-driven co-production' which has been most visible in the production of IAMs and associated scenarios – there has been a sharp increase in IAM publications ahead of each cycle of IPCC reports (van Beek et al., 2020a). The centrality of the IAM community to the IPCC's mapping of mitigation options – such as taking 2 °C and 1.5 °C as targets for pathway modelling – has constrained the research questions being addressed. In a circuitous way, this feedback loop has led to the prominence of BECCS among potential climate-change measures (Low & Schäfer, 2020). In sum, the IPCC, with its substantial involvement in emissions scenario production and use, has had a central role in orchestrating the scientific literature on climate change. Some important questions have not therefore been researched by the academic community that might otherwise have been (Hulme, 2016).

From a systems perspective, positive feedback loops can be identified. For instance, being a lead author leads to advantages in scholarly publishing, which leads such authors to become more influential within the IPCC, and so on (Hughes & Paterson, 2017). This is another instantiation of the 'Matthew effect' – the rich getting richer and the poor getting poorer – that has been studied in the sociology of science since the 1960s. At the institutional level, the IPCC plays a major role in the orientation, rhythm and domain of applicability of some fields of climate research (Cointe et al., 2019). For example, the current prominence of IAMs to explore low-carbon futures is a result of complex historic science–policy dynamics involving the IPCC, a central part of this being IAMs' anchoring of relationships among the three IPCC WGs (van Beek et al., 2020a). A similar positive feedback loop had also been observed earlier in the case of complex climate models (e.g. Petersen, 2000, [2006] 2012; Demeritt, 2001; Yearley, 2009).

On the other hand, there have also been calls for the IPCC to exercise a *larger* impact on academic disciplines. The lack of integration of disciplinary knowledge within the IPCC, beyond the natural sciences and economics, is partly related to the way academic institutions are organised around separate disciplines (Bjurström & Polk, 2011). For some scholars, a successful transformation within the social sciences and humanities towards systematic and integrated knowledge generation is seen as needed to help increase the policy relevance of IPCC assessments (Minx et al., 2017). The recent establishment in universities of numerous 'Schools of Sustainability' and similar academic units can be seen to contribute to this goal.

12.5 Achievements and Challenges

The IPCC, through its rigorous procedures, has been able to successfully create credible assessments of the evolving state of expert knowledge on climate change. However, there have been some drawbacks to the way that the IPCC has relied on academic disciplines. For example, the IPCC's focus on peer-reviewed publications has devalued other types of less academically formalised expert knowledge, such as practitioner and engineering expertise and legal reports, or Indigenous knowledge (Beck & Forsyth, 2015).

I suggest that major changes are needed in the way the IPCC engages with disciplinary and other expert knowledge. The information needs of decision-makers and practitioners around the world are varied and increasingly urgent. Yet, as these needs have expanded, there has been a widening gap between what most IPCC authors understand to be useful information and what decision-makers see as informative (Petersen et al., 2015). It has been argued that the addition of a fourth WG on 'historical, cultural, and social contexts' could assist in re-framing climate change as an ethical, cultural and political phenomenon. This could counter the observed epistemological hierarchy, with biases in the existing WGs towards physical and economic sciences (O'Neill et al., 2010).

However, I judge that this has only limited potential of success in terms of integration with the other IPCC WGs and its ability to function within the UN system. Since governments want to control the IPCC's statements about social behaviour, or statements that implicate policy choices, it is mostly politically non-controversial 'high confidence' statements that make it into the Summaries for Policymakers. Such statements are more likely to emerge from 'positivist' disciplines than from interpretative ones. A parallel process to the IPCC – but non-governmental – would be needed to address controversial topics such as how best to design international agreements or how to govern the use of geoengineering technologies (Victor, 2015).

Finally, the presence of positive feedback loops described in this chapter not only shows the presence of a potential conflict of interest – with for instance Lead Authors filling the research gaps that they themselves identify – but also highlights the fact that the IPCC has now increasingly become self-referential. This raises questions about the notion of the IPCC's 'policy relevance'. More specifically, who decides what policy relevance is? There is a danger that researchers – finding eager receptors in particular policymakers involved in UNFCCC processes – are deciding what disciplines are policy-relevant for IPCC assessments. The IPCC should find ways to become more reflexive about this issue, while a wide set of decision-makers should seek to construct a larger ecosystem of science–policy institutions that meet their practical needs.

Three Key Readings

Cointe, B., Cassen, C. and Nadaï, A. (2019). Organising policy-relevant knowledge for climate action: Integrated Assessment Modelling, the IPCC, and the emergence of a collective expertise on socioeconomic emission scenarios. *Science and Technology Studies*, 32(4): 36–57. http://doi.org/10.23987/sts.65031

This article provides an analysis, based on interviews, of the way the integrated assessment modelling community organised itself around AR5 (2014).

O'Reilly, J., Oreskes, N. and Oppenheimer, M. (2012). The rapid disintegration of projections: the West Antarctic Ice Sheet and the Intergovernmental Panel on Climate

Change. *Social Studies of Science*, 42(5): 709–731. http://doi.org/10.1177/0306312712448130

This article provides an analysis, based on interviews, of the way expert judgement lost out from modelling in estimating future sea-level rise in AR4 (2007).

Vasileiadou, E., Heimeriks, G. and Petersen, A. C. (2011). Exploring the impact of the IPCC Assessment Reports on science. *Environmental Science and Policy*, 14(8): 1052–1061. http://doi.org/10.1016/j.envsci.2011.07.002

This article applies bibliometric methods to identify the impact of IPCC reports (AR1–AR4) on academic disciplines, one of the very few studies that tackles this question.

13

Indigenous Knowledge Systems

BIANCA VAN BAVEL, JOANNA PETRASEK MACDONALD
AND DALEE SAMBO DOROUGH

Overview

The Intergovernmental Panel on Climate Change (IPCC) has begun to acknowledge, albeit slowly, the importance of Indigenous knowledge (IK) systems in contributing to understandings of climate change and effective climate action. Yet Indigenous Peoples (IPs) and IK systems remain largely excluded and marginalised from the IPCC global assessment reports. IPCC scientists and leaders have a unique and specific obligation to IK systems that does not extend to other knowledge systems. IK is the knowledge of rights holders and therefore acknowledging and respecting the self-determination of IPs over their knowledge – including how it is used, interpreted and synthesized – is imperative. There are examples of IPs organising themselves in other international spaces that could inform how the IPCC can approach a stronger, more durable engagement with IPs. Perhaps the ultimate challenge for the IPCC is that when bringing IK systems together with other knowledge systems, the framing of evidence must reflect the diversity of these distinct and discrete ways of knowing. Examples from the lived experience of the Inuit Circumpolar Council (ICC) in engaging with the IPCC demonstrate diverse channels for engagement, yet significant limitations persist.

13.1 Introduction

As it stands, the IPCC 'knowledge base' consists largely of peer-reviewed and internationally available academic literature with some selected non-peer reviewed – so-called 'grey' – literature (see **Chapter 12**). Given the nature and scope of the peer-review publication process, this translates into assessing evidence predominantly through a Western scientific lens. Widening the knowledge base is not just about including more diverse peer-reviewed literature. It is about engaging with diverse knowledge systems and forms of evidence originating outside a scientific system of understanding, crucial among these being IK systems.

Excluding or failing to adequately and appropriately engage with IK systems results in a failure to capture in-depth and extensive evidence that could (i) significantly enhance the understanding of environmental, biophysical and climatic systems; (ii) provide crucial information about the interconnections between humans, more-than-humans and the environment, and (iii) strengthen the knowledge base in such a way that could help to advance evidence-based climate policy and create better-informed rigorous climate action responsive to all, including IPs. This chapter makes a case for widening the IPCC's knowledge base to include IK systems. But it also outlines how this might be done by discussing what it means to ethically and equitably engage with IK systems.[1] To do this we draw both from published academic literature and from lived experience of the IPCC's exclusive processes and limitations to its knowledge base.

13.2 IK Systems

IK systems have been largely excluded from IPCC reports to date and from climate research broadly (Ford et al., 2012; Smith & Sharp, 2012; Ford et al., 2016; van Bavel, 2021). However, IK systems have been recognised as essential to understanding the environment and human-environment relationships, and to developing solutions to mitigate and adapt to the climate crisis (e.g. Laidler et al., 2011; Nalau et al., 2018; IPCC, 2019g; Sawatzky et al., 2020). Furthermore, IPs live in environments and ecosystems that are often heavily impacted by climate change and therefore have extensive lived experience and an intimate knowledge of climate change (Maldonado et al., 2016; Savo et al., 2016; Forest Peoples Programme et al., 2020). Indeed, the profound relationship that IPs have with their lands, territories and resources – and their collective rights to their lands, territories and resources – is a unique and unparalleled connection. It is therefore essential for the IPCC to make linkages between IK systems and impacts of climate change on Indigenous lands.

IPs own, protect, manage or have tenure rights to more than a quarter of the Earth's land territory, comprising 40 per cent of all protected land and ecologically conserved landscapes with high biodiversity and carbon storage (Garnett et al., 2018; Forest Peoples Programme et al., 2020). This intimate knowledge and stewardship expands the understanding of the impacts of climate change, and how to respond to them. IK has been defined in many ways and will not be defined in one way here; rather, it is essential to recognise the various definitions of IK, such as that offered by the ICC[2] (see Box 13.1). We note that IPs have the right to define IK as they understand and engage with their own knowledge.

Box 13.1
One of many definitions of Indigenous knowledge

Inuit Circumpolar Council (2013)

Indigenous knowledge is a systematic way of thinking applied to phenomena across biological, physical, cultural and spiritual systems. It includes insights based on evidence acquired through direct and long-term experiences and extensive and multigenerational observations, lessons and skills. It has developed over millennia and is still developing in a living process, including knowledge acquired today and in the future, and it is passed on from generation to generation. Under this definition, IK goes beyond observations and ecological knowledge, offering a unique 'way of knowing'. This knowledge can identify research needs and be applied to them, which will ultimately inform decision makers. There is a need to utilise both Indigenous and scientific Knowledge. Both ways of knowing will benefit the people, land, water, air, and animals within the Arctic.

Regardless of the term or definition, IK is the knowledge of rights holders. IK systems are therefore tied to Indigenous rights and any engagement with IK systems requires a rights framework or rights-based approach. IK systems cannot be taken out of the specific cultural context from which they emerge. It is also crucial to recognise that IK systems and Indigenous languages are inextricably connected. Serious rights safeguards are imperative in relation to IK systems[3] and such safeguards must be recognised and respected. Article 31 of the UN Declaration on the Rights of Indigenous Peoples affirms 'the right to maintain, *control*, protect and develop their intellectual property' (emphasis added). This must be understood as directly linked to exercising the elements of the right to free, prior and informed consent – here, the term 'control' in its plain meaning suggests that the peoples concerned have power over, to influence, manage, restrain, limit or prevent something from taking place (United Nations, 2007). Article 31 must also be read in the context of the whole of the instrument and all the interrelated rights affirmed therein. A rights-based approach means acknowledging and respecting the self-determination of IPs, their governance systems, their right to define their knowledge systems and to be equal partners in knowledge translation and mobilisation. It also means understanding IPs' rights to represent their people in regional, national and international processes, whether this be knowledge production, knowledge assessments or policy development. In applying an Indigenous worldview, knowledge cannot be separated from governance. To capture the richness and depth that IK systems can offer, Western models of knowledge production, synthesis and decision-making should welcome IPs and recognise them as fellow experts, decision-makers and distinct knowledge holders.

Lastly, it is important to understand that IPs are well organised in international climate spaces. IPs have self-organised to effectively and directly participate in various international systems including the International Union for the Conservation of Nature (IUCN), the Convention on Biological Diversity (CBD), and the UN Framework Convention on Climate Change (UNFCCC). While the organisation of IPs around each system varies in operation and membership, the structural framework and core principles remain consistent. In dealing with such international bodies, IPs are formally recognised within the UN system and are engaged and organised into seven UN socio-cultural regions – Africa, Asia, Latin America and the Caribbean, Russia, the Arctic, the Pacific, and North America. IPs in these regions coordinate regionally to discuss and determine shared interests and priorities. They then come together under one Indigenous body – for example, for the UNFCCC, IPs gather under the International Indigenous Peoples Forum on Climate Change (IIPFCC), also referred to as the IP caucus[4] – to build consensus around shared Indigenous positions and messages.

These bodies and organisational structures have been in place for decades and are well recognised. They uphold principles of diversity, inclusivity, collaboration, fluidity, and respect for local and regional governance structures. IPs can engage with the Indigenous body while at the same time engage with advocacy and actions specific to their organisation, country, priorities, strategies or region. Recognising the centuries-old debates concerning the status, rights and roles of IPs and the historical antecedents of IPs as objects and subjects of international law, the world community has embraced IPs. Yet, challenges such as the engagement of IK remain. It is therefore important to recognise these structures because they demonstrate IPs' in-depth knowledge and experience in engaging with international climate processes and are exemplary in respecting self-determination. There is extensive expertise within and readiness from IPs to engage with the IPCC and examples of how to facilitate this (see Section 13.7).

13.3 Engaging with IK Systems in Equitable and Ethical Ways

Widening the knowledge base to ethically and equitably include IK systems in the IPCC is two pronged. The first important element is to engage with IPs directly and to provide opportunities for partnership and direct participation in the IPCC process. Responsible engagement includes processes of partnership and participation that are initiated in mutual agreement with or by IPs (David-Chavez & Gavin, 2018). This is contrary to the extractive models of engagement often applied when attempting to access IK systems externally from Western scientific contexts of research and evidence assessment. Developing relationships with IPs and organisations is one initial effort that will aim to ensure IK systems are present in IPCC assessments.

The other crucial element is ensuring that the ongoing machine of knowledge production that feeds into the IPCC prioritises the co-production of knowledge. Knowledge co-production is a process in which multiple distinct and separate paradigms are applied simultaneously at all stages of knowledge generation (Tengö et al., 2014; Johnson et al., 2016; Berkes, 2018; Hill et al., 2020). While being considered together in this generative process of co-production, the integrity and quality of each knowledge system is still valued as it continues to engage in its independent production processes (IPCC, 2019f; their Fig. CB4.1). According to a recent report produced by the ICC, aiming for genuine co-production of knowledge is a crucial part of ethically and equitably engaging with IK systems. It requires essential elements of trust, respect and relationship, as well as full acceptance of agreed values (ICC, 2021). Further guidance towards genuine co-production processes involves acknowledging IK 'as a unique knowledge system that comes with its own evaluation and validation processes' (ICC, 2021: 20). This guidance extends to the IPCC assessment process and its synthesis of a diverse knowledge base and highlights the existing tensions between fundamentally different knowledge-handling processes that must be recognised and resolved for new knowledge to be co-produced.

Research assessing how IK has been used as evidence to shape IPCC assessments – from the Fourth (AR4) to the Sixth Assessment Report (AR6) – has demonstrated that, despite an increase in Indigenous-focused content over time, the IPCC process has no established procedures or guidance for ethically and equitably engaging with IK systems, especially where it is highly relevant (Ford et al., 2012, 2016; Smith & Sharp, 2012; van Bavel, 2021). Furthermore, the underlying principles and procedures that guide IPCC assessments have been shown to actively restrict the knowledge base from equitably and ethically engaging with IK systems (van Bavel, 2021). Here, an excerpt taken from publicly available IPCC expert reviewer comments also reveals some of the challenges encountered when working within the existing IPCC assessment process:

It is somewhat difficult to use 'published' IK – first of all because very little is published, second, because it can easily be taken out of context and be misinterpreted, since it is very complex. The context/analysis should ideally always be confirmed by the knowledge holders – Expert Reviewer 22590 SROCC

IPs highlight protocols and methodologies that belong to the worldviews and paradigms of IK systems (e.g. Kovach, 2009; Inuit Tapiriit Kanatami, 2018; Whyte, 2018; ICC, 2021). They can offer a process, outside of Western scientific forms of validation, for widening the knowledge base through knowledge co-production (e.g. Tengö et al., 2014; Parsons et al., 2016). Multiple, distinct and separate knowledges coming together requires a framing of evidence that reflects such diversity – including fundamental differences in epistemology, ontology, methodology and axiology (see **Chapter 18**). Critically, this need for reforming the assessment process to widen the knowledge base has been echoed by Indigenous persons and organisations navigating their own engagement with the IPCC. One such organisation is the ICC, which has called for and exemplified the importance of a two-pronged approach to widening the knowledge base. This is through direct participation, engagement and partnership of IPs in the IPCC process, and through prioritising the co-production of knowledge. ICC has shared this message and embodied this approach in various ways including as an expert reviewer, as a contributing author, as a member of a government's delegation to plenary sessions, and most recently as an official observer.

13.4 IPs and IPs Organisations as Expert Reviewers

The existing IPCC review process plays a significant role in engaging the IPCC's knowledge claims through experts beyond academia, including those from government, non-government and industry (see **Chapters 10** and **11**). As an expert reviewer, the ICC has made substantial comments and fed directly into IPCC assessments during this review process. The extent to which these comments are addressed has varied, but has allowed for the ICC to consistently call for more engagement with IK systems and qualify what that engagement should look like. Despite the significant demand on time and resources that is required to adequately complete the IPCC review process, ICC has continuously provided expert Indigenous-specific input and analysis on how the various reports have used IK systems. It has also provided detailed expert advice on appropriate language, framing, literature and other source materials. For example, it has ensured that when IK is introduced in the Summary for Policymakers it is alongside concepts of Indigenous rights and self-determination within the research and evidence assessment process (Expert Reviewer 3088, SROCC). As an expert reviewer, ICC has flagged the absence of Indigenous authors and emphasised in numerous review processes the importance of partnership and direct participation. It has called for genuine opportunities to contribute co-authored content, especially where the IPCC refers to the work and knowledge of ICC and other IPs:

Ideally, Indigenous knowledge holders should participate in the development of these reports so that they stand as an example of HOW to be engaging with Indigenous knowledge ... there are many communities and individuals from this population whose voices, knowledge, and experience would have strengthened the writing of this report had they been brought in from the beginning – Expert Reviewer 9604, SR1.5

13.5 Indigenous Authorship

During the most recent IPCC assessment cycle, ICC has worked with an IPCC author who understands what it means to ethically and equitably engage with IK systems. This author has sought to provide more meaningful opportunities to include Indigenous voices and knowledge in IPCC assessments. Through this relationship, ICC has contributed text to the IPCC SROCC and IPCC AR6 WGII Polar Regions Cross-chapter Paper. Ensuring the integrity and robustness of a contribution can be very challenging when facing word limits, restrictions to peer-reviewed sources, requirements to fit into a Western framing, and comments from other authors, expert reviewers or government representatives who do not understand IK systems, IPs or Indigenous rights. In addition, as with the review process, authorship requires allotting staff time and resources to IPCC work, often without having allocated funding for this work. However, this opportunity to contribute has provided ICC greater insight into the process and allowed for a stronger understanding of where to find intersections and common points of convergence that can facilitate the utilisation of IK systems. Including Indigenous authors in the IPCC reports is certainly one step towards meaningful engagement. Continuing to include and support Indigenous authors should be a priority for the IPCC (Ford et al., 2012).

13.6 IPs as Part of a Member Government Delegation

The ICC has also been invited to join the Canadian delegation at Panel's plenary meetings. As part of the Canadian delegation, ICC can participate in the final approval of reports, voice concerns that have not been addressed in the review process, and request changes to wording to ensure respectful and appropriate framing of IK systems and Indigenous perspectives. Support from governments by making space for Indigenous representation on the delegation is a significant step in the right direction. Yet Indigenous participation in this capacity remains limited and ultimately IPs should have their own autonomous and equal seat at the table. A step in this direction occurred in February 2020 when ICC was granted formal observer status to the IPCC (see **Chapter 10**). This is the first time an Indigenous Peoples Organisation (IPO) has been recognised as a formal observer and may provide new opportunities for engagement. ICC can now fully participate in its own right and represent itself at plenary sessions and when interacting with the Panel, the Bureau and the Technical Support Units. Observer status also may be useful for ICC to contribute to training workshops or expert meetings on the topic of IK systems. The absence of other observer IPOs further points to the lack of examples of IPOs intersecting or engaging with the IPCC.

13.7 Achievements and Challenges

Recognising that there are many ways of knowing – which must be considered together to inform the transformation of our understandings of climate change – is a recent awakening in the IPCC. We can trace the evolution of the treatment of IK systems in IPCC reports. This started with simply the recognition of IK systems as sources of knowledge in their own right, to having representations of IK in reports – albeit sometimes through inappropriate means – to seeing original contributions from an IPO, to having the first IPO accepted as an observer. We recognise that these are fledgling efforts from a regrettably small body of examples. And yet, there is the expertise, will and desire from within IPOs, including the ICC, to effectively and meaningfully engage with the IPCC process to ensure IK systems are included equitably and ethically within the knowledge base.

True transformation towards equitable and ethical engagement of IK systems and IPs requires going beyond fledgling practices of engagement. It requires changing the current paradigm, framing of evidence, and developing processes of the IPCC to reflect the diversity between and within knowledge systems and co-produce the transformative understandings of climate change needed today. Starting points would be having IPOs as full members of the IPCC and Indigenous representation in the Bureau; supporting Indigenous authorship/leadership early and often in the assessment cycle; recognising Indigenous peer-reviewed processes; and citing Indigenous-led materials in reports. There are many challenges and tensions, especially within the academic world, that restrict such transformation, some of which have been characterised in this chapter. It is not an easy task and the IPCC remains in the infancy of this unchartered territory. Yet engaging and mainstreaming IK systems in assessments like the IPCC perhaps offers a way forward for their adoption of new processes, paradigms and understandings. Certainly IPOs such as the ICC deem their engagement efforts worthwhile, despite the challenges and the glacier-paced change. Indeed, the benefits of being involved in the IPCC process and championing knowledge co-production and transformation, to the extent possible, will always outweigh the costs of time and resources because Indigenous lives, cultural integrity, ways of life and knowledge systems are at stake.

The extraordinary developments in favour of IPs within the field of international human rights law at the UN, Organisation of American States (OAS), International Labour Organisation (ILO), and elsewhere, suggests that the IPCC may have a responsibility to prioritise and value the ethical and equitable engagement of IK systems that does not extend to other knowledge systems. Here, we refer to the unique and specific set of obligations to understand Indigenous perspectives and worldviews, engage with IK systems and rights holders, and co-produce knowledge. This includes IPCC scientists and leaders questioning their assumptions, perspectives and approaches to knowledge production. To date, the burden of furthering increased understanding between IK systems and science has largely fallen on the shoulders of IPs and Indigenous academics. Such individuals understand the distinct cultural context of the Indigenous world, but they have been trained in the Western or non-Indigenous academic realm and understand both systems. These individuals who can act as bridges are rare, but have been essential in making these important connections (cf. multi-positional thematic bridges described in **Chapter 18**).

Beyond the IPCC, there are various bodies and mechanisms that offer opportunities from which the IPCC can learn about facilitating equitable and ethical engagement with IK holders and IK systems. Again, this is being done through Indigenous partnership and direct participation as well as prioritising the co-production of knowledge. For example: the Facilitative Working Group of the Local Communities and Indigenous Peoples Platform (LCIPP)[5] under the UNFCCC, the UN Permanent Forum on Indigenous Issues (UNPFII)[6], the Arctic Council[7], as well as the IIPFCC (see Section 13.2). These are examples to learn from, but these bodies also continue to be challenged with fully embodying the equitable and ethical engagement of IK systems and co-production of knowledge in its fullest and truest form. IPOs like the ICC continue to work in these spaces to encourage and cultivate an understanding of IK systems. An expansive understanding of IPs based on their relationship with their lands, territories and resources can never be captured by Western science. The IPCC must strive to make its assessment processes ethical and equitable in a way that has relevance and validity for IPs, in Indigenous contexts. This could have resounding reciprocal benefits for climate research, policy and practice, as well as enhancing the recognition of IPs and implementation of their distinct rights globally.

Notes

1 Making Indigenous knowledge systems the focus, this chapter will not engage with questions around local or practitioner knowledges, or any other knowledge systems, since these are distinct from Indigenous knowledge.
2 The Inuit Circumpolar Council (ICC) is an Indigenous Peoples Organisation, founded in 1977 to promote and advance the unity of 180,000 Inuit from Alaska, Canada, Greenland, and Chukotka. ICC works to promote Inuit rights, safeguard the Arctic environment, and maintain the Inuit way of life. Working for recognition of and respect for IK systems is a priority of the ICC. https://www.inuitcircumpolar.com/
3 Such as the American Declaration on the Rights of Indigenous Peoples (2016), a human rights instrument that is complementary to the UNDRIP, which contains more comprehensive provisions addressing "systems of knowledge" and their relationship to identity, land, territory, resources, etc.
4 The IIPFCC organises meetings around the UNFCCC COPs and intersessional sessions. Engaging with IPOs through this forum could be one option for the IPCC to consider.

5 LCIPP is a new and important space mandated to facilitate knowledge exchange and develop the capacity of state parties for engagement with IK systems and holders. Activities most relevant to the IPCC include training webinars on Indigenous knowledge, seminars on Indigenous climate change curricula, and a co-produced web portal (https://lcipp.unfccc.int/) with information about how to engage with Indigenous perspectives and knowledge of climate change.

6 UNPFII acts an advisory to the UN Economic and Social Council regarding areas of concern and rights of IPs. Members of the UNPFII have been engaging in research and synthesis reports regarding IK systems, including the treatment of IK within the UNDRIP framework (ECOSOC and Permanent Forum on Indigenous Issues, 2015), analysis of customary laws pertaining to IK (ECOSOC and Permanent Forum on Indigenous Issues, 2007), the resilience and protection of IK systems in African contexts (ECOSOC and Permanent Forum on Indigenous Issues, 2013b, 2014), and connecting IK systems, history, and social circumstances within the education system (ECOSOC and Permanent Forum on Indigenous Issues, 2013a). More information available at https://www.un.org/development/desa/indigenouspeoples/unpfii-sessions-2.html.

7 The Arctic Council recognises Arctic IPOs as Permanent Participants who share the same table as eight Arctic state party members and who are actively engaged in all aspects of the Council, including its working groups. The fact that the Arctic is the homelands of these respective Indigenous Peoples Organisations, they are accorded equal and direct access to every issue of Arctic Council concern, above and beyond that of non-Arctic nations. https://arctic-council.org/

Three Key Readings

Inuit Circumpolar Council (2021). Ethical and Equitable Engagement Synthesis Report: A collection of Inuit rules, guidelines, protocols, and values for the engagement of Inuit Communities and IK from Across Inuit Nunaat. Available at: www.inuitcircumpolar .com/project/icc-ethical-and-equitable-engagement-synthesis-report/

This synthesis report illustrates what it means for Inuit to secure the ethical, equitable, fair and just engagement of Inuit knowledge. It does so by synthesizing Inuit-developed rules, laws, values, guidelines and protocols from across Inuit Nunaat–Inuit homelands and territories. This report is instrumental in the collective development of circumpolar engagement protocols and guidelines that support Inuit sovereignty, self-determination and self-governance.

Inuit Tapiriit Kanatami (2018). National Inuit Strategy on Research. Ottawa. Available at: www.itk.ca.

This strategy presents an Inuit vision for research in Inuit Nunangat, the Inuit homeland and territory in Canada, that can be achieved through the equitable and ethical engagement with Inuit and their knowledge, governance and rights. It emphasizes how ensuring the right to Inuit self-determination in research, and research relationships, is a means for ensuring that Inuit Nunangat research is efficacious, impactful and useful for Inuit.

Whyte, K. (2018). What do Indigenous knowledges do for Indigenous Peoples? In: Nelson, M. K. and Shilling, D. (eds.), *Keepers of the Green World: Traditional Ecological Knowledge and Sustainability*. Cambridge: Cambridge University Press. pp. 57–82. http://doi.org/10.1017/9781108552998.005

This book chapter highlights the significance of what IK systems do for IPs. Whyte calls on Western scientists seeking to engage in knowledge exchange and co-production processes to recognize the irreplaceable value of IK systems not only in terms of what they can do for Western science, but what they do for IPs themselves.

14

Climate Models

HÉLÈNE GUILLEMOT

Overview

Climate computer models are irreplaceable scientific tools to study the climate system and to allow projections of future climate change. They play a major role in the assessment reports of the Intergovernmental Panel on Climate Change (IPCC), underpinning palaeoclimate reconstructions, attribution studies, scenarios of future climate change, and concepts such as climate sensitivity and carbon budgets. While models have greatly contributed to the construction of climate change as a global problem, they are also influenced by political expectations. Models have their limits, they never escape uncertainties, and they receive criticisms, in particular for their hegemonic role in climate science. And yet climate models and their simulations of past, present and future climates, coordinated via an efficient model intercomparison project, have greatly contributed to the IPCC's epistemic credibility and authority.

14.1 Introduction

The role of models in IPCC assessment reports cannot be overestimated. Models provide the core content of the IPCC's reports; all assessment reports and their Summaries for Policymakers (SPMs) are illustrated by figures, graphs and maps based on the outputs of climate models. By providing climate simulations that made it possible to distinguish between anthropogenic and natural influences on twentieth-century climate, from the IPCC's Third Assessment Report (AR3, in 2001) onwards, climate models were central for attributing observed climate change to anthropogenic greenhouse gas emissions with high confidence. Models therefore have a political role. They affirm the reality, form and intensity of climate change, but they also shape the IPCC's particular conception of climate change with which governments engage. Conversely, the development of models and the organisation of climate modelling on an international scale has been in large part driven by the need to produce future climate projections for the IPCC.

In this chapter, I explain how climate models are constituted and how they have evolved and become essential instruments for predicting global climate change. I show how the models and scenarios used by the IPCC have been the target of attacks by climate sceptics, have been subject to critical scrutiny by social scientists, and aroused debates among climatologists about research biases, inadequacies and research strategies. I show how the modelling community has organised itself internationally to make climate simulations comparable by building a powerful 'knowledge infrastructure' (Edwards, 2010), the Coupled Model Intercomparison Project (CMIP). Finally, I return to the achievements of climate models and their limitations and ask what their new role could be in shaping future directions for the IPCC. The chapter focuses exclusively on climate models (see Box 14.1) and does not consider a different genre of models – Integrated Assessment Models (IAMs) – which are also central to the IPCC's work; these are discussed in **Chapter 15**.

14.2 Instruments of Globalisation and Prediction

Climate models, originally called General Circulation Models (GCMs), are numerical programs run on computers to produce simulations of the evolution of the atmosphere. The atmosphere is represented by a three-dimensional grid and the computer calculates for each cell and at each time step the variables characterising the atmospheric state (temperature, pressure, wind, humidity and so on) by solving algorithms based on the physics of the atmosphere. GCMs were initially developed from the end of the 1950s on the very first mainframe computers, at first to calculate the weather and, by the mid-1960s, to study climate.

For more than six decades, climate models have kept their original structure while increasing considerably in size – from thousands to millions of lines of computer code. This evolution has been driven by the exponential increase of computing power, by the extension of observation networks, the rise of earth sciences, and by the growing political importance of the climate problem (Weart, 2008). The algorithms of the models have been improved and their spatial resolution increased. Above all, atmospheric circulation models have included more and more phenomena affecting the climate through parametrisations or by coupling with other models. In the 1980s, scientists succeeded in coupling an atmosphere model with a model of the ocean. In the 1990s, climate models gradually encompassed representations of continental surfaces and sea ice and, from the 2000s, aerosols, dynamic vegetation, atmospheric chemistry, land ice and the carbon cycle. Models that include biogeochemical cycles are often referred to

---

Box 14.1
Varieties of numerical climate models

A wide range of numerical models – i.e., programs run on computers to produce numerical simulations – are used to study the climate system and climate change across multiple temporal and spatial scales.

GCM: General Circulation Model – or, more recently, Global Climate Model. GCMs are computer programs representing the evolution of the atmosphere. They build on the fundamental laws of physics that govern atmospheric dynamics and on more empirical representations of the other processes affecting the atmosphere (absorption of solar radiation, clouds and so on). GCMs are used on a daily basis for weather forecasts, and to simulate the climate over several decades, centuries or millennia – these long simulations being analysed in statistical terms.

AOGCM: Atmosphere-Ocean coupled General Circulation Model. AOGCMs are numerical models consisting of an atmospheric general circulation model coupled with an ocean circulation model – both based on the laws of fluid dynamics.

ESM: Earth System Model. ESMs seek to simulate all relevant aspects of the Earth system and its physical, chemical and biological processes. In practice, ESMs are atmosphere-ocean coupled models incorporating biogeochemical processes such as the carbon cycle. ESMs can also include models of dynamic vegetation, atmospheric chemistry, ocean biogeochemistry, and continental ice sheets.

EMIC: Earth System Models of Intermediate Complexity. EMICs are simplified models compared to ESMs. They have lower spatial resolution and include processes in a more parameterised form. EMICs are used to investigate the climate on long timescales, for example, for simulations of palaeoclimates.

IAM: Integrated Assessment Model. IAMs are large-scale models composed of modules representing environmental, technological, and human systems in a single integrated framework. They model the evolution of the interaction between these systems by integrating contributions from various disciplines (environmental sciences, economics, engineering and so on) to produce quantified scenarios of global socio-economic developments.

Simple models and emulators: Simple models and emulators are heavily parametrised models, quick to run on laptops or even iphones, and tuned to reproduce the responses of more complex models. Emulators in particular are used to transfer knowledge between the IPCC WGI and other Working Groups (WGs).

---

as Earth-system models (ESMs). Since the creation of the IPCC, the number of climate models in use around the world has grown enormously – even if the development of climate models and ESMs remains largely restricted to developed countries; see Figure 14.1.

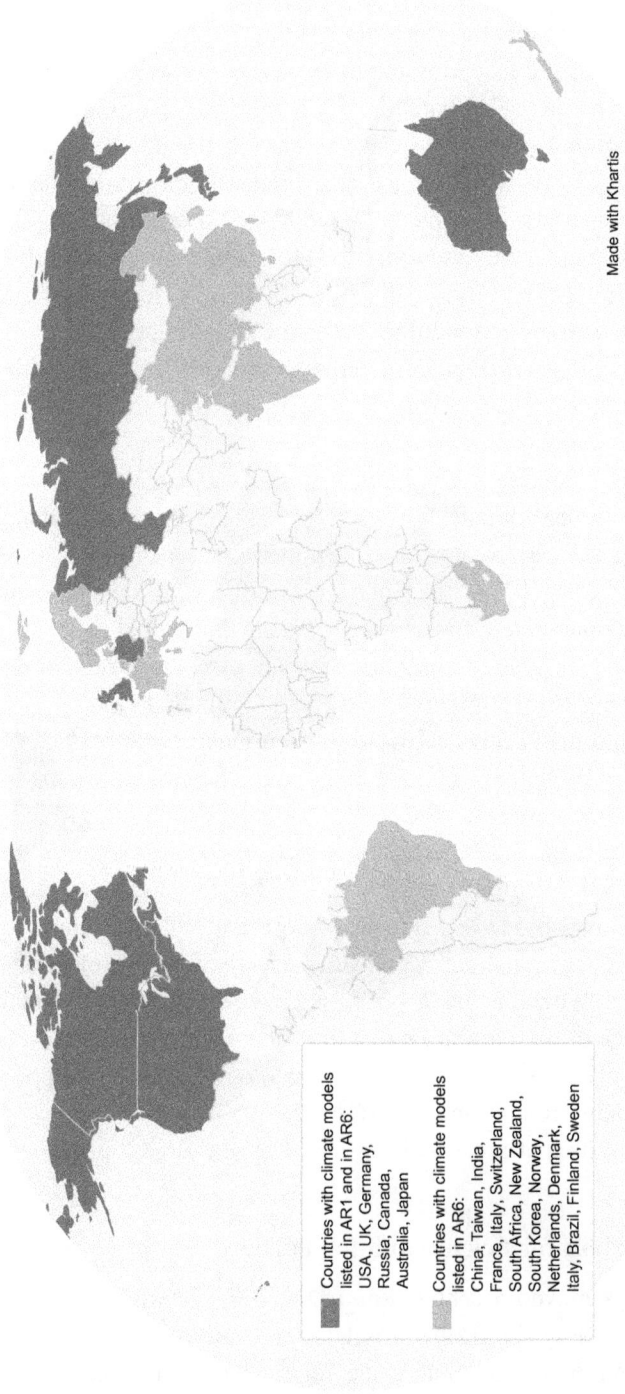

Figure 14.1 Countries with climate models.
In dark grey, countries with climate models listed in AR1 and AR6. In light grey, countries with climate models listed in AR6.

Computer models have greatly contributed to imposing a global vision of climate and climate change (Hulme, 2010), a vision central to the work of the IPCC. The global physico-mathematical vision embedded in these models has thus ousted the plural and geographical conception that prevailed previously – regional climates defined as types of weather (Heymann, 2010). Scientific reasons are often put forward to justify this global scale: for example, carbon dioxide molecules emitted at any point mix quickly with the air and integrate the atmospheric circulation on a planetary scale. But other factors have helped to co-produce this global conception in climate science and policy (Miller, 2004): a powerful infrastructure of observational networks (Edwards, 2010); a long-standing internationally organised scientific community; the huge scientific exploration programs of the American military during the Cold War, relayed by worldwide scientific programs and institutions, such as the World Climate Research Program (WCRP).

GCMs – and later ESMs – are the only simulation tools capable of making quantitative projections of future climate. GCMs were used to assess climate change as a result of increased carbon dioxide atmospheric concentrations long before the creation of the IPCC. In 1979, 'the Charney report' for the US National Academy of Sciences first calculated from three models the global warming corresponding to a doubling of the atmospheric carbon dioxide level, while recognising considerable uncertainties (National Research Council, 1979).

Models' ability to integrate many physical factors when making predictions of future climate have given comprehensive climate modelling a hegemonic status in climate science and, similarly, within the IPCC. But models also contain flaws, gaps and uncertainties (Petersen, [2006] 2012), which modellers attempt to characterise and communicate in IPCC reports (see **Chapter 17**). To build confidence in their simulations, modellers devote a large part of their work to validating models against observational data. Validating future climate projections poses a particular challenge. There is no a priori guarantee that a model that reproduces the characteristics of the current or past climate will also perform well in predicting future climate (Oreskes et al., 1994). Climatologists have developed multiple strategies to compare simulations and observations in a statistical way (Guillemot, 2010), comparisons that are widely assessed by the IPCC.

14.3 Tools for Science and for Policy

Climate models have always played a central role in the IPCC, starting with the First Assessment Report (AR1) in 1990. Models generate climate change projections, underpin attribution studies and guide regional impact assessments, which form the substance of the report. They validate essential concepts in the climate debate – such as global mean temperature, the climate sensitivity and the global carbon budget. Conversely, and importantly, the IPCC has a major influence on the development of climate models. Thus, the improvement of model parametrisations or the introduction of new components into ESMs takes into account the need for future climate projections that IPCC reports demand. As with academic disciplines – see **Chapter 12** – the IPCC is active in shaping the creation of knowledge, via its influence on models, institutions, research programs and careers.

Climate models have a crucial role in predicting, evaluating and attributing anthropogenic climate change, and so the results from climate models inform a range of major policy issues. Social scientists have analysed the effects that both scientific and political objectives have on climate modelling. Because climate change is often framed as a problem in which science is assumed to guide policy decisions, political disagreements are frequently transposed to the scientific field (Pielke, 2002; Sarewitz, 2004). Models have often lain at the centre of such disputes. In the 1990s, debates erupted – especially in the United States – about the difficulties of verifying or validating models in a rigorous fashion (Oreskes et al., 1994). Climate sceptics questioned the scientific credibility of climate models by opposing model simulations to 'sound science' based on 'raw data'. Yet historian Paul Edwards has shown that observed data and climate models are interdependent, this relationship being 'symbiotic', with each gaining legitimacy from the other (Edwards, 1999).

Social scientists studied how the political stakes of climate change influence modelling practices, highlighting the elements of co-construction in climate models and simulations. They showed how some parts of climate modelling result from negotiations, or from an anticipation by scientists of the needs of policy makers – notably the representation of uncertainties (Shackley & Wynne, 1996), the estimate of climate sensitivity (van der Sluijs et al., 1998), and recourse to flux adjustments (Shackley et al., 1999).

The hegemonic position of models in climate science – and subsequently in the IPCC – prompted critical analysis of the conception of climate change and the future induced by these 'global kinds of knowledge' (Hulme, 2010). In 1991, two Indian scholars criticised the accounting of greenhouse gases based on a physical indicator named Global Warming Potential (GWP). By abstracting these gases molecules from their production context, they claimed, climate models do not distinguish survival emissions of the poor – e.g. methane from rice paddies – from the luxury emissions from the rich – e.g. carbon dioxide from cars and planes (Agarwal & Narain, 1991). According to science and technology studies (STS) scholars, this 'physico-chemical reductionism' of climate models obscures the social, economic and historical dimensions of greenhouse gas emissions (Demeritt, 2001). Geographical differences and political contexts are erased. Moreover, models' hegemony within climate change research 'reduces the future to climate' – being partly predictable, climate marginalises other environmental or social factors shaping the future (Hulme, 2011a).

Arguing historically that a 'culture of prediction' often gains traction within environmental issues, scholars such as Matthias Heymann have suggested that climate modelling shifted from offering a heuristic approach to understanding climate to offering predictions for decision-making (Heymann & Hundebol, 2017). The central role that models played in IPCC assessment reports was crucial for this shift. Along the same lines, philosophers of science note that due to the multiplicity of processes interacting in climate models, it is almost impossible to link the characteristics of the simulated climate to a particular component of the model. This 'holism', they claim, 'makes analytic understanding of complex models of climate either extremely difficult or even impossible' (Lenhard & Winsberg, 2010: 253). However, some modellers claim conversely that physical understanding is even more necessary in climate modelling, since the future climate cannot be observed (Bony et al., 2013).

The increasing complexity of climate models is partly a consequence of the need to produce climate predictions. Models have evolved by encompassing more and more environmental phenomena (Dahan-Dalmedico, 2010) because they are supposed to integrate all the processes potentially important for future climate. But climate is subject to a huge range of biogeophysical processes, and the relative importance of any single process is not known until its influence has been tested within the climate system. However, according to some climatologists, this race for complexity, encouraged by a logic of expanded instrumentation and greater funding, should not come to the detriment of research on other climate processes whose role in climate change is known to be essential – for example, concerning cloud feedbacks (Bony et al., 2013).

14.4 A Worldwide Research Infrastructure: CMIP

Since the early 2000s, climate change simulations have been standardised and coordinated through the international CMIP. These multi-model datasets, providing the basis for thousands of peer-reviewed papers, have come to play a prominent role in IPCC reports. In 1990, the WCRP first approved the Atmospheric Model Intercomparison Project (AMIP) in order to compare the output of atmospheric GCMs under similar conditions – same simulation period, same boundary conditions, same carbon dioxide concentrations and so on. Most modelling groups took part in the intercomparison, using the computer facilities of the Lawrence Livermore National Laboratory in California. Having shown the capacity of intercomparison projects to coordinate and organise research (Gates et al., 1999), AMIP paved the way to subsequent 'MIP' exercises.

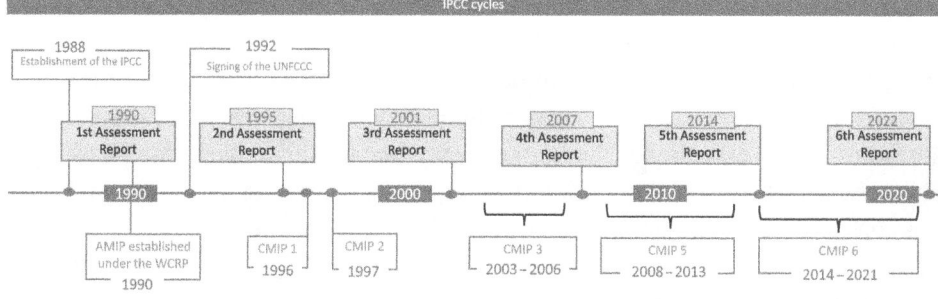

Figure 14.2 Timeline of AMIPs/CMIPs and IPCC assessment cycles.

In 1995, the first phase of the CMIP (CMIP 1) coordinated the comparison of 15 atmosphere-ocean coupled models, soon followed by CMIP 2. CMIP 1 and 2 outputs were included in the IPCC's AR3 report and a few years later, CMIP 3 was designed primarily to provide assessments for the Fourth Assessment Report (AR4), with projections of model simulated climate change under different emission scenarios (Touzé-Peiffer et al., 2020) (see Chapter 15). By 2007, CMIP made outputs from climate change simulations freely available to the scientific community at large, and the simulations for CMIP became synchronised with IPCC reports.

Since 2007, CMIP intercomparison experiments coordinate and pace the work of most modelling groups so as to make it as timely and useful as possible for the IPCC (see Figure 14.2). From CMIP 5 (there was no CMIP 4), the modelling community within WCRP expressed the will to use CMIP to focus not merely on carbon dioxide emissions scenarios, but also on a range of scientific questions. Through an extensive process of consultation across the broad climate community, the simulations comprising CMIP 5 were discussed and prioritised. CMIP 5 included control and historical simulations, climate change scenarios, as well as experiments on regional downscaling, decadal prediction, and a range of 'idealised' experiments to help advance understanding of physical processes. CMIP 6 design was also based on a survey amongst climate scientists (Stouffer et al., 2017). Organised under the auspices of the WCRP to support IPCC reports, CMIP has evolved considerably from a few simulations performed by 18 models in 14 modelling groups for CMIP 1, to thousands of simulations performed by over 100 models in 49 modelling groups for CMIP 6.

The CMIP-standardised dataset allows researchers to align and compare different model simulations and to construct multi-model ensembles of future projections. However, the scientific interpretation of these ensembles is not obvious: an output common to several simulations is not necessarily a guarantee of robustness – it might arise from an error common to all models, and an 'average' result is not necessarily more credible than others. More importantly, different models are not fully independent of each other, since they are tied to predecessor versions or else they exchange ideas and codes with other modelling groups. The spread of model outputs does not therefore systematically explore the uncertainty about future climate change (Knutti et al., 2013). Nevertheless, by making it possible to distinguish the patterns common to all models from those that differ, CMIP has made it possible to advance understandings of the multi-model ensemble outputs that now lie at the heart of the IPCC reports.

CMIP has transformed the way climate scientists work by strengthening coordination, encouraging the standardisation of scientific practices, and considerably widening the user community. This would unlikely have happened – or not have happened as quickly – without the presence, and demand, of the IPCC. The free availability of multi-model output far beyond the modelling teams 'ushered in a new era in climate change research' (Stouffer et al., 2017). But it also created a growing gap between model developers and model users, who still regard GCMs as a 'black box' (Touzé-Peiffer et al., 2020).

14.5 Achievements and Challenges

Today, climate models are rarely called into question in the public sphere, as was still the case as recently as in 2009/10 when climate scepticism was rising in Northern America and Europe (see Chapter 6). Climate models have made it possible for the IPCC to formally attribute global climate change to anthropogenic greenhouse gas emissions. They have shown their ability to reproduce twentieth-century and palaeoclimates, and to produce credible future climate projections, even pre-empting the detection of global warming in climate observations. But now that the IPCC has successfully relied upon climate models to raise awareness of human responsibility for climate change, and pointed to the range of magnitudes of possible future climate change, what is the future role of models in the IPCC?

Two often-cited and growing uses of climate models are for the attribution of extreme climate events to anthropogenic climate change, and for generating climate forecasts at regional or local scales in order to guide necessary adaptations. However, the demand for local forecasts brings into focus the limits of climate modelling. Climate change is more detectable and predictable on large continental scales than on smaller ones: as the spatial scale of climate predictions decreases, uncertainties increase, making it more difficult to distinguish anthropogenic climate change from natural climate variability. Moreover, at local scales, meteorological and social causalities become increasingly intertwined. For example, it can be problematic to attribute to climate change disasters that also arise from socio-political causes, such as social vulnerabilities, inequalities or poor management (Lahsen et al., 2020).

How should models evolve to improve understandings of climate and to better predict future climate? Debates have arisen among modellers. How far should climate models be made ever more complex? Some scholars are considering models that would include 'human systems' as an integral part of the Earth system (e.g. Schellnhüber, 1999). Social scientists have criticised this global and systemic vision of modelling the entirety of the planet *and* of human action. Their argument is that such a vision invites a techno-managerial approach to shaping Earth's future (Lövbrand et al., 2015), obscuring the multiplicity of cultural values, the inequality of social situations, and the importance of power relations in making decisions.

Other climatologists believe that despite incontestable achievements, the pace of progress in climate modelling is too slow, the uncertainties decrease by too little, and systematic errors remain for many years. Some advocate very high-resolution models (Shukla et al., 2009; Voosen, 2020). But this approach, according to others, does not provide the sets of climate simulations necessary to explore climate variability. Some suggest joining forces to build a unique model from scratch, but others stress the importance of keeping open a diversity of modelling approaches – because of the complexity of the climate system and for fear about the hegemony created by international super-models. Others propose replacing all or part of the model with machine-learning algorithms.

There is no consensus among climatologists about whether GCMs will be able to produce regional quality forecasts, whether they will continue to evolve towards greater complexity, towards very high resolution models, or even towards another type of simulation tool – or even what the place of models will be in future IPCC reports. These debates might seem to be reserved for a handful of climate modellers. But the future of climate modelling will determine much of the future knowledge that will be evaluated and synthesised by the IPCC. The future of climate models therefore concerns not just climate modellers, but decision-makers, policy advisors and, indeed, all people on Earth.

Three Key Readings

Edwards, P. (2010). *A Vast Machine. Computer Models, Climate Data, and the Politics of Global Warming*. Cambridge, MA: MIT Press.

This book tells the story of climate science as a 'global knowledge infrastructure' and shows how observation networks and climate models have made the global warming problem emerge and grow.

Shackley, S., Risbey, J., Stone, P. and Wynne, B. (1999). Adjusting to policy expectations in climate change modeling: an interdisciplinary study of flux adjustments in coupled atmosphere-ocean general circulation models. *Climatic Change*, 43: 413–454. http://doi.org/10.1023/A:1005474102591

This article, based on a survey in 15 modelling groups, is an early STS study of climate modelling showing the diversity of the practices of these groups and of their relationship to the political implications of their research.

Touzé-Peiffer, L., Barberousse, A. and Le Treut, H. (2020). The Coupled Model Intercomparison Project: History, uses, and structural effects on climate research. *WIREs Climate Change*, e648. doi.org/10.1002/wcc.648

This article retraces the history of the CMIP, highlighting its close links with the IPCC and its effect on climate research.

15

Scenarios

BÉATRICE COINTE

Overview

Scenarios are among the most visible and widely used products of the Intergovernmental Panel on Climate Change (IPCC). Many kinds of scenarios are used in climate research, but emissions scenarios and the socio-economic assumptions that underpin them have a distinct status because the IPCC orchestrated their development. They have evolved from assessment cycle to assessment cycle and serve as 'boundary objects' across Working Groups (WGs) and as instruments of policy-relevance. The field of Integrated Assessment Model (ling) (IAM) has emerged to produce these scenarios, thereby taking centre stage within the IPCC assessment process. Because these scenarios harmonise assumptions about the future across disciplines, they are essential tools for the IPCC's production of a *shared* assessment of climate research and for ensuring the policy-relevance of this assessment. Yet, the reliance on a relatively small set of complex models to generate scenarios spurs concerns about transparency, black-boxed assumptions, and the power of IAMs to define the 'possibility space'.

15.1 Introduction

Scenarios are everywhere in IPCC reports, from the climate change projections of WGI (**Chapter 14**) to the mitigation pathways of WGIII. Often encountered as graphs displaying arrays of roads-yet-to-be-taken, scenarios are in fact complex sets of interrelated numerical variables. Among them, the scenarios projecting long-term evolutions of greenhouse gases (GHG) stand out because the IPCC has orchestrated their development. They are a cornerstone of the IPCC's outlook on the future. Through them, the IPCC has contributed to the elaboration of a new approach to scenarios, distinct from scenario planning or futurology. This chapter focuses on these scenarios and on the IAMs that produce them.

The IPCC initially produced projections of GHG emissions as input for Global Climate Models (GCMs), but the function of emissions scenarios has greatly increased in scope and ambition. In 2006, the IPCC moved from scenario producer to 'catalyst', entrusting the elaboration of new scenarios to the 'scientific community' (IPCC, 2006b). Rather than a catalogue of projections, the resulting scenario framework became a toolbox used for various purposes across WGs. This reflects an ambition to integrate the increasingly diverse domains of climate research. As explained in the WGIII contribution to the Fifth Assessment Report (AR5), 'scenarios can be used to integrate knowledge about the drivers of GHG emissions, mitigation options, climate change, and climate impacts' (IPCC, 2014a: 48). Their development has harmonised the futures considered by climate research, ensuring some compatibility and comparability across disciplines. It has also accompanied and shaped the emergence and evolution of IAMs, now the main providers of scenarios.

Scenarios are not just outputs of IPCC reports. They are, first, a cornerstone of IPCC assessments and of the broader ambition to construct a consistent and policy-relevant body of knowledge on climate change. They are also a research infrastructure, enabling the organisation, harmonisation and circulation of data across disciplines. Last, they are now a field of research whose emergence was fostered by the IPCC. Considering these three dimensions of scenarios, this chapter first retraces the evolution of IPCC scenarios since the First Assessment Report (AR1). It then clarifies the role of IAMs, and reviews ongoing debates on IAM-produced scenarios.

15.2 The IPCC as Scenarios Producer

To project future climate change, climate modellers need estimates of the future evolution of GHG and other emissions. Providing 'scenarios of possible future greenhouse gas emissions for the use of the three IPCC Working Groups' was one of the first tasks undertaken by WGIII in the preparation of the IPCC's AR1 (IPCC, 1990b: xxxi). Since then, scenario development has gone hand-in-hand with the IPCC assessment cycles. Emissions scenarios have been regularly updated to take into account real-time evolutions in GHG emissions and to meet the evolving needs of climate research and policy.

To date, there have been four generations of scenarios (Table 15.1). They differ in their scope, characteristics and development process (Girod et al., 2009). The first set of scenarios, labelled 'SA90', was developed in 1989 by an expert group formed by the 'Response Strategies Working Group' (IPCC, 1990b: 17). Its four scenarios were intended as inputs for GCMs (van Beek et al., 2020a).

The IPCC requested an update in 1991 (IPCC, 1991) and the resulting 'IS92' scenarios – standing for 'IPCC Scenarios 1992' – were published in a supplement to AR1 (Leggett et al., 1992). As noted in the foreword to the Special Report on

Table 15.1. *Four generations of IPCC scenarios*

Assessment cycle	Scenarios	Models used	Development period	Key publications
AR1	SA90 4 scenarios	ASF (US EPA) IMAGE (NL)	1988–1990	Tirpak and Vellinga (1990)
AR2	IS92 (a to f) 6 scenarios	ASF (US EPA)	1991–1994	Leggett et al. (1992) Alcamo et al. (1995)
AR3, AR4	SRES (A1B, A1F, A1T, A2, B1, B2) 6 markers, 40 in total	*Open process* AIM (Japan) ASF (US EPA) IMAGE (NL) MARIA (Japan) MESSAGE (IIASA) MiniCAM (US)	1996–2000	Nakicenovic et al. (2000)
AR5 onwards	Initially 4 RCPs (2.6, 4.5, 6, 8.5) 5 SSPs (1 to 5) After 2016, 7x5 Scenario matrix (Figure 15.1)	One model for each RCP (selected from the literature): AIM, IMAGE, GCAM, MESSAGE Open process for the SSPs, many models	RCP: 2005–2010 SSP: 2010–2016 Scenario matrix: 2016 onward	Moss et al. (2008) IPCC (2012b) Special issues in *Climatic Change* (vol. 109, 2011 and vol. 122, 2014) and *Global Environmental Change* (vol. 42, 2017). O'Neill et al. (2016) for AR6

Source: Author.

Emissions Scenarios (SRES), these IS92 scenarios were 'pathbreaking' as 'they were the first global scenarios to provide estimates for the full suite of greenhouse gases' (Nakicenovic et al., 2000). The IPCC-requested evaluation of the IS92 scenarios (Alcamo et al., 1995) was possibly even more influential. At the time, there were few emissions scenarios in the literature and no established criteria for their evaluation (Alcamo et al., 1995: 242). The 1995 evaluation set an evaluation framework, recommended good practice, and categorised the potential uses for scenarios. Its guidelines have remained benchmarks for the development and assessment of scenarios.

The 'SRES scenarios' were developed between 1996 and 2000 and published in a 600-page Special Report (Nakicenovic et al., 2000). They marked an increase in ambition and scope. Based on an extensive literature review, they were designed for a broader range of purposes and users. The process of constructing the scenarios was also more open, with a 50-author writing team and a call for participation issued to researchers. It produced a set of 6 marker scenarios picked among a total of 40 scenarios, all published in an internet database. One of the main innovations was the development of four storylines to map scenarios along two axes – regional vs. global, economic vs. environmental. With this structuring compass, the SRES scenarios offered a framework for organising and communicating uncertainties surrounding climate change.

The SRES scenarios were used as reference points by all three WGs in the AR3 (2001) and AR4 (2007) reports. By 2003, the scenarios literature had considerably expanded and so the IPCC raised 'the question of new scenarios for the AR5' (IPCC, 2003). This initiated a major overhaul of the scenario framework and a redefinition of the IPCC's role in it.

15.3 The IPCC as Catalyst: Towards a New Scenario Framework

During the revision of the scenario framework, initiated in 2005, the IPCC shifted from being the producer of scenarios to being the catalyst of their production. At its 25th Panel session in 2006, the IPCC delegated the development of new scenarios to the scientific community at large, whilst retaining a facilitating role. The Integrated Assessment Modeling Consortium (IAMC) was founded to coordinate scenario work.[1] The delegation of this work was possible because the emerging IAM community convinced the IPCC chair of its ability to coordinate the process (Cointe et al., 2019). In fact, this community comprised many of the same people involved in previous scenario developments – the three founders of the IAMC included two SRES authors. The process involved IPCC-sponsored meetings (where the main features of scenarios were agreed upon), annual IAMC meetings and a string of research workshops. Reflecting the change of process, there was now not *one* document presenting the scenarios, but a collection of multi-authored workshop reports, journal articles and special issues (Table 15.1).

The process was bottom-up and had to accommodate the technical specifications of climate models, the requirements of diverse scientific and policy users, the IPCC timeline, and the capacities of existing models. It was guided by two aims: first, to make scenarios suitable for more purposes, especially policy analysis and impact assessments; and, second, to decouple climate change projections from socio-economic assumptions, so as to enable climate modelling, impact studies, and the elaboration of socio-economic scenarios to progress independently in a 'parallel process' (Moss et al., 2010).[2] The resulting framework is quite intricate, and cannot be understood independent of its development process.

Between 2005 and 2017, two types of scenarios were elaborated: Representative Concentration Pathways (RCPs) and Shared Socioeconomic Pathways (SSPs). The RCPs are emissions scenarios leading to specified levels of radiative forcing and designed as inputs for climate models. The radiative forcing profiles serve as a common currency to connect mitigation pathways with climate scenarios. Within the AR5 timeline, four RCPs were selected among published IAM scenarios. They were adapted to the data requirements of climate models (Moss et al., 2008: xv) without harmonising the underpinning socio-economic assumptions. They had to satisfy scientific soundness, requirements from WGI researchers, and expectations for policy-relevance. The choice of the low-emissions pathways illustrates this latter demand. The compatibility of RCP2.6 with the '2°C policy objective' made it a favourite scenario in policy negotiations, but it was only approved after a scientific check (Weyant et al., 2009; Moss et al., 2010; Beck & Mahony, 2018b).

The SSPs, which took longer to develop, provide both narrative (storylines) and quantitative sets of socio-economic assumptions – for example, population and economic growth – that form coherent pictures of how the world might develop *without* climate change and climate policy (O'Neill et al., 2014). IAMs use these assumptions to project future emissions, combining them with policy assumptions to reach lower emissions levels. In the lead-up to AR6, eight new reference scenarios – combining one SSP storyline with one radiative forcing level – were selected for WGI (O'Neill et al., 2016). This updated the RCPs by expanding their scope and harmonising their socio-economic assumptions.

Rather than a fixed library of scenarios, the new (and current) IPCC scenario framework is a method for organising assumptions in order to harmonise and coordinate different types of climate-relevant projections. This method is encapsulated in the 'scenario matrix' (Figure 15.1) designed as a common reference to map the range of assumptions about the future. Thus, contrary to previous versions used by the IPCC, the current scenario framework is an

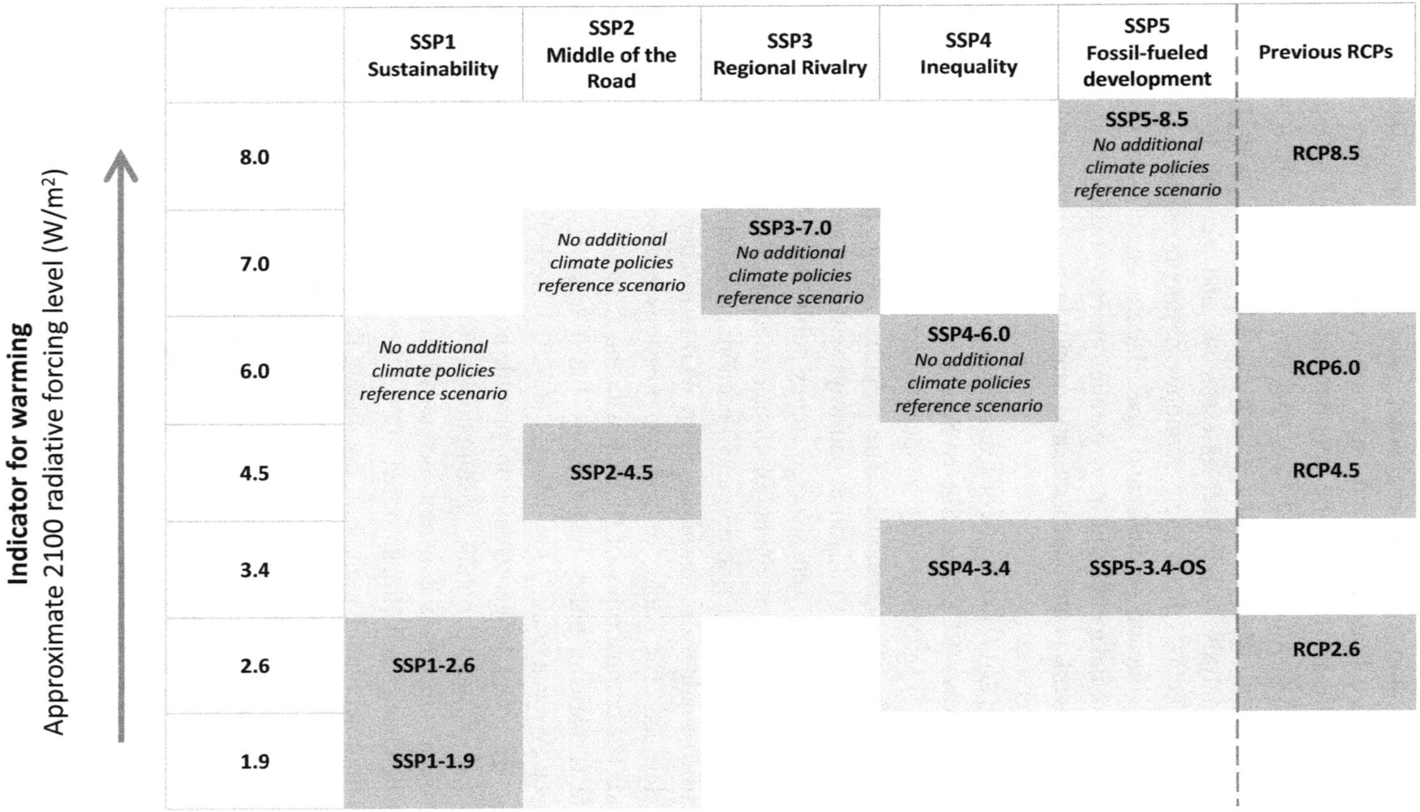

Figure 15.1 The scenario matrix combines the five SSP storylines with seven radiative forcing levels.
White boxes: no scenarios available; **SSPx-y:** scenarios used by WGI in AR6.
Adapted from O'Neill et al. (2016) and Fuglestvedt et al. (2021) (their Figure 1)

infrastructure to organise model inputs and outputs across research communities, which can be rediscussed, refined and adapted.

15.4 The 'Mapmakers': Integrated Assessment Models

The elaboration of the scenario framework established the models used to produce emissions scenarios as a cornerstone of climate research. The emergence of IAMs as a category of models and a tightly bound research community is inseparable from the development of scenarios for the IPCC. The original website of the IAMC emphasised this co-evolution, stating that 'scenarios to underpin the 1st Assessment Report of the IPCC were elaborated with 1st generation IAMs' (IAMC, 2017).

IAMs are complex numerical models that represent the interactions between environmental, human and technological systems. They do not build upon a shared theoretical basis, but combine disciplines and intellectual traditions including environmental sciences, systems analysis, macroeconomics and engineering. About 30 IAMs are referenced in the AR5 (Clarke et al., 2014), most of them developed in Europe, the United States and Japan. As tools to assess mitigation trajectories and policy options on a global scale, they constitute an important part of the research assessed by WGIII, especially in AR5 where they were the basis for 'the exploration of the solution space' (IPCC, 2014a: ix).

Although IAMs are widely used outside the IPCC scenario process, their emergence is closely tied to the IPCC and its WGIII (see **Chapter 12**). Corbera et al. (2016) note that a number of WGIII authors have organised their careers around the IPCC, which is the case for several prominent figures of IAM research. Most IAM group leaders have been IPCC authors and have participated in scenario development – some, such as Jae Edmonds, Priyadarshi Shukla, John Weyant or Nebosja Nakicenovic, since the 1990s. The IMAGE model – developed originally by the Netherlands Environmental Assessment Agency (PBL) – has also been a consistent feature of scenario development, except for the IS92.

These links intensified after 2005. The delegation of scenario development to the scientific community, and the central position of IAM-produced mitigation scenarios in the WGIII AR5, drove the organisation and professionalisation of IAM research (Cointe et al., 2019). The combination of an intense schedule of IPCC-sponsored 'expert meetings' to work on scenarios, together with several large EU-funded IAM research projects, meant that involved researchers met almost every other month for a few years. This effectively fostered a small and close-knit community. The IAMC, initially created to prepare the RCPs, turned into a disciplinary organisation, and its annual meeting became a fully fledged conference. This emerging community also set up an infrastructure for collaboration and data exchange – partly to be able to work together, partly because it was a requirement for IPCC scenarios. The database created at the International Institute for Applied Systems Analysis (IIASA) to host RCP data now serves as a repository of scenarios for IPCC-related work and for research projects; model documentation and codes are increasingly available; and the IAMC curates a Wiki documenting existing IAMs.

This considerably improves the transparency of IAMs, but it also exposes them to scrutiny and criticism (Robertson, 2021). The prominence of IAM-produced scenarios indeed gives the models' underlying assumptions, worldviews and solving mechanisms considerable influence in defining the scope of action presented by the IPCC.

15.5 The Contested Influence of IAMs

The position of IAMs-generated scenarios at the interfaces between different domains of climate science and between science and policy puts them at the heart of lively – if mostly academic – debates. These debates highlight the difficulty of disentangling the process of scenario production from the substance of scenarios.

One core issue is the lack of transparency of models. IAMs are complex, interdisciplinary models that are hard to communicate even among experts. They are thus often perceived as 'black-boxes' (Haikola et al., 2019). In fact, much of the work undertaken in the IAMC and in modelling projects aims to enable modellers from different groups to understand each other's models. Transparency about model structure, assumptions and data is necessary to assess the soundness and reliability of IAM projections. This is not only an epistemic concern. Because IAMs-generated scenarios are used to explore the 'possibility space', their structure, inputs and underlying assumptions constrain the range of futures brought to the attention of policy-makers (Beck & Mahony, 2018b; Beck & Oomen, 2021; also Chapter 21). According to Robertson (2021), failure to answer calls for transparency risks undermining trust in the IPCC. To some degree, the IPCC has heeded such critiques in expert meetings and publications attempting to tackle the challenge (IPCC, 2017b; Skea et al., 2021).

Criticism of the reliance of IAMs on negative emission technologies (NETs) – and in particular on bioenergy with carbon capture and storage (BECCS) – to achieve scenarios compatible with the 2 °C and 1.5 °C policy objectives of the UN Framework Convention on Climate Change (UNFCCC) has spurred examination of the inner workings of IAMs. This has brought social sciences and science and technology studies (STS) scholars into the discussion (Beck & Mahony 2018b; Haikola et al., 2019; Carton et al., 2020; Low & Schäfer, 2020). These analyses suggest that the tendency of IAMs to favour NETs comes from their representation of technological progress, their focus on least-cost options, and their discounting assumptions. Many limitations of IAMs have been highlighted: they are better at representing technological change than lifestyle changes; they use economics as a basis for decision-making; they tend to consider a limited range of market-based policies; many (not all) are cost-optimisation models; and they hardly consider no-growth or degrowth futures. For critics like Kevin Anderson, this makes them 'the wrong tool for the job' (Anderson & Jewell, 2019). However, not all of these limitations are hard-wired into the models, and modellers are reflecting on how to address them (O'Neill et al., 2020; Keppo et al., 2021).

Another issue of concern is the interpretation and use of IPCC-sanctioned scenarios. Scenarios have a life of their own, and their assumptions and limitations often do not travel with them, even when they are acknowledged in the original publications (see also Box 15.1). The performativity of scenarios often escapes

---

Box 15.1
'Business-as-usual' scenarios

An important choice when making climate scenarios is whether to consider increased climate policy action. Scenarios *without* additional climate policies, often referred to as 'business as usual', serve as baselines against which to assess the effects, costs and benefits of climate action. The SA90 scenarios included policy and no-policy scenarios. As requested by the IPCC, the IS92 and SRES scenarios were all 'business as usual'. The later scenario matrix is more flexible, but retains the idea of a no-policy baseline: while the SSP storylines do not include climate policies, modellers add policies (usually a carbon price) to reach lower concentrations from the same socio-economic assumptions. The term 'business as usual' can be misleading when used to refer to a single scenario. There is not one, but many possible, scenarios without additional policies (Figure 15.1). Scenario experts insist that all can serve as baselines and none should be considered more likely than any other. In practice, however, all are not used equally. Reviewing the use of IS92 scenarios, the SRES report noted that the high-emission IS92a scenario was often used as a baseline, despite explicit recommendations to use the full range of IS92 scenarios for climate assessment (Nakicenovic et al., 2000: 32). More recently, Pielke and Ritchie (2021) and Hausfather and Peters (2020) warned against considering RCP8.5 as a 'business as usual' scenario, arguing that its assumptions – especially for future coal consumption – were implausible and outdated. This reignited a longstanding debate about the assignment of probabilities to scenarios to aid interpretation – something that modellers have so far resisted so as not to liken scenarios to predictions (This issue is discussed in AR6; Chen et al., 2021: 109–111.) Rather than 'mis-uses', these debates reflect different understandings of the status of baseline scenarios. They highlight the challenges that arise from the use of scenarios as boundary objects and from their appropriation by increasingly diverse users.

their creators. The reason NETs are controversial is that their ubiquity in IAM scenarios makes them seem inescapable – even though these technologies do not exist at scale – to the expense of alternative options, perhaps more realistic but not as frequently modelled by IAMs. NETs-heavy scenarios have thus been criticised for sustaining the discrepancy between policy ambitions and real-world policy action, and for maintaining the chimera that gradual emission reductions can ever be enough (Anderson & Peters, 2016; Beck & Mahony, 2018b; Carton et al., 2020).[3]

15.6 Achievements and Challenges

Since its first report, the IPCC has driven the establishment of scenarios as boundary objects (see **Chapter 24**) among climate research communities. In orchestrating the development of emissions scenarios, the IPCC has defined an approach to scenarios that puts IAMs centre stage. It has also 'charted out' the future. Scenarios work as boundary objects that harmonise assumptions about the future across disciplines, thereby enabling the circulation and comparison of projections.

The development of scenarios has encouraged integration across WGs (see **Chapter 18**) and supported the emergence of a shared scientific understanding of climate change. Thanks to debates around the new scenario framework, both IAMs and the IPCC scenario infrastructure have become more transparent and open to alternative perspectives. Although there is still much room for improvement, the IPCC is at the forefront of these efforts. Because IAMs are now essential tools for navigating the climate challenge, they are (rightly) held to higher standards of accountability than other models. They need to be subjected to *both* scientific and political scrutiny.

The opaqueness of IAMs is to an extent irreducible given their complexity and diversity. The intricacy of the scenario framework and the proliferation of scenarios add to the challenge of transparency. However, this opaqueness also stems from the ambition for scenarios to meet the requirements of increasingly diverse users. These users can have different understandings of the usefulness, validity and plausibility of scenarios, a challenge likely to be amplified as scenarios are taken up in political discourses or juridical trials.

Indeed, despite its ambition for comprehensiveness, the scenario framework used by the IPCC offers an incomplete map of the future. Its success has enshrined a quantified, model-based approach largely framed by the requirements of GCMs, at the expense of alternative scenario methods. The next major challenge for the IPCC is to incorporate more diverse and more radical versions of possible world futures into their assessment process.

Notes

1 Source: IPCC (2007) 'Consortium EMF, NIES and IIASA, among others', Compilation of replies on IPCC request to the scientific community on scenario activities. Available at: http://web-old.archive.org/web/20071031113709/http://www.mnp.nl/ipcc/docs/index0407/Compiled%20replies_v3.pdf (retrieved 31 October 2007) and http://web-old.archive.org/web/20071031113640/http://www.mnp.nl/ipcc/ (retrieved 31 October 2007).
2 In contrast, under the previous SRES framework, climate impact studies needed outputs from GCMs/ESMs which in turn needed socio-economic scenarios. This meant that there was a considerable lag between the publication of socio-economic scenarios and the climate impact assessments based on them. It also required climate scenarios to be re-run every time socio-economic scenarios were modified.
3 It should be noted, however, that RCP2.6 does involve drastic and rapid emissions cuts in all sectors, and that the IPCC SR15 clearly states the necessity for radical and rapid changes to stay within the 1.5 °C target.

Three Key Readings

Cointe, B., Cassen, C. and Nadaï, A. (2019). Organising policy-relevant knowledge for climate action: Integrated Assessment Modelling, the IPCC, and the emergence of a collective expertise on socioeconomic emission scenarios. *Science and Technology Studies*, 32(4): 36–57. http://doi.org/10.23987/sts.65031

This article provides a detailed analysis of the emergence and organisation of the IAM community as a provider of scenarios for the IPCC during the AR5 cycle.

van Beek, L., Hajer, M., Pelzer, P., van Vuuren, D. and Cassen, C. (2020). Anticipating futures through models: the rise of Integrated Assessment Modelling in the climate science-policy interface since 1970. *Global Environmental Change* 65: 102191. http://doi.org/10.1016/j.gloenvcha.2020.102191

This article retraces the history of global modelling and IAMs since the 1970s, highlighting links with policy-making and with the IPCC process.

Low, S. and Schäfer, S. (2020). Is bio-energy carbon capture and storage (BECCS) feasible? The contested authority of integrated assessment modeling. *Energy Research & Social Science*. 60: 101326. http://doi.org/10.1016/j.erss.2019.101326

This article dissects controversies about the representation of NETs in IAMs and the way they challenge the authority of IAMs; it discusses competing views on how to organise relations between scenarios and policy-making.

16

Controversies

SHINICHIRO ASAYAMA, KARI DE PRYCK AND MIKE HULME

Overview

Over three decades, the Intergovernmental Panel on Climate Change (IPCC) has been no stranger to controversies. Given its institutional character as a boundary organisation working between science and policy, it is no surprise that IPCC reports often reflect wider controversies in the scientific and political life of climate change, especially those concerning its consequences and potential solutions. In this chapter, we explain why controversies about the IPCC's knowledge assessment are inevitable and point out how the IPCC could use controversies for adapting and developing its assessment processes in constructive ways. That is, we show how controversies serve as 'generative political events' for the IPCC's own learning process. To do so, we classify IPCC knowledge controversies into four types (*factual, procedural, epistemic* and *ontological*) and, using two illustrative cases, distinguish between controversies that the IPCC *triggers* and those that the IPCC *absorbs* into its knowledge assessment.

16.1 Introduction

Scientific or knowledge controversies do not have a good reputation. They are thought to reveal the uncertainty of scientific knowledge, to undermine the authority of science, and to slow down the quest for 'universal truth'. It may seem that controversies are best avoided. Yet, in practice, controversies are routine in the production of scientific knowledge. They are important drivers of scientific progress. They are also expressions of the inherent 'social games' (Skrydstrup, 2013) embedded in all human activities. In the case of climate change, controversies have been used to discredit the work of climate scientists –and in some cases they are deliberately manufactured for the purpose of stalling policy regulation (Oreskes & Conway, 2010). However, controversies have also contributed to deepening the scientific understanding of climate change – its impacts and potential solutions – and have led to increased transparency and reflection in scientific practices. The Climategate affair that erupted in November 2009 is a good example of this (Raman & Pearce, 2020; see also **Chapter 6**).

From a science and technology studies (STS) perspective, controversies offer a good entry point for studying the production of scientific knowledge and investigating how science and technology transform society (Pinch, 2015; Jasanoff, 2019). STS researchers may disagree amongst themselves about precisely what constitutes a 'scientific controversy'. Nevertheless, they would agree that controversies can be regarded as key moments that open the black box of scientific facts and provide a lens through which to explore the solidity (or the fragility) of the institutions that produce scientific knowledge, as well as those who make decisions based on science. By following controversies, researchers are better able to understand 'science in the making' and 'science in society'. As Pinch (2015) points out, it is during a controversy – or a 'moment of contention' – that the normally hidden social and cultural dimensions of science may become more explicit. Given that at such moments knowledge claims become subject to public dispute, knowledge controversies can act as 'generative events' that create an opportunity to arouse a different awareness of the problem and facilitate the negotiation of new practices and procedures (Stengers, 2005; Whatmore, 2009).

In this chapter, we first look at different types of knowledge controversies that have invested the IPCC, before then highlighting the role of the organisation in both generating and stabilising wider political controversies. In doing so, we view the IPCC as an institution that establishes, stabilises or disrupts the knowledge order about climate change, its impacts and potential solutions (see **Chapter 12**).

16.2 A Typology of IPCC Controversies

Controversies have been central objects of study in the sociology of scientific knowledge and STS since the 1970s (Pinch, 2015; Jasanoff, 2019). Controversies have become a method by which to study the complex entanglement between science and society. Broadly speaking, controversies are 'situations where actors disagree' – that is, they are *moments* of contention that 'begin when actors discover that they cannot ignore each other' and 'end when actors manage to work out a solid compromise to live together' (Venturini, 2010: 261). Controversies usually come to an end through the process of 'closure', the point in which an agreement emerges.

Controversies can be distinguished from 'scandals' or 'affairs' – the transgression of values that are dear to a society. Also, a distinction is often made between scientific and political controversies, typically by the different processes of closure. While scientific controversies are considered to be closed through the application of epistemic and methodological standards, political controversies are thought to be resolved by the negotiation of political and economic interests (Pinch, 2015). However, the entanglement between science and society tends to blur this boundary. Controversies are 'the crucible where collective life is melted and formed' (Venturini, 2010: 264) such that the science–society boundary is unremittingly constructed, deconstructed and reconstructed during a controversy.

In the context of climate change, scientific controversies rarely remain confined within the scientific domain. Studying controversies therefore facilitates exploration of the underlying dynamics of science and its relations with society (Limoges, 1993; Whatmore, 2009). This does not mean that all scientific controversies spark wider societal disputes. But controversies get particularly 'hot' during politically charged situations, for example when the Summaries for Policymakers (SPMs) are approved (see **Chapter 20**) – or when IPCC conclusions enter public debate.

Below, we classify knowledge controversies surrounding the IPCC into four types according to their 'origin' – whether they emerged from *factual errors*, *procedural irregularities*, *epistemic disagreements* or *ontological disputes*. These types of controversies are not mutually exclusive.

Factual errors: Controversies have occasionally arisen from factual errors contained in IPCC reports. Most prominent was the erroneous statement about the melting rate of the Himalayan glaciers in the AR4 Working Group II (WGII), which surfaced early in 2010. This error gained widespread media attention at the time and, following the 2009 Climategate affair, further fuelled public scrutiny and criticism of the IPCC (Beck, 2012). The controversy led the UN and the IPCC to ask the InterAcademy Council (IAC) to undertake a review of the procedures of IPCC assessment and to make recommendations for change. This controversy was defused by the IPCC revising its procedures and improving its communication practices in response to the IAC recommendations (see **Chapter 3**).

Procedural irregularities: A second way of characterising controversies that have erupted around IPCC reports are those that have been caused by irregularities – or claimed irregularities – in the IPCC's own internal procedures. A prominent example is the controversy that followed the AR2 WGI plenary meeting. This concerned the allegation made by climate sceptics against the IPCC that 'unauthorised' alterations had been made to the text of WGI's Chapter 8 on climate detection and attribution after the final IPCC approval plenary had closed, hence violating its own rules of procedure (Lahsen, 1999; Edwards & Schneider, 2001; Oreskes & Conway, 2010). Despite the accusation being unfounded, this Chapter 8 controversy exposed unclear rules of peer review and led the IPCC to formalise its rules of procedure and to add the 'Review Editor' role for overseeing the review process (see **Chapter 11**).

Epistemic disagreements: A third set of controversies arises from disputes amongst scientists and experts about how particular statements about the current state of knowledge should be crafted and communicated. These controversies are grounded in epistemic disagreements *within* science about how valid, reliable and/ or useable knowledge is best generated and assessed. Some of these controversies remain largely contained within the scientific community and the IPCC, like the one regarding projections of future sea-level rise in AR4 WGI (O'Reilly et al., 2012; see Box 12.1). Others, however, have the potential to trigger wider political controversies. For example, calculation of the statistical value of human life in AR2 WGIII led to political conflict between economists and developing country delegations (see Box 16.1). Similarly, the so-called 'hockey-stick graph' – used prominently in AR3 WGI – triggered wider disputes both within and beyond the palaeoclimate science community about the reconstruction and representation of millennial scale temperature change (Zorita, 2019). While an iconic figure, the hockey-stick graph is one of the most contested visualisations in the history of climate science (see **Chapter 25**).

Ontological disputes: A fourth type of controversy relates not to how questions are answered by the IPCC but, rather, which questions are asked in the first place and by whom (Venturini & Munck, 2021). Here, disputes emerge about the scope of the problems to be assessed by the IPCC and the values and worldviews in which its assessment work is rooted. For example, the IPCC has been criticised for its narrow focus on quantitative modelling analyses and for being heavily dominated by natural science disciplines, i.e., a lack of epistemic plurality (Hulme, 2011b; see also **Chapter 12**). Similarly, the IPCC is criticised for poorly engaging with indigenous knowledge about the climate (Ford et al., 2016; see **Chapter 13**). Although these ontological disputes in IPCC assessments are yet to spark public controversy, growing calls for greater ontological diversity might push the IPCC into considering further reforms if it is to address the broader social and cultural dimensions of climate change.

16.3 Triggering and Absorbing Controversies

As well as categorising IPCC controversies according to their origins, another way of looking at knowledge controversies is to examine how IPCC assessments get entangled with wider (geo)political disputes. Here, we can distinguish between the IPCC *triggering* wider political controversies and the IPCC *absorbing* external political controversies. To illustrate this, we consider two particular cases from earlier stages in the IPCC's history. The first is the controversy in AR2 WGIII about the economic valuation of climate change damage – in particular, monetary valuation of mortality risk from climate change (see Box 16.1). The second case is the contested political negotiations over the methodology and accounting rules for calculating forest carbon sinks in the approval of the 2000 Special Report on Land Use, Land Use Change and Forestry (LULUCF) (see Box 16.2).

Box 16.1
The controversy over the 'value of human life'

In July 1995, the IPCC WGIII session in Geneva was in disarray. Government delegations were supposed to approve the AR2 WGIII SPM, but the approval process was stalled due to a bitter dispute over the economic valuation of climate impacts addressed in Chapter 6 of the report (Masood & Ochert, 1995). The authors of this so-called 'social costs chapter' had reviewed the literature on the estimated monetary value of the costs and benefits of climate change, including that assigned to human mortality. The 'value of human life' number given by the authors became the subject of intense debates because it valued the lives of people in developed nations 15 times higher than those in developing nations. Delegates from developing countries and environmental groups furiously criticised this estimate and called for the chapter to be rewritten or else to be removed entirely (Masood & Ochert, 1995).

The chapter authors refused to revise their calculation, instead defending their approach (Pearce, 1997). They insisted that most attacks against their valuation were rooted in the misreading of what is actually meant by the term 'value of statistical life' (VOSL). Notwithstanding the confusing terminology, VOSL was not representing the *value* of life. It measured people's attitude to mortality risk – or more precisely, people's willingness to pay to avoid the risk of death. Because what people are willing to pay is constrained by their ability to pay – i.e., their income – VOSL estimates necessarily vary between rich and poor. For this reason, the chapter authors argued that their regionally differentiated VOSL estimates simply reflected 'a fact of life' (Fankhauser & Tol, 1998).

Interestingly, the IPCC authors' rebuttals revealed how they demarcated 'science' (economic valuation) from 'politics' (intergovernmental negotiations). Some criticisms were rejected as attempts to 'hijack an essentially scientific process for political and ideological ends' (Pearce, 1996: 8). This also points to a difference between economists and general publics in their views on the notion of monetisation. Economists often use money as a common metric for the cost-benefit analysis – a sort of a 'politically neutral measure of social value' (Demeritt & Rothman, 1999). Irrespective of the technicality of valuation, however, monetary estimates inherently carry political and ethical implications (Fearnside, 1998). The very idea of monetising human lives was indeed the reason for the moral outrage of developing countries.

A few months later, after the disarray of the Geneva meeting, the AR2 WGIII SPM was nevertheless approved, and WGIII's Chapter 6 kept intact. But the wording in the SPM was modified to effectively disavow many of its conclusions by stating that '[t]here is no consensus about how to value statistical lives or how to aggregate statistical lives across countries. Monetary valuation should not obscure the human consequences of anthropogenic climate change damages, because the value of life has meaning beyond monetary considerations' (Bruce et al., 1996: 9–10). This change in the SPM was a compromise acceptable to developing nations, but the underlying ethical question about the monetisation of human life remained unanswered.

Box 16.2
The controversy over accounting rules for forest sinks

Within the UN Framework Convention on Climate Change (UNFCCC), the concept of biological sinks from land use activities such as afforestation and reforestation has always been at the centre of political disputes (Fry, 2002). Throughout the 1990s, several developing countries raised concerns that an inclusion of forest sinks in the Kyoto Protocol would be a 'loophole' to delay early mitigation efforts. Despite such concerns, the Protocol allowed carbon removals by forest sinks to be accounted for in meeting emissions reduction commitments. This marked the beginning of a long and complex process of political struggle – what Fry (2002) described as 'twists and turns in the jungle' – to determine the scope and limit of forest sinks.

Due to a lack of consensual knowledge and no shared normative commitments among negotiating parties – the situation in which Lövbrand (2009) called 'epistemic chaos' – the carbon sink negotiations after Kyoto became a tug of war between two opposing political positions (Lövbrand, 2004). On the one hand, a group of industrialised economies including the United States, Canada and Japan viewed sinks as a 'cost-effective alternative' to emissions reduction. On the other hand, the European Union (EU), some developing nations and most environmental NGOs considered sinks an 'obstacle' to serious efforts to cut emissions from fossil fuels and thus argued for the restricted use of forest sinks. The controversy was so intense that negotiators could not agree on even a simple technical question about the definition of a forest (Fry, 2002).

Under this highly politically charged atmosphere, the IPCC was asked to prepare a Special Report on LULUCF to set the scientific context for the negotiations. Although the IPCC was expected to insert 'science' into politics and hence tame the controversy, the IPCC instead became the site of politicised negotiations about forest science (Fry, 2002; Fogel, 2005; Lövbrand, 2009). During the planning and writing of the Special Report, IPCC authors were attacked from all sides. The IPCC plenary discussions on the SPM approval were nearly as intense as the negotiations at the UNFCCC Conferences of the Parties. Every word in the SPM was subject to close scrutiny from government representatives who sought to shape its conclusions (Fogel, 2005).

Notwithstanding the initial expectations, the IPCC Special Report on LULUCF by itself could not end the sink controversy. Due to a lack of agreement on the issue, the COP6 (Conference of the Parties to the UNFCCC) negotiations in the Hague collapsed. However, the US withdrawal from the Kyoto Protocol changed the political landscape of the negotiations. For the sake of 'saving the Kyoto Protocol', the EU and those parties critical of forest sinks compromised by agreeing to more generous sink provisions. This led to the adoption of the Marrakesh Accords at COP7 in November 2001, which marked a turning point at which sink negotiations moved from 'epistemic chaos' towards 'epistemic validity' (Lövbrand, 2009).

Continued

Box 16.2 (cont.)

Although the approval of the Special Report on LULUCF became the site of a politicised debate, the IPCC's engagement nevertheless certified the abstract sink concept as a scientifically sound mitigation strategy, contributing to the closure of the controversy (Lövbrand, 2009). And yet, whilst political controversy receded, the ethical question about using terrestrial carbon sinks as a substitute for reducing fossil carbon emissions remained unresolved. This ethical concern over forest sinks has lingered, and recently resurfaced with the increased attention being paid to the role of afforestation for meeting the Paris climate goals (Carton et al., 2020).

The two cases illustrate different ways in which the IPCC became embroiled in political controversies. For the dispute over the 'value of human life', the IPCC itself was a trigger for political and ethical contestation among different actors. On the other hand, in the forest sinks dispute, the IPCC was drawn into the controversy by the UNFCCC with an expectation that the IPCC would absorb and defuse political conflict. What these two cases illustrate however is how epistemic controversies within the IPCC are inevitably and intricately bound up with normative disputes in political negotiations within the UNFCCC. At the same time, both cases reveal ethical questions that remained unresolved even after the closure of political controversies. This suggests the likelihood that the IPCC will face similar ethical and ontological controversies in the future.

16.4 Achievements and Challenges

Despite often appearing unwelcome in science, controversies need not always be feared. While sometimes a destructive force, controversies can also act as 'generative events' that create new opportunities for organisational learning (Whatmore, 2009). Controversies are likely unavoidable for the IPCC and therefore the management (or at least acknowledgement) of controversy has to be an integral part of IPCC activities.

In order to maintain its epistemic authority amid controversies, the IPCC has tended to engage in 'boundary work' (Gieryn, 1995), discursively separating its work from politics and hence maintaining its appearance of 'policy neutrality' (see **Chapter 21**). Through this boundary work, the IPCC seeks to contain *scientific* controversies within its domain, and at the same time to keep *political* controversies at bay. However, as seen in the case of the 'value of human life' controversy, the IPCC assessment itself can spark intense political controversies. Inversely, as seen in the case of the Special Report on LULUCF, the IPCC can be brought in to pacify political controversies. Scientific and political disputes are thus often inseparable during controversies.

In some cases, the IPCC succeeds in stabilising epistemic controversies and black-boxing scientific facts. As a result, the wider ethical or political disputes from which such controversies emerged – or which they provoked – also reach a point of closure, at least temporarily. Nevertheless, some normative disputes are often not fully resolved and may therefore resurface in other circumstances. The emergence (and cessation) of controversies is always context-dependent.

Given the complex ways in which climate change is embedded in social, economic and political worlds, the IPCC will continue to find itself always positioned on the brink of controversy. There is no easy escape for the IPCC from this exposed position. Perhaps, only through being a learning organisation (see **Chapter 6**) – constantly revising procedures for knowledge assessment and developing new modes of engagement with diverse audiences – will the IPCC be able to live through moments of controversy. The learning from past controversies might also help the IPCC anticipate issues on the horizon from which unseen controversies might arise in the future.

Three Key Readings

Lövbrand, E. (2009). Revisiting the politics of expertise in light of the Kyoto negotiations on land use change and forestry. *Forest Policy and Economics*, 11(5–6): 404–412. http://doi.org/10.1016/j.forpol.2008.08.007.

This article offers a valuable case study of the 'carbon sinks controversy' that enveloped the IPCC in the UNFCCC negotiation; Lövbrand emphasises how scientific controversies in climate change are always bound up with political questions about power and governance.

Edwards, P. N. and Schneider, S. H. (2001). Self-governance and peer review in science-for-policy: the case of the IPCC Second Assessment Report. Chapter 7 in: Miller, C. A. and Edwards, P. N. (eds.) *Changing the Atmosphere: Expert Knowledge and Environmental Governance*. Cambridge, MA: MIT Press. pp. 219–246. http://doi.org/10.7551/mitpress/1789.003.0010

This chapter offers a useful case study of how the alleged controversy over the rule of procedures led the IPCC's own learning to set the clear rule of peer review process.

Whatmore, S. J. (2009). Mapping knowledge controversies: science, democracy and the redistribution of expertise. *Progress in Human Geography*, 33(5): 587–598. http://doi.org/10.1177/0309132509339841.

This article offers a useful guide to how to think about controversies in science in general: why they occur, who perpetuates them, what is at stake.

Part IV

Processes

This part deals with some of the most important internal processes by which the assessments of the Intergovernmental Panel on Climate Change (IPCC) are crafted, drawing attention in particular to some of the practices, norms and principles that guide these processes. **Jessica O'Reilly** (Chapter 17) evaluates how scientific uncertainties have been treated and managed in IPCC assessments, in particular how uncertainties are understood and operationalised by the different Working Groups (WGs), as well as by government representatives. **Mark Vardy** (Chapter 18) assesses how integration between disciplines, experts and concepts is handled within and between the WGs and how the integration of knowledge made by the IPCC has come to be supported by orchestration efforts occurring outside the IPCC. **Mike Hulme** (Chapter 19) examines why and how the IPCC seeks scientific consensus and some of the limits of such consensus-seeking. In similar fashion, **Kari De Pryck** (Chapter 20) examines the process through which shared ownership of IPCC reports is reached between authors and governments, in particular during the line-by-line approval of the Summaries for Policymakers (SPMs). Finally in this part, **Martin Mahony** (Chapter 21) carefully interrogates the injunction for IPCC assessments to be policy relevant yet policy neutral, and the practices by which the institution navigates this boundary.

17

Uncertainty

JESSICA O'REILLY

Overview

In reports of the Intergovernmental Panel on Climate Change (IPCC), calibrated language is used to communicate confidence and/or agreement in claims. This language is highly specialised and has developed over time to account for diverse sources of knowledge and types of agreement. Currently, the IPCC uses two typologies for calibrated language – a qualitative confidence scale that assesses the amount of evidence, and expert agreement about that evidence, and a more quantitative scale that measures and expresses uncertainty. IPCC leadership intends for calibrated language to help make their reports scientifically clearer, although the resulting stylised language raises readability challenges. Calibrated IPCC language is also used, cynically, as a diplomatic tool during the report adoption plenaries of the Panel, as government delegates raise questions about the characterisation of climate facts. Uncertainty language in the IPCC, then, signifies both technical advancement in the characterisation of uncertainty and the challenges of communicating climate science in diverse contexts.

17.1 Introduction

There is no uncertainty here, or very little. It is at most an alibi.
Jean-Pierre Dupuy (2012: 586).

In his article, beautifully titled 'the precautionary principle and enlightened doom-saying', French philosopher Jean-Pierre Dupuy gets right to the heart of why IPCC authors spend countless hours of volunteer labour pouring over their uncertainty language, carefully calibrated with their chapter group of expert assessors, ensuring that the terms align with the research at hand and the guidance provided by the IPCC. It is work of care and standardisation, precise depictions of what is known and what isn't, what has been fully investigated and what is emergent as a topic of

159

research, and where and how experts agree about climate science. Uncertainty, in IPCC documents, emerges from managed, calibrated epistemic and authorial processes – processes that the IPCC has taken up with incredible technocratic enthusiasm.

Calibrated language in IPCC reports, specifically in their Summaries for Policymakers (SPMs), is intended to provide scientific clarity and precision to the text. However, this is often perceived to be at the expense of readability, particularly among lay people or non-expert decision makers as the IPCC seeks to expand its audience beyond environmental ministries (Barkemeyer et al., 2016). The highly stylized language, requiring specific knowledge to comprehend, is a barrier to accessing climate information in IPCC reports.

Uncertainty is also an alibi. Using uncertainty language offers an alternative to providing statements of fact, which may take scientists decades or even centuries (if ever) to come to agreement upon. Formal uncertainty language helps shade in details about knowledge that always comes in the form of ranges of possible future outcomes – like climate modelling – or knowledge that is partial, underway, incomplete or currently in a state of some expert disagreement. Uncertainty allows for plausible hedging. It is protective and, like much of scientific dispositions, it is conservative, offering ranges that may narrow or widen as more becomes known.

Uncertainty is also used cynically. Dupuy contrasts epistemic uncertainty to the uncertainty of random variables in life. Scientists know this well, characterising different types of uncertainty in response to how it is generated – through computer models or through conflicts in expert agreement, to name two examples. But climate contrarians have regularly taken the deployment of uncertainty by scientists to underscore what is not known, suggesting that action cannot be taken until knowledge is complete. This approach does not hold up well in the face of the overwhelming evidence of human-caused climate change.

Instead, the cynical approach to uncertainty is used in increasingly sophisticated ways, including using the careful process of calibrated language in IPCC reports as a tactic for stalling and derailing the adoption of these reports at a political level, as described later. But first, this short chapter will provide an overview of the history and typology of uncertainty language before examining a case study of political re-interpretations of IPCC uncertainty guidance.

17.2 A Brief History and Typology of Calibrated Language in the IPCC

Scientific uncertainty is a means for communicating precision in ranges of outcomes. There are two main types of uncertainty – model uncertainty and socially derived uncertainty – which further encompasses conflict uncertainty, judgement uncertainty and ethical uncertainty. Model uncertainty can reflect parameters of climate models or the structural uncertainty inherent in making decisions about the code (Funtowicz & Ravetz 1990; Draper 1995; Patt, 2007). Conflict uncertainty (Patt, 2007) is generated by subjective, expert disagreement relating to how to interpret evidence. Judgement uncertainty (O'Reilly et al., 2011), like conflict uncertainty, is socially derived and is generated through the cultural specificity of the group of experts charged with assessing information. The IPCC is just beginning to consider the ethical implications of model choices as Integrated Assessment Models (IAMs) continue to gain power as epistemic and political tools (see Chapter 15). The IPCC communicates model uncertainty and, to an extent, conflict uncertainty. The social act of performing the assessment creates judgement uncertainty, which the IPCC generally does not assess.

The history of uncertainty treatment in the IPCC originates with attempts to standardise the communication of model uncertainty and, over time, develops into more elaborate devices to calibrate socially derived uncertainty (see also Swart et al., 2009). In the First Assessment Report (AR1), only Working Group I (WGI) used uncertainty language and this hewed closely to quantitative, probabilistic statements familiar to earth systems modellers. In the Second Assessment Report (AR2), WGII included qualitative confidence statements in their Executive, Summaries as well (Mastrandrea & Mach, 2011: 661). The AR3 provided the first attempt to standardise IPCC approaches to assessing and communicating uncertainty, although this was only picked up by WGI and WGII (for an insider's account, see Petersen, [2006] 2012). Moss and Schneider (2000) wrote the guidance document, a wide-ranging article that offered advice on how to match a style of uncertainty communication with the type of uncertainty being assessed. This guidance was applied interpretively, chapter by chapter, as the expert authors iterated on the guidance to suit the publications they assessed. While this makes intuitive sense from a scholarly perspective, it did not help the report readers more clearly understand the information assessed. AR4 leadership worked towards a more systemised approach, at least within – and for the first time, across all – WGs.

AR4 was written with a four-page guidance document for calibrating uncertainty (IPCC, 2005). This note built upon Moss and Schneider's advice, along with the substantial proceedings of a 2004 IPCC workshop titled 'Describing Scientific Uncertainties in Climate Change to Support Analysis of Risk and of Options' (Manning et al., 2004). Each of the three WGs could, in essence, choose one of several approaches to calibrating their confidence language depending on the epistemic traditions of their WG, including how best to communicate uncertainty for the type of literature generally assessed (IPCC, 2005). The InterAcademy Council (IAC) report, an independent assessment of the IPCC, took place after the plaudits and scandals emerging from AR4 (see **Chapters 3** and **6**). An entire chapter is devoted to 'IPCC's evaluation of evidence and treatment of uncertainty' (IAC,

2010: 27). After analysing the three different WG uncertainty standards, the IAC review authors recommended that the WGIII approach – using a qualitative level-of-understanding scale describing the amount of evidence available and the degree of agreement among experts – was 'convenient' and recommended that this become the standard across all three WGs, supplemented with qualitative uncertainty judgements when possible (IAC, 2010: xiv–xv).

The IPCC took this advice into account for AR5 and AR6, both of which used the AR5 guidance note on uncertainty, although they have elaborated their approach slightly. This is because, while 'level-of-understanding' language can help readers understand the knowledge basis that guides the authors' judgement, this language does not communicate their likelihood assessment. Authors communicate their qualitative level-of-understanding and then – depending on the type of knowledge being assessed – calibrate their assessment with formalised, qualitative confidence language or quantified uncertainty language. Specifically, the guidance note (Mastrandrea et al., 2010) instructs authors to:

1. 'evaluate the validity of a finding': type, amount, quality, consistency of evidence
2. If high agreement and robust confidence, do one of the following:
   a. Qualitative level of confidence based on author judgement (very low, low, medium, high, very high) (Mastrandrea et al., 2010: 2)
   b. Quantitative measure of uncertainty (virtually certain, very likely, likely, about as likely as not, unlikely, very unlikely, exceptionally unlikely) (Mastrandrea et al., 2010: 2)
      i. Statistical analysis to determine probability distribution
      ii. Alternately, a formal, quantitative survey of expert views can determine probability distribution (Mastrandrea et al., 2010: 4)

The AR5 (and AR6) uncertainty guidance included a figure and a table to help visualise the ranges of uncertainty, along with the appropriate calibrated language. The qualitative 'confidence scale' combines the level-of-understanding along axes of evidence and agreement (Figure 17.1). Confidence, because it is a collective judgement by the authors about the state of the literature being assessed, can be evaluated even when evidence is limited if existing literature is generally in agreement (Mastrandrea et al., 2011: 679).

When the information at hand allows assessors to make quantitative judgements about uncertainty, another scale of language is used to describe likelihood. Figure 17.2 helps authors align their probabilistic assessment with likelihood language, articulating the numerical range behind the prose. The table's footnote suggests that some additional likelihood terms from AR4 can be carried forward if that probabilistic estimate is more appropriate for the assessment.

High agreement Limited evidence	High agreement Medium evidence	High agreement Robust evidence
Medium agreement Limited evidence	Medium agreement Medium evidence	Medium agreement Robust evidence
Low agreement Limited evidence	Low agreement Medium evidence	Low agreement Robust evidence

Agreement →

Evidence (type, amount, quality, consistency) ⟶

Confidence
Scale

Figure 17.1 Confidence scale comparing evidence and agreement.
Adapted from Figure 1 in Mastrandrea et al., 2010: 3

Likelihood Scale	
Term*	**Likelihood of the Outcome**
Virtually certain	99–100% probability
Very likely	90–100% probability
Likely	66–100% probability
About as likely as not	33–66% probability
Unlikely	0–33% probability
Very unlikely	0–10% probability
Exceptionally unlikely	0–1% probability

Figure 17.2 Likelihood scale matching terms to probability ranges.
Adapted from Table 1 in Mastrandrea et al., 2010

Figure 17.1 and the table in Figure 17.2 function as devices for IPCC authors to align their assessment with the calibrated language expected in the full assessment reports. Along with these reference tools, IPCC authors working on internal IPCC documents – such as uncertainty guidance – often publish more conceptual versions of their IPCC-adjacent work in peer-reviewed journals. This allows for additional scrutiny, as well as ensuring that their work is attributable (read: citable) to a broader audience than the universe of IPCC authors (see Manning et al., 2004; Mastrandrea et al., 2011 for key examples related to IPCC uncertainty). For AR5, the IPCC guidance note – with its clear, stepwise, user-guide style – contrasts with the longer scholarly style of the lengthier concept paper, although the content remains consistent. Significantly, the peer-reviewed concept paper lays out the importance of creating a 'traceable account' of all uncertainty statements in the

IPCC, moving from individual chapters through to the SPM and Technical Summary. Such traceable accounts are important for rigour and precision, as well as for assisting those representing the IPCC at the approval plenaries (Mastrandrea et al., 2011). Additionally, these publications provide guidance for assessing uncertainty related to 'key findings', which suggests that key findings should be those with robust evidence and agreement along with relatively high levels of confidence or likelihood.

This process has become increasingly legible, transparent and standardised. But the fact that an IPCC 'key finding' must be adorned with varying linguistic levels of uncertainty further relegates knowledge that cannot be treated in this way to findings that are not, by default, 'key'. Adler and Hirsch Hadorn (2014) note several critiques about scholarship that is either difficult or impossible to calibrate. This includes scholarship coming from models of linear expertise (Beck, 2011a), small scale, holistic studies that are the hallmark of anthropology (Bjurström & Polk, 2011), and a lack of inclusion of interpretive social sciences (Hulme & Mahony, 2010). The totalising demands of the IPCC's uncertainty language marginalises entire forms of knowledge and sets of disciplinary expertise, while at the same time paints over the knowledge that *is* assessed with a veneer of completeness and authority.

What is thereby left out of the IPCC's 'key findings' may well be knowledge that is essential to understanding how to survive the climate crisis. For example, this might be knowledge from the interpretive social sciences that reveals the possibilities or barriers to behavioural, political and cultural change in different contexts, or Indigenous knowledge or otherwise marginalised knowledge (see **Chapter 13**). What is left *in* the text is often conceptually vague, either because of slippage in the use of formal uncertainty language or else due to more fundamental misunderstandings. Aven and Renn (2015) note that the conceptual and theoretical underpinnings of risk and uncertainty in IPCC reports remain unclear, even as guidance over the assessment process has become more directed and authors attempt to take a more standardised approach to calibrated language.

The requirement for deploying rigid uncertainty language raises another concern about what is left *out* of IPCC texts. This is the way the IPCC communicates low-probability, high-risk events, such as the rapid disintegration of the polar ice sheets (O'Reilly et al., 2012). In the case of the ice sheets, AR4 authors did not include assessments of 'rapid dynamical flow', although they noted the exclusion – a wispy, flagging gesture towards a serious conflict in this part of the report (see Chapter 12 and Box 12.1). For AR5, uncertainty guidance included encouragement to consider such events, exhorting author teams to 'provide information of the range of possible outcomes, including the tails of distributions of variables relevant to decision-making and risk management' (Mastrandrea et al., 2011: 681).

Building levees that address the middle range projections for sea-level rise is very different from building levees that account for the higher-end projections.

The users of the IPCC reports – who are sometimes framed as decision-makers, other times as 'consumers' of the products of the reports – also have diverse lenses through which they read these apparently clear words. In their literature review categorising IPCC approaches to and critiques of uncertainty, Adler and Hirsch Hadorn (2014: 669) included a box about end users titled 'pluralism of epistemic standards and values of users'. These different standards and values become apparent in the example offered in the following section, as the WGI AR6 report travelled to the report adoption IPCC plenary in July and August 2021.

17.3 When Calibration Veers Off Course: Political Re-interpretations of Uncertainty

Comparing the AR4 and AR5 reports, the use of calibrated language in IPCC texts increased in both frequency and diversity across the three scales: evidence/agreement, confidence and likelihood (Mach et al., 2017). Janzwood (2020) extended this analysis to note further increases in calibrated uncertainty language use in the Special Reports of the AR6 cycle. Mach et al. – a team of experts who have held roles as IPCC authors, co-chairs, advisors, and Technical Support Unit staff – are clear about the goals underpinning the more sophisticated set of AR5 uncertainty guidance: 'a harmonised, more broadly applicable approach, enabling consistent treatment of uncertainties in communicating the assessed state of knowledge' (Mach et al., 2017: 3). However, I additionally suggest that the increase in confidence language is not just about institutional decision-making by the IPCC and increased maturity in uncertainty guidance for the authors. It is also in anticipation of – or in direct response to – governmental requests for clarification at the approval plenary stage.

IPCC reports undergo several rounds of expert and government review before taking a final step at the report adoption plenary (see Chapter 11). At this meeting, the governments that form the Panel approve the SPM, sentence by sentence. Delegates come to the meetings ready to intervene on matters of style and substance. Unsurprisingly, these interventions often take up matters of national interest. These interests range from assuring the correct scientific representation of climate change and concerns about due process from various states, to acting as an upholder of particular scientific values, to ensuring that scientific understanding accelerates the energy transition from petroleum to renewables – or not (see De Pryck, 2021a).

Over the course of the AR6 WGI report adoption plenary – conducted virtually from 26 July to 6 August 2021 – particular delegates offered interventions that were important for their countries to communicate. These interventions became dependable and predictable in their repetition. One illustrative example was the Saudi Arabian delegate's interventions on calibrated language, the characterisation of statements of facts, and ensuring that textual statements could be associated with quantification. In their opening statement, as reported by the *Earth Negotiations Bulletin* (ENB), 'SAUDI ARABIA pointed to instances in the report where non-calibrated language is used, and called for clarifying uncertainties relating to the use of models and projections' (ENB, 2021: 3). Additional, representative interventions along these lines (and the outcomes) in the ENB report include:

SAUDI ARABIA objected to "unequivocally." Delegates noted compromise on explicit reference to warming of "atmosphere, ocean, and land," rather than "climate system," as these are unequivocally associated with human influence. INDIA opined that human influence has varying levels of confidence and likelihood across the three. Co-Chair Masson-Delmotte said this is a statement of fact and the authors concurred. After some discussion, SAUDI ARABIA accepted the compromise formulation with a small editorial change and the Headline Statement was approved. (ENB, 2021: 4, regarding A.1)

SAUDI ARABIA preferred to keep "main," arguing "dominant" is not IPCC-calibrated language and that "more than 50%" refers to something being "likely" rather than "very likely." The paragraph was approved with no further amendments (ENB, 2021: 5, regarding A.1.3)

Saudi Arabia was not the only delegation at the approval Plenary to intervene about calibrated language and quantification, but they were the most persistent. Nor was this topic the only point that they brought into the Plenary. Their delegation used quantification – and the IPCC's turn towards increasing quantification – as a means for slowing down the proceedings, as well for raising doubts about the validity of statements if they were not easily translated in quantifiable – or quasi-quantifiable – prose. As evident from the statements above, sometimes the suggested changes were incorporated into the SPM, sometimes the authors conferred and made small edits, sometimes the authors explained their rationale and the original wording was accepted. And sometimes others – like WGI co-chair Dr. Masson-Delmotte – benchmarked the language against past practice or against the broader narrative of the report.

While the Saudi Arabian delegation regularly urged deletion of text if their concerns could not be quantified, or at least clarified, the German delegation worked on calibrated language from the other end of the spectrum. That is, several times a German representative noted that statements of fact did not need calibrated language attached. For example:

GERMANY asked why the first sentence states it is "virtually certain" that the land surface will continue to warm more than the ocean surface rather than a statement of fact. The authors clarified it is not a statement of fact because the assessment concludes that, in the near term or for low levels of global warming, internal variability can be high and temporarily mask warming (ENB, 2021:12, regarding B.2.1)

The pull-and-push over uncertainty language at the low- and high-uncertainty ranges shows that the edges of uncertainty continue to matter as points of political and scientific import. The removal of calibrated language represents the point at which a claim becomes fact. The inclusion of low-likelihood, but high-impact, information becomes a point of policy relevance, even policy demand, even as the scientific information at hand remains unresolved. Janzwood (2020) notes that authors know that these critiques are imminent at the adoption Plenary and may consider leaving out information in anticipation of the debate that might ensue at the political level. In an interview Janzwood conducted with an IPCC author, this author noted that being made to consider levels of confidence when elevating statements to the level of the SPM constitutes a 'reality check' (Janzwood, 2020) : 1666). Authors decide in advance that some matters are too politically contentious to withstand the scrutiny and the slowing of the approval process, choosing some statements to defend and others to remain only in the main report or the Technical Summary, both of which receive less scrutiny.

17.4 Achievements and Challenges

As an institution, the IPCC has demonstrated enthusiasm for creating and implementing increasingly sophisticated means for calibrating uncertainty language. Most importantly, the move towards systematising qualitative information has encouraged trust and comparison between the quantifiable and probabilistic findings typical of natural and physical sciences and forms of knowledge coming from different disciplinary traditions. In AR6, the concept of risk was also scaled up into rubrics, decision matrices and standardised, calibrated language, building off the apparent success of IPCC uncertainty guidance (Reisinger et al., 2020). IPCC authors, leadership and staff regularly convey that this elaboration of uncertainty guidance reflects community values within the IPCC – values including traceability, transparency, professionalism, rigour and care.

However, this trajectory has some sticking points, both epistemic and political. In terms of knowledge, the process of standardising calibrated language, even as it seeks to be more inclusive of diverse methodological and disciplinary traditions, excludes some forms of knowledge that don't easily adhere to formal uncertainty calibration due to their descriptive or interpretive nature. As an in-language, frequent use of formal uncertainty calibration can alienate the audience that the IPCC hopes to engage. And in diplomatic spaces, the rhetoric of precision can be cynically deployed to slow the approval process, obfuscate or remove findings that cannot clear the language bar, or else engender debates about the nature of scientific facts.

Three Key Readings

Adler, C. E. and Hirsch Hadorn, G. (2014). The IPCC and treatment of uncertainties: topics and sources of dissensu s. *Wiley Interdisciplinary Revi ews: Climate Change*, 5(5): 663– 676. http:// doi.org/10.1002/wcc.297

This article lends critical purchase to the epistemic commitments and absences in IPCC uncertainty communication practices.

Mach, K. J., Mastrandrea, M. D., Freeman, P. T. and Field, C. B. (2017). Unleashing expert judgement in assessment. *Global Environmental Change*, 44: 1–14. http://doi.org/10 .1016/j.gloenvcha.2017.02.005

This article, written by IPCC authors and leaders, demonstrates the pragmatic and inclusive state of uncertainty thinking within the institution.

Swart, R., Bernstein, L., Ha-Duong, M. and Petersen, A. (2009). Agreeing to disagree: uncertainty management in assessing climate change, impacts and responses by the IPCC. *Climatic Change*, 92(1): 1–29. http://doi.org/10.1007/s10584–008-9444-7

This article provides a comprehensive historical overview of the development of uncertainty guidance in the IPCC through AR4.

18

Integration

MARK VARDY

Overview

In the Sixth Assessment Report (AR6) of the Intergovernmental Panel on Climate Change (IPCC), the chapters of each of the three Working Groups (WGs) are structured with the intention of integrating 'cross-cutting themes' and 'handshakes' between them. While integration received special emphasis in AR6, it is not new. The IPCC has long considered how to treat issues such as representations of uncertainty and scenario data consistently across WGs. The IPCC's effort to integrate knowledge across WGs raises important epistemological and ethical questions related to how the humanities, natural sciences and social sciences shape understandings of climate change. To illustrate the theme of integration as applied within the IPCC, this chapter focuses on how risk is integrated across WGI and WGII in the AR6.

18.1 Introduction

The expectation of integration in the AR6 is clear in the vision statement that the IPCC Chair submitted to the IPCC's 46th plenary session, held in Montreal in 2017:

Producing an AR6 which documents different levels of transformational societal changes requires different types of knowledge ranging from physical science, to ecological and economic sciences, to humanities and social sciences, as well as knowledge drawn from the practitioner community. This will require the experts involved in the scoping and writing exercises of the AR6 to undertake concerted multi- and interdisciplinary conversations, across-WGs but also intra-WGs, and to be mindful of the needs of the practitioner community, especially as the AR6 is meant to adopt a risk and solution-oriented framing. (IPCC, 2017a: 22–23)

This integration of social and natural sciences and humanities across WGs – while considering practitioners and focusing on solutions – can be understood as 'anti-boundary' work; instead of maintaining boundaries between WGs, they are intentionally bridged (De Pryck & Wanneau, 2017: 206–207).

The emphasis in the AR6 on integrating knowledge within and between WGs is motivated in part by the imperative to provide policymakers with solutions-focused science. This could lead to reductionist or abstract generalisations. It could potentially strip away political-economic contexts in which climate change is produced and in which solutions might be implemented (Schipper et al., 2021). This problem can be put differently. If different forms of knowledge have different ways of understanding what the problems and appropriate solutions to climate change are, then there may well be disagreement between IPCC authors when it comes to integrating their home disciplines into a common framework (Schipper et al., 2021).

The implications of integration across WGs are discussed in the literature in reference to adaptation, mitigation, and development (Ayers & Huq, 2009; Nightingale et al., 2020), food security (Porter et al., 2019; Rivera-Ferre, 2020), and Negative Emission Technologies (NETs) (Beck & Mahony, 2018b). This chapter focuses on the topic of risk, and introduces the theme of integration by tracing the development – through informal and formal venues – of the approved AR6 chapter outline.[1]

18.2 A Typology of Integration

The tensions identified above by Schipper et al. (2021) can usefully be situated alongside the typology developed by Barry et al. (2008) in their study of 'the logics of interdisciplinarity', which draws from science and technology studies (STS), political theory and empirical case studies. Barry et al. (2008) articulate three ideal-typical modes through which a range of actors and organisations have attempted interdisciplinary work: service-subordination, integrative-synthesis and agonistic-antagonistic.

The *service-subordination* mode integrates knowledge through a 'hierarchical division of labour' that subordinates the social sciences and humanities to a framework established by the natural sciences. The expectation is that the social sciences will 'serve' the natural or physical sciences. It is plausible that some of the historical tensions between the cultures of the three WGs could be traced to this mode (see **Chapter 12**). However, the *integrative-synthesis* mode provides the dominant discourse through which interdisciplinarity is attempted in the AR6. This mode is characterised by the ways that 'social' factors (e.g. the economy) and nature are accounted for in the same model. Its prevalence in the IPCC is evidenced in the dominance of concepts of resilience, adaptive capacity and vulnerability, which each draw upon complexity theory and social-ecological systems theory. As Barry et al. (2008: 28) point out, the synthesis enacted in this mode can lead to closure, not 'new heterogeneous fields'. This speaks to the tension identified by Schipper et al. (2021) between a holism that imposes a totalising unity on the one hand, and the complex and deeply rooted ways that climate intersects with existing relations of power on the other.

The third mode discussed by Barry et al. (2008) is the *agonistic-antagonistic* mode. This draws from Chantelle Mouffe's concept of the role of opposition as a constitutive element of the political. In this mode, 'interdisciplinarity springs from a self-conscious dialogue with, criticism of, or opposition to, the intellectual, ethical or political limits of established disciplines or the status of academic research in general' (Barry et al., 2008: 29). In other words, the norms and assumptions of different disciplines are challenged as they are brought into conversation with each other. The agonistic-antagonistic mode highlights the potential for creative and novel ways of understanding and responding to climate change to emerge from the intermingling of received ideas. At the same time, it highlights the potential for incommensurability. For example, as discussed in **Chapter 13**, seeking to integrate Indigenous knowledge into a framework dominated by Western science might diminish the integrity and meaning of Indigenous knowledge by removing it from the context within which it is produced.

18.3 A Historical Snapshot: Networked Relationality, Uncertainty and the TGICA

Treating 'cross-cutting issues' consistently between WGs is a long-standing issue in the IPCC. For example, a set of four guidance papers produced over 20 years ago in the lead up to AR3 argued for the 'consistent use of terms and approaches to the assessment and reporting of information that is relevant to the cross-cutting issues' (Pachauri et al., 2000: 2). The four cross-cutting issues treated in the guidance papers were: costing methodologies; uncertainties; decision analysis frameworks; and development, equity and sustainability. Additional cross-cutting issues that were dealt with in special reports at that time were: integrated assessment; scenarios; biogeochemical/ecological feedback; and sinks (Pachauri et al., 2000: 2).

In their guidance paper produced for the AR3, Moss and Schneider (2000: 48) detailed how uncertainties are represented in different ways in previous assessments, and called for 'more explicit and consistent treatment of uncertainties in future assessments for all working groups'. Despite Moss and Schneider's

(2000) plea, however, uncertainty was not always treated in a uniform manner (see **Chapter 17**). As reported by the InterAcademy Council (IAC, 2010: xiv), WGs in the AR4 'used a different variation on IPCC's guidance to describe uncertainty'. This hampered the IPCC's ability to communicate uncertainty and, in the aftermath of the controversies of 2009–2010 (see **Chapters 3** and **6**), the IAC (2010: 69) echoed statements made in the cross-cutting papers with their recommendation for 'strengthening coordination across Working Groups where appropriate and productive'.

Despite the evident desire for integration, coordinating this across WGs is no easy task. Each of the three WGs has its own culture, which is not necessarily shared (Beck, 2011a; Fløttum et al., 2016). This is due, in part, to the IPCC's organisational structure. The IPCC has relatively few permanent paid staff members; at the time of writing, the Secretariat headquartered in Geneva had 16 positions, not including three interns. Each WG is supported by a paid Technical Support Unit (TSU) of a similar number, and each of the three TSUs is formed anew by different host nation states for each new assessment cycle. The work of actually writing the assessment reports is undertaken by volunteers who are selected for each specific report. Given this organisational structure, it is helpful to understand the IPCC as a 'network organisation' in which change can be mediated through key individuals (Venturini et al., 2022). Integration within and between WGs is worked towards through key individuals whose roles span more than one WG; they occupy what Venturini et al. (2022) call 'multipositional thematic bridges'.

Lead Authors, Coordinating Lead Authors, and IPCC Bureau members, which includes WG Co-chairs, can all provide bridges between and within WGs in both formal and informal spaces (see Figure 18.1). As depicted in the figure, informal spaces allow for interaction to build support for key concepts that can then enter the formal structure of the IPCC at Panel/WG plenaries.

The controversies of 2009–2010 heightened the need for transparency and consistent treatment of issues across WGs. This must have been on the minds of some of the roughly 50 individuals – many of whom act as multipositional thematic bridges – who participated in the 2016 IPCC Expert Meeting on the Future of TGICA (Task Group on Data and Scenario Support for Impacts and Climate Analysis). The meeting was convened to consider how the TGICA should respond to changing conditions, including the massive increase in computing power that had occurred since its inception. The TGICA was formed in 1997 as a reformulation of a similar group that had formed the previous year (Vaughan, 2016: 1). One of the main tasks of the TGICA was to coordinate and provide consistent scenario data to all three WGs. Another of its tasks was to provide input on 'cross-cutting issues' that were thought to be relevant to all three WGs (IPCC,

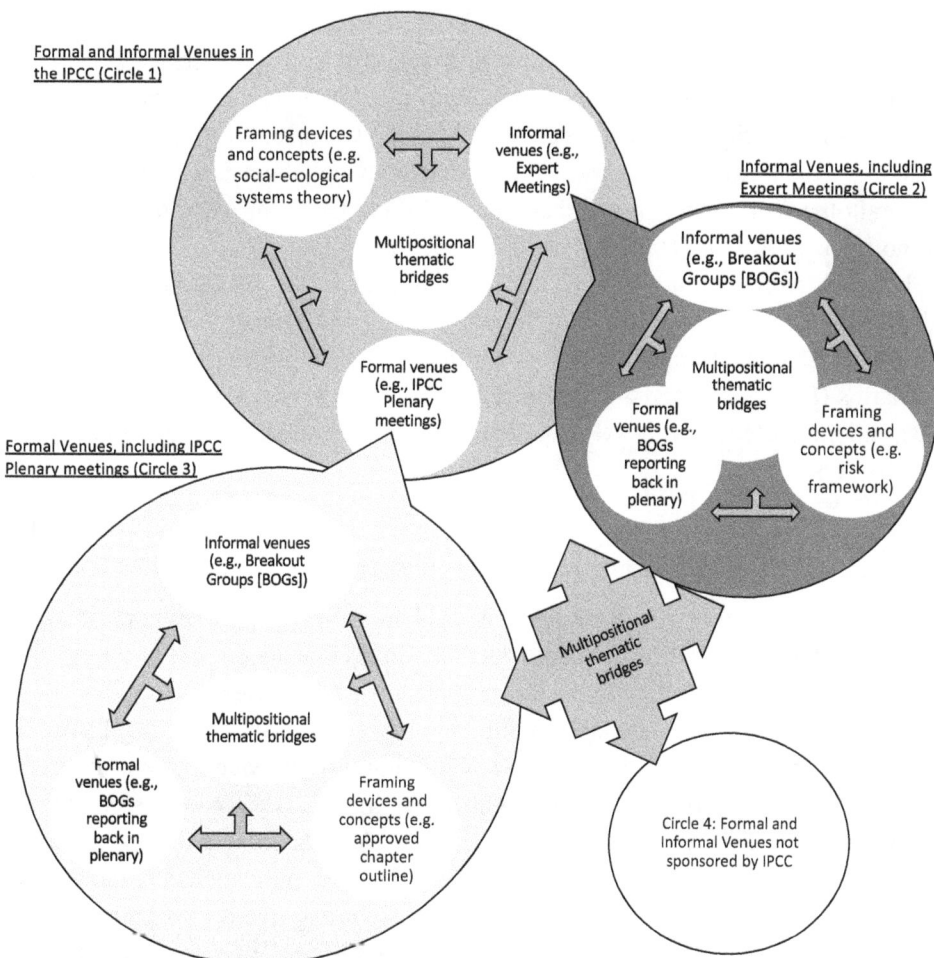

Figure 18.1 Networked integration.

Key actors who occupy multiple positions between and within WGs can communicate thematic framing devices and concepts in informal and formal venues. IPCC processes (Circle 1) include informal venues, such as Expert Meetings (Circle 2), and formal venues, such as WG/Panel Plenaries (Circle 3). This interplay between informal and formal venues takes place on a smaller scale within each type of venue. That is, both informal venues (Circle 2) and formal venues (Circle 3) include informal and formal elements. Thematic bridges, who occupy multiple positions in informal and formal venues, allow for framing devices and concepts, such as the risk framework, to be communicated between and within WGs. As indicated by Circle 4, venues outside of the IPCC can also be connected in this manner.

Figure made by the author

2018f: 13). As Vaughan (2016: 2) states in her report written for the 2016 Expert Meeting: 'Many current and past TGICA members cite its role in facilitating informal communication between Working Groups that does not have many other avenues for exchange as critically important'.

The Expert Meeting on the Future of TGICA in 2016 was an informal venue (Circle 2 in Figure 18.1) that featured a series of plenary presentations and breakout discussion groups, one of which was titled 'Collaboration within IPCC – including facilitating interaction between Working Groups'. One participant noted that in AR5, it was left to individual authors to collaborate with other WGs. Several other participants noted that some LAs and CLAs in AR5 'had very little or no interaction with TGICA' (IPCC, 2016d: 14).

In 2018, two years after the Expert Meeting, the IPCC decided to rename the TGICA as the Task Group on Data Support for Climate Change Assessments (TG-Data) and change its mandate to focus primarily on the management of data and scenarios (IPCC, 2018d: 14–16). The TG-Data is not expected to be a conduit for integration; instead, with AR6, integration is structured into the outline of its chapters.

18.4 Achieving Integration through Informal and Formal Venues

The Scoping meeting for the AR6 was held in Addis Ababa, Ethiopia. There, themes and topics that were first addressed in venues that are outside of the IPCC's formal processes – specifically the meeting on Integrating Science across the IPCC on Climate Risk and Sustainable Solutions (Stockholm, Sweden, 29–31 August 2016) and the International Conference on Climate Risk Management (Nairobi, Kenya, 5–7 April 2017) – were brought inside the IPCC's formal processes via thematic bridges (Circle 4 in Figure 18.1). The AR6 Scoping Meeting in Addis Ababa included breakout group discussions that not only included topics and themes addressed in prior venues but that also, according to the Co-Chairs of WGI and WGII, 'provided a unique opportunity for the three WGs to coordinate the development of their respective assessments, [which is] critical to have early in a cycle where more integration across WGs is expected than in previous cycles, building on the cross-WG Special Reports that are currently underway' (IPCC, 2017c: 6).

The outline developed at the AR6 Scoping Meeting was approved in Montreal, Canada, in 2017 at the IPCC's 46th session, where the following cross-cutting issues were discussed in a series of breakout groups: Regions, Scenarios, Risks, Cities, Global Stocktake, Geoengineering, Adaptation and Mitigation, and Approaches and Processes for Integration (IPCC, 2017a: 7–13).

Integration was built into the approved chapter outlines for each of the three WGs. The final chapter of WGI, for example, 'Chapter 12: Climate change information for regional impact and for risk assessment' was intended to synthesise hazards identified by WGI for further integration into the risk framework in WGII. As stated by the WGI co-chairs report: 'this chapter will contribute to the hazard component of a quantitative assessment of present and future climate risks, resulting in a key 'handshake' point between WG I and II' (IPCC, 2017c: 28). Integration is structured into the approved outline for WGII, in which the final cluster of three chapters synthesise previous chapters. The concluding chapter of WGII, 'Chapter 18: Climate resilient development pathways', was intended to act as a 'connection' to WGIII (IPCC, 2017d: 6). Another key 'handshake' was the online interactive atlas that was published in August 2021 (IPCC, 2021b).

After the formal adoption of the AR6 outline, the dynamic process of integration depicted in Figure 18.1 continued through the work of writing the AR6, which can be seen in the case of risk and regionalisation. As stated by the WGI co-chairs in their report for the IPCC's 46th meeting: 'Two major areas that require coordination across WGI and II are regional information in the assessment of climate mechanisms and linking climate variability and change and related uncertainties to the risk assessment framework' (IPCC, 2017c: 9).

The Expert Meeting on Assessing Climate Information for Regions, 16–18 May 2018, was held in Trieste, Italy, several months before the first Lead Author Meeting for AR6 WGI. The Expert Meeting reports:

For the IPCC AR6 Working Groups main contributions to comprehensively inform regional risk assessment and decision making, it is important to evolve from the traditional one-direction approach … to a more integrated approach in which regional climate information, projections, vulnerabilities and impacts, and response options are considered altogether [across all three WGs]. (IPCC, 2018g: 11)

One of the main recommendations made by the meeting, which was structured around the familiar form of informal breakout groups and formal plenary sessions, was to: 'Make an improved and consistent use of the risk assessment framework across WGI and WGII, and regions' (IPCC, 2018g: 9). Indeed, the risk framework is a key way in which WGI and WGII achieve integration.

As made explicit in Figure 1.5 of AR6 WGII report, one of the significant differences between risk framework used in AR5 and that used in AR6 is the addition of 'response' along with the trio of hazard, exposure and vulnerability established in previous assessment cycles (Begum et al., 2022: 35; see also Simpson et al., 2021). In other words, the risk framework recognises the possibility that maladaptation contributes to the risks that humans experience.

18.5 Achievements and Challenges

To integrate WGs in the AR6, the IPCC explicitly pursues approaches that fall within the integrative-synthesis mode of integration identified by Barry et al. (2008) and that guided the risk and resilience frameworks that were structured into the approved chapter outlines. However, the networked quality of the IPCC means that integration cannot be achieved through top-down imposition. Actors occupying multipositional thematic bridges champion the vision for integration in formal and informal venues. But it is up to authors – Lead Authors, Coordinating Lead Authors, Chapter Scientists and Contributing Authors – to actually write the assessments. This means that, in the actual writing of AR6, the service-subordination or agonistic-antagonistic modes discussed by Barry et al. (2008) might be attempted by different individuals or groups (see **Chapter 12**).

The risk framework in AR6 represents an achievement of the IPCC. Several decades ago, the IPCC adopted a risk framework that centred on biophysical hazards. But as discussed earlier, the AR6 updates the risk framework to include human responses to climate change as an additional source of risk. As stated in the AR6 WGII Summary for Policymakers, 'the risk that can be introduced by human responses to climate change is a new aspect considered in the risk concept' (IPCC, 2022: 5). This extension of the IPCC risk framework to further include 'the social' should be seen as an achievement.

Another achievement accomplished in AR6 is the high degree of cooperation between the Co-chairs of the three WGs, which appears to be greater than that achieved in AR4 or AR5. Similarly, anecdotal information suggests that in AR6 more multipositional thematic bridges participated in LA Meetings for WGs *other than their own* than was the case in previous assessment cycles. These individuals are key to the success of the IPCC's attempt for integration, but they are also rare. It takes considerable social, economic and cultural capital to be able to communicate between different disciplinary paradigms. A challenge the IPCC faces is how to support those thematic bridges who better represent geographical and gender diversity. The scope of this challenge for the IPCC increases when Indigenous knowledge is included along with the humanities, and the social and natural sciences.

Some IPCC authors might censor themselves and not include text that they suspect might be opposed by governmental delegates. For example, there may be ample peer-reviewed evidence that political–economic contexts and social relations of power exacerbate the vulnerability of impoverished people to climate change. But it could be a challenge for IPCC authors to include such knowledge into an integrative framework in such a way that retains critical and political clout while also being approved by all government delegates (see **Chapter 20**).

Considering the challenges described earlier, the IPCC should confront the question of what can and should be done with incommensurable forms of knowledge that come from Indigenous Peoples or critical scholars. This knowledge may provide vital insight into the problem of climate change, but it may remain incommensurable with the IPCC's chosen integrative frameworks, posing significant ethical and epistemological challenges.

Note

1 Although not discussed in this chapter, IPCC Special Reports are another important venue for integration. For example, the SREX (2012) includes chapters co-authored by WGI and WGII authors, and the Special Report on Global Warming of 1.5 °C, or SR15 (2018), was the first time that authors from all three WGs collaborated to work on the same chapter. See Chapter 5.

Three Key Readings

Barry, A., Born, G. and Weszkalnys, G. (2008). Logics of interdisciplinarity. *Economy and Society*, 37(1): 20–49. http://doi.org/10.1080/03085140701760841

This article provides an empirically and theoretically grounded analytic framework for studying the various ways in which the natural and social sciences and the humanities are brought together.

De Pryck, K. and Wanneau, K. (2017). (Anti)-boundary work in global environmental change research and assessment. *Environmental Science and Policy*, 77: 203–210. http://doi.org/10.1016/j.envsci.2017.03.012

This article provides the historical and political context of the push for integration in the AR6 by tracing the development of discourses related to solutions-oriented science.

Schipper, E. L. F., Dubash, N. K. and Mulugetta, Y. (2021). Climate change research and the search for solutions: rethinking interdisciplinarity. *Climatic Change*, 168(3): 18. http://doi.org/10.1007/s10584-021-03237-3

This article, co-authored by scholars with extensive insider experience of the IPCC, provides a detailed and critical analysis of the imperative to integrate knowledge for solutions within the IPCC.

19

Scientific Consensus-seeking

MIKE HULME

Overview

A widely shared expectation of science is that it speaks authoritatively about how the physical world works and therefore about what the consequences of different human actions and policy interventions are likely to be in that world. Science, and therefore the scientist, is believed to offer public life something different – something more truthful and hence more authoritative – than offered by politicians, journalists, lawyers, priests or celebrities. Scientists 'reaching a consensus' and 'speaking with one voice' are integral to science's projection of epistemic authority. This is especially the case with the Intergovernmental Panel on Climate Change (IPCC), where its authority is perceived to rest on its communication of a scientific consensus. This chapter first summarises the nature of consensus-making in science in general, before examining the IPCC's consensus-seeking practices. It then evaluates some of the arguments for and against the pursuit of consensus by the IPCC and concludes by highlighting some future challenges for the IPCC with respect to its pursuit of consensus.

19.1 Introduction

The pursuit of consensus has been central to the mission, procedures and communication of the IPCC's knowledge assessments. This pursuit has been grounded in the belief that an intergovernmentally owned and transnational knowledge consensus about climate change is a prerequisite for effective policymaking. From its beginning, the IPCC has sought and delivered a consensus on what is deemed to be known scientifically about climate change. For example, in the foreword to the IPCC's very first assessment – the Working Group I (WGI) First Assessment Report (AR1) published in 1990 – the Co-Chair Sir John Houghton wrote 'peer review has helped *ensure a high degree of consensus* amongst authors and reviewers regarding the results presented' (IPCC, 1990a: p.v, emphasis added). This aspiration for authority-through-consensus has been evidenced in the rhetoric of IPCC communications. For example, in November 2007, just ahead of the publication of AR4's Synthesis Report, the IPCC promoted its consensus processes thus: '2500+ scientific expert reviewers; 800+ contributing authors; and 450+ lead authors; from 130+ countries; 6 years work; 4 volumes; 1 report. The core findings of the three volumes integrated in the most policy-relevant scientific document on climate change for the years to come'. The sheer weight of expertise compressed into 'one report' is offered by the IPCC, tacitly, as evidence of its epistemic authority.

This association between consensus and authority is used by social and political actors and commentators outside the IPCC, whether they be politicians, lobbyists, advocates or critics. The stronger the consensus, it is claimed by advocates, the greater the authority the IPCC has in public or policy debates. Critics on the other hand, seek to challenge the IPCC's consensus in order to weaken its public authority. Politicians also draw upon the language of consensus. For example, Kevin Rudd, the then Australian Prime Minister, announced in a speech on 6 November 2009, just before COP15 in Copenhagen:

This is the conclusion of 4,000 scientists appointed by governments from virtually every country in the world . . . Attempts by politicians in this country and others to present what is an *overwhelming global scientific consensus* as little more than an unfolding debate . . . are nothing short of intellectually dishonest. They are a political attempt to subvert what is now a *longstanding scientific consensus* (emphases added).

The role of the IPCC's consensus in public debates and political negotiations about the goals and instruments of climate policy continues to provoke vigorous arguments. Some scientists are critical of consensus-seeking practices in the IPCC because of their ostensibly conservative outcomes. Oppenheimer et al. (2007), for example, argued that the IPCC's search for consensus with respect to future sea-level rise deflected attention from the full exploration of scientific uncertainties, to the detriment of robust policymaking. On the other hand, some political philosophers accuse consensus-driven knowledge assessments of subverting good scientific practice, by masking legitimate epistemic *dis*sensus (Beatty & Moore, 2010). These arguments about the legitimacy, outcomes and effects of the IPCC's consensus-seeking practices highlight long-standing debates in the history and philosophy of science about the nature of epistemic consensus (e.g. Fuller, 2002) and in science and technology studies (STS) about the legitimacy of knowledge consensus practices in science–policy interactions (e.g. Jasanoff, 2004). They also reflect debates in political science about the role and status of expert representation and deliberation in healthy democracies (e.g. Brown, 2009). These academic debates about the nature and impact of consensus in regulatory scientific institutions and knowledge assessments are interesting in general terms. But they become crucially important for public policy with respect to specific concerns such as climate change.

This chapter first summarises the nature of consensus-making in science in general, before examining the IPCC's consensus-seeking practices. It then evaluates some of the arguments for and against the pursuit of consensus by the IPCC and examines whether such consensus is epistemically appropriate and politically desirable. It concludes by highlighting some future challenges for the IPCC with respect to its pursuit of consensus.

19.2 The Nature of Scientific Consensus

Making and defending a scientific consensus can be understood to fulfil a number of different functions. For example, a consensus can validate specialist knowledge about some physical phenomenon and hence act as a 'truth claim'. Establishing such a consensus can bring a new epistemic community into being or else consolidate the perceived authority of an existing epistemic community (Haas, 1992). A consensus can also offer a pragmatic way of bringing authoritative knowledge into public circulation when important policy decisions loom. Oreskes (2019) argues that consensus-making – 'scientists speaking with one voice' – is central to the practice of science. On the other hand, none of these functions of consensus-making in science stands unchallenged; there has long been a strand of philosophy that interrogates the nature of consensus in science. Thus Rescher (1993) argues against the desirability of consensus, claiming that cognitive pluralism in science is inescapable, while Miller (2013) points out that the lack of social diversity in an epistemic community undermines its claim to forge a legitimate consensus. In a similar vein, Stirling (2010) argues that democratic decision-making is better served by epistemic pluralism – 'keeping things open' – than by seeking a knowledge consensus.

The slippery and contested nature of a knowledge consensus prompts STS scholars such as Harry Collins to claim 'we don't really know what scientific consensus is' (quoted in Jomisko, 2013: 28). And it results in a proliferation of knowledge consensus typologies and the recognition of multiple practices of consensus-making. Scholars also talk about 'strong' and 'weak' consensuses. Gilbert (2002), for example, puts forward a non-summative account of group belief (i.e. consensus), which distinguishes between the group's collective belief in a claim and the range of beliefs of the individual members of the group. Similarly, Fuller (2002: 207–232) distinguishes between 'essential' (group belief arrived at through deliberation) and 'accidental' (convergence of autonomous individual beliefs) consensus. And there seems no consensus about *how* a scientific consensus should best be arrived at. Guston (2006), for example, proposes the use of voting procedures in scientific assessments, whilst Verheggen et al. (2014) enumerate consensus in climate science through expert surveys.

When applied to matters of significant public policy concern – such as climate change – these questions about the nature and legitimacy of a knowledge consensus become important to answer. There may be a general recognition in philosophy of science that cognitive diversity is inevitable, that consensuses are unstable over time, and that what matters for the cultural authority of science is the legitimacy and integrity of *the process* of consensus-making (Beatty & Moore, 2010). But this theoretical understanding of consensus in science begs two important practical questions when it comes to pursuing and interpreting knowledge consensus in the IPCC: When is making a knowledge consensus *epistemically appropriate*? And when is it *politically desirable*?

In relation to the first question, Miller (2013) asks under what conditions might an epistemic consensus be deemed 'a mark of knowledge'. He suggests three conditions need to be satisfied:

- the *social calibration condition* – the use of common evidential standards and ontological schemes;
- the *apparent consilience of evidence condition* – different lines of evidence seem to converge;
- the *social diversity condition* – parties to a consensus should have diverse social profiles.

The case of the IPCC presents particularly challenging circumstances for these three conditions to be met. Social calibration and the consilience of evidence are more exacting conditions when dealing with a wide range of disciplinary epistemologies and traditions (Jasanoff, 2011b), such as the IPCC embraces. And the social diversity condition reveals the tension between parties to a consensus being selected on the basis of formal expertise versus national allegiance or other non-epistemic criteria (see **Chapter 7**).

With respect to the second question – when is a consensus politically desirable – a range of factors come into play. These can broadly be captured by the idea of civic epistemology (see **Chapter 23**), which challenges the universal legitimacy and efficacy of a knowledge consensus generated by a transnational body such as the IPCC. *How* a knowledge consensus is made, and whether these processes are perceived as credible and legitimate within any given polity, will then determine how – and how effectively – consensus claims are used in public discourse and policy advocacy. What is politically effective in Germany, for example, may be very different from what is effective in the United States. Policy traps lurk if a singular transnational knowledge consensus is used to guide or justify the design of policy instruments to be applied across different political cultures of risk management (Rothstein et al., 2012).

19.3 Consensus Practices in the IPCC

Little systematic theoretical or empirical attention has been given to exactly *how* knowledge consensus within the IPCC is constructed or how these processes have evolved historically. Where such consideration *has* been given to the nature of the IPCC's consensus, it has often been poorly grounded in empirical evidence (e.g. exchanges with regard to the early IPCC consensus; see Boehmer-Christiansen, 1996; Shackley, 1997), or else been approached using insights from limited disciplinary perspectives. For example, Elzinga (1996) reflected from an STS perspective on the shaping of the IPCC's 'worldwide consensus' and Goeminne (2013), likewise, using STS and political science. Conversely, Curry and Webster (2013) examined the IPCC's consensus in terms of scientific practice, but without drawing upon the insights of STS or philosophy of science. The clutch of studies which have sought to enumerate the strength of the 'climate consensus' (e.g. Oreskes, 2004; Verheggen et al., 2014) have done so with little engagement with political science (Pearce et al., 2017b).

IPCC reports generate different types of consensus statements. For example, in Summaries for Policymakers (SPMs) there is line-by-line agreement between government representatives and scientists, which is a different form of consensus than that which emerges within chapter teams. For SPMs, IPCC procedures allow for issuing formal 'minority reports', although this option is rarely utilised (Livingston et al., 2018). Central to the IPCC's consensus practices is how the final assessment products capture and represent uncertainty in scientific knowledge. The IPCC has evolved an elaborate series of guidelines for communicating uncertainty in its knowledge statements (see **Chapter 17**). Yet among observers and participants of the IPCC, there are ambiguities about whether consensus statements reflect 'a lowest common denominator consensus view of the vast majority of scientists' (Edwards & Schneider, 1997: 13), or whether the IPCC 'brings controversy within consensus, capturing the full range of expert opinion' (Edwards, 2010: xvii). Guidance issued ahead of AR6 asked chapter teams to seek the 'full range of views', but stopped short of saying exactly what this means or how this should be done. It is also important to recognise the distinction between consensus-as-product – offering the 'lowest common denominator' between varying expert opinions – and consensus-as-process – negotiating between different scientific interpretations of theory or evidence (see Box 19.1).

Box 19.1
Controversies and IPCC consensus

The ambiguity about whether an IPCC consensus captures the 'lowest common denominator' about which all experts can agree or the 'full range of expert opinion' is present in a number of controversies. One example concerns the case of the IPCC's estimates of future sea-level rise in AR4 (O'Reilly et al., 2012). Hansen (2007) argued that these sea-level rise projections were troublingly conservative, because the need for consensus meant that emerging and still uncertain work about ice sheet dynamics was discounted by the relevant IPCC chapter team. Hansen painted the IPCC's consensus projections as a lowest common denominator, identifying 'scientific reticence' by experts in their avoidance of exploring more extreme possibilities. For Oppenheimer et al. (2007: 1506), the need for potentially consequential information in the 'tails' of probability distributions meant that the 'establishment of consensus by the IPCC is no longer as critical to governments as a full exploration of uncertainty'. This controversy about sea-level rise reflected uncertainties in different modelling strategies.

Epistemic controversies in the IPCC about the value of human lives, the contribution of different countries to atmospheric greenhouse gas levels or links between climate change and violent conflict, cast the problem of consensus-seeking in a different light (see **Chapter 16**). Despite the apparent 'mechanical objectivity' of the scenarios and models that underpin the IPCC's knowledge claims, a growing emphasis has been placed on 'expert judgement' as the key process for generating consensual knowledge (Mach & Field, 2017). And in WGII and WGIII, disagreement can be observed over where exactly the boundary between 'facts' and 'values' lies. This leads to conflicts between authors and governments, the latter perceiving their interests to be threatened by overly subjective constructions of climate risks. On the one hand, this boundary work can be read as the naked defence by governments of their political–economic interests. Equally, it can be understood as an expression of different expectations of what constitutes 'scientific assessment', of where science ends and politics begins (see **Chapter 21**). In pursuing consensus, the IPCC's WGs are therefore not just engaged in resolving epistemic uncertainties. They are mediating between different ideals of what knowledge consensus means in practice.

19.4 Arguments in Favour of Consensus

The argument in favour of the IPCC seeking a scientific consensus on climate change is that by doing so it reflects what science supposedly is uniquely disposed to be good at – applying rules of reasoning and inference, which lead unambiguously and universally from evidence to conclusion. The same evidence presented to the same disciplined minds leads to precisely the same conclusion. In this view, a *lack* of consensus would undermine the authority of science. It might suggest that sufficient effort had not been made to reconcile conflicting views among experts, or else that personal or cultural biases and values had protruded into the reasoning process.

This is the position implicitly assumed by Sir John Houghton in the foreword to the AR1 WGI report cited earlier. His comments on IPCC's consensus were immediately preceded by the observation that: 'Although … there is a minority of opinions which *we have not been able to accommodate*, the peer review has helped ensure a high degree of consensus amongst authors and reviewers regarding the results presented. *Thus*, the Assessment is an authoritative statement of the views of the international scientific community at this time' (IPCC, 1990: p. v, emphasis added). The IPCC's assessment of knowledge is authoritative *because* it is a consensus. Paradoxically, this is also the view of many critics of the IPCC who assert that science properly conducted – through unbiased and structured reasoning processes – *should* lead to unanimous consent (Oreskes, 2019). On such a reckoning, simply pointing to the existence of a minority dissenting position that contradicts an IPCC consensual statement is sufficient to undermine the authority of the IPCC's consensus. The symbolic and political power that a scientific consensus affords the IPCC would thereby be undermined (Pearce et al., 2018). This view of consensus in science is one that offers a wide variety of protagonists a useful defence against cultural relativists.

19.5 Arguments against Consensus

The earlier defence of consensus reflects a very particular (purist) view of scientific knowledge, which scholars such as Bruno Latour (1993) have described as the 'modernist illusion of science'. Silberzhan et al.'s (2018) experiment, for example, shows that random groups of similarly qualified experts can reach quite different conclusions when presented with identical empirical evidence.

There are three main groups of arguments against the pursuit of a knowledge consensus by the IPCC. First, the requirement of consensus can be pernicious; in order to protect the authority of a group it encourages premature agreement among experts where there is none (Beatty & Moore, 2010). Some argue that the IPCC should more openly embrace the idea of expert elicitation, or even expert voting: 'A scientific body that does not partake in … a politics of transparent social choice – one that hides both its substantive disagreements and its disciplinary and sectoral interests beneath a cloak of consensus – is not a fully democratic one' (Guston, 2006: 401). For example, such an approach to capturing disagreement could usefully have been applied to the case of the sea-level rise controversy in AR4 (see Box 19.1). Expert elicitation makes disagreements explicit and better reflects the quasi-rationality of scientific deliberation.

Second, the presence of officially sanctioned credible minority views – thereby revealing the extent of expert dissensus – can enhance the authority of science in public and political life (Rescher, 1993). It would show that the deliberative procedures of the IPCC were fair and accommodating to the full range of accredited views. The implication of this argument is that the IPCC assessment process should not just *allow* minority reporting in its rules of procedure, but ensure that minority reporting is *actively facilitated*. 'Science would provide better value to politics if it articulated the broadest set of plausible interpretations, options and perspectives, imagined by the best experts, rather than forcing convergence to an allegedly unified voice' (Sarewitz, 2011: 7).

A third group of arguments against the necessity of scientific consensus works by analogy. Majority rule works very effectively in maintaining order in social institutions, such as parliaments and the courts that involve voting MPs and juries. Consensus is not required for a legal ruling or judgement to carry authority in wider public settings. And whatever differences between the nature of scientific enquiry and political (or jury) debate might be insisted on, it must be recognised that scientific assessments such as the IPCC are established explicitly as social (i.e. deliberative) institutions. They scrutinise and evaluate evidence, much like a judicial process (Shapin, 2010). There are many other dimensions beyond just 'unanimity of view' if institutions are to become trusted and authoritative amongst members of a polity – for example, fair and agreed procedure, respect for dissent, and acceptance of outcomes.

Even if one accepts that a scientific consensus is desirable, in many fields of climate change consensus is elusive. Agreement – i.e., 'high confidence' – exists within some specific research communities, for example among detection and attribution studies leading to affirm the reality of human influence on the climate system. But in other fields relevant to climate change impacts and policy such a consensus does not hold. For example, there is 'low confidence' in the magnitude of the contribution of permafrost thawing to carbon cycle feedbacks, on whether – and with what speed – Antarctic ice sheets might contribute substantially to sea-level rise and on whether Arctic sea-ice thawing causes increases in mid-latitude climate variability (IPCC, 2021a).

19.6 Achievements and Challenges

Over its 34-year history the IPCC has brought a substantial degree of 'epistemic order' to scientific knowledge about climate change. The founding chairman of the IPCC – Bert Bolin – sought to bring order out of what he perceived in 1988 to be 'chaos' in the public perception of climate science (Bolin, 2007: 49). Reflecting this desire, the IPCC has managed to organise the scientific community to increasingly approximate a univocal stance on climate change knowledge. As a social accomplishment, this was already recognised nearly 25 years ago by van der Sluijs et al. (1998) in their analysis of the IPCC's consensus statement about the climate sensitivity; this consensus estimate – a range of 1.5–4.5 °C – 'anchored' the scientific terms of the policy debate.

However, the IPCC's search for consensus across all areas of relevant scientific and social scientific knowledge has not always been easy and there are new challenges ahead. As the IPCC seeks to respond to changing political and public expectations about its role, how it establishes and communicates a knowledge consensus on climate change will come under ever closer scrutiny. As future assessments engage more directly with policy solutions to climate change – and as the IPCC furthers its enlistment of more diverse forms of knowledge and expertise – informal modes of consensus-making relying on unstructured deliberation will be found wanting. For example, future engagement by the IPCC with more explicitly value-based forms of knowledge (see **Chapter 13**) will question whether consensual statements are epistemically, or even ontologically, appropriate or politically desirable. These tensions have already surfaced in previous ARs and will require more direct handling in the future. Formal procedures such as voting, expert elicitation and minority reporting – far from weakening the authority of the IPCC – may in fact be the only way in which the IPCC can remain authoritative and relevant for policy.

Three Key Readings

O'Reilly, J., Oreskes, N. and Oppenheimer, M. (2012). The rapid disintegration of projections: the West Antarctic Ice Sheet and the IPCC. *Social Studies of Science*, 42(5): 709–731. http://doi.org/10.1177/0306312712448130

> This article offers a very good case study of how the IPCC handled disagreement among experts about the contribution of ice-sheet dynamics to future sea level, and hence the practical difficulties of reaching consensus.

Pearce, W., Grundmann, R., Hulme, M., Raman, S., Kershaw, E. H. and Tsouvalis, J. (2017a). Beyond counting climate consensus. *Environmental Communication*, 11(6): 723–730. http://doi.org/10.1080/17524032.2017.1333965

> Using the case of climate change, this review article explains the political uses and limits of scientific consensus, in particular when that consensus is arrived at through non-deliberative techniques.

van der Sluijs, J., van Eijndhoven, J., Shackley, S. and Wynne, B. (1998). Anchoring devices in science for policy: the case of consensus around the climate sensitivity. *Social Studies of Science*, 28(2): 291–323. http://doi.org/10.1177/030631298028002004

> This was one of the first published studies that explored how and why consensus in climate science emerged through the IPCC's knowledge assessment practices; it takes the seminal case of 'the climate sensitivity'.

20

Governmental Approval

KARI DE PRYCK

Overview

The reports of the Intergovernmental Panel on Climate Change (IPCC) are not produced by scientific experts disconnected from policy. They are produced within a political framework. The governmental endorsement of IPCC reports is a key element of the perceived success of the organisation. In particular, the approval of the Summaries for Policymakers (SPMs) makes the member states of the IPCC active participants in the assessment process and creates ownership of their content. At first sight, the involvement of governments in the IPCC reveals a genuine exercise of co-production between science and politics. It is expected to make the reports more legitimate and policy-relevant. Yet a closer look at the practices through which governmental ownership of IPCC reports is produced shows that governments may in some cases contribute to making them policy-*ir*relevant.

20.1 Introduction

Presenting the Fourth Assessment Report (2007) (AR4) at the United Nations Summit on Climate Change in 2009, the former chair of the IPCC, Rajendra K. Pachauri (2009) stated that 'the uniqueness of this mammoth exercise lies in the fact that all the governments of the world – your own governments – approved of this report, and therefore have full ownership of its contents'. More recently, Chris Field and Vicente Barros (2015: 36), two former members of the IPCC Bureau, praised the 'added value' of IPCC approval sessions, which 'generate broadly shared ownership of scientific knowledge on climate change – a key contribution to the influence of IPCC reports'. These quotes are illustrative of the 'perceived binding force' (Riousset et al., 2017: 263) that emerges from governmentally negotiated documents like the SPMs. It is generally expected that, once approved, the summary statements cannot be questioned in other multilateral fora, and in particular in the UN Framework Convention on Climate Change (UNFCCC).

For a long time, the IPCC approval process was presented by its leadership as exempt from political interference. For instance, another Bureau member, Sir John Houghton (2007: 14), argued that 'it can be said with confidence that no wording was included or added, and no changes were made [in the SPMs] for political or ideological reasons'. Social scientists, however, have increasingly challenged such views and presented a more complex, social and political analysis of the approval process. It has been argued that such a process, while creating a 'shared scientific understanding' of climate change (Lidskog & Sundqvist, 2015: 12) can also be conflictual and lead to 'least-common denominator generalities' (Vardy et al., 2017: 59). It has also been suggested that the approval process offers the member states of the IPCC (i.e. the 'principals') much scope to shape the knowledge and policy perspectives put forward in the SPMs (Compagnon & Bernstein, 2017).

This chapter discusses how governmental ownership is forged through the approval process and ultimately how IPCC member states contribute to shaping the meaning of climate change. In this chapter we understand the IPCC as we would any other UN organisation, i.e., one that remains 'accountable to governments, its founders and funders, both individually ... and collectively' (Ghaleigh, 2016: 69). This does not mean that IPCC authors and Bureau members do not have agency in shaping the SPMs. Quite the contrary. But IPCC authors do need to take governments' multiple and sometimes contradictory interests into account while drafting the reports.

This chapter thus explores how the scientific 'facts' presented in the SPMs are translated into diplomatic 'facts' (Ruffini, 2017: 120). It shows that the SPM approval process reveals disagreements about scientific interpretations and policy relevance. But it also shows that, crucially, when statements contained in the SPMs become entangled with interstate relations and UNFCCC negotiations, the approval reveals multilateral diplomacy at work. The chapter is based on the available literature, on participants' accounts, as well as on the author's own observations of plenary sessions of the Panel (2014–2022). The following sections discuss governmental approval as a process, as a negotiation and as an output.

20.2 Approval as Process

Governmental ownership is not only created at the end of the assessment process, when IPCC authors submit their reports, but through the whole process (see Chapter 3). First, governments agree on whether or not to produce a report and decide on the timeline for its production. Following a scoping meeting – which brings together representatives from governments, observer organisations and academia – a first outline is submitted for approval to the member states of the IPCC. This outline sets the overall narrative of the report and contains chapter titles and indicative bullets. The approval of the outline offers an opportunity for governments to define the mandate of the reports and to suggest policy-relevant questions. It is also a moment in which the messages and terminology proposed in the document are scrutinised and may become enmeshed in controversies.

During the approval of the outline, government representatives may ask for clarifications and changes in the structure and the bullet points. Because they come from diverse national institutions (e.g. from meteorological agencies or ministries of foreign affairs), their interventions can be both scientific and political. Some government representatives may want the IPCC to address specific scientific and technical debates or to discuss issues relevant for their domestic and international policies. Others may also seek to raise issues in the IPCC in order to move forward discussions in the UNFCCC because of the historical proximity between the two institutions (see **Chapter 2**).

At this stage, much time is already spent 'weighting' (Hughes & Vadrot, 2019) the terms and concepts proposed in the outline, by testing how they can be interpreted by different audiences and assessing whether they have a 'policy context' – for example, whether they relate to policy documents beyond the IPCC. Governments may also seek to *prevent* certain topics from being discussed in the IPCC. For example, references to terms such as 'fossil fuel' or 'Nationally Determined Contributions' (NDCs) have sometimes been opposed, because oil-producing countries wanted to divert attention from the main drivers of climate change or because of unresolved conflicts in the UNFCCC (Hermansen et al., 2021). While the outline still leaves much leeway to authors in how they address each topic, its approval reflects struggles over the control of the narrative of the reports and of the assessment process more broadly. These struggles often re-emerge in subsequent meetings of the IPCC.

Following the approval of the outline, authors then work autonomously in their Working Groups (WGs) and draft the reports. Governments get involved in the review process by providing comments on the Second Order Draft (SOD) of the reports, as well as on their SPMs (see **Chapters 5** and **11**). At that stage, they may ask for clarification and additional information, make suggestions to improve the text, but also express disagreement with certain statements. The governmental review process helps authors and Bureau members identify issues that are likely to become controversial in the approval session of the SPMs. They assess whether each statement or figure is grounded in well-founded and traceable reasoning – and are thus 'defendable' – and make sure it does not constitute

Figure 20.1 Plenary Session of the IPCC Member States, UNESCO, 24–28
February 2020.
Photo by IISD/ENB Leila Mead

a 'red line'. This may lead to self-censorship, but authors and Bureau members
may also decide to go forward with their analyses and 'fight' for it in plenary
(Broome, 2020).

The approval of the SPMs usually takes one week, two weeks when approved
online (see **Chapter 4**, Box 4.1). These sessions are performances of multilateral
diplomacy where government delegates scrutinise the document line by line and
agree, in dialogue with the authors, on a common position that satisfies them all. The
IPCC uses deliberative procedures that have been refined over 30 years and closely
follow UN practices. These include the arrangement of the main plenary room
(Figure 20.1), where delegates are seated in alphabetical order by country, the use
of the track-changes mode to amend the draft documents, and the availability of
breakout rooms to pursue parallel discussions in smaller and less formal settings.
At the same time, the detailed scrutiny that the SPMs undergo is unique. Few other
international institutions give member states such control over their outputs.

Sitting on a podium, the authors – usually the Coordinating Lead Authors or
Lead Authors, see Chapter 7 – and the Bureau members assess the requests made
by governments and suggest more consistent formulations. Arguments put
forward concern issues of 'clarity of the message', 'scientific accuracy', 'balance',

'policy-relevance', 'policy prescriptiveness' and 'procedural consistency' (Petersen, 2011: 3). In other words, statements contained in the SPMs must be clear and consistent with the underlying literature reviewed in the WG reports. Statements also need to be balanced in such a way that they do not single out particular perspectives, and yet are deemed relevant to a wide range of policymakers, while leaving unconstrained the range of development pathways and policy options (to avoid policy prescriptiveness) (see Chapter 21). While government comments are sometimes politically motivated, when their countries' interests are at stake, most contribute to make the SPM clearer – and provide at times a much needed 'reality check' to some of the theoretical and abstract statements proposed by the authors.

The SPMs must be approved in a transparent process that does not leave any country behind. The approval process renders visible the tensions between two views of consensus that coexist more generally in the IPCC (see **Chapter 19**). On the one hand, is the view in the singular. This type of consensus tends to reduce the diversity of perspectives by converging on the most robust and unanimous conclusions. On the other hand, consensus is also viewed in the plural. This view seeks to accommodate the concerns of all parties and to balance a variety of perspectives. This second type of consensus abides by principles of pluralism to ensure that 'everybody is on board' (Kouw & Petersen, 2018).

20.3 Approval as Negotiation

Studies of intergovernmental expert bodies like the IPCC – but also of the Intergovernmental Science-Policy Platform on Biodiversity and Ecosystem Services (IPBES) – have conceptualised SPM approval sessions as 'negotiating sites' (Hughes & Vadrot, 2019: 15). The SPM 'negotiations' involve much arguing, a great deal of compromising and some bargaining (De Pryck, 2021a). The deliberations are generally dominated by a small group of countries (see **Chapter 9**).

The approval process is complex (Figure 20.2), contingent on the negotiating capabilities of delegates *and* authors and is influenced by a variety of factors. These include: the epistemic features – for example whether quantitative or qualitative knowledge is under discussion – and 'controversiality' of the sentence or figure under scrutiny; the strength of the arguments raised; the scientific and political resources of the delegations supporting/opposing it; and the personality and argumentative skills of the delegates, authors and chairs of the sessions. In general, the modification of a statement without the consent of the authors cannot be accepted without exposing the organisation to severe criticism. Yet, authors are strongly encouraged to seek consensus and accept compromises, even if they might not always want to.

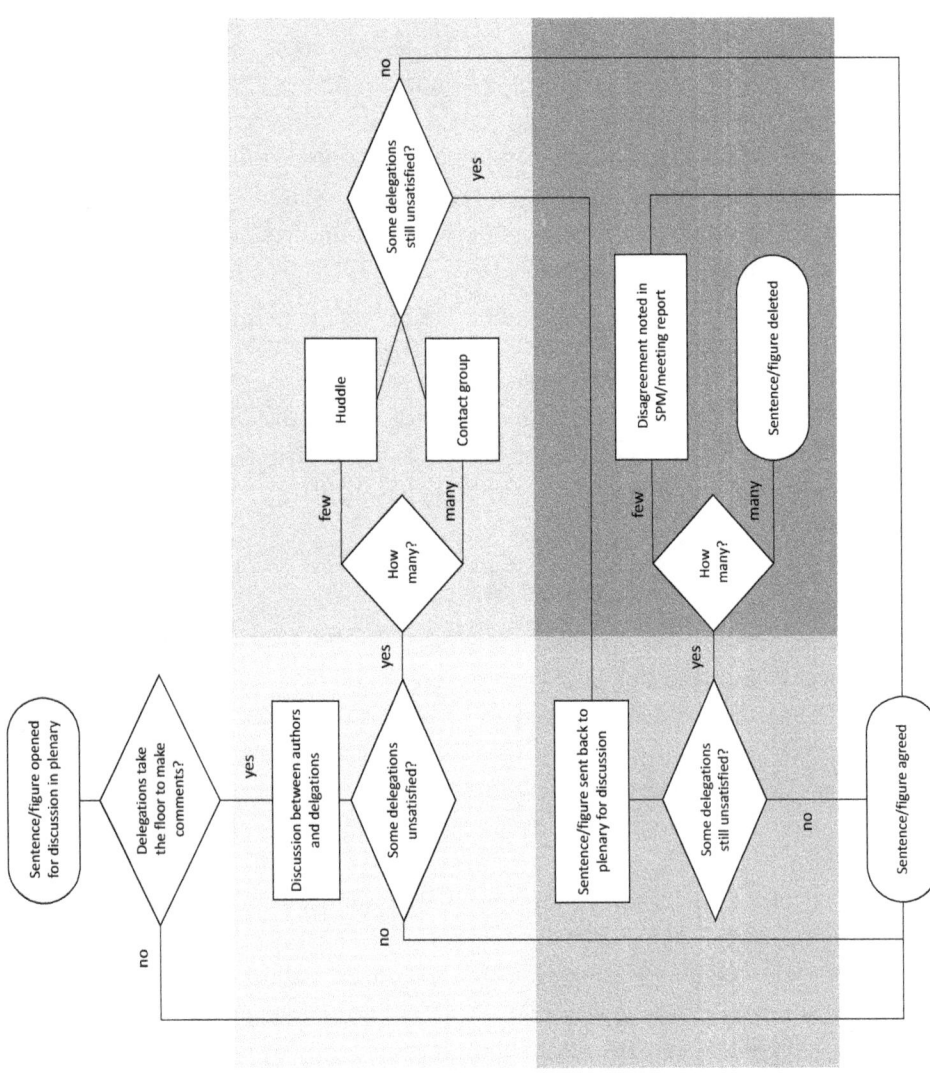

Figure 20.2 Flowchart representing the process of negotiating an SPM sentence or figure. The shades of grey show the level of controversiality. Flowchart produced by the author

The authors and Bureau members use various strategies to respond to governments' comments. They may enjoin governments to respect the voice of the authors or ask for additional time to consider their requests. When an issue cannot be resolved in plenary, the discussion with disagreeing parties is moved to 'a contact group', a formal parallel meeting in a dedicated room, whose proceedings are carefully communicated. Or 'a huddle' may be formed – an informal meeting, decided on the spot, which generally takes place in the back of the plenary or in the corridors. The choice of one or the other of these devices is made at the discretion of the chair of the session and depends on the number of disagreeing parties. Contact groups are chaired by two government delegates – one from a developed country and one from a developing country – mandated to remain neutral and bring parties to an agreement. They can span several days and generally multiply towards the end of the week. When a consensus is found, it is brought back to the plenary and accepted.

When a compromise consistent with the position of the authors *cannot* be found, the IPCC procedures allow for the diverging views to be acknowledged in the document, for example in a footnote. Government delegates are, however, reluctant to be publicly named in the SPMs and generally request to see their reservations expressed in the minutes of the session. Governments may also consensually agree to delete the contentious issues from the document, a decision that generally creates great frustration among the authors. John Broome (2020), for example, recalls a moment in which a paragraph on climate justice in the AR5 Synthesis Report came close to being deleted by governments. Yet, when the authors threatened to resign from the process, 'this made the delegates suddenly more cooperative. They did not really want us to go. Consequently, agreement was reached following some shuttle diplomacy between the two camps the next day' (Broome, 2020: 105).

Closure is reached when silence fills the room, in the absence of delegates asking for the floor. It reflects their agreement to let a document stand as the position of the group and the 'suspension of disagreement ... signalled by the absence of objections to a consensus proposal' (Moore, 2017: 127). Once approved, the SPMs become a 'black box' that masks the disagreements that went into the deliberations. Their conclusions are widely disseminated in the media, through outreach events in different countries and at UNFCCC side events (see **Chapters 22** and **26**). In the UNFCCC, they are discussed in the Subsidiary Body of Scientific and Technological Advice (SBSTA) and in other ad hoc mechanisms – for example, in the Structured Expert Dialogue (SED). Yet, agreement on *which* conclusions to identify as most relevant for the UNFCCC and *how* they should be integrated in decisions of the Conference of the Parties (COP) is generally difficult to reach (Lahn & Sundqvist, 2017).

20.4 Approval as Output

In general, the approval of the SPMs is deemed necessary by many participants and researchers for whom such a process reflects a delicate exercise of co-production between scientists and government representatives to produce 'usable knowledge' (Haas & Stevens, 2011). There is no doubt that it generally helps increase its policy relevance and speak to a wide range of perspectives. At the same time, questions have been raised about the implications of the approval on the framing of climate change. In the early work of the IPCC, observers have documented numerous attempts by Saudi Arabia and the United States to focus the debate on the remaining uncertainties related to anthropogenic climate change in order to delay action (Franz, 1998). It has also been suggested that governments may seek to weaken the language of the SPMs by inserting vague and consensual terms, caveats and qualifications that render statements too generic.

Social scientists have also drawn attention to the 'epistemic selectivity' (Vadrot, 2017: 69) at play in intergovernmental expert bodies – the dominance of 'specific forms of knowledge, problem perceptions, and narratives over others' – and to the tendency to put forward a global and technical framing of environmental problems. It has been suggested that governments contribute, as much as scientists, to presenting an abstract and global story of climate change, which downplays more regional and local information and asymmetries (Livingston et al., 2018). Such language also avoids implicating actors or sectors and contributes to framing climate change in a non-political manner (Victor, 2015). Researchers have also challenged the tendency of some governments to privilege a technical framing of climate solutions by down-playing the political feasibility and socio-economic implications of certain technologies (Fogel, 2005).

Finally, social scientists have elucidated the challenges that the IPCC faces when introducing issues that have implications for the UNFCCC, because governments are unlikely to accept statements that could compromise their positions. For example, in the approval of the AR5 WGIII SPM, conflicts arose over a graph showing anthropogenic greenhouse gas emissions aggregated by country-income groups (Victor et al., 2014) and a paragraph on the effectiveness of the Kyoto Protocol (Stavins, 2014). Both examples carried important implications for the ongoing negotiations of the Paris Agreement that several governments did not want reflected in the SPM. In response to the controversy, authors shared this frustrating experience, suggesting that the SPM had become a summary *by* policymakers rather than a summary *for* them (Wible, 2014).

20.5 Achievements and Challenges

The endorsement of IPCC's reports by its member states and, in particular, the approval of their SPMs, is a unique institutional feature of the organisation. It is undeniably one of the main reasons for the IPCC's high legitimacy among policymakers. Because of the perceived success of the IPCC as a science–policy interface, several other global environmental assessments have adopted a similar framework. Both IPBES and UNEP (in its Global Environmental Outlook) submit SPMs for the approval of their member states.

At the same time, as this chapter shows, social scientists have increasingly highlighted the limits of these governmentally negotiated documents. First, the approval of key scientific conclusions does not mean that governments accept them and will take more informed decisions. For instance, following the approval of the Special Report on Global Warming of 1.5 °C (SR15), the United States – under the administration of Donald J. Trump – requested to insert in the report of the meeting a statement noting that the 'approval of the SPM ... should not be understood as U.S. endorsement of all of the findings and key messages included in the SPM' (IPCC, 2018c: 16). Later, at COP24, the United States, with Saudi Arabia, Kuwait and Russia, opposed 'welcoming' the report out of concern that it could be used to call for more stringent action.

Second, despite its intergovernmental nature, the IPCC has increasingly been struggling with meeting the multiple information needs of policymakers. On the one hand, IPCC reports tend to produce decontextualised knowledge that is difficult to translate at the national, regional and local levels. On the other hand, by shying away from some of the most relevant (geo)political aspects of climate change, they may contribute to supporting the international status quo and the ossification of the UNFCCC. In that context, the policy-relevance of the IPCC has been questioned. Interestingly, however, other actors, and civil society groups in particular, have started to leverage the political status of the SPMs, using them for instance as legal evidence in climate change litigation.

Social and political pressure on the IPCC is likely to intensify in the context of an increased interest in solutions to climate change. If the IPCC is to meet these challenges and remain policy-relevant, it will need to rethink how governmental approval is produced. Several researchers have proposed giving more visibility to the individual chapters of the WG reports and to the Technical Summaries, whose language and scope is less likely to have been tuned down (Victor et al., 2014). Others (Hulme et al., 2010; Victor, 2015) have suggested that the most controversial political questions should be addressed in parallel processes independent from the IPCC and from governmental influence.

Three Key Readings

Broome, J. (2020). Philosophy in the IPCC. Chapter 7 in: Brister, E. and Frodeman, R. (eds.), *A Guide to Field Philosophy Case Studies and Practical Strategies.* London: Routledge. pp. 95–110.

   This chapter provides a witty account of the IPCC approval process from the perspective of a philosopher involved as Lead Author.

De Pryck, K. (2021). Intergovernmental expert consensus in the making: the case of the Summary for Policy Makers of the IPCC 2014 Synthesis Report. *Global Environmental Politics*, 21(1): 108–129. http://doi.org/10.1162/glep_a_00574

   This chapter draws on ethnographic methods to study the SPM approval process, using the case of the IPCC AR5 Synthesis Report.

Hughes, H. and Vadrot, A. B. M. (2019). IPBES and the struggle over biocultural diversity. *Global Environmental Politics*, 19(2): 14–37. http://doi.org/10.1162/glep_a_00503

   This chapter provides a detailed analysis of the SPM approval process in the IPBES and draws parallels with the IPCC.

21

Policy Relevance and Neutrality

MARTIN MAHONY

Overview

This chapter reviews the history of the efforts of the Intergovernmental Panel on Climate Change (IPCC) to achieve and maintain policy relevance while remaining policy-neutral and staying far away from 'policy prescriptiveness'. The chapter argues that the boundaries between policy relevance, neutrality and prescriptiveness are a practical achievement – they must be constantly negotiated as the science and politics of climate change evolve. The chapter uses historical case studies to illustrate this point, such as the controversy over the so-called 'burning embers' diagram. It ends by discussing recent debates about the IPCC's new role in the post-Paris Agreement policy landscape. While IPCC actors call for greater policy relevance, observers and critics contend that the IPCC will always and inevitably be policy-prescriptive, even if on a tacit and unintentional level. Achieving even greater policy relevance may therefore mean jettisoning or modifying the aspiration to be policy-neutral.

21.1 Introduction

> Because of its scientific and intergovernmental nature, the IPCC embodies a unique opportunity to provide rigorous and balanced scientific information to decision makers. By endorsing the IPCC reports, governments acknowledge the authority of their scientific content. The work of the organisation is therefore policy-relevant and yet policy-neutral, never policy-prescriptive.
>
> — IPCC (2013b)

For anyone with an interest in the history of scientific objectivity, authority and science-politics relations, there's a lot going on in the above self-description of the IPCC's status and *modus operandi*. The institution is both *scientific* and *governmental* by nature, concerned both with understanding the world and with governing it, and thus must presumably negotiate the occasional contradictions of those natures. The scientific information it offers is both *rigorous* – it offers the very highest quality of analysis – and *balanced* – it accounts for various interpretations and arguments, some of which presumably will be less rigorous than others. And the process of governmental *endorsement* is a performative demonstration of states' deferment to scientific expertise in offering the most *authoritative* description of the world under climate change, even where those descriptions may have profound implications that run contrary to some states' self-interests.

All these sources of potential tension lay behind the IPCC's oft-quoted mantra of being policy-relevant but policy-neutral, never policy-prescriptive. The IPCC offers a science that describes and predicts potential policy problems, and that increasingly evaluates the impacts of different policy options. But it offers a science that is neutral when it comes to political choice. The IPCC won't tell you what to do, just that something needs to be done, and that there is a range of possible things that you might do (Havstad & Brown, 2017). But working at these many interlinking boundaries – between description and prescription, knowing and governing, rigour and balance, scientific authoritativeness and real-world relevance – is neither easy nor straightforward. Indeed, the policing of these boundaries is arguably a defining feature of all the various disputes and controversies that have punctuated the IPCC's history to date (see **Chapter 16**).

This chapter reviews and summarises studies of the IPCC's efforts to navigate the relevance/neutrality boundary. Most of this research is informed by science and technology studies (STS), a field which largely offers its own consensus that science and politics (or policy) cannot be neatly separated and that values, norms and interests structure scientific work in similar ways to how they shape political decision-making. STS scholars would therefore conclude that defining a science–policy boundary is a *practical* achievement – something which must be continually worked at, as situations and contexts change.

21.2 Beyond 'Truth to Power': Fashioning Policy Relevance

From the outset, the IPCC moved beyond a model of science–policy interaction by which an autonomous science 'speaks truth' to a separate, political domain of 'power' (see **Chapter 2**). The IPCC has, since its founding, created and operated within a uniquely 'hybrid' space of science and policy, where problem framings, the selection of relevant questions and foci, modes of assessing reliability (**Chapter 11**), expressing uncertainty (**Chapter 17**) and communicating findings (**Chapters 25** and **26**) have been the product of negotiation between scientists and policymakers (**Chapters 9** and **20**). Although much copied since, the IPCC was for many years unique in following this hybrid model in producing regular global environmental assessments. But the nature of this hybridity has changed over time.

Over its first assessment cycle (1988–1990), this science–policy hybridity was particularly intense, and the IPCC was essentially *the* global setting for negotiating both the science and politics of climate change. In the First Assessment Report (AR1), Working Group III (WGIII) was a space for debating policy alternatives, whereas its next manifestation in 1995 became the more prosaically framed 'Economic and Social Dimensions of Climate Change'. Several developing countries expressed dissatisfaction at the first report's ambiguous positioning at the science–policy boundary, and were wary of the IPCC, with its numerical dominance of participants from the global North (see **Chapter 7**), becoming the chief setting where a climate policy architecture would be worked out (Miller, 2009). The Intergovernmental Negotiating Committee (INC) was therefore established in 1990, and was the institutional setting for the drafting of the UN Framework Convention on Climate Change (UNFCCC) (Bodansky, 2001). This act of boundary making subsequently strengthened the IPCC's self-identification as a scientific body, with a clear 'firewall' established between policy relevance and policy neutrality.

Beginning with the Second Assessment Report (AR2), new modes of fostering policy relevance were developed. Government representatives took on a larger role in the review process, and the processes for producing a Synthesis Report (SYR) and Summary for Policymakers (SPM) were formalised (see **Chapter 3**). The SYR offered an interdisciplinary, policy-relevant synthesis of the three WG reports and, Shaw (2005) contends, acted as a firewall between the science-facing WG chapters and the more policy-oriented SPM. Parts of the assessment process were increasingly pointed towards the requirements of the COP – such as Article 2 of the UNFCCC and the definition of dangerous anthropogenic interference (DAI) with the climate system (Oppenheimer & Petsonk, 2005). In the AR3 report (2001), attempts were made to further enhance the policy relevance of the SYR by including a number of 'policy-relevant scientific questions' (PRSQs). The intention was to draw policymakers not just into the review and approval of the provisioned information, but into the process of framing the very questions addressed. But as Shaw (2005) reports, the process of defining the PRSQs was fairly ad-hoc, involving just a select number of national governments.

This trajectory of the IPCC seeking to further increase the policy relevance of its assessment products, while strengthening both the internal and external boundaries between science and policy, has continued to date. It extends to the much-heralded 'solution-oriented' turn (Kowarsch & Jabbour, 2017) and to the increased regularity of 'special reports', some of which – like that on the implications of 1.5 °C of global warming (SR15) – have been very directly mandated and framed by policymakers (Livingston & Rummukainen, 2020). Later in this chapter, we will return to these recent developments; what follows next is an exploration of how the pursuit of ever more policy relevance has always been accompanied by contestations and struggles over the boundaries of relevance, neutrality and prescriptiveness.

21.3 Policing the Boundaries

In the Third Assessment Report (AR3), a new way of visually engaging with the possible definition of DAI was developed by the authors of WGII, Chapter 19. The 'burning embers' diagram offered a visual depiction of authors' estimates of when different impacts would occur at different levels of temperature rise (for an example, see Figure 25.3 in **Chapter 25**). The blurred colours were intended to convey the inevitable uncertainties involved in aggregating already-uncertain knowledge about regional impacts to a global scale, and to convey the role that 'expert judgement' (see Mach et al., 2017) played in evaluating the significance and meaning of findings in the scientific literature.

The diagram was intended to be policy-relevant in the sense of furnishing policymakers with information by which they could come to their own judgements as to the meaning of DAI. Interviews with the diagram's creators revealed the complex, and not always consensual, intersection of epistemic, aesthetic and 'value' judgements.[1] Ultimately the diagram was designed to separate the primarily *epistemic* judgements of the authors from the subsequent *normative* judgements to be made by policymakers with the diagram's assistance. But this distinction was challenged in the review process, most notably by government representatives. A reviewer for the US government suggested that the implication that there was enough scientific evidence to inform a judgement of DAI was itself far too close to being policy-prescriptive, while other reviewers thought the diagram offered far too conservative a view of when dangerous impacts might begin. The subsequent AR4 version of this chapter met with similar issues. For a US reviewer, the whole thing was far too normative and prescriptive, even verging on the 'theological'. In contrast, for a German reviewer, the chapter needed to engage much more closely with the emerging political discourse around 2 °C as being an appropriate threshold of DAI, and thus serving as a policy target (Mahony, 2015). In the draft AR5 version of the burning embers figure, a much closer engagement with both 2 °C and 1.5 °C targets was proposed, but at the government plenary where approval was sought for the SPM, the 'UK, supported by Slovenia, proposed removing all dotted lines so as to appear scientifically neutral' (IISD, 2014: 12).

Throughout the history of the burning embers diagram, which has become 'a cornerstone of the IPCC assessments' (O'Neill et al., 2017: 28), the authors were praised by some for consistently acknowledging the role of 'value judgements'. For others, however, the presence of such judgements in any form ran counter to the IPCC's stated mission to be policy-neutral. For such critics, even venturing a possible definition of DAI constituted unwelcome policy prescriptiveness. These tussles can be interpreted as instances of 'boundary work' – the social processes whereby distinctions are drawn between science and non-science (Gieryn, 1999). Conventionally, 'boundary work' has been seen as something done by scientists to maintain their own intellectual authority and autonomy. In boundary organisations like the IPCC however, boundary work is something engaged in by both scientific and policy participants, in struggles to stabilise an ever-moving field of scientific and political facts and arguments, and to retain the respective autonomy of zones of scientific and political reasoning.

One lesson of the burning embers example – and of comparable cases discussed in **Chapter 24** – is that different conceptions of where the science/policy (or relevant/neutral/prescriptive) boundary lies exist in different policy communities. In relation to the burning embers, Jasanoff's notion of civic epistemology can help interpret the wildly diverging views of different government representatives (see Chapter 23). Sociotechnical controversies in the United States and Germany, for example, reveal very different ideas about where science ends and politics begins (also Jasanoff, 2011b). The challenge for an international body like the IPCC is that there is no universally accepted definition of that distinction. The IPCC is a space where international actors engage in constant negotiation over how to bring science and policy together, and how to produce policy-relevant knowledge that does not stray into the realm of policy prescription. IPCC statements and representatives may allude to an apparently universal definition of where the boundaries lie. But the IPCC's history of practically managing science–policy interactions shows that drawing a line between science and policy, relevance and neutrality, is a product of negotiation within particular contexts. The line can never be settled once and for all, and more negotiation will always be required as contexts change.

21.4 Incredible Futures: From Relevance to Performativity?

The political world after the Paris Agreement of 2015 is very different: countries are busy deliberating their own Nationally Determined Contributions (NDCs) to the mitigation effort, as well as trying to think about adaptation at more local scales (see **Chapter 22**). Thus, the meaning of policy relevance for the IPCC is undergoing some quite radical changes (Lahn, 2018), and the intensification of mitigation debates has put the economics-heavy work of WGIII in the spotlight (Hughes & Paterson, 2017). WGIII participants have themselves become active participants in debates about the future of solution-oriented global environmental assessments (GEAs), most notably former WGIII Co-Chair Ottmar Edenhofer in his collaborations with philosopher Martin Kowarsch. They have argued that GEAs have a duty to provide much better knowledge of the implications and co-benefits of different policy choices, and to better accommodate diverse normative viewpoints. These authors say that the IPCC needs to reach out beyond conventional national government audiences to the diverse array of actors that make up the new landscape of polycentric climate governance. They contend that IPCC authors can work as 'map-makers' and 'cartographers of pathways', helping policymakers to think about different routes to intended policy outcomes – like keeping global warming to 1.5 °C or 2 °C – and to think through the interdependencies of policy goals, means and outcomes (Edenhofer & Kowarsch, 2015).

Edenhofer and Kowarsch's model recognises that maintaining policy relevance will require the IPCC – or at least parts of it – to engage more readily with thorny normative and political questions. They do not propose that the IPCC become 'policy-prescriptive', but rather that policy relevance be maintained through ever-closer engagement with the goals and values of policymakers and diverse stakeholders. Much of the earlier controversial work of the IPCC sought to help policymakers identify policy goals, such as not exceeding a point of DAI. Now, however, knowledge controversies are more likely to rage around pathways to pre-agreed policy outcomes (see **Chapter 15**).

Following the publication of AR5 several commentators criticised the inclusion of speculative 'negative emission technologies' (NETs) like bioenergy with carbon capture and storage (BECCS) in modelled pathways prepared for the assessments. For Oliver Geden, Kevin Anderson and others, this was evidence of the modelling community, which underpinned the work of WGIII, trying to keep policymakers engaged by telling them what they wanted to hear – that their targets were still achievable despite the continued lack of real mitigation effort (Anderson, 2015; Geden, 2015). By loading the models with *deus ex machina* technologies that would, at some point in the future, come along and save the day, policy goals could be retained while the means and outcomes of the pathways to them changed radically. For some, this represented an abnegation of scientific integrity; for others, the presence of speculative technologies in authoritative mitigation scenarios raised another prospect – that of the 'performativity' of scenarios and forecasts.

While the inclusion of high levels of BECCS may not have been an overt *prescription* by WGIII authors – i.e., a statement of 'this is what the world should do' – perhaps it could nonetheless become a self-fulfilling prophecy. Sociologists of science and technology have long observed that visions of the future can become self-fulfilling by shaping what is deemed to be possible and desirable, by directing funding decisions, and lending an air of credibility to what otherwise might be considered speculation (Merton, 1948). Economic theory and forecasts have been noted to be particularly performative, with public policy used to shape markets and societies such that positive forecasts come true. The real world is increasingly shaped by the concepts and principles of mainstream economics, rather than the other way around. It is the supposed 'neutrality' of economics as a science that gives it the authority to exercise such world-making power (MacKenzie, 2006).

In the climate context, theoretical technologies like BECCS have, since 2015, increasingly been positioned in national policy scenarios and toolkits (e.g. National Grid, 2021). This seemingly bears out the idea that BECCS, as an illustrative possible means to a certain end in IPCC scenarios, has come to be seen as indispensable to achieving certain ends. It appears as a fully-fledged policy option under consideration by powerful actors, even if the technology may be unproven and lacking societal consent (Beck & Mahony, 2018b).

The inclusion of BECCS-heavy low-emission scenarios in AR5 was a laudable attempt to keep the possible 'solution space' for policymakers as open as possible, in line with the principles proposed by Edenhofer and Kowarsch (2015). However, Beck and Oomen (2021) argue that in pursuing its role as a 'map-maker', the IPCC has also functioned as a 'corridor-maker'. It has limited ideas of possible routes to predefined emissions goals to a series of consensually agreed and scientifically authoritative pathways. The concern is that in relying on technologies that can pass the economic sniff-tests of integrated assessment modelling, other, more radical policy options may be left off the table. Many are now asking how assessments like the IPCC can instead broaden the solution space in a way which goes beyond those solutions deemed feasible within economic models designed to tend towards global economic optimisation (Kear, 2016; Pielke Jr, 2018). What if, to deal with decarbonisation properly, the rules of mainstream economics, and of political and social feasibility, need rewriting? What would that mean for the IPCC?

The integrated assessment community is starting to explore scenarios that unsettle the assumption that economic growth should be a default policy goal (O'Neill et al., 2020). In assessing such scenarios the IPCC could further expand the possible solution space. But with economic growth being such a powerful default public policy (Barry, 2021), would this be to the detriment of policy relevance and credibility? By challenging – or at least questioning – some basic political-economic assumptions, the IPCC will inevitably attract criticism for being too normative or prescriptive, or maybe even 'theological'. But as the IPCC seeks policy relevance in a polycentric climate governance context, and as it aims to pivot from identifying the climate change problem to assessing solutions, it will need to increasingly engage with thorny normative and political questions (Maas et al., 2021). Indeed, Noel Castree and colleagues recently called for a new mode of GEA that is openly political, offering 'visibility to a wide range of worldviews', particularly those which would challenge the base assumptions of other worldviews, such as the nature of power, what counts as valid argumentation, and the desirability of endless economic growth (Castree et al., 2021: 72). Remaining 'neutral' in such a context would be impossible – indeed remaining so would *itself* be an exercise of power, an unspoken backing for a certain way of thinking about and organising the world (Delvenne & Parotte, 2019).

21.5 Achievements and Challenges

The IPCC has often been accused by reviewers and critics of being 'too political' and 'alarmist', and of not sticking to a sober deliberation of scientific facts (Shaw & Robinson, 2004). Others have observed that the push for consensus and rigorous assessment has sometimes undermined the policy relevance of reports. For example, reflecting on the exclusion of more extreme, but highly uncertain, projections of future sea-level rise (SLR) from the AR4 WGI report, Oppenheimer et al. (2007) argued that the IPCC was doing policymakers a disservice (see Box 19.1). Surely those charged with governing coastlines and littoral cities would want to know about 'high-magnitude' potential events – like an SLR of 7 metres or more – no matter how unlikely the best models may currently say they might be (see also **Chapter 17**). In a later paper, Brysse et al. (2013) looked across a range of IPCC projections and argued that the knowledge-making structures and processes of the IPCC mean that the reports tend to 'err on the side of least drama'. Avoiding scientific and political 'hot potatoes', in a bid to preserve scientific credibility and authority, means that information that may be highly relevant to policymakers can be excluded because of its uncertain or controversial nature. As the IPCC strives towards ever more policy relevance, it runs up not only against its own policy of remaining neutral, but also against its other practices for maintaining credibility and authority, such as consensus-seeking (see **Chapter 19**).

The distinction between policy relevance and neutrality may seem straightforward in theory, but it is something that must be worked out continuously in practice. Stabilising the boundary between science and policy is always a practical, context-bound achievement – a product of ongoing negotiations between IPCC authors, reviewers and government representatives. The IPCC can claim some success in stabilising this boundary sufficiently over time such that its reports continue to be considered a scientific gold standard as well as having demonstrable policy impact. But the IPCC and the communities that constitute it will need to reflect on the new political context of climate change, and on the challenge of the relevance and neutrality of IPCC reports being in more direct tension as the organisation pivots towards a more solution-oriented and risk-management framing of its assessments (see **Chapter 18**).

Rather than simply seeking relevance to policy and policymakers, perhaps the IPCC should take as a guiding mantra the enlargement of the solution space, for example through engaging with a wider range of scenarios of, and pathways to, global sustainability (O'Neill et al., 2020). Through this and other means the IPCC could build relevance with diverse stakeholders and publics, while helpfully laying the foundations for informed democratic debates about the broad suite of policy options available for limiting the trajectory and impacts of global warming. The challenge here would be to reconcile new tensions between relevance and neutrality. Perhaps enlarging the scope of the former is worth the cost of jettisoning some of the latter.

Note

1 'We were looking at the evidence and then using value judgements, and portraying that by being cloudy and making the colours sort of mesh into each other'; another: 'We changed things to a bit more red than we actually had agreed on, but everybody was so exhausted of fighting about this' (quoted in Mahony, 2015: 157–159).

Three Key Readings

Beck, S. and Mahony, M. (2018). The IPCC and the new map of science and politics. *WIREs: Climate Change*, 9(6): e494. http://doi.org/10.1002/wcc.547

  This paper reconstructs the history of 'boundary work' within and around the IPCC, and describes the new challenges the IPCC is likely to face in an evolving climate policy landscape.

Edenhofer, O. and Kowarsch, M. (2015). Cartography of pathways: a new model for environmental policy assessments. *Environmental Science & Policy*, 51: 56–64. http://doi.org/10.1016/j.envsci.2015.03.017

  This paper succinctly describes the 'IPCC-as-map-maker' approach to reconciling the competing demands of policy relevance and neutrality.

Havstad, J. C. and Brown, M. J. (2017). Neutrality, relevance, prescription, and the IPCC. *Public Affairs Quarterly*, 31(4): 303–324. http://doi.org/10.2307/44732800

  This paper argues that the IPCC's stated goal of being 'policy-neutral' can be interpreted in many different ways, some of which have generated misunderstandings and damaged the IPCC's credibility. The authors argue that being non-prescriptive is a better characterisation of the IPCC's overall mandate.

Part V

Influence

The final part of the book explores the influence of the work of the Intergovernmental Panel on Climate Change (IPCC) on different audiences. **Rolf Lidskog** and **Göran Sundqvist** (Chapter 22) review the different ways in which the IPCC has had influence on international and domestic decision-making processes, and the extent of this influence in the post-Paris context. **Jean Carlos Hochsprung Miguel** and **colleagues** (Chapter 23) examine this same question using the concept of 'civic epistemology', which helps to explain the different ways in which IPCC reports are perceived in different national political cultures. They in particular show how the legitimacy and credibility of the IPCC is context-dependent. **Bård Lahn** (Chapter 24) uses the idea of 'boundary objects' to also explore the successes and limits of the IPCC's influence over different political actors and institutions, using examples of objects that circulate between the IPCC and the UN Framework Convention on Climate Change (UNFCCC). **Irene Lorenzoni** and **Jordan Harold** (Chapter 25) explore the production, role and efficacy of IPCC 'visuals' as a means of communicating climate change to different audiences. **Warren Pearce** and **August Lindemer** (Chapter 26) pursue this question about the effectiveness of IPCC communications by examining the IPCC's communication strategy and the appropriation of IPCC reports by different publics. The final chapter of this section offers a more personalised view of the IPCC's influence and its future. **Clark Miller** (Chapter 27) takes a broader view of the production of global knowledge for policy and its related challenges, and offers a proposal of what the IPCC should evolve into over future decades.

22

Political Context

ROLF LIDSKOG AND GÖRAN SUNDQVIST

Overview

The explicit aim of the Intergovernmental Panel on Climate Change (IPCC) is to influence policymaking. By synthesising research on climate change and presenting it to policymakers, the IPCC tries to meet its self-imposed goal of being policy-relevant and policy-neutral, but not policy-prescriptive. The hallmark of the IPCC has been to offer a strong scientific voice demonstrating the necessity of climate policy and action, but without giving firm political advice. Yet scholars have contested the idea of maintaining such a strong boundary between science and policy in the IPCC, questioning whether upholding this boundary has been successful and whether continuing to do so offers a viable way forward. The Paris Agreement provides a new political context for the IPCC, implying a need for solution-oriented assessments. The IPCC itself has also argued that large-scale transformations of society are needed to meet the targets set by the Agreement. To be relevant and influence policymaking in this new political context, the IPCC needs to provide policy advice.

22.1 Introduction

The IPCC is a political organisation in the sense that its assessment reports are designed, decided upon and approved by national governments. Its ambition, however, is to determine the state of knowledge on climate change, and this knowledge assessment is undertaken by researchers. An additional aim of the IPCC is to perform this scholarly work in a way that is policy-relevant (see **Chapter 21**). This mainly means being relevant for political negotiations and decision-making under the UN Framework Convention on Climate Change (UNFCCC), which constitutes the primary political context for the IPCC. Hence the two organisations mutually influence each other.

An early study by Agrawala (1998b) qualifies the discussion on political influence by making a distinction between *process* and *outcome*. He argued that the IPCC had been influential in terms of process – generating and maintaining societal interest and concern regarding climate change – but also in terms of outcome. Without the IPCC, neither the UNFCCC nor the Kyoto Protocol, with its binding agreements on emission reductions, would have been possible. Furthermore, the many lobby groups funded by the fossil fuel industry and devoted to finding weaknesses in the IPCC reports are (indirect) evidence that the IPCC has influenced policy and politics (Agrawala, 1998b: 639–640).

Other researchers have, however, questioned these conclusions, stressing that it is difficult to distinguish cause from effect when so many factors other than knowledge influence climate policies (Grundmann, 2006). De Pryck (2018) argues that unilateral causal connections between the IPCC assessments and climate policies are claimed rather than shown, and that this *assumed* influence is an important part of the IPCC's self-image. It is far too simple to claim that the IPCC's First Assessment Report (AR1) in 1990 (AR1) led to the formation of the Convention (1992), the Second in 1995 (AR2) to the Kyoto Protocol, the Third in 2001 (AR3) to a focus on climate adaptation, the Fourth in 2007 (AR4) to the 2 °C target, and the Fifth in 2013/2014 (AR5) to the Paris Agreement. This oversimplified view of how science influences policy is based on a unidirectional linear model in which scientific knowledge constrains and guides policy actors.

In this chapter we present the political context of the IPCC. This context is external to the Panel, but is also an inherent and crucial factor in the design of its activities. We are therefore critical of a linear understanding of the IPCC's work, because it separates science from policy and politics, and assumes that knowledge is a necessary prerequisite for political action (Beck, 2011a; Lidskog & Sundqvist, 2015; Mahony & Hulme, 2018). Nevertheless, a linear understanding of the interplay between science and policy is an important part of the IPCC's self-conception, and is also presupposed by many commentators (Sundqvist et al., 2018). Contrary to the linear model, we hold that the work of the IPCC involves ongoing, close interaction between science and policy – something which, instead of being denied, should be fully acknowledged.

This contribution begins by presenting the relationship between the IPCC and the UNFCCC and its Paris Agreement. We argue that the Paris Agreement constitutes a new political context for the IPCC and thus imposes new conditions for how scientific knowledge can influence policy and political decision-making (see **Chapter 18**). We then analyse this new situation through one of the IPCC's best-known reports: the 1.5 °C report published in 2018 (hereafter SR15) and its demand for transformative change to meet the political goal of limiting global warming to 1.5 °C. To what extent does the IPCC influence policies and politics when the crucial political task is more about initiating and governing transformative change than creating awareness of climate threats? We finally discuss our results in relation to the IPCC's ambition of not being policy-prescriptive, which means not giving advice to policymakers.

22.2 Solution-oriented Assessments

The use of synthesised assessments is well established today and characterises the international policy landscape on global environmental issues. These global environmental assessments (GEAs) have increased in scope and complexity over time, both in terms of content and focus. A survey shows a large increase in the amount of assessed material, as well as in the number of experts involved in the assessment work. This trend toward increased complexity in content and focus has been described as a shift from scientific evaluations to solution-oriented assessments (from GEAs to SOAs) (Edenhofer & Kowarsch, 2015; Jabbour & Flachsland, 2017). SOAs require more explicit treatment of the values, objectives and assessments of policy proposals, which makes them more obviously political than GEAs (Haas, 2017; Castree et al., 2021). The IPCC is no exception to this trend.

A radical change in the political context of the IPCC occurred with the adoption of the Paris Agreement in 2015. The Agreement stipulates that signatories must work to keep global warming below 2 °C whilst 'pursuing efforts' to limit the temperature increase to 1.5 °C. As part of the Agreement, the IPCC was asked to compile a Special Report on Global Warming of 1.5 °C (2018) (SR15), comparing the effects of temperature increases of 1.5 and 2 °C, and describing possible ways to achieve these goals. The Panel accepted this request, even though the task was more specified than usual for the IPCC (see **Chapter 5**). The requested report was solution-oriented; its aim was to present possible ways to achieve the temperature target. Yet there was not much research to compile; few studies had been conducted on possible ways to reach the 1.5 °C target (Hulme, 2016; Livingston & Rummukainen, 2020).

The SR15 report states that to achieve the goal, radical measures will be needed, including new technologies (negative emissions technologies, NETs) such as bioenergy with carbon capture and storage (BECCS). However, these technologies have not been tested on a large scale or brought up for political discussion (Beck & Mahony, 2018a). Being commissioned to deliver this special report created a new context for the IPCC, both in terms of knowledge evidence and of policy relevance, and necessitated a substantial change in the Panel's working methods (Ourbak & Tubiana, 2017; Beck & Mahony, 2018a; Livingston et al., 2018). In SR15, the Panel compiled relevant scientific evidence to a lesser extent than in previous assessment reports, and contributed to formulating policy proposals to a greater extent. As a result, the report had a more solution-oriented and prescriptive role, which is strengthened by its strong focus on scenarios – what SR15 calls 'pathways'. When the Panel includes large-scale investments in nuclear power and NETs as important components of many of the presented pathways, this can and will be interpreted as the Panel advocating these technologies.

The IPCC chairman Hoesung Lee has argued strongly for the use of solution-oriented assessments in order to better serve the UNFCCC (Lee, 2015). In practice, however, the IPCC has not taken advantage of this new post-Paris situation in any deeper sense (Hermansen et al., 2021), and it still sticks to its original position of being policy-neutral, not policy-prescriptive.

The challenge for the IPCC is not only to present conclusions with high certainty, or projections derived from scenarios, but also to address controversial policy-relevant topics that demand greater inclusion and involvement of the social sciences. Similarly, Carraro and colleagues claim that the IPCC must become better at evaluating policy options on various scales – subnational, national and international – including alternative options for measuring equity and efficiency (Carraro et al., 2015). However, this emphasis may lead to controversy; few governments would gladly have their policies evaluated by an international panel, and researchers may not be equipped to handle value-laden and politicised questions in the sensitive manner they require. According to Victor (2015), one of the few social scientists who served as a Coordinating Lead Author in AR5, the IPCC's ambition to seek consensus and avoid controversial topics has increasingly made it largely irrelevant to climate policy.

In our estimation, the shift to SOA means that the IPCC needs to present policy options and possible ways forward, i.e., pathways. But it must also assess the feasibility and viability of these pathways in order to provide decision-makers with relevant knowledge. This means that social scientific studies need to be better integrated into the assessment work of the IPCC.

22.3 The National Turn in the Paris Agreement

The basic design of the Paris Agreement consists of two interrelated parts. One is national, and is based on the signatory countries' own voluntary decisions about reducing greenhouse gas emissions – Nationally Determined Contributions, NDCs. The other is global, and sets the common target that the combined measures of the various countries should keep the global average temperature well below 2 °C, and preferably limit it to 1.5 °C.

The Paris Agreement implies a more decentralised global policy regime than previously envisaged, with a national focus and a strong, bottom-up governance system (Jordan et al., 2018; Aykut et al., 2021). After years of conflict over global distribution principles and which countries should reduce their emissions by how much and by what year, it is now up to individual states to set their own climate targets and deliver on them. Complicated international negotiations can no longer be used as an excuse for prevarication at the national level. However, every fifth year (starting in 2023), the NDCs will be globally reviewed in a process called the Global Stocktake of the Paris Agreement.

This national turn shifts the focus towards defining potential pathways for reaching specified goals (Beck & Mahony, 2018a). The IPCC now finds itself in a position where national-level policy processes will be decisive, while the global level will continue to be relevant with the Global Stocktake process ratcheting up national ambitions. Of great importance is how the IPCC can fulfil its mandate and remain policy-relevant in this more complex, polycentric and nationally oriented post-Paris policy terrain, where the responses to climate change are becoming more diverse (Hermansen et al., 2021). As argued earlier, in this situation characterised by a national turn, the IPCC will have to give more thought to how to support and inspire ongoing work on national and regional levels (Carraro et al., 2015; Victor, 2015; Livingston et al., 2018; see also Hulme et al., 2010). The need for this kind of support will increase, as exemplified by NGO initiatives such as 'Climate Action Tracker', 'Climate Analytics' and 'Climate Interactive'.

In line with the design of the Paris Agreement, it is mainly at the national level that decisions will be taken that can make the IPCC's knowledge relevant and thereby increase its ability to influence climate policy. An important reason why the UNFCCC invited the IPCC to produce SR15 in the first place was to 'inform the preparation of nationally determined contributions' (UNFCCC, 2015: §20), and SR15 is accordingly expected to support policy formation at the national level, in line with post-Paris global climate policy. Thus, there is a strong link between the Paris Agreement's national turn and the SR15 report, something which the IPCC has not reflected on to any greater extent. In our view, the IPCC needs to become more self-aware of its important role of providing support, including advice, to ongoing and future national climate-transformation efforts.

22.4 The IPCC on Transformative Change

The topic of transformation, or transformative societal change, in response to climate change has increasingly attracted research attention in the social sciences (O'Brien, 2012; Linnér & Wibeck, 2019). It has been argued that the IPCC plays an instrumental role in producing the visions of societal change used by those arguing for its necessity (Beck et al., 2021). In SR15, it is explicitly claimed that 'limiting global warming to 1.5 °C would require substantial societal and technological transformations' in terms of energy production, land use (agriculture and food), urban infrastructure (transport and buildings) and industrial systems

(IPCC, 2018a: 56). It also states that the work of achieving a resilient future is fraught with complex moral, practical and political difficulties and inevitable trade-offs.

SR15 presents a manifold of pathways to reach the 1.5 °C target, four of which are selected as illustrative model pathways (IPCC, 2018a: Chapter 2). These involve different portfolios of mitigation measures combined with different implementation challenges, including potential synergies and trade-offs with sustainable development. At the same time, they all presuppose a decoupling of economic growth from energy demand and carbon dioxide emissions, and new low-carbon, zero-carbon or even carbon-negative technologies. The differences between the pathways are presented with the help of global indicators, such as final energy demand, renewable share in electricity, primary energy source, and carbon capture and storage. Thus, the SR15 report strongly stresses the need and opportunity to make changes in energy supply.

When it comes to necessary change in the social and economic order, which is stressed at a general level, the pathways do not propose any radical changes. Societal conditions are only taken into consideration in so far as they enable or obstruct technological development. This is the case for all the different pathways that rely heavily on BECCS, whether they are based on reduced energy demand, include a broad focus on sustainability, or imply intensive use of resources and energy. SR15 states that to implement the pathways it is crucial to strengthen policy instruments, enhance multilevel governance and institutional capacities, and enable technological innovations, climate finance, and lifestyle and behavioural change (IPCC, 2018a: section 4.4). But apart from these sweeping statements, there is no further elaboration on how to create these conditions in relation to different pathways.

SR15 thus exhibits a paradoxical view of transformative change. It stresses its necessity, but in practice places great hope in technological fixes – technical solutions that do not require structural changes in the current economic and social order. The economic and social order is reduced to a resource for facilitating technical innovation. This view is reinforced in the report's discussion of the risks and trade-offs – for the environment, people, regions and sectors – that are associated with the pathways. For example, the novel technology of BECCS is recognised to be unproven and to pose substantial risks for environmental and social sustainability (IPCC, 2018a: 121), but it is considered manageable. It is only *if* BECCS and other NET options are poorly implemented that trade-offs will be required (IPCC, 2018a: 448). Similarly, risks associated with nuclear power (IPCC, 2018a: 461) are mentioned, but nothing is said about whether these should have any bearing on which pathways to choose. Thus, despite the overall stress on trade-offs in the report, there seems to be a strong belief that they will be manageable and will not constitute any substantial obstacles to implementing the pathways. This makes it possible for the IPCC to present risks and trade-offs, while at the same time not according them any implications for the suggested pathways, and thereby not politicising them.

SR15's recommendations – the pathways – have a radical view of technology, putting great faith in future technological innovations, but are conservative in their view of societal change: they do not propose any transformation of the economic and social order. This is remarkable, since no connections are made between technological and social change. For decades, research in the social sciences has stressed the need for *societal* changes and *social* or *socio-ecological* transformation (Díaz et al., 2019), in the sense of fundamentally redirecting social organisation and human activities, including technology. SR15 on the other hand, when presenting possible pathways for limiting global warming, puts its hope in technological innovations isolated from social change. If the IPCC wants to be policy-relevant, it needs to adopt a wider and more comprehensive understanding of transformative change when developing pathways, and conceptualise society as more than just a set of conditions enabling or restricting technological innovation.

We thus find that the IPCC needs to incorporate more profound knowledge about transformative change into its assessments, including a deeper understanding of the mechanisms of social change on different spatial and temporal scales. A prerequisite to being influential is being policy-relevant, and in the post-Paris context this means presenting and assessing different options for how to initiate and facilitate transformative change without losing sight of social factors.

22.5 Achievements and Challenges

The IPCC is undoubtedly one of the most ambitious efforts ever undertaken to develop and communicate science to inform environmental policy globally. Among its greatest successes is its impressive mobilisation of the scientific community to allocate substantial resources – in the form of researchers' time – to produce knowledge syntheses on an urgent issue. Determining whether this mobilisation has influenced policymaking, however, is more difficult. The IPCC has been surprisingly stable in its method of working: making systematic assessments and delivering – on a regular, if not frequent, basis – comprehensive reports that accurately summarise the current state of knowledge. The cornerstone of their work is not to be policy-prescriptive and thereby not to politicise the results. In practice, this means that the IPCC has primarily focused on developing and maintaining its epistemic authority, and only to a very limited extent has been interested in providing guidance to policymakers. However, this strategy is an insufficient way to proceed in the post-Paris political context.

There are several ways to further increase the relevance of the IPCC's work to support national (and thus global) societal transformation. With the shift towards

SOAs and the need for transformative change, the Panel should pay more attention to the socio-political aspects of these extremely demanding challenges, and adopt a deeper understanding of how politics (and society) works. For example, proposed technical innovations and solutions need to be embedded in realistic social conditions, otherwise the pathways will work on paper only. This demands better integration of social science in the IPCC's assessments, which will be a challenge, because the Panel's assessment work is not well-suited for assessing social science with its diverse epistemologies and methodologies. In the post-Paris political context, the Panel should focus more on regional and national contexts to be policy-relevant for national climate policies. This includes emphasising realistic policy options that consider regional and national variation, not least in relation to the development and implementation of technological solutions.

This does not imply that the IPCC needs to be policy-prescriptive in a narrow sense, telling governments what they should do. It is possible to assess studies on transformative change and present policy options – including evaluating their feasibility – without advocating one particular way forward. Social science has a long history of assessing policy development, analysing political experiments and exploring the conditions for transformative change, while not being prescriptive in the sense of giving firm advice. However, assessing such studies will require addressing controversial topics. To increase its policy relevance, the IPCC needs not only to outline possible policy options, but also to provide knowledge about their feasibility and viability. By utilising social science research, the IPCC can assess different options, which in fact means to give policy advice.

Three Key Readings

Castree, N., Bellamy, R. and Osaka, S. (2021). The future of global environmental assessments: making a case for fundamental change. *The Anthropocene Review*, 8(1): 56–82. http://doi.org/10.1177/2053019620971664

This article gives an overview of global environmental assessments and proposes a fundamental change of them in order to be of political relevance.

Hermansen, E. A. T., Lahn, B., Sundqvist, G. and Øye, E. (2021). Post-Paris policy relevance: lessons from the IPCC SR15 process. *Climatic Change*, 169(7): 1–18. http://doi.org/10.1007/s10584–021-03210-0

This article concludes with a set of empirically grounded recommendations for how the IPCC may approach its goal of policy relevance after the Paris Agreement and the IPCC SR15.

Linnér, B.-O. and Wibeck, V. (2019). *Sustainability Transformations: Agents and Drivers Across Societies*. Cambridge: Cambridge University Press. http://doi.org/10.1017/9781108766975

This book provides an overview of the meanings of sustainable transformation and examines examples of societal transformation across the world.

23

Civic Epistemologies

JEAN CARLOS HOCHSPRUNG MIGUEL, RENZO TADDEI
AND MARKO MONTEIRO

Overview

This chapter discusses the concept of 'civic epistemology' in relation to the
Intergovernmental Panel on Climate Change (IPCC) and the governance of climate
change. Civic epistemology refers to 'the institutionalised practices by which
members of a given society test and deploy knowledge claims used as a basis for
making collective choices' (Jasanoff, 2005: 255). Differences in civic epistemologies seem to be directly related to how scientific climate knowledge, presented in
IPCC assessment reports, relates to political decision-making at different scales –
national, regional, global. The concept is especially rich because it enables a
nuanced understanding of the role of IPCC assessments in national climate
governance and in meeting the challenges of building more cosmopolitan climate
expertise. Both of these aspects are important if emerging institutional
arrangements that seek to govern global environmental change are to be
understood. Through a critical review of the civic epistemology literature related
to the IPCC, this chapter investigates how the cultural dimensions of the science–
policy nexus, in different national and geopolitical contexts, conditions the
legitimation and uptake of IPCC knowledge.

23.1 Introduction

Environmental governance regimes are enacted and legitimised by states and
epistemic networks. The role of science in such regimes has been the subject of
much debate, and many have considered knowledge consensus-building to be a
crucial factor in shaping policy (Haas, 1992). However, the history of the IPCC
shows that the influence of climate change knowledge is not restricted to a linear
idea of agreed-upon science directing policy (see **Chapter 22**). For example,
scientific consensus often appears less relevant for policy than the persuasive

powers of those speaking *for* science (Jasanoff, 2011). Understanding the science–policy interface therefore requires explaining how scientific claims gain policy-relevance in specific, sometimes divergent, ways across different countries (Agrawala, 1998a; Hulme & Mahony, 2010). At the national level, scientific consensus becomes one factor among many in the public deliberation of how to govern climate change or how to incorporate scientific claims into national or local policies (Hulme, 2009).

The IPCC has attempted with relative success to provide a common and reliable scientific knowledge base for international climate dialogues, but its credibility in the eyes of citizens and policymakers varies significantly from country to country. The multiplicity of modes of validation of the legitimacy of knowledge and the different forms of interaction between science and politics (Beck, 2012) challenges the supposedly abstract universality of climate science – represented as the 'view from nowhere' (Borie et al., 2021) institutionally maintained by the IPCC. This poses several problems for understanding the IPCC's role in global politics. Several authors have called for the building of a more 'cosmopolitan climate expertise' as a way to navigate these challenges (Hulme, 2010; Beck, 2012; Raman & Pearce, 2020). Cosmopolitan knowledge has been defined as expertise which is comfortable with multiplicity and ambiguity, yet amenable to integration in a critical debate and a 'reasoning together' about a broader public good (Raman & Pearce, 2020: 3).

This chapter explores this challenge by using the concept of 'civic epistemologies' (Jasanoff, 2011), an idea which alludes to the historical, social and political dimensions of the different publicly accepted and institutionally sanctioned ways of performing trust and validating knowledge. We will explore the case of Global South nations – Brazil and India – to show how the reception and appropriation of knowledge organised by the IPCC occurs in contexts of scant public participation in the assessment and deliberation of science. We reiterate that the idea of civic epistemologies moves beyond the linear model of science for policy. We emphasise how this idea helps to understand the politics of climate knowledge not just in the Global North – for which there are many examples in the literature on the IPCC – but also in the Global South, even though there are fewer published examples available.

23.2 Civic Epistemologies and Climate Change

The concept of civic epistemologies emerged in science and technology studies (STS) and refers to 'the institutionalised practices by which members of a given society test and deploy knowledge claims used as a basis for making collective choices' (Jasanoff, 2005: 255). These practices include the following:

institutionalised or explicit norms, protocols and systematic ways of producing and testing knowledge; tacit and implicit forms of deliberating; cultural predispositions and value judgements; and historical traditions that impinge upon the ways knowledge helps order social and institutional life. These epistemologies include 'the styles of reasoning, modes of argumentation, standards of evidence, and norms of expertise that characterise public deliberation and political institutions' (Miller, 2008: 1896). They make it possible to analyse and understand the myriad ways publics and states arrive at agreements collectively regarding how knowledge can become a foundation for public decisions.

To illustrate how the idea of civic epistemologies can be applied to climate change, Jasanoff (2011) compared three cases: the United States, Britain, and Germany. These nations share many cultural, technological and political characteristics, but have fundamentally divergent understandings of how climate science relates to climate policy. In the United States, a country 'founded on common law's adversary system' (Jasanoff, 2011: 135), information is usually generated by parties with vested interests in the issues at hand and tested in public through overt confrontation, for example in courts. In opposition to the United States, 'the British approach has historically been more consensual. Underlying Britain's construction of public reason is a long-standing commitment to empirical observation and common-sense proofs' (Jasanoff, 2011: 136). The trustworthiness of the individual expert is the focus of concern in Britain. In Germany, by contrast, it is believed that 'building communally crafted expert rationales, capable of supporting a policy consensus, offers protection against a psychologically and politically debilitating risk consciousness ... The capacity to form inclusive consensus positions functions as a *sine qua non* of stability and closure in German policy making' (Jasanoff, 2011: 138, 140). Through this comparison, Jasanoff shows how practices of public reasoning and validation of knowledge are culturally situated. These examples demonstrate that scientific consensus does not move policy in the same directions in different countries; simple applications of the linear concept of the science–policy relationship are therefore questionable.

23.3 Brazil and India: Epistemic Sovereignty and Political Culture

One factor related to civic epistemologies that Jasanoff (2011) did not explore concerns the geopolitical influences on the acceptance of the IPCC reports by different countries. Developed nations produce climate science that is well-represented in the IPCC's scientific assessments. This is not the case with Global South countries, where issues related to a lack of 'epistemic sovereignty' over climate change knowledge (Mahony & Hulme, 2018) might be far more important for influencing national policy than the existence of a 'global consensus'.

Being represented in IPCC assessments through patterns of authorship (see **Chapter 7**) can begin to explain differential national uptake and trust in the assessments produced. Studies show that the United States, Britain, and Germany are the highest contributors to the IPCC in terms of the number of authors (El-Hinnawi, 2011). For nations like India and Brazil – albeit less present in terms of IPCC authorship – having large populations and extensive territory makes them central players in any global effort to curb climate change. One of the common characteristics of the civic epistemologies of these latter countries is that lower participation in the IPCC's assessments – alongside other political and economic variables – may be associated with a reduced level of trust in the associated scientific conclusions and weaker engagement with the political agendas that emerge from them.

After the Fourth Assessment Report (2007) (AR4), climate change became an increasingly charged political issue in India and Brazil in different ways and with divergent consequences in terms of political action in these countries. A series of errors were discovered in the AR4 report, including one claim that Himalayan glaciers might completely disappear by 2035. This statement was challenged by the Government of India in the review process. Still, it remained in the final report and, three years later, circulated publicly in international media as a warning to the subcontinent about the perils of climate change and the need – for India as much as for the rest of the world – to act. The claim even appeared in a speech by John Kerry, then the US Senate Foreign Relations Committee chair, who argued that unchecked climate warming could reignite geopolitical tensions between India and Pakistan. The Indian Government responded by commissioning local glaciologists to conduct their own assessments of the prospects of Himalayan glaciers and by setting up what some dubbed an 'Indian IPCC' – the Indian Network for Climate Change Assessment (Mahony, 2014b). This example suggests that the absence of locally accepted knowledge on glaciers – or the presence of claims produced by an international assessment with little participation of Indian scientists and with potentially disruptive political consequences – drove the Indian state to produce counter-assessments to the IPCC. This relates both to the specificities of Indian civic epistemologies and to India's specific political history under British colonisation.

In the case of Brazil, dissatisfaction with what some dubbed 'Northern' framings of climate change – most notably concerning deforestation and the role of the Amazon in the carbon cycle – caused controversy about the validity of scientific claims for directing national policy. Northern climate models used parameters that were considered inadequate by local scientists for simulating the effects of tropical forests on the carbon cycle. Among elected officials, the historical view that the Amazon region should be integrated into the national economy through economic exploitation was pervasive throughout the twentieth century. In that context, Brazilian Government officials felt that scientific assessments, such as those of the IPCC, directed deliberations over mitigation strategies towards the interests of global North countries (Lahsen, 2009; 2016). The Amazon historically occupies a sensitive spot in Brazil's environmental policy, and fears over foreign interference have long roots (Monteiro et al., 2014). Like elsewhere, local histories and cultures therefore condition how deliberation over technical expertise is applicable to environmental policy, specifically expertise produced outside the country in question. Brazilian civic epistemologies, like those in India, are related to longstanding concerns over sovereignty, albeit for different reasons.

The question of scientific credibility in the Brazilian case was not just about whether models and observations assessed by the IPCC were right or wrong. It was about fundamental inequities in national capacities to produce and frame knowledge (Miguel et al., 2019). For the historically dominant Brazilian civic epistemology, local scientists working in national scientific infrastructures are seen as more trustworthy and credible than those from the global North, especially in politically sensitive issues like Amazon deforestation. The creation of a Brazilian Panel on Climate Change (BMPC) to produce systematic reviews of the scientific literature clearly reflects concerns of scientists and decision-makers about epistemic sovereignty (Duarte, 2019). This is in direct relation to Brazil's role in international negotiations on greenhouse gas emissions and securitisation extended to territorial control.

One important shared idea of civic epistemologies emerging from Global North countries discussed by Jasanoff (2011b) is that governmental decisions pertaining to climate change should be deemed acceptable by the public and directed by scientific principles. It can also be noted that these nations have well-established and well-funded scientific infrastructures, well-educated publics, and pathways of public deliberation about science. However, these political cultures and infrastructural conditions are radically different in the Global South. Issues of sovereignty, for countries like Brazil and India, play a role in different ways than in other places when technical decision-making is concerned; these issues become important elements of both scientific and political discussions related to climate change.

Civic epistemologies in Latin America for example – as part of broader political cultures – tend to be marked by top-down, non-participatory approaches to decision-making, which relate to the historical role of military dictatorships in the region. In addition, scientific systems and infrastructures were built across the continent in waves of centrally induced rapid modernisation; these mixed technocracy and the radical depreciation of local, popular forms of understanding reality. Such hierarchical patterns of deliberation are a legacy of authoritarianism and often persist intermingled with democratic processes. These structural elements weaken the inclusion of civil society in the assessment of government and expertise, and limit public participation in the decision-making processes related to climate governance. Lahsen (2009: 360), for example, argues that science and decision-making on matters of environmental risk in Brazil reflect a general attitude that assumes that 'high-ranked decision-makers can be trusted to define national policy single-handedly, and that they better serve the common good than the processes of democratic politics'. In Brazil, a 'technocratic civic epistemology' keeps decision-making centralised in the hands of experts located in government bodies, which constantly alienates civil society from technically based political decisions.

In the Indian case, the emergence of civil society organisations after India's independence – with objectives ranging from popularisation to the democratisation of science and related policy making – pressed against the Indian government's resistance to public debate around scientific questions. The country also adopted a technocratic model of governance, directed at furthering the geopolitical interests of the state. At the same time, the memory of British colonialism in the country built a political culture focused on the search for sovereignty and the need to place political and scientific processes under the central control of the government (Agarwal et al., 1982; Mahony, 2014b).

Comparing the Indian and Brazilian cases with the UK, United States, and Germany, two factors emerge as distinct in their respective civic epistemologies. First, for nations of the Global North the issue of the authorship of scientific works assessed by the IPCC is not seen as a problem of legitimacy. In contrast, in many nations of the Global South, epistemic sovereignty is an important factor in the legitimacy of science in politics. Second, while the Global North frames climate science as an object of public scrutiny, Global South countries tend to frame climate science as a 'science for the administration of the state' and thus as part of the geopolitical process. These examples illustrate the different 'epistemic geographies of climate change' (Mahony & Hulme, 2018) and the importance, for users and observers of the IPCC, of knowing about different civic epistemologies. Box 23.1 offers another case – that of Russia – which helps to illustrate the diversity of climate change civic epistemologies in non-Western nations.

Box 23.1
Russia: the 'policy-follower' civic epistemology

Elena Rowe (2012) discusses how internationally produced expert knowledge claims are taken up domestically in climate policy-making and debates in Russia. This provides an example of the national reception of international expert knowledge such as offered by the IPCC and 'the role of experts in a quasi-democratic State' (Rowe, 2012: 712). Rowe's argument is that Russia's successful engagement in international climate policy is likely to be based on appeals to the country's political and economic interests and power aspirations, rather than on scientific knowledge that involves Russian authors or scientific institutions (Rowe, 2012). According to Rowe, Russian IPCC participants 'did not seem to play a role in deliberative processes leading to key decision-making moments' (Rowe, 2012: 713). However, 'these experts were certainly called to legitimise decisions taken for other political and economic reasons' and also to provide 'input and guidance' to Russian policy-makers in 'navigating' international forums and deliberative processes (Rowe, 2012: 713). The international scientific consensus is thus received in Russia as part of a 'political package deal' (Rowe, 2012: 723). Rowe concludes: 'in a climate-politics "follower" State like Russia, the intervention of Russian experts was not needed to ensure that international science would diffuse into Russian policy circles' (Rowe, 2012: 723).

23.4 Achievements and Challenges

In this chapter, we have shown the rich potential of the concept of civic epistemology to make sense of difficulties in enacting global climate governance through the IPCC. We have illustrated the need for further comparative research into how global environmental assessments result in robust policy impact across different countries, notably in non-Western ones. From our discussions about different civic epistemologies of climate change, a central question arises: Can the IPCC stimulate a more effective scientific and political arena for climate governance in the face of such globally diverse civic epistemologies?

Authors have suggested that the IPCC could prioritise a more cosmopolitan climate expertise (Raman & Pearce, 2020). The promise of cosmopolitan knowledge is to recognise the diversity and ambiguity of forms of knowledge-making and knowledge appropriation as a strength rather than a weakness for engaging with climate change. However, matters of epistemic sovereignty pose a more profound question related to inequality in the production of global climate science. How can the IPCC deal with the claim that climate science produced in developed countries does not fully represent underdeveloped nations in global climate governance? Global governance means dealing with global inequalities on several levels, two of the more important ones being unequal means of producing knowledge, and unequal access to economic and scientific resources that are essential to adaptation and mitigation of climate change. These inequalities condition how countries enter global climate debates and engage with policy development. They also influence the variety of civic epistemologies that condition how international scientific assessments, such as the IPCC, and global governance structures are accepted, deemed legitimate, and incorporated into national and local governance.

Three Key Readings

Miller, C. A. (2008). Civic epistemologies: constituting knowledge and order in political communities. *Sociology Compass*, 2: 1896–1919. http://doi.org/10.1111/j.1751-9020 .2008.00175.x

> This article reviews the concept of civic epistemology, exploring its intellectual origins and its heuristic potential for political and social analysis, including current issues like globalisation and sustainability.

Jasanoff, S. (2011). Cosmopolitan knowledge: climate science and global civic epistemology. In: Dryzek, J., Norgaard, R. B. and Schlosberg, D. (eds.), *Oxford Handbook of Climate Change and Society*. Oxford: Oxford University Press. pp. 129–143. http://doi.org/10.1093/oxfordhb/9780199566600.001.0001

> This book chapter discusses the need for culturally situated understandings of science and its place in climate governance, incorporating distinct civic epistemologies and suggesting institutional changes to build cosmopolitan knowledge for climate action.

Beck, S. (2012). The challenges of building cosmopolitan climate expertise: the case of Germany. *Wiley Interdisciplinary Reviews: Climate Change,* 3(1): 1–17. http://doi.org/10.1002/wcc.151

> This article advances the discussion on the situated ways in which countries incorporate supposedly universal scientific expertise in relation to climate change, focusing on the case of Germany. It also offers a discussion on the concept of a more cosmopolitan climate knowledge using the example of the Climategate controversy.

24

Boundary Objects

BÅRD LAHN

Overview

Research on the interaction between climate science and policy has pointed to the production of so-called 'boundary objects' as one way in which the Intergovernmental Panel on Climate Change (IPCC) has influenced climate policymaking and broader climate discourses. By providing a common framework that enables interaction across social worlds, while still allowing more localised use by different groups of actors, such objects have been key in bringing together climate science and policy, in turn shaping the trajectory of both. This chapter reviews several concepts that have been analysed as boundary objects – such as the concept of climate sensitivity and the 2 °C and 1.5 °C targets – and explains how they have been productive of new science/policy relations. It also points to new challenges for the IPCC as climate policy development moves towards implementation and increases demand for more 'solution-oriented' knowledge.

24.1 Introduction

Much analysis of the IPCC – and indeed the IPCC's traditional self-understanding – assumes that its influence and authority is premised on a strong demarcation between science and policy. In practice, however, the ways in which the IPCC may come to influence policy development or wider public perceptions of climate change is by making connections across these two spheres of science and policy (see Chapter 22). This presents a puzzle that requires solving in order to understand the IPCC's influence: How can ideas about a clear separation between science and policy coexist with practices that constantly criss-cross or undermine the presumed boundary between them (cf. Sundqvist et al., 2018)?

One way of attending to this puzzle is by analysing the specific *objects* that bring the IPCC and its contributing scientists into contact with policymakers, political activists or other groups of actors on different sides of the presumed boundaries. The notion of *boundary object*, originally proposed by Star and Griesemer (1989; Star, 2010), describes some 'thing' – whether concrete or abstract – that holds together across different social worlds, allowing actors with different interests and views to act without the need for consensus on the object's precise meaning. In studies of the IPCC and its relationship to publics and policymaking, the notion of boundary objects offers a way of focusing not simply on the construction of boundaries between social worlds or on how actors on one side of the boundary influence the other. Rather, the idea of boundary objects begins to explain how these actors *produce new realities together.* Analysing boundary objects is thus a way of going beyond general assertions about 'co-production' to study what exactly is produced at the intersection of science and policy, and with what effects.

This chapter employs the notion of boundary objects to show how the work of the IPCC has been closely intertwined with climate policy development, and how this interplay has shifted over time. It reviews existing studies of boundary objects that have been important for the IPCC's influence on climate policy – and that have simultaneously worked to influence the IPCC's own assessments and the wider trajectory of climate science. Two sets of such objects are identified. The first one represents features of the physical climate system, namely the concepts of Equilibrium Climate Sensitivity (ECS) and Global Warming Potentials (GWP). These objects illustrate the influence of the IPCC on the early features of the emerging international climate policy regime.

The other set of objects is a series of future-oriented limits, targets and scenarios, which have come to strongly structure both IPCC assessments and climate policy discourse in recent years. Most prominent among these are the 2 °C and 1.5 °C targets. These objects serve to connect the IPCC more closely to policy goals and explicitly normative considerations of desirable futures. They thereby increase the potential influence of IPCC knowledge on policy development. At the same time, they challenge the idea of a strong demarcation between science and policy on which the IPCC's self-understanding has been premised. The concluding section discusses what this challenge might mean for the IPCC's future role, and how the notion of boundary objects may help in understanding the influence of the IPCC more broadly.

24.2 Climate Sensitivity and Emission Equivalents: Epistemic and Governable Things

A key challenge in assessing climate change for policy purposes is how to align a scientific understanding of climate change – as a complex and insufficiently understood phenomenon – with the certainty and simplicity required for policymaking and governing. Knowledge about future climate change originates in complex models that are not easily understood outside the community of modellers (see **Chapter 14**). Research on the interaction between climate science and policy has pointed to the production of boundary objects as one way in which knowledge from climate models has become stabilised and taken up in policy processes.

Van der Sluijs and colleagues (1998) analysed the concept of *climate sensitivity* as a case of a particularly stable boundary object. The IPCC defines climate sensitivity as 'the change in the surface temperature in response to a change in the atmospheric carbon dioxide concentration or other radiative forcing' (IPCC, 2021a). The concept emerged as a way of comparing and summarising model results in a way that enabled new forms of interaction between climate modellers, other scientific communities and policy actors. It was initially used as a heuristic tool for comparing different climate models, as modellers tested the sensitivity of models by comparing the temperature response of a doubling of atmospheric carbon dioxide concentration. With the need to communicate model results to policymakers through assessment reports, the concept was deployed for a different purpose – as a shorthand for summarising the expected magnitude of climate change given continued carbon dioxide emissions.

In early climate assessments reports, the sensitivity of different models was summarised in an estimated range for climate sensitivity of between 1.5 °C and 4.5 °C for a doubling of atmospheric carbon dioxide (van der Sluijs et al., 1998: 299). When IPCC chair Bert Bolin delivered the IPCC's statement to the first Conference of the Parties to the UN Framework Convention on Climate Change (UNFCCC) in Berlin in 1995 (COP1), this estimate was among his key messages from the scientific community to the attending government representatives. In this way, the understanding of climate sensitivity as a measurable property of the physical climate system became a key reference point for climate policy discussions (van der Sluijs et al., 1998: 311).

Making the climate sensitivity relevant for policy actors in this way, impacted not only policy and public understandings of climate change. It also influenced the further scientific use of the concept, since it created a new demand for estimating and constraining climate sensitivity – not just as a metric for comparing models, but as an actually existing property of the climate system – in order to better inform policymaking (van der Sluijs et al., 1998).

Climate sensitivity originated from climate modelling, but was made relevant in new ways for policy communities. A different example from the IPCC's early years illustrates that boundary objects may also originate from a specific policy need. When international discussion about how to govern climate change began in the late 1980s, some countries – the United States in particular – favoured a 'comprehensive approach' which dealt not only with carbon dioxide emissions, but also with other greenhouse gases (Shackley & Wynne, 1997: 91). To address the need for a simple way of comparing the climate effects of different gases, the metric of *Global Warming Potentials* (GWP) was developed and published in the IPCC's First Assessment Report (AR1). The GWP metric allows for a conversion of gases by calculating their 'CO_2-equivalent' warming effect. The metric was later adopted by the UNFCCC to underpin quantified emission reduction commitments and international carbon trading (MacKenzie, 2009).

Among IPCC scientists, GWP was understood as an ambiguous and potentially problematic simplification (Shackley & Wynne, 1997). For example, because the warming effects of greenhouse gases differ depending on their atmospheric lifetime, the choice of time-horizon for comparing them greatly influences the result.[1] In AR1, GWPs for three different time horizons were presented 'as candidates for discussion' (quoted in Shackley & Wynne, 1997: 91). Thus scientists saw the development of GWP as opening up a scientific area of inquiry – a discussion of how gases could usefully be compared in order to inform policy. Meanwhile, in the policy arena, the GWP metric was quickly adopted and put to use as an unambiguous fact of the climate system, as a basis for calculating exact amounts of allowable emissions, or the price at which carbon credits can be sold in international markets (MacKenzie, 2009).

Similar to the concept of climate sensitivity, the GWP metric became an object that stabilised and simplified complex and ambiguous knowledge. The objects thereby enabled interaction between different social worlds, while also generating new problems and practices both in scientific and policymaking circles. Crucially, however, although both objects were flexible enough to mean something rather different in policy discussions among climate modellers, they also maintained their distinct use in both arenas (van der Sluijs et al., 1998). In this way, the boundary objects that resulted from the interaction between the IPCC and policy communities in the organisation's early years held a dual role – on the one hand enabling scientific knowledge-production about the climate system, and on the other hand underpinning new projects for governing it.

In the first role, these objects are similar to what Hans-Jörg Rheinberger (1997) has labelled 'epistemic things'. These are objects to be studied and worked on through the scientific process, which are characterised partly by the things not yet known and the questions they open up for study. In this sense, they embody an 'irreducible vagueness' (Rheinberger, 1997: 28). On the other hand, for policy purposes these objects take on a much more definitive character, representing something that is already known, and that can therefore be governed. They become objects or technologies of government, imbued with quantified precision and premised on a belief in scientific certainty and rigour (Porter, 1995; cf. Asdal, 2008).

This 'tacking back-and-forth' (Star, 2010: 601) between a 'weakly structured common use' and a 'strongly structured individual-site use' (Star and Griesemer, 1989: 393) is what makes climate sensitivity and GWP usefully understood as boundary objects. Their value lies in enabling the IPCC to interact with non-scientific actors through a common language, while at the same time meeting the requirements of each group necessary to uphold internal credibility and thereby the idea of a clear separation between science and policy.

24.3 Targets and Pathways: Dangerous Anthropogenic Objects?

The examples above show how boundary objects enabled the IPCC to influence the early stages of the international climate regime. As policy development has progressed, however, a different set of objects have emerged, which are directed less towards the physical climate system and more towards future policy action. Most prominent among these is the target to keep warming below 2 °C (and later the ambition of 1.5 °C), which has frequently been analysed as a boundary object (Randalls, 2010; Cointe et al., 2011; Lahn & Sundqvist, 2017; Morseletto et al., 2017; Livingston & Rummukainen, 2020).

The UNFCCC in 1992 established the goal to avoid 'dangerous anthropogenic interference' with the climate system, yet without specifying at which level climate change would be considered 'dangerous'. Partly informed by the concept of climate sensitivity – which summarised the climate system in the metric of temperature rise – discussions about how to define 'dangerous' and 'tolerable' levels of climate change came to centre on a global temperature limit (Randalls, 2010). The EU adopted the 2 °C limit in 1996, and was its main proponent internationally until its formal adoption in the UNFCCC in 2010 (Morseletto et al., 2017).

The EU adopted the 2 °C target based on 'trust in the underlying scientific content' (Morseletto et al., 2017: 661), regarding the target as derived from scientific knowledge about climate impacts. In public discourse, it has also been widely represented as a 'scientific' target, often with implicit reference to the IPCC (Shaw, 2013: 567). In the scientific literature, however, it is usually considered a political target, and has even been critiqued as not sufficiently scientifically grounded (e.g. Knutti et al., 2016). In other words, while the target provides an intuitive and simple metric capable of bringing together a range of actors, its precise meaning varies widely among them.

The IPCC has arguably played an important role in enabling and upholding this multiplicity of meaning. Although IPCC reports have never endorsed any specific temperature limit as a marker of 'dangerous' climate change, they have increasingly been framed around temperature increase as a unifying metric. This is seen, for example, in the so-called 'Reasons for Concern' framework, which was introduced in the Third Assessment Report (AR3) and lent credibility to the idea of considering climate impacts in relation to global temperature rise (Mahony, 2015; Asayama, 2021; see Chapter 21).

In this way, the 2 °C target became established as a unifying object that is 'neither scientific nor political in essence, but instead co-produced by both' (Livingston & Rummukainen, 2020: 10). Its influence on climate policy discourse has been such that even criticism of it came to be framed in the same terms. Thus, developing countries or activists arguing that 2 °C represents an 'unsafe' level of warming did not criticise the framing of IPCC reports around temperature targets. Rather, they asked for alternative targets such as 1 °C or 1.5 °C to be included for scientific analysis and policy debate, both in IPCC assessments and in UNFCCC negotiations (Cointe et al., 2011: 18; Lahn, 2021: 21; for more on the 1.5 °C target, see Guillemot, 2017; Livingston & Rummukainen, 2020).

The formal adoption of 2 °C in 2010, and the further inclusion of 1.5 °C as an additional ambition in the Paris Agreement, marks a (provisional) end to discussions about how to define 'dangerous anthropogenic interference'. Attention has thereby shifted from overall goals towards scenarios, pathways and technologies that may achieve those goals. Bringing together policy goals and scientific knowledge in a common representation of futures to be achieved or avoided, such as pathways and scenarios, may well be seen as new boundary objects in the making (cf. Garb et al., 2008).

Examples of such new boundary objects are the Representative Concentration Pathways and the Shared Socioeconomic Pathways, which have been produced for, but organised independently from, the IPCC (see **Chapter 15**). The goal of these new scenarios is explicitly to provide a common framework through which different groups within the IPCC can work together, thus producing an 'epistemic thing' that links (for example) climate modelling, integrated assessment modelling and research on climate impacts. At the same time, as Beck and Mahony (2018a, 2018b) have shown, the new pathways also bring new governable objects into being. By legitimising new technologies such as bioenergy with carbon capture and storage (BECCS), they serve to make some mitigation measures 'politically legible and actionable' while potentially obscuring others (Beck & Mahony, 2018a: 8).

This double character makes the new pathways similar to the boundary objects from the IPCC's early years, as described earlier. However, in contrast to concepts such as climate sensitivity – which came to be seen as a feature of the physical climate system – the future-oriented and goal-directed character of the pathways make them explicitly 'anthropogenic' in origin. They are directly implicated in the 'world-making' work of rendering certain futures more or less thinkable or desirable. For this reason they challenge any notion of a clear-cut divide between scientific fact and political or societal values – thus 'raising new questions about the neutrality of climate science' (Beck & Mahony, 2018a).

Following international agreement on how to define 'dangerous anthropogenic interference', then, a new class of 'dangerous anthropogenic objects' are rising to prominence in the work of the IPCC. What makes them 'dangerous' to the IPCC is not so much that they make scientists engage more explicitly with policy goals in a 'solution-oriented' mode. Rather, the danger lies in how they challenge the IPCC's self-understanding based on a strong demarcation between science and policy, thus potentially forcing a reassessment of the IPCC's role in relation to policy development. This is illustrated in the controversy that arose around the Bali Box (see Box 24.1).

Box 24.1
The Bali Box controversy

In the Fourth Assessment Report (2007) (AR4), the IPCC presented a box quantifying the emission reductions that would be required by developed countries as a group in order to achieve the 2 °C target. The numbers became key to discussions about equitable effort-sharing between developed and developing countries during the UNFCCC negotiations in Bali, and was subsequently dubbed the 'Bali Box' (Lahn & Sundqvist, 2017).

In their analysis of the Bali Box as a boundary object, Lahn and Sundqvist (2017) show that the numbers of the box initially enabled a relatively broad group of actors to come together around a common understanding of effort-sharing. However, the IPCC scientists who developed the numbers later published an analysis that also quantified emission reductions required by developing countries. At this point, the numbers were contested from an equity perspective and the Bali Box became a source of controversy both in UNFCCC negotiations and in the scientific literature.

The disagreement that ensued can be seen as a form of 'ontological controversy', as described in Chapter 16 – a disagreement over the underlying values and presuppositions of scientific findings. The result was that the Bali Box – initially successful in bringing together actors around a shared understanding of a difficult issue – did not retain its authority when the interdependencies of science and policy became exposed. It thus eventually failed to do the coordinating work of a successful boundary object.

24.4 Achievements and Challenges

As the examples above have shown, the IPCC's influence has in part been enabled by the establishment of boundary objects that allow different groups of actors to interact while maintaining their distinct identities and commitments. The notion of boundary objects, however, also points to a broader understanding of 'influence' than a simple one-way transmission of scientific knowledge to policymaking. Indeed, the objects described in this chapter produce new realities in both spheres, simultaneously raising new scientific questions and enabling new forms of governing.

An important aspect of several boundary objects reviewed in this chapter is that they have allowed for close interaction and mutual influence between science and policy, while still permitting an understanding of the two spheres as clearly separated. With new demands being placed on the IPCC for solutions and roadmaps for achieving societal goals, this may no longer be the case. Rather than upholding the idea of separation, new boundary objects emerging in the post-Paris terrain of climate science and policy – such as pathways towards global or national targets – may instead prompt recognition of how climate science and policy are intricately interlinked. This presents an obvious challenge to the IPCC's traditional self-understanding (Hermansen et al., 2021).

Beck and Mahony (2018b) have suggested that the IPCC could deal with this challenge by substituting its self-understanding as 'neutral arbiter' with the goal of producing 'responsible assessment'. This would include 'opening up to a broader and more diverse set of metrics, criteria and frameworks' for assessing responses to climate change (Beck & Mahony, 2018b: 6). Analysing the IPCC from the perspective of boundary objects shows that influence and relevance is achieved through mutual adjustment and the development of shared meaning across various groups of actors. However, as the controversy around the Bali Box illustrates, such achievements stand in danger of being eroded if the interdependencies between science and policy are denied or ignored. This suggests that the IPCC should be more reflexive about how it helps bring about new science–policy realities. It should therefore think through what kinds of objects might result from a new and more 'responsible' assessment mode in the future.

Note

1 The time-horizon for GWPs refers to the length of time over which the radiative forcing effect on climate of the respective gas is integrated. Thus the ratio between GWPs of two given greenhouse gases – and hence their relative importance for climate change – will vary depending on the time-horizon selected.

Three Key Readings

van der Sluijs, J., et al. (1998). Anchoring devices in science for policy: the case of consensus around climate sensitivity. *Social Studies of Science*, 28(2): 291–323. http://doi.org/10.1177/030631298028002004.

This article provides a classic study of an early boundary object in climate science/policy, i.e. the concept of climate sensitivity.

Lahn, B. and Sundqvist, G. (2017). Science as a 'fixed point'? Quantification and boundary objects in international climate politics. *Environmental Science & Policy*, 67: 8–15. http://doi.org/10.1016/j.envsci.2016.11.001.

This article examines the so-called Bali Box as a case of a failed boundary object.

Beck, S. and Mahony, M. (2018). The politics of anticipation: the IPCC and the negative emissions technologies experience. *Global Sustainability*, 1: e8. http://doi.org/10.1017/sus.2018.7.

This article discusses the challenges ahead for the IPCC as a result of the increasing demand for 'solutions-oriented' knowledge.

25

Visuals

IRENE LORENZONI AND JORDAN HAROLD

Overview

This chapter reviews the types, use, production, accessibility and efficacy of data visuals contained in the assessments and special reports of the Intergovernmental Panel on Climate Change (IPCC), drawing upon available published literature. Visuals of different types are key to the communication of IPCC assessments. They have been subject to academic interest among social and cognitive scientists. Furthermore, wider societal interest in the IPCC has increased, especially since the publication of its Fifth Assessment Report (AR5). In response, the IPCC has revisited its approach to communication including visuals, which has resulted in a greater professionalisation of its visualisations – involving information designers and cognitive scientists – and in new forms of co-production between authors and users.

25.1 Introduction

IPCC visuals[1] are integral to the communication of IPCC assessments, and have been the subject of academic research since the late 1990s. Visuals provide diverse representations of evidence, primarily in the form of graphs, maps, diagrams, tables, and more recently, icons and infographics, such as those in the Technical Summary of the IPCC's Special Report on the Ocean and Cryosphere in a Changing Climate (IPCC, 2019f). The focus of research on this topic has broadly addressed four questions:

- What types of visuals are used in reports, and how?
- How have they changed over time and why?
- How are visuals produced?
- How well do they convey the messages they intend to, and how well are they understood by different audiences?

As societal interest in the work of the IPCC has expanded, the accessibility of IPCC communications has been scrutinised in more detail (see Chapter 26). Studies by social and cognitive scientists have explored the effectiveness of IPCC visuals and how they are interpreted and understood by a variety of users, including policy-makers and non-experts. This chapter explores these aspects in detail, with reflections on how these intersect with the nature, role and authority of the IPCC and on its response to calls for change in its communication processes.

25.2 Types of IPCC Visuals

IPCC visuals are provided to communicate data and information, consonant with the tradition in scientific literature of illustrating specific evidence through visuals. Visuals are bespoke to Summary for Policymakers (SPM) reports, but typically evolve from figures contained in Working Group (WG) chapters or in Technical Summaries, which in turn may have their origins in published literature. The bespoke nature of SPM visuals reflects the purpose and format of IPCC assessments. Although visuals are embedded within the written narrative of the reports, there is a paucity of research exploring how readers use text and visuals in isolation or in relation to each other, and the effectiveness of these approaches.

There is wide variation in the type and content of visuals used within and between reports and over time. Box 25.1 shows an example for the changing visualisation of observed global temperature between the First Assessment Report (AR1) in 1990 and the Sixth Assessment Report (AR6) in 2021. These differences are related in part to scientific and social advances – knowledge, modelling capacity, understanding of uncertainty, data availability – and partly to representational choices (discussed later). The visuals provide representations of a range of topics – for example, observational data (in time series format or geographically referenced), projections, processes, comparisons of change, model

---

Box 25.1
Development of visuals of global temperature change

These two visuals (Figures 25.1 and 25.2) – with original captions included – drawn from IPCC SPM reports in AR1 (1990) [top panel] and in AR6 (2021) [lower panel], show the evolution in the way IPCC has depicted observed trends in global temperature. The visual from the AR6 WGI SPM denotes the causes, as well as the changes, of recent warming. It uses titles and annotations to help guide the reader, and includes a detailed caption about the data presented. Reproduced here from AR1 WGI (IPCC, 1990a: SPM, p. 23, original greyscale), and AR6 WGI (IPCC, 2021a: SPM, p. 6, original in colour).

Continued

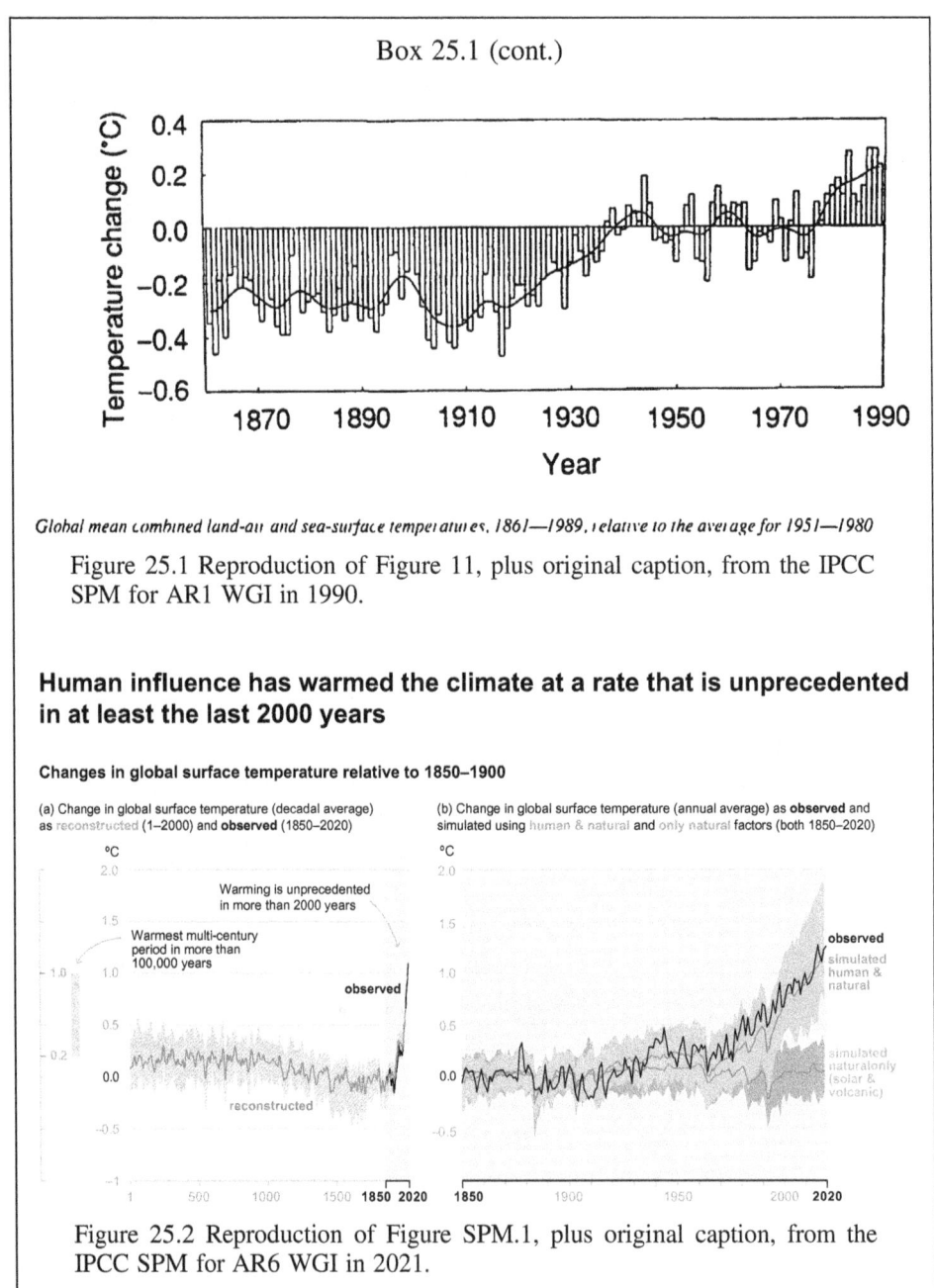

Box 25.1 (cont.)

Global mean combined land-air and sea-surface temperatures, 1861—1989, relative to the average for 1951—1980

Figure 25.1 Reproduction of Figure 11, plus original caption, from the IPCC SPM for AR1 WGI in 1990.

Human influence has warmed the climate at a rate that is unprecedented in at least the last 2000 years

Changes in global surface temperature relative to 1850–1900

Figure 25.2 Reproduction of Figure SPM.1, plus original caption, from the IPCC SPM for AR6 WGI in 2021.

outputs, risk assessments – drawing upon a variety and diversity of data sources as well as expert judgement. Multiple aspects of climate change are often represented in a visual – for example the 'burning embers' diagram, discussed later – reflecting the need to synthesise information as part of an assessment. The media through which visuals in IPCC reports are disseminated has evolved over time – from print-only copies of the earlier assessments to more recent digital online availability supported by multimedia (for example WGI's short video of its AR6 contribution, FAQs, an Interactive Atlas, Regional Fact Sheets, Data Access, and Outreach Materials).

25.3 Presentation and Use of Visuals

The varied foci and key messages contained in visuals, as well as the need to convey these to multiple audiences effectively, can be challenging for their production. Doyle (2011) and Nocke (2014) mention that the production and presentation of visuals in the first four of the IPCC's assessment reports were influenced by a focus at the time on datasets capturing global observations to monitor and project global change, facilitated by the emergence of institutions with a global remit. Observational data in early IPCC visuals is often presented in graphs showing temporal change on one axis, with environmental and ecological variation depicted as linear change, its complexity thus constrained by the representational medium used (see Doyle, 2011).

In maps, variation in ecological processes is expressed in spatial terms. These have until recently lacked regional specificities (Doyle, 2011; Nocke, 2014) and have been critiqued for removing the local relevance of change and connection to a sense of place. Temporal change was also more challenging to present in maps of earlier IPCC reports. It has been argued that the use of these formats denotes the power of western cartography in terms of which features are represented and how (see discussion in Doyle, 2011). To enhance the accessibility of visuals for wider audiences, choices were made in regard to presentation, style and aesthetics (Doyle, 2011: 57). For example, the graphs in the AR3 Synthesis Report included a wider range of colours; this was accompanied by specific choices for typeface and borders to draw attention to specific content.

Static visuals may be useful for presentational purposes, although these can be perceived as being simplistic (Nocke, 2014). More in-depth and comprehensive exploration of data can be enabled through interactive options, made possible through recent digital advances. Conversely, interactive data platforms can be challenging for users if they lack knowledge of how to navigate the complex datasets and portals available (Hewitson, et al., 2017). In recognition of the potential for interactive data visual products displaying tailored information, the AR6 WGI assessment developed an Interactive Atlas (IPCC, 2021d). This enabled users to customise representations of regional information and access the underpinning data.

Studies have highlighted how the representation of visuals in IPCC reports is affected by the complex relationships between those who create, review, shape and

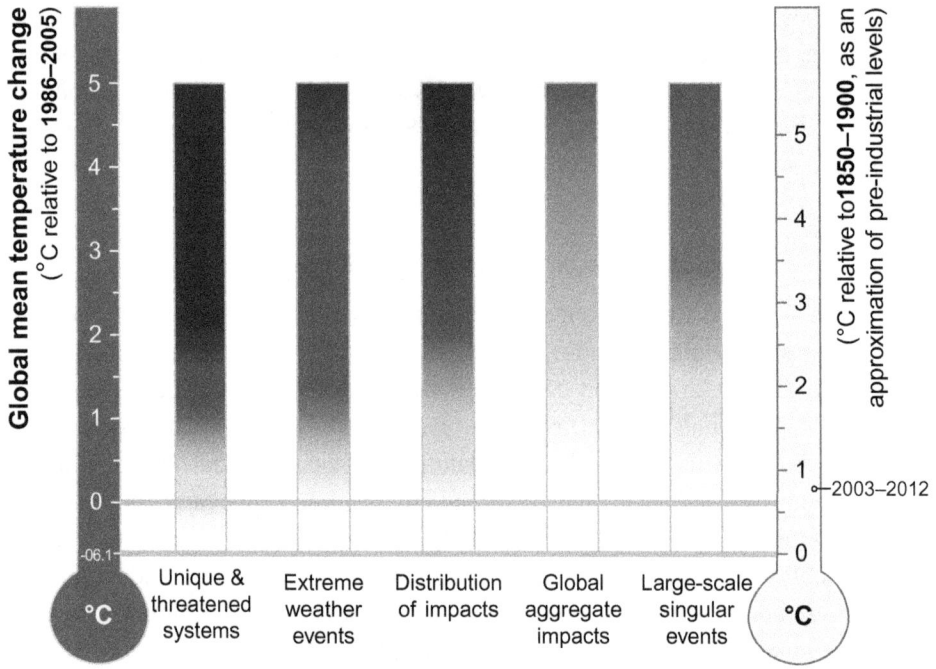

Level of additional risk due to climate change

| Undetectable | Moderate | High | Very high |

Figure 25.3 Risks associated with Reasons For Concern at a global scale are shown for increasing levels of climate change.

The so-called 'burning embers' diagram, reproduced here in greyscale from colour visual in IPCC (2014b) AR5 SYR, Box 2.4, Figure 1 (p. 73)

use such visuals. Visuals may evolve over time, acquiring diverse social and political significance. One well-known visual that was produced to represent and convey the likelihood of future risk and uncertainty is the 'burning embers' diagram (see Figure 25.3; see also **Chapter 21**). Mahony's (2015) study of the origins and development of the visual examines how its representation of thresholds at which climate change may become dangerous was revisited, debated and embraced/rejected, through processes underpinned by a range of interpreta-tions and 'political objectives' (Mahony, 2015: 153). These were, he concludes, indicative of tensions and debates among different knowledges and practices of sense-making. Recognising these differences opens up opportunities for further understanding the iterative creation of visual forms of knowledge through multiple disciplinary perspectives. Zommers et al. (2020) note how lessons learnt from debates about the burning embers diagram have translated into more formalised processes – protocols, standardised metrics for risk thresholds – in recent IPCC reports that aim to increase transparency. Another contested visual is 'the hockey-stick' graph in AR3, showing a significant rise in temperatures in the twentieth century in the context of the last thousand years. Its visual presentation and the statistical methods used to represent the data (Walsh, 2010) received criticism, in part fomented by the rise of internet communications (Zorita, 2019).

Research on visuals has mainly focused on the physical science of climate change, typically reports produced by WGI. As a point of departure, Wardekker and Lorenz (2019) evaluated the content and framing of visuals in WGII from AR1 to AR5. Their work shows that the majority of the over 700 visuals examined focus on impacts (problems), but few on solutions and adaptation. The authors point to the importance of understanding how visual information is framed (presented), given its influence on how information is interpreted, perceived and used in decision-making. Wardekker and Lorenz (2019) also acknowledge the potential for debating the visual framing of information in internal IPCC processes. Such debates can be highly politicised with competing interests at stake. The aforementioned authors note how opportunities may arise for tailoring visuals – for example more specific national and regional foci in regional chapters or increased interaction across drafting teams earlier in the SPM process – and for learning from the use of visuals in other contexts, for example on climate adaptation by national agencies.

25.4 Accessibility and Efficacy of Visuals

Studies have examined how individuals cognitively interpret visuals, providing insights into their comprehensibility and usefulness. Understanding a data visual involves the direction of visual attention to specific visual features, and the sense-making of features using prior knowledge. Hence, comprehension is influenced both by visual aspects – for example format, colour, text – and by user characteristics, for example the reader's goal, knowledge of graphs, knowledge of the content (Harold et al., 2016). McMahon et al. (2015) examined representation and understanding of two types of uncertainty – scenario uncertainty and climate response uncertainty – through interviews with people similar to the IPCC target audience. This was presented in the IPCC AR4 WGI SPM visual of modelled global surface temperatures according to various scenarios. Their work indicated that individuals often attributed most of the uncertainty to climate models – the participants interpreted the visual using their own prior assumptions – whereas scenario uncertainties were largely unnoticed; this was due to the design choices included in the visual which were not interpreted in the same way by the scientists creating the figure and the readers viewing it. The findings point to the need for involving users during the process of designing visuals to identify different interpretations, and to inform how the communication of information might be improved.

A more recent study on AR5 WGI SPM visuals identified a tension between the need to retain scientific accuracy in visuals – as expressed by the IPCC authors – and the desire for increased accessibility (Harold et al., 2020). Non-specialists found the more complex figures more difficult to understand, which the IPCC authors also recognised. The authors of this study suggested that visuals be evaluated for complexity and be co-designed and tested with users. This may provide opportunities to produce visuals that could better enable the different goals of scientific accuracy and user accessibility to be constructively considered and possibly balanced. A further consideration is the perceived association of the format of a visual with expectations of scientific content and 'authority'. McMahon et al. (2016) showed that visuals perceived to be more scientific – graphs, maps and so on – were more closely associated with the authority of a scientific source. Both McMahon et al. (2015) and Harold et al. (2020) propose that IPCC visuals are created with input from the stakeholders for whom they are devised, and tested for comprehensibility at various opportunities during the drafting process.

An important recent development that has affected IPCC communications is the exponential evolution of societal interest in visual communication over the past 30 years and extensive use of social media for discussion and exchange. IPCC reports have regularly received print and television media attention. More recently, their communication has also increasingly occurred through social media – either through direct recirculation of IPCC materials or through indirect reference to the IPCC visuals themselves. The IPCC has also had to keep up with such visualisation trends (see Section 25.5). When analysing the media coverage and framing of IPCC AR5 reports – both text and visuals – O'Neill et al. (2015) found that the 'newsworthiness' of the WGIII report was lower than that of WGI and WGII. The authors suggest this may be due in part to the visuals in the WGIII report – despite some visually attractive images – not speaking to the requirement of dramatisation and personalisation, which news outlets frequently draw upon for presenting their stories. To inform future IPCC assessments, O'Neill et al. (2015) advocated co-produced research by academics and media outlets about the place of visuals in the production of news, and research into how audiences interact with media narratives and visuals, expanding the work to non-English speaking nations.

The visual portrayal of climate change in legacy media may not make frequent use of IPCC visuals, even when reporting IPCC assessments. One study used a sample of print newspaper articles reporting the IPCC AR5 to show that accompanying visuals tended to be photographic material, even if consonant with the content of the related article text (Dahl & Fløttum, 2017). The authors indicated that selection of visuals continues to present a challenge for news producers. Imagery of human beings 'taking action' or 'being impacted' has the potential to engage audiences more than decontextualised representations which often characterise IPCC visuals – in other words imagery *without* an explicit human or geographical reference. Walsh (2015) offers a similar perspective, arguing that the rhetorics embedded in, and associated with, IPCC graphics may be distancing people from engaging with climate change. Other (more local) forms of visualisation may therefore be more effective for inducing action on climate change. However, the contents of visuals used to communicate IPCC reports require careful attention. Nerlich and Jaspal (2014) analysed images of extreme weather in English-speaking media following the publication in 2011 of a draft IPCC report on extreme weather and climate adaptation. They found that the images studied may have 'largely negative emotional meanings' (Nerlich & Jaspal, 2013: 253) and conveyed some sense of helplessness; they may, therefore, disengage audiences from climate change.

25.5 Co-producing Visuals

The IPCC has pioneered new features to support improved communication, for example the use of headline statements to provide a concise summary of the overall assessment (Stocker & Plattner, 2016: 637). However, despite such innovations, the accessibility of IPCC reports was critiqued following the publication of AR5 (2013/2014). In an Expert Meeting on Communication held in February 2016, the IPCC (2016b) acknowledged 'growing calls from policymakers and other users to do more with its communications', having faced criticism that even its SPMs are 'unreadable and inaccessible for non-specialists' (for further context, see **Chapters 6** and **26**).

Starting with the AR6 cycle, co-production of visuals has taken centre stage within the IPCC SPM process. This is based on recognising the importance of co-developing scientifically accurate and rigorous visuals and of meeting the needs of 'users', even if there are challenges in such co-production (Morelli et al., 2021). This approach was pursued in both the Special Report on Global Warming of 1.5 °C (2018) (SR15) and the Special Report on Climate Change and Land (2019) (SRCCL), where visuals were collaboratively produced and guided by design and cognitive psychology principles. These principles were to establish and agree upon a clear intent (message) of the visual (see Box 25.1) as a main reference point. The visual could then be built iteratively with chapter authors as the content and focus of the IPCC report became better defined and with consideration of feedback elicited through user testing.

Concurrent with the growing social attention to visuals, visual design within the IPCC has also been professionalised, for example through collaboration with designers and recruitment of graphics officers within Technical Support Units (TSUs). This professionalisation supports authors in their preparation of visuals and also enhances the efficacy of the resulting visuals in terms of reach and understanding. The visuals featured in the AR6 WGI SPM are therefore substantially different from visuals in previous reports, both in terms of the cognitive insights adopted to convey data and information, and their visual presentation and format. Having been coordinated by the IPCC, co-created by professional designers in association with authors and cognitive experts, and refined through testing with policymakers, they may turn out to be more 'usable', 'intuitively understood' and 'enhance climate literacy' (Gaulkin, 2021).

25.6 Achievements and Challenges

Published research increasingly recognises the role of visuals in IPCC reports as key components of communication, in association with and complementing relevant text. Concurrently, the IPCC has acknowledged the relevance of its reports to audiences much more diverse and broader than the policymakers to whom its SPMs are explicitly addressed. The context within which the IPCC operates has also evolved, with now much wider societal interest in novel tools for digital and instant communication. The IPCC has responded to critiques by embarking upon innovative co-design for some visuals included in its reports, as part of a wider focus to improve its communications. The attention to the IPCC's visuals in a variety of settings by a diversity of social actors reflects a development in IPCC processes. Co-production of visuals presents opportunities for widening participation and for more meaningful inclusion of diverse perspectives. However, new visual designs and formats raise questions about how these are evaluated by expert reviewers and national delegates.

There is a paucity of research on the effects of these new processes. Research is needed to understand how the SPM visuals in the AR6 reports have been reviewed and evaluated by national delegates, how they are received and used by policymakers, how they are communicated by print and social media, and how they are understood, used, and (re)circulated by different societal actors with an interest in communicating climate change. For example, to what extent are IPCC visuals circulating in other media and contexts, outside of the IPCC processes, perhaps detached from the original report in which they were included? This is especially relevant given the widespread use and accessibility of social media. Little is known about how public and media framing of IPCC visuals occurs and how this influences their circulation and reframing (O'Neill et al., 2015; Mahony,

2015; see also van Beek et al., 2020b). Nor is much known systematically about the knowledges and perspectives that are highlighted or excluded as a visual is subsequently iterated, (re)used and recast across different media platforms.

Furthermore, in the context of media and user-generated content inspired by the IPCC communications, there is a need to understand how this downstream visual content expresses new or diverse meanings and perspectives around climate change, beyond those intended by the IPCC's authors. Of relevance too is better understanding how key climate change messages are communicated. Do IPCC visuals circulate widely, and for which purposes? Or do its visuals have a limited efficacy in certain regions or amongst particular publics, for whom perhaps other visuals more effectively represent key messages on climate change? Expanding current understandings and drawing together existing work to inform and continue building on the reflections and new processes initiated within the IPCC could help its visuals, products and messages be relevant to those it wishes to reach.

Note

1 A 'visual' indicates a representation perceived through sight, encompassing a wide range of publishable media (videos, photographs, maps, graphs etc.). In this chapter we focus on data visuals (i.e. figures).

Three Key Readings

Lynn, J. (2018). Communicating the IPCC: challenges and opportunities. In: Filho, W. L., Manolas, E., Azul, A. M., Azeiteiro, U. M. and McGhie, H. (eds.), *Handbook of Climate Change Communication: Vol. 3*. Cham: Springer. pp. 131–143. http://doi.org/10.1007/978-3-319-70479-1_8

This chapter provides an overview of the opportunities and challenges in the IPCC's communication of climate change, following the reflections instigated in 2016.

McMahon, R., Stauffacher, M. and Knutti, R. (2015). The unseen uncertainties in climate change: reviewing comprehension of an IPCC scenario graph. *Climatic Change*, 133 (2): 141–154. http://doi.org/10.1007/s10584-015-1473-4

This article examines how interpretations of a visual can vary and significantly affect its comprehension.

Wardekker, A. and Lorenz, S. (2019). The visual framing of climate change impacts and adaptation in the IPCC assessment reports. *Climatic Change*, 156: 273–292. http://doi.org/10.1007/s10584–019-02522-6

This article provides an in-depth examination of framings of IPCC visuals on impacts and adaptation.

26

Communications

WARREN PEARCE AND AUGUST LINDEMER

Overview

This chapter analyses the development of the policy of the Intergovernmental Panel on Climate Change (IPCC) for the communication of its reports, the content and style of its communication, and how its knowledge becomes reappropriated for alternative, often political, purposes. In doing so, we review IPCC policy documents, key literature on the IPCC and climate science communication, as well as providing a case study of a recent controversy in IPCC communication: the reappropriation of a paragraph from the IPCC Special Report on Global Warming of 1.5 °C (SR15) to headline a political campaign that there were only 12 years to prevent dangerous climate change. This controversy highlights the huge transformations in the political and media landscapes since the IPCC's formation in 1988 and opens up the question of whether its communication approach remains fit for purpose. We highlight how the IPCC's communication dilemma stems from the historic decision to design it to be an authoritative voice rather than a deliberative space.

26.1 Introduction

The importance of communicating authoritative scientific knowledge to multiple audiences was integral to the IPCC from its establishment in 1988. In his history of the IPCC, Bert Bolin, its first chairman, argued that 'forthcoming reports must be written by renowned scientists and in such a manner that ... would be read far outside the scientific community' and that 'there would be a need to reach out to the public, stake-holders, decision-makers and politicians' (Bolin, 2007: 48). Bolin's successor as IPCC chairman, Robert Watson, similarly described outreach and communication as one of the characteristics necessary to make scientific assessments useful (Watson, 2005: 473). With particular regard to public communication of climate science, Bolin identifies how a stringent assessment of the science could help to resolve disagreement between scientists and prevent a 'chaotic' debate with citizens (Bolin, 2007: 49). He further noted that 'the scientific community does not yet fully appreciate the way politicians make use of and the general public interprets the information that scientists provide' (Bolin, 2007: 199).

The imagined model here is one where different strands of the climate science literature are transformed by IPCC processes into a coherent and consensual knowledge product (see **Chapter 19**), which is then communicated to different groups outside climate science communities. However, this model could be more accurately referred to as 'science distribution' than science communication, with a view to persuading these groups as to the robustness and importance of the knowledge (Trench, 2008). While this model of science communication has been prevalent far beyond climate change, it was particularly embedded into the IPCC from the organisation's inception (see **Chapter 2**). Clark Miller identifies how, although the IPCC has an ostensibly global orientation in its framing of the climate system, a single political culture – that of the United States – has had a disproportionate influence on the organisation's design. This has established the IPCC as a means of projecting scientific authority, rather than as a space for deliberation around competing framings and meanings of climate change (Miller, 2009: 158–159). This quest for authority over and above the political fray has led the IPCC to prize global framings, scientific disinterestedness and consensus over local issues, policy relevance and plurality (Pearce et al., 2018). These trade-offs have implications for the IPCC's communication model, and while its 'just the facts' approach has established scientific authority, recent developments have reinforced the model's structural weakness in a world where media technology has transformed and methods for validating public facts are rapidly evolving (Marres, 2018).

This chapter takes these issues in turn. First, we review recent developments in the IPCC's communications strategy, which reinforce the importance of objectivity and authority. Second, we highlight key issues in the social science literature on IPCC communication and how these relate to the organisation's structural issues. Third, we focus on the recent '12 years' controversy as an example of how both epistemic authority and climate politics have changed in the last three decades, and the dilemmas this opens up for the IPCC in its communications strategy.

26.2 IPCC Communication Strategy: Authoritative Objectivity with Multiple Audiences

Notwithstanding the IPCC's involvement in outreach activities since the release of the Third Assessment Report (2001) (AR3), and despite controversies and increasing pressures from outside under the chairmanship of Rajendra Pachauri, it was not until 2012 that the organisation first adopted an official communications strategy (IPCC, 2021e; De Pryck, 2021b). This strategy was last revised in March 2021 and is guided principally by two policy documents produced by the IPCC Secretariat in consultation with the IPCC's Communications Action Team. These documents are, one, a review of the IPCC's Communications Strategy (IPCC, 2021e) and, two, the subsequently updated IPCC Communications Strategy of 2021 (IPCC, 2021f). In these documents, the IPCC adopts two central goals for its strategic communication efforts: to communicate the issue of climate change and to communicate its own organisational processes and structures. Phrased differently, it aims to communicate the scientific knowledge it produces and also how this knowledge is produced. The former centres on providing 'clear and balanced information on climate change' (IPCC, 2021f: 1), and the latter on underpinning this information with the IPCC's 'reputation as a credible, transparent, balanced and authoritative scientific body' (IPCC, 2021f: 1). Together, these goals construct the principal aim 'to establish the IPCC as the key science/ policy interface organisation for climate change' (IPCC, 2021f: 2).

In its communications strategy, the IPCC defines for itself two 'primary target audiences' (IPCC, 2021f: 3), namely the United Nations and its intergovernmental processes – in particular the UN Framework Convention on Climate Change (UNFCCC) – on the one hand, and 'governments and policymakers at all levels' on the other (IPCC, 2021f: 3). Next to these two primary targets the IPCC lists a wide range of secondary audiences including the scientific, education, business and non-governmental organisation (NGO) sectors, and names various strategic communication goals, such as to build relationships with the media and to produce context specific 'tailor-made outreach activities' (IPCC, 2021f: 3). While their communications strategy points to third parties as intermediary communicators of IPCC assessments, it makes unmistakably clear that such third-party communication products must not be considered 'in any way products of the IPCC' (IPCC, 2021f: 3).

The IPCC's concern for authoritative objectivity is made explicit in its discussion of the selection and training of spokespeople, who are expected to 'focus on communicating a factual, objective presentation of information from the approved IPCC reports and refrain from public statements that could be interpreted as advocacy and compromise the IPCC's reputation for neutrality' (IPCC, 2021f: 5). In the review of its 2019 communications strategy (IPCC, 2021e), the IPCC positions this choice of audience as the central decision of any communication strategy. In particular, it posits a tension between targeting a specific core audience on the one hand and, on the other, reaching 'as many people as possible' (IPCC, 2021e: 9). The importance of the former is expressed as concerning climate policy relevance, while the latter 'matters for overall impact and visibility' (IPCC, 2021e: 9). It is this distinction that underlies the demarcation between primary and secondary target audiences mentioned earlier. Interestingly, the IPCC does not position its attempts to reach a wider audience as a response to an impetus emerging from within the organisation itself. Rather, it is a response to the 'widespread and growing interest of the non-specialist public in our work' (IPCC, 2021e: 9). Notably, the IPCC expresses a need to 'understand advances in climate communications specifically, such as behavioural science' (IPCC, 2021e: 4) in order to pursue these objectives.

In addition to the review and strategy documents, in September 2020 the IPCC published a guidance note for authors of its Sixth Assessment Report (AR6) specifically on communicating climate change-related risks and risk management options. The note is in many ways similar to its much earlier guidance note on communicating uncertainties for the authors of its Fifth Assessment Report (AR5) (see Chapter 17). The issue of uncertainty, in fact, is one of the central points of discussion in its guidance concerning risk, with attempts to harmonise uncertainty communication across the IPCC's three Working Groups (WGs) proving challenging (Janzwood, 2020; see also Chapter 25).

26.3 Issues in IPCC Communication

The IPCC's approach to communication has been subject to wide-ranging criticisms in the social scientific literature. The majority of this literature assumes a linear model of communication by which the IPCC's efforts produce varyingly inadequate or insufficient outcomes among the so envisioned audiences. A long-standing and central element of this critique is the IPCC's communication of risk and uncertainty, an issue the IPCC is itself concerned about as seen in its author guidance documents. The issues discussed by the literature on the IPCC's approach to risk and uncertainty have included the following four: ambiguity in wording and subsequent invitation of interpretive biases by different readerships (Patt & Dessai, 2005); inconsistencies in communicating the distinctions between the different sources of uncertainty such as climate system response and future emissions (Ekwurzel et al., 2011); a too narrow communication of risks as statistical expectations detached from the strength of the knowledge supporting them (Aven, 2020); and a lack of concrete representations and efficacy information to motivate action (Poortvliet et al., 2020). In recent years the academic literature has raised a wider array of concerns regarding the IPCC approach to climate change communication. These concerns include the persistent reliance on a consensus policy in communication (Hoppe & Rödder, 2019), an unhelpful use of complex language and its subsequent misinterpretation (Bruine de Bruin et al., 2021) and, most radically, the prominence of an economic growth framing that some see as hindering a transition towards carbon-neutral societies (Kanerva & Krizsán, 2021).

Many of these critiques relate to the reception of IPCC communications by different audiences. Yet as Beck (2012) pointed out a decade ago, the relationship between the IPCC and wider publics cannot be reduced to whether or not communication is effective when the linear model of expertise that the IPCC operates under itself conditions transparency, accountability and public trust. Dudman and de Wit (2021) have recently pushed further in this more fundamental rethinking of forms of scientific appraisal and models of expertise and communication. These authors argue for the IPCC to adopt a reciprocal rather than a unidirectional approach in its communication efforts. Instead of focusing on further strengthening the voice of the IPCC, they propose a new approach to communicative thinking built around both speaking and listening that 'makes space for social complexity within the machinery of the institution' (Dudman and de Wit, 2021: 8). Nightingale et al. (2020) similarly argue that what guides current responses to climate change is a techno-scientific apparatus represented by organisations such as the IPCC. This apparatus insufficiently addresses how climate change acquires meaning and value – how it is known and experienced – while simultaneously disempowering people. In contrast, they argue that climate change needs to be addressed 'with contested politics and the everyday foundations of action, rather than just data' (Nightingale et al., 2020: 348). Many of the debates reviewed in this section map onto trends in the wider science communication literature; in particular, the shift from a deficit model of communication to greater dialogue between scientists and their audiences (Smallman, 2016). Next, we look at an emerging focus of science communication studies that is more specific to the IPCC: appropriation.

26.4 The Appropriation of IPCC Communication

Whether distributing knowledge or starting to engage in a more dialogic process, the IPCC remains a key actor in the communication of its knowledge. However, as climate change becomes ever more political, the likelihood increases that the IPCC's scientific knowledge will be appropriated by other actors without prior consultation. For example, Sanford et al. (2021) draw parallels between the responses to the 2019 IPCC Special Report on Climate Change and Land and the 2018 SR15 report, in particular the '12-year deadline' narrative emerging from the latter report that was appropriated by activists (see Box 26.1). It is in this context that the authors charge the IPCC to 'respond more effectively to distortions of the content of its reports' (Sanford et al., 2021: 21). Boykoff and Pearman (2019: 285) similarly identify the '12-year "deadline" trope' in the appropriation of SR15 and

---

Box 26.1
The IPCC's communication dilemma over '12 years'

The recent '12 years' communication controversy demonstrates both the persistence of challenges identified in the early days of the IPCC, as well as the changing social context that the organisation finds itself in regarding climate change knowledge politics. SR15 was an important report, focusing on the global temperature target contained in the Paris Agreement and the first time that all three WGs collaborated on a single report (Bounegru et al., 2020). In Bert Bolin's terms, it provided a new iteration in the IPCC's efforts to resolve scientific disagreement and bring order to climate change knowledge. However, this impressive achievement did not have the effect Bolin envisaged of preventing a chaotic public debate. Rather, a new scientific and political controversy was sparked when an article in the UK national newspaper, *The Guardian,* interpreted two statements in the report as a warning that there were only '12 years to limit climate change catastrophe' (Asayama et al., 2019).

The '12 years' claim was taken up by newly prominent climate activists such as Extinction Rebellion and Sunrise Movement (Asayama et al., 2019), as well as becoming widespread in more establishment organisations such as the World Economic Forum and the UN Environment Programme (UNEP). The easy mobility of this claim arguably marked one of the greatest political impacts of any IPCC report. However, it provided both the IPCC and the wider scientific community with a dilemma: should they attempt to retake control of the narrative by pointing out the wider context for the statements underpinning '12 years', or accept – as Wimsatt and Beardsley argued 75 years ago – that the report is 'detached from the author at birth, and goes about the world beyond his [sic] power to intend about it or control it' (Wimsatt & Beardsley, 1946: 470). As it turned out, the IPCC did not issue any official clarification regarding the accuracy of the 12 years claim, although some prominent climate scientists did provide strong criticism of the idea that there was any 'cliff edge' in climate change related to 12 years (Freedman, 2019). This was a resolution of sorts to the dilemma. But it highlighted a new problem for the IPCC: having spent years crafting an authoritative, consensual voice of climate science as a bulwark against climate sceptics, accusations of misinterpretation were now being levelled at those wanting an acceleration in climate action.

---

its potentially obstructionist effects. The effect, they claim, induces fear and disengagement and points to a 'critical need for more creative, co-produced, and innovative ways to meet everyday people where they are on the existential collective-action problem of climate change' (Boykoff & Pearman, 2019: 287).

Similarly to the discussions summarised earlier, some scholars argue for a more fundamental shift away from concerns about the communication of knowledge to concerns about how the IPCC's knowledge is produced and applied. Drawing on surveys and interviews with, among others, policy-makers – and using the IPCC's AR5 report – Tàbara et al. (2017) argue that it is not the adequacy or inadequacy of assumptions about knowledge that stand to be critiqued and transformed. Rather, it is the assumptions of the IPCC's knowledge systems, their interactions and normative positions. What climate policy requires, they conclude, are 'new knowledge integration spaces in which meaningful dialogues leading to solutions and new forms of communication strategies can be jointly elaborated' (Tàbara et al., 2017: 36), rather than further attempts to fill knowledge gaps and deficits (Hulme, 2018).

It is also noteworthy that much literature on the IPCC's communication efforts is concerned almost exclusively with a universalisation of climate change and its communication. The literature on the appropriation of IPCC's knowledge, however, shows more concern for particularities, especially in local appropriations. Studies illustrating this critique would include analysis of the coverage of IPCC reports in Japanese mass media, domesticating the global to the national and blurring lines between science and politics (Asayama & Ishii, 2014), or the particularised perceptions and representations of climate change as a social phenomenon emerging out of political and media contexts in Spain (Teso-Alonso et al., 2021).

26.5 Achievements and Challenges

The IPCC has unquestionably transformed the production and communication of climate change knowledge, and there is now widespread awareness and acceptance of some basic facts about climate science, even in the traditionally sceptical USA (Pearce et al., 2017b). By projecting its authority as a novel organisation at the interface of climate science and policy, the IPCC has established a widely accepted baseline of climate knowledge, with reports prompting discussions of climate science across mainstream and social media, and frequently referred to by a broad range of actors. The IPCC has attempted to learn from previous missteps, developing a more comprehensive communications strategy in response to criticisms from the InterAcademy Council regarding uncertainty communication and the acknowledgement of errors (Beck, 2012). The IPCC is also starting to demonstrate increased reflexivity on the context for its science communication, with a section in Chapter 1 of the AR6 WG1 report (IPCC, 2021a) explicitly addressing the new media context for its work.

However, despite these advances, the IPCC remains faced with structural challenges to communication. As the IPCC has helped broaden awareness of scientific knowledge about the physical processes of climate change, so the focus of opposition has shifted to the efficacy and impacts of 'policy options and solutions' (Bounegru et al., 2020). For example, in 2021 the Global Warming Policy Foundation – a UK body renowned for its climate scepticism – transmogrified into Net Zero Watch. In its previous incarnation, the Foundation gave prominence to a flatlining global temperature graph. Now it focuses on the economic impacts of net zero, where values are likely to play a prominent role in choosing, for example, how future damage from climate change should be valued in the present (Jasanoff, 2010b). The IPCC has less leverage in these areas, as the institution remains explicitly *not* 'policy-prescriptive' and does not engage in controversies about their reports.

Looking forward, the IPCC could, in theory, adopt a radically different deliberative model closer to that envisaged by Clark Miller (see **Chapter 27**), more attuned to the shift in attention to political climate change issues where values are more prominent. This 'cosmopolitan' approach could enable a shift from knowledge distribution to more genuine dialogue (Raman & Pearce, 2020). For example, the IPCC could provide space for people to declare and discuss their hopes and fears about climate change, prompted by normative questions such as 'how shall we live?' (Corner & Groves, 2014). Such a move would require the re-structuring of IPCC reports, providing a means of directing the IPCC assessment agenda towards topics of public interest. Undoubtedly such a shift would bring risks for the IPCC and for its position as an epistemic authority in climate politics. Equally risky perhaps, would be for the IPCC to persist in its commitment to policy neutrality in a world where these climate politics are becoming ever more contested and urgent. Either way, the IPCC cannot afford to proceed without a meaningful reflection on the impacts and implications of its communication practices within a rapidly evolving political climate.

Three Key Readings

Asayama, S., Bellamy, R., Geden, O., Pearce, W. and Hulme, M. (2019). Why setting a climate deadline is dangerous. *Nature Climate Change*, 9(8): 570–572. http://doi.org/10.1038/s41558–019-0543-4

This paper focuses on the rise in 'deadline' rhetoric following the IPCC SR15, and the challenge of maintaining policy neutrality when its assessments are used for political purposes.

Hoppe, I. and Rödder, S. (2019). Speaking with one voice for climate science – Climate researchers' opinion on the consensus policy of the IPCC. *Journal of Science Communication*, 18(03): a04. http://doi.org/10.22323/2.18030204

This article shows how support for the IPCC's consensus model of communication varies according to researchers' disciplinary background, with greater support coming from climate scientists than from social scientists.

O'Neill, S. and Pidcock, R. (2021). Introducing the topical collection: 'Climate Change Communication and the IPCC'. *Climatic Change*, 169(3): 19. http://doi.org/10.1007/s10584–021-03253-3

This editorial introduces a topical collection of research on the IPCC and climate communication, and suggests that the IPCC could shift from a communication strategy to an engagement strategy, as well as 'road testing' more deliberative and dialogic approaches to communication.

27

Re-imagining the IPCC

A Proposal

CLARK MILLER

Overview

This chapter positions the Intergovernmental Panel on Climate Change (IPCC) in the context of global efforts to understand and combat climate change. Throughout its first three decades, as nations have sought to understand and prioritise climate change in global policy, the IPCC has served as the world's principal knowledge-making institution. It has created, authorised and narrated a new kind of global knowledge; profoundly shaped global public imagination of the climate emergency; and provided epistemic support to the call for collective global action to tackle it. Looking forward, however, it is less clear whether the IPCC is well positioned to help support the work of institutions around the world to end fossil fuel use and reduce greenhouse gas emissions. The chapter asks, therefore, whether the IPCC needs to be re-imagined if it is to help advance the transition to a climate-neutral global economy and energy systems.

27.1 Introduction

When the IPCC was established in 1988, it was intended as a space of global politics for translating climate science into the design and negotiation of coordinated global action (Miller 2004). That idea quickly broke down after the signing of the 1992 UN Framework Convention on Climate Change (UNFCCC). Instead, the IPCC was rebuilt as a scientific advisory body to review and synthesise scientific and social scientific knowledge about climate change for global policymakers. It has exercised that responsibility for nearly three decades (Beck et al., 2014).

The shift to science advice did not ultimately reduce the IPCC's political significance. In packaging assessed scientific knowledge for public and policy consumption, the IPCC constructed out of the cacophony of disjointed scientific work *a global fact base* that establishes the existence of the Earth's climate system, illuminates the dangerous risks threatening that system, and demonstrates humanity's responsibility for creating those risks (Borie et al., 2021). In short, the IPCC helped fashion *the imaginary of a climate emergency* now shared broadly in the global public imagination (for one illustrative framing, see Ripple et al., 2021) and positioned its knowledge as the definitive source for understanding this planetary crisis. There are, to be sure, many framings of the climate emergency – and how to tackle it. Yet, there are also continuities: that climate change is an emergency; that it is a disturbance of the global climate system; and that solutions must be global. The IPCC has contributed deeply to shaping these continuities. It is no accident that the UN Secretary General specifically identified the 2021 IPCC Sixth Assessment Report (AR6) Working Group I (WGI) report as a 'code red' for humanity (Guterres, 2021).

This chapter reviews the IPCC's intertwined epistemic and political work over the past three decades. Scholars in science and technology studies (STS) label such work *co-production*, meaning the ways in which knowledge and social order are configured together (Jasanoff, 2004). The IPCC epitomises co-production, simultaneously helping create three key 'products': a new kind of global knowledge; a new class of global knowledge institutions to make it; and a new form of global politics centred on forging global policy responses to global problems (Miller, 2004). Few such exercises of global power go uncontested, however. From the 1990s through the 2010s, the IPCC was a lightning rod for opposition in fights over global climate science and policy. Critics challenged many aspects of the IPCC, and for many reasons (Feder, 1996; Hulme, 2009; Hajer, 2012; Martin, 2014; Beck & Mahony, 2018a; Sanford et al., 2021). Two sets of criticisms are especially relevant to this chapter. From one direction, opponents of climate action sought to undermine the credibility of *specific IPCC knowledge claims* and of the IPCC as a scientific institution in an attempt to protect fossil fuel industries. Others criticised *the IPCC's ways of knowing* as an illegitimate approach to making global knowledge and organising global governance. They argued that the IPCC excluded important groups and their knowledges, and inappropriately framed climate change as a singular, universal global problem.

The IPCC has largely defeated the first set of criticisms, amid broader shifts in climate policy and public opinion toward the foreseeable elimination of fossil fuels. Since 2020, global climate debates have passed an important turning point (see Fink, 2020, for an illustration of an influential financial institution adopting climate change as central to its own transformation). As witnessed at COP26 in Glasgow, a substantial majority of the world's governments and industries now publicly support systematic action to create a climate-neutral future and transform the global economy and energy systems by 2050 (for example EU, 2021).

Accomplishing this goal will not be easy, and knowledge will remain critical to informing world action. The kinds of knowledge and politics needed, however, may differ significantly from those developed and curated by the IPCC to date. This makes the second set of criticisms of the IPCC all the more poignant. What kinds of knowledge should guide action to end fossil fuel use and decarbonise the global economy? Who should participate in that knowledge-making? Is the global construction and organisation of knowledge that underpins imagination of the climate emergency what is now needed? It concludes, therefore, by asking 'Now what?' for the IPCC. The chapter argues that the IPCC should carefully consider the kind of knowledge and politics it is bringing into being and informing – and re-imagine itself as fit-for-purpose for the task(s) ahead. Understanding the challenge of transitioning to a post-carbon economy and the different possibilities for replacing it, and helping different communities and places advance that agenda, in differentiated ways, is a critical problem to which the IPCC could potentially contribute. Or not. Different pathways forward could lead to very different futures, and how both the science and politics of those pathways is narrated matters (Hulme, 2019).

27.2 The Organisation of Global Knowledge-making

At its most basic meaning, the idea of co-production emphasises (i) that new knowledge is made – i.e., it is a product of human work – through the design and organisation of new social and institutional practices; and (ii) that new ways of ordering social organisation and practices are orchestrated through the making and application of new kinds of knowledge (Miller & Muñoz-Erickson, 2018). The emergence of a new kind of politics of planetary emergency is no exception. Throughout its history, the IPCC has pioneered both the globalisation of knowledge-making and its use to inform and drive global politics (Miller & Edwards, 2001). The IPCC has worked to characterise and establish the ontological reality of the climate system as a global object at risk from human affairs (Edwards, 2010). It presents itself as an institution that represents and synthesises scientific and social scientific knowledge from all peoples and countries (Ho-Lem et al., 2011); can thus present its findings credibly to policy audiences across the globe (Mahony, 2014a); and is capable of identifying and analysing global problems so as to inform and coordinate collective global action to correct them (Turnhout et al., 2016). See **Chapters 7** and **23** for a thorough and appropriate critique of that self-image.

Even the earliest statements of the IPCC present the basic outlines of this framework. In presenting the findings of the IPCC First Assessment Report (AR1) in 1990, for example, Bert Bolin, the first chair of the IPCC, emphasised the factual reality of climate change – 'there is a greenhouse effect'; its global ontology – 'how the global climate system operates'; and the ability of the IPCC to guide collective action – 'clear justification for the need to start the process of combating climate change now' (Bolin, 1991: 19–20). Over time, these core elements of IPCC knowledge-making became even clearer and more ambitious, as the IPCC incrementally ratcheted up the immediacy of its warnings and the need for rapid, global action to combat it (IPCC, 2021a).

This epistemic and narrative work by the IPCC played a central role in establishing climate change as a widely shared global fact in the imagination of publics around the globe. It has also shaped and delimited what people know about climate change, and built causal narratives that connect these evidentiary foundations to visions and values of action within a global imaginary of climate emergency. In a recent survey of 1.2 million people in 50 countries, 'nearly two-thirds (64 per cent) of people in 50 countries believe that climate change is a global emergency' (UNDP, 2020: 15), including 58 per cent in the least developed countries and 61 per cent or more in every region of the world.

The drip, drip, drip of three decades of IPCC reports, responses to and criticisms of them by policymakers, business leaders, activists and scientists around the globe – and its coverage in global media – has had an enormous impact on global public imagination (Kunelius et al., 2017). Today, the IPCC stands at the centre of a world-spanning – admittedly somewhat decentralised – global machinery, extending throughout diverse policy, economic, media, social media and non-governmental institutions in every country, dedicated to creating and distributing knowledge about climate change among global publics (Boykoff & Yulsman, 2013). Within those networks, the ideas about climate change that the IPCC articulates are the grist around which all sorts of knowledge-making gets spun (Boykoff & Pearman, 2019).

27.3 The Conflict over Global Knowledge-making

The IPCC's success in creating a global fact base for understanding and acting on climate change catalysed a multi-decade conflict over global knowledge-making. One facet of this conflict has centred on attacks on the credibility of the IPCC and its knowledge claims (Hulme, 2013). These attacks have come from very different directions – some motivated by a narrow desire to protect carbon economies, some by a fear that knowledge of global risks will support rising calls for stronger global governance, and some by deep concerns about the narrative of emergency that circulates in and around IPCC reports. These attacks – and responses to them – have done little to slow the global spread of the imaginary of a climate emergency. They have, however, done damage – for example polarising the IPCC among some groups, slowing policy responses, and contributing to the rise of post-truth knowledge politics in global discourses, especially but by no means exclusively in the United States (Fischer, 2019).

A second facet of the conflict has focused on efforts to extend the model of the IPCC into other domains of global governance. This criticism has focused more on the legitimacy of the IPCC's ways of knowing, practices of inclusion and governance, and role in framing climate change. In important ways, the IPCC has become the model for making knowledge about global risks, especially in the health, environmental and biological sciences (Beck et al., 2014). In biodiversity conservation, for example, scientists have sought to articulate the diversity of life on Earth as 'an irreplaceable natural heritage' at risk of a global 'biodiversity crisis' and to establish 'a mechanism akin to the IPCC' to build a global fact base that justifies global action to halt the loss of species and habitats around the world (Loreau et al., 2006). The World Health Organisation (WHO) adopted similar strategies on tobacco and emerging diseases. It cast both as 'global health risks'. It established, in 2003, a Framework Convention on Tobacco Control – note the similarity in language to the Framework Convention on Climate Change. Finally, in 2005, upgrades to the WHO's International Health Regulations allowed the WHO to declare global health emergencies (Miller, 2015a).

These efforts to globalise science, risk, and governance for biodiversity and health ultimately backfired. Viewing them as threats to national sovereignty – over, respectively, the ownership of national biological resources and health security decision-making – key countries refused to countenance the globalisation of either knowledge-making or policy authority. Under Chinese leadership after 2006, WHO capacity to detect and respond to infectious diseases was systematically dismantled. This contributed to slower and less effective responses to Ebola in 2013–2016 and COVID in 2020–2021, as well as to political conflict over the scientific guidance and proper role of the WHO in both instances. In parallel, opposition from Brazil, Indonesia and other large, biodiverse countries, slowed the development of international scientific advisory processes for biodiversity conservation. When the Intergovernmental Science-Policy Platform for Biodiversity and Ecosystem Services (IPBES) was finally established in 2012, it followed a very different model to the IPCC. It emphasised cultivating distributed and diversified scientific capacity and governance at local and national scales (Beck et al., 2014; Borie et al., 2021). This was despite repeated agitation by the scientific community for stronger, more centralised knowledge-making and action (Wilhere, 2021).

27.4 Knowledge-making and Public Imagination

The tremendous impact of the IPCC in shaping global public imagination – and the conflicts it engendered – is a reminder that it matters *how* global knowledge is chosen to be made and *how* global knowledge is made to entwine with global politics. Scholarship on knowledge politics has long emphasised this point – knowledge is power, forms of knowledge-making are forms of governance, and the modern state incorporates a wide diversity of institutional arrangements for making knowledge and applying it to the exercise of political muscle (Jasanoff, 1990; Ezrahi, 1990; Foucault, 1991; Miller, 2015b). It is no surprise that similar dynamics are at play in global governance.

What next, then, for the IPCC? The current form of knowledge politics produced by the IPCC – global, emergency, centred on the threat to planetary systems – demands a global policy response and mirrors those that, historically, have helped buttress the creation of strong national states (Scott, 1995) and state regulatory apparatuses for controlling resources and protecting against risk (Rueschemeyer & Skocpol, 1996; Hays, 1999). Thus, given the current IPCC orientation, it is no surprise to note high levels of anxiety over the persistent failures of the UNFCCC Conferences of Parties (COP) to write strong global climate rules (Dauvergne, 2021), recurring calls to establish a world environment organisation (Biermann, 2020), or calls for emergency global powers to address the climate crisis (Gills & Morgan, 2020).

Is that really the way to go, however? Mike Hulme has argued that the politics of emergency are a treacherous foundation on which to build a sustainable future for humankind (Hulme, 2019). Especially at a time when democracy seems fragile, and many see a growing gap between the world's citizens and the governments that represent them (Castells, 2018), it is appropriate to ask whether an alternative politics of climate change might exist.

Although the IPCC has always framed its work as informing and motivating global policymakers, an alternative, bottom-up social movement has also formed to accelerate climate action. Worldwide, cities, communities, businesses, energy organisations, local governments, countries and other kinds of organisations are setting their own targets to achieve climate-neutral futures and, more importantly, making plans and investments to reduce greenhouse gas emissions (Kuramochi et al., 2020). This movement – far more than the prospects of a global treaty or extensive new national investments in clean energy infrastructures (IEA, 2021) – gives me hope that climate change will be tackled over the next few decades.

I see in all of this frenetic activity a validation of recent scholarship on *sociotechnical imaginaries* – the shared, socialised forms of public imagination that permeate modern societies (Jasanoff & Kim, 2015). Two aspects of this literature are especially interesting: the centrality of organised practices of fact-making to the creation of sociotechnical imaginaries among democratic publics; and the decentralised processes of knowledge uptake, engagement and interpretation through which those epistemic claims are transformed into social organisation and collective action. In his book *Imagined Communities*, Benedict Anderson depicts the contribution of maps, museums and censuses, all products of State knowledge-making, to the rise of collective national identities in the transition from colonial and monarchic rule to democracy (Anderson, 1991). Similarly, in *Imagined Democracies*, Yaron Ezrahi argues that a foundation of 'reality' – built on shared factual resources, often produced by the state, describing what exists in the world and the causal relationships among its parts – forms an important element in the imaginative resources of publics through which they imagine themselves as democratic (Ezrahi, 2012; Miller, 2015b).

The question is whether there are ways that the IPCC could leverage its power in global knowledge-making to help create new kinds of knowledge capabilities that both support decentralised, polycentric climate action (Ostrom, 2009; Keohane, 2015) *and* strengthen democratic public imaginations around the world. Unfortunately, the current focus of the IPCC on knowledge of global environmental systems offers little to no informational value to sub-global entities seeking to map out paths to reducing greenhouse gas emissions, for example the world's ten thousand electric utilities. Nor is it immediately clear how the current approach of the IPCC helps support the imagination and construction of post-carbon futures by diverse communities around the world.

Maybe the IPCC shouldn't try to help communities find local climate solutions. The power of global scientific institutions like the IPCC to crowd out local ways of knowing must be taken seriously. However, it is worth also taking seriously the possibility of redesigning the IPCC to provide support to regional knowledge institutions and energy transitions. Ending humanity's addiction to fossil fuels will be complex, arduous and tricky. It will take different forms in different communities and places, yet also need to be coordinated to avoid catastrophic risks to regional energy infrastructures – especially in the context of growing weather and climate extremes.

Could the IPCC help develop and distribute the know-how necessary to undertake this work, in a way that supports rather than imposes itself on local communities and actors? For example, the IPCC could leverage its position as an influencer of global public imagination to advocate for new investments in developing the substantial sub-global knowledge capabilities needed to inform decentralised climate action. And it could re-orient and re-imagine its own work in terms of engaging, motivating and supporting polycentric action. Such an approach could potentially help strengthen communities and facilitate democratic imagination and action by helping foster public understanding of what is happening, in detail, at sub-global scales. This would improve deliberation of the adequacy, orientation and justice of sub-global economic and energy transitions (Dryzek, 2012). At the same time, the IPCC could serve as a counterweight to other global actors seeking to inappropriately influence and shape local efforts to imagine and create post-carbon futures. These are ideas worth exploring.

27.5 Achievement and Challenges

In this moment of deep despair for the prospects of the planet, democracy and the human future, it is worth reflecting on what the IPCC has achieved, despite its shortcomings. Today, publics and institutions worldwide understand the need for and are working to achieve climate neutrality by 2050. That new climate social movements and shared climate imaginaries exist is – in no small part – due to the work of the IPCC.

What responsibilities does the IPCC have to these movements to support their work? Correspondingly, what risks does the IPCC face in continuing to support a narrative of climate emergency without also supporting those working, at all levels, to tackle climate change? Up to this point, the IPCC has chosen not to invest substantially in helping diverse actors mobilise or build distributed capacity for the knowledge and expertise necessary to understand how the world's diverse energy systems work, how these energy systems intertwine in complex ways in particular places with a host of other critical infrastructure systems, and what it will take to transform them to achieve a climate-neutral future. Nor has the IPCC sought to track or assess in any significant way the work underway by distributed actors to transform the global economy and global energy systems. The result, unfortunately, is that the IPCC helps perpetuate the idea that the world is not acting sufficiently to tackle climate change, while simultaneously also not working to help those institutions that *are* pursuing that effort.

If the IPCC is to help the world's diverse peoples tackle climate change through collaborative action – and in the process help usher in a transformation of the global economy and energy systems – it needs to reflect on and re-imagine itself as a maker of global *social order*, not simply a maker of global *facts*. It needs to ask what kind of global social order it wants to help call into being. This would be a radical departure for the IPCC and the alternatives are stark. Continued climate emergency is one possibility, along with the treacherous forms of global politics it entails. Another possibility is for the IPCC to reconstitute itself to support a robust, decentralised movement to undertake the essential work of navigating the transition to climate-neutrality – which has to happen everywhere, anyways. Such a movement might make real contributions to shoring up, or even reconstituting, global democracy.

Three Key Readings

Miller, C. A. (2004). Climate science and the making of a global political order. Chapter 3 in: Jasanoff (ed.), *States of Knowledge: The Co-Production of Science and Social Order*. London: Routledge. pp. 46–66.

   This chapter provides an overview of the IPCC as an agent of co-production in climate science and politics.

Jasanoff, S. (2015). Future imperfect: science, technology, and the imaginations of modernity. Chapter 1 in: Jasanoff, S. and Kim, S.-H. (eds.), *Dreamscapes of Modernity: Sociotechnical Imaginaries and the Fabrication of Power*. Chicago: University of Chicago Press. pp. 1–33.

This chapter introduces readersto the concept of sociotechnical imaginaries.

Beck, S. et al. (2014). Towards a reflexive turn in the governance of global environmental expertise. The cases of the IPCC and the IPBES. *GAIA-Ecological Perspectives for Science and Society* 23(2): 80–87. http://doi.org/10.14512/gaia.23.2.4

This article highlights the design differences between the IPCC and IPBES and their implications for the variations of science and politics co-produced by the two institutions.

28

What Has This Book Achieved?

KARI DE PRYCK AND MIKE HULME

Overview

In this chapter we offer concluding remarks based on issues raised in the book and informed by discussions between its contributors at a workshop held in December 2021. We emphasise the need to understand the Intergovernmental Panel on Climate Change (IPCC) as a complex epistemic, social, political and human institution and we evaluate its activities, achievements and challenges using three metaphors. First, we suggest opening the 'black box' of the IPCC to examine its internal workings, to understand how it functions and where its authority comes from. Second, we call for thinking of the IPCC as a 'ship on the ocean' to help situate its work within the scientific and (geo)political contexts in which it evolves. Finally, we caution against thinking of the IPCC as a 'Swiss army knife' that can successfully be all things for all people. These reflections on the design, function and future of the IPCC have implications for the study of other expert institutions.

28.1 What This Book Has Achieved

In *A Critical Assessment of the Intergovernmental Panel on Climate Change*, we have brought together more than 30 social scientists who have each studied the IPCC as an institution, and some of whom have been involved in its activities. These authors bring different disciplinary perspectives to the study of the IPCC, assessing, with a critical eye, the main features of the institution and evaluating its influence. They draw upon the available literature and their own experiences. Taken individually, each chapter offers an analysis of key questions relating to, among other things, the governance of the IPCC, the participants involved, the types of knowledge assessed, the processes guiding its work, and its influence in society. Taken as a whole, the book offers the first comprehensive and detailed overview of the procedures, principles, practices and products that, together, comprise the IPCC and which underpin its authority and project its influence.

The book refrains from treating the IPCC as a unitary actor with a singular function, identity and culture. The starting point for many of the chapters has been recognising the heterogeneity of the institution, which brings together diverse scientific, social scientific, practitioner and political communities. The book therefore presents the IPCC as a complex epistemic, cultural, political and human knowledge institution whose ramifications extend well beyond its organisational boundaries. It shows that the procedures put in place to guide the assessment process, the types of knowledge assessed, as well as the individuals and institutions involved in the organisation, matter for how we think about the knowledge that produces. The IPCC is not a neutral loudspeaker for the voice of climate experts worldwide, but an active participant in producing such a voice. And its reports, products and messages – what that voice speaks – are not interpreted the same way around the world. The IPCC's procedures and modus operandi have implications not only for the framing of climate change in its reports, but also for the construction of its authority in various national and international contexts.

By compiling this book we also seek to start a debate about the perceived successes of the IPCC. We give contributors space to identify and discuss its various achievements, as they understand them, and the range of challenges it faces. 'Success' is not only defined in terms of impact and communication, but also in terms of governance, participation, diversity, transparency and reflexivity. The different chapters thus assess the IPCC with regards to its ability (or failure) to reach across different audiences, to develop inclusive, transparent and fair practices and processes of knowledge assessment, and to reflect on its own role in society.

In this conclusion, we draw out several threads that run through the book, using three different – and deliberately incommensurable – metaphors: the IPCC as a 'black box', as a 'ship in the ocean' and as a 'Swiss army knife'.

28.2 Opening the 'Black Box' of the IPCC

The IPCC is primarily known for the authoritative and scientifically rigorous reports that it periodically publishes and that make headlines in media outlets worldwide. From the outside, like many successful institutions, it resembles a 'black box' – a complex organisation whose internal workings are hidden or, at least, not well understood. The contributions in this book have demonstrated the importance of opening the black box of institutions like the IPCC to describe how expert claims are produced, how their legitimacy and credibility are constructed, and how they are interpreted by a wide range of public audiences. These perspectives have shown that the IPCC is many things: it is a panel of member states; it is three distinct Working Groups (WGs) and a Task Force; it is a small secretariat; and it is a network of researchers, government representatives and bureaucrats spread around the world in different national and international institutions. The chapter contributors have also offered a nuanced reading of some commonplace assumptions about how the IPCC selects its authors, produces its reports and communicates its findings.

First, opening the black box of the IPCC allows us to see how it is a unique experiment of co-production between scientific and social scientific experts and government representatives. It has evolved into a distinct professionalised space of encounter between these different worlds, with its own norms, codes, culture and philosophy. Applying a sociohistorical perspective to the IPCC makes two things clear. First, the institution was imagined, founded and originally designed in the late 1980s, within a particular geopolitical context that shaped its institutional form and governance procedures, and within an epistemic context that recognised a particular relationship between (scientific) knowledge and policymaking, namely, a 'science-first' approach. But, second, in its subsequent history, the institution has been continuously re-shaped by scientific advances, knowledge controversies, and national and international politics; for example, by climate contrarians, by UN Framework Convention on Climate Change (UNFCCC) negotiations and by shifts in geopolitical power. For all these reasons, the IPCC was 'born political', has never escaped subsequent politicisation and never will. All the contributions in this book deconstruct the carefully defended narrative that the institution is able to separate science from politics and that the IPCC is neutral with respect to policy. Yet they also observe that the political nature of the IPCC is not necessarily a problem, if acknowledged and reflected upon.

Second, opening the black box of the IPCC draws attention to how its knowledge assessments are constructed. This construction occurs through both the micro-practices of its participants and through the Panel's orchestration efforts that reach well beyond its institutional boundaries. Over time, the IPCC has developed one of the most sophisticated machineries of all global knowledge assessments, one which mobilises thousands of experts, hundreds of research institutions and scores of bureaucrats, working together over several years. Contributions in this book reveal the importance of the internal rules that guide the work of the institution, manage interactions between authors and government delegates, and respond to criticism. At the same time, they caution against thinking that procedures act as a proxy for objectivity. Rather, such procedures reveal the informality and learning-by-doing approach that prevails in many aspects of the IPCC's assessment process.

Third, opening the black box of the IPCC foregrounds the importance of participation for the legitimacy of its global assessments. Participation in the IPCC is multifaceted. It is characterised by a high level of turnover among expert authors and government representatives, but also by the existence of a small group of individuals building their career and work around IPCC assessments. Participation is also limited. Despite efforts to increase the involvement of various groups – experts from developing countries, civil society, early career researchers, Indigenous Peoples, social scientists, humanities scholars, women – contributions to the book show the difficulties the institution still faces in developing procedures to enhance their participation. Contributors also argue that participation is less about quotas and statistics than it is about strengthening the capacity of these participants to contribute effectively, and with influence, to the IPCC's assessment work. Enhancing such capacity is not only essential to strengthen participants' engagement with the IPCC, but also to improve the quality and relevance of knowledge assessments produced by the IPCC.

Fourth, opening the black box of the IPCC renders visible some of the power asymmetries that characterise relations between disciplines (the natural and social sciences) and epistemologies (scientific and non-scientific systems of knowledge), between authors and governments, and between governments (for example, fossil fuel exporters, small island states, forest-rich countries). IPCC deliberations do not occur in a vacuum; they are subject to the same asymmetries that characterise, more broadly, interdisciplinary and transdisciplinary research, and the distribution of knowledge production between the Global North and the Global South. Many of the chapters identify moments in the assessment process where these asymmetries become visible and limit the consensus strategy pursued by the IPCC. They can restrict meaningful participation and deflect the overall narrative of the assessment.

Finally, and drawing upon the above insights, opening the black box of the IPCC helps situate the particular kind of knowledge that the institution produces and puts into global circulation. Several contributions to the book emphasise the IPCC's reliance on numerical modelling and quantitative analysis to tell the story of climate change, its impacts and potential solutions. Such framing comes at the expense of presenting plural narratives, grounded in perspectives from the social sciences, humanities, and Indigenous knowledge systems, which could reflect how climate change is experienced and interpreted differently around the world. The IPCC's particular framing of climate change also comes at the expense of acknowledging – especially in the Summaries for Policymakers – some of the disagreements and asymmetries of power that run deep within and between societies. And this framing further tends to support technocratic climate solutions that run the risk of locking in certain futures and narrowing the policy options available.

Who the IPCC's experts are (from which country, discipline or societal group) and how they arrive at their conclusions (the content of the black box) are thus as important as what they say (the reports).

28.3 'A Ship on the Ocean'

To use this metaphor of a ship on the ocean, *A Critical Assessment of the Intergovernmental Panel on Climate Change*, while focusing on the IPCC ('the ship'), is also about the context ('the ocean') in which the institution evolves and operates.[1] The IPCC navigates an ocean of variable depth and with dynamic currents and it regularly needs to adapt its sailing techniques. Its architecture and navigation system has evolved over time as the profile of its passengers and crew diversified, as conflicts over its destination arose, and as the physical properties of a warming ocean changed. This is not to say that the 'ship' does not also shape the ocean when its hull enters the water. Quite the contrary. Contributions in the book argue that the IPCC has played a key role in giving prominence to climate science, supporting international climate negotiations and raising global awareness on climate change. And they also show how these processes have, in turn, shaped the IPCC.

First, the authority of the IPCC derives not only from its internal procedures and practices, but from a large network of scientific and research institutions – principally located in Europe, Australia and North America – that have historically supported its work. The IPCC would not be what it is if it could not rely on the resources of these institutional actors whose own activities have, over the years, become increasingly organised around the IPCC's assessment cycles. In turn, these research institutions occupy key positions in the Panel's operations, creating feedback loops whereby the knowledge that these semi-independent and powerful institutions produce becomes even more prominent and influential in shaping and communicating the story of climate change as told by the IPCC.

The 'ship' of the IPCC, through its institutional proximity with the UNFCCC, is also closely connected to 'the ocean' of international climate negotiations. As shown by several contributions in the book, the IPCC has on several occasions become enmeshed in controversies over issues relevant to the negotiations – for example, when the UNFCCC commissioned a Special Report on Land Use, Land-Use Change, and Forestry (SRLULUCF) in 2000, or requested a Special Report on Global Warming of 1.5 °C (SR15) in 2015. In these situations, the IPCC is explicitly called upon to settle a political conflict between parties. The hope is that a rational and technical management of a political problem through IPCC knowledge assessment procedures may ease normative disagreements – such as, in the examples given earlier, what a carbon sink is and why 1.5 °C of warming is safer than 2 °C.

The IPCC is not insulated from the 'winds and currents' of external influences and often ends up trying to respond to them through internal deliberations. So far, the ship of the IPCC has not run aground in these tempestuous storms, although as several of our chapters illustrate it came close to doing so in 2010 following the 'Climategate' controversy and some errors found in the Fourth Assessment Report (2007) (AR4). Several contributions also delve into the implications of the new role taken up by the IPCC in the post-Paris (after 2015) context. The IPCC's principal mandate, dating back to 1988, of assessing what is known about the changing climate and its impacts is evolving into an expectation for the IPCC to pay more attention to the assessment of solutions. In these chapters, our contributors express concern about the prominent place given in IPCC reports to putative solutions to climate change whose technical, social and political feasibility is uncertain – for example, afforestation and bioenergy with carbon capture and storage, also known as BECCS. By promoting certain technocratic solutions that have not been debated through democratic means, the IPCC can be seen by some as exceeding its role as an assessor and synthesiser of knowledge. There are some dangerous rocks here around which the ship of the IPCC needs to navigate.

The IPCC is also connected to other institutions producing global environmental assessments through the links that are made with other problems, such as ozone depletion, biodiversity, desertification, chemical waste pollution and so on. For many interested observers, the IPCC sets an institutional precedent. As an exemplar of a science–policy interface, the IPCC's internal arrangements – consensus-based, intergovernmental, science-focused – serve as a design template for other advocated global environmental assessments. However, the fact that the IPCC ship is still afloat after more than 30 years does not mean that the same ship design and navigating principles are appropriate for the different challenges of different oceans. The establishment in 2012 of the Intergovernmental Science-Policy Platform on Biodiversity and Ecosystem Services (IPBES) is a good illustration of adopting some design features of the IPCC, but choosing a ship and a crew that looked and moved rather differently in order to navigate a different ocean. The IPBES, for example, brings together more diverse types of knowledge and explicitly includes capacity building in its mandate (which the IPCC formally does not).

To continue with this metaphor, the contributions to this book also draw attention to the multiple layers of various depths of the ocean the IPCC navigates. IPCC reports are relevant not only for global governance, but also for different regional, national and local decision-making processes. At the same time, IPCC reports – their framing of climate change, the analytical techniques adopted, their assessment of uncertainties and promotion of visuals – are circulated, used and interpreted in many different ways around the world. The perceived legitimacy of its reports, and their usefulness for various actors, vary significantly over time, and depending on context. In the wake of increased public attention to climate change in recent years – and the worldwide mobilisation of a youth climate movement – IPCC reports are under the spotlight in many countries and are being used by various groups to call for more ambitious national action. But the IPCC also faces contestation by other actors who question its legitimacy and credibility for a variety of reasons. For instance, in the Global North, the IPCC has been the target of climate contrarian groups that sought to delay climate action by discrediting its work. In the Global South – where inequalities in knowledge production and access to resources hinder participation in the IPCC – its reports are criticised for underrepresenting the perspectives of developing countries. And as is made clear in one of our chapters, many Indigenous Peoples feel that the IPCC has not done justice to the Indigeneous knowledge systems held by peoples who feel excluded from participation and yet whose knowledge needs formal means of recognition by the IPCC.

The metaphor of the ship in the ocean draws attention to how the IPCC (the ship) shapes and influences the social, political, cultural and epistemic context (the ocean) in which it is embedded. But the metaphor also points to how this changing environment within which the IPCC operates prompts adjustments to the staffing, the navigational protocols and even some infrastructural elements of the ship.

28.4 'The Swiss Army Knife' Problem

While *A Critical Assessment of the Intergovernmental Panel on Climate Change* has been more concerned about what the IPCC is than about what the IPCC ought to be, this normative question is considered in many contributions. They reveal the diverse expectations that societal actors have about how the IPCC should function and what kind of knowledge it should produce. These ambitious expectations are a reflection of how successful the IPCC is in the eyes of many.

After each assessment cycle, reform of the IPCC is called for. For some, the IPCC should adapt its work so as to produce more tailored and context-specific regional and local information relevant for actors in charge of developing mitigation and adaptation policies. In contrast, for others the IPCC should listen more closely to the needs of the UNFCCC and adjust its publication timeline to key mechanisms, such as the Global Stocktake due to be completed by 2023. Contributors to this book also offer their own expectations for the IPCC. Several of them call for a greater integration of insights from the social sciences, Indigenous knowledge systems, practitioners and even the public at large. Others call for the IPCC to acknowledge its political role and for it to be more reflexive about the policy choices and value judgements that underpin its assessments. One of our contributors calls for the IPCC to redesign itself to be an engine for constituting a new form of global democracy.

As a result of the diversity of its stakeholders, there is no shortage of expectations about what the institution of the IPCC should become. This is what the contributors to this book recognise as the 'Swiss army knife' problem.[2] A Swiss army knife is a unique handy tool that can be used in multiple ways and situations to perform multiple functions. While the IPCC might want its reports to be multifunctional and address a wide range of audiences across the world, in practice this is a difficult and problematic task. It might even be an impossible mission because it is difficult to imagine that the IPCC can simultaneously fulfil all the functions that different societal actors ascribe to it and satisfy all their needs. First, from a human resource perspective, it is complicated because the IPCC may not have the necessary capacity or resources – authors are volunteers for whom the assessment process is already very cumbersome and the volume of literature to assess keeps expanding. Second, from an epistemic perspective, as the contributions to this book have shown, the IPCC is already hardly all things for all people. It is an institution whose reports satisfy some scientific or knowledge communities, and some countries, more than others. Letting in new stakeholders would require substantial re-imagination of the rules and the intricately orchestrated process of assessment writing, and require the redistribution of power within the institution.

Finally, as several contributions suggest, the conflicts that arise in IPCC deliberations are becoming increasingly unresolvable, because they concern clashing worldviews, paradigms and values. While the IPCC might have overcome earlier controversies – for example about the attribution and detection of climate change – it is still struggling to use knowledge to reach a global consensus on how to tackle climate change, and how fast. Such a struggle might not even be necessary anymore, since the Paris Agreement and its Nationally Determined Contributions have in fact allowed for different tracks and different speeds. It might be time for the IPCC to recognise that the issue of climate change divides societies as much as it unites them, and that a rational and technical management of the climate crisis is unlikely to bring about major societal changes.

28.5 Looking Ahead

With the help of the three metaphors discussed, we now circle back to the argument that opened this conclusion – the IPCC is a complex knowledge institution that means a lot of different things to different people. Instead of making the IPCC ship bigger to satisfy all, it may be worth considering building smaller ships to acknowledge the multiple and sometimes contradictory ways of thinking about climate change and its solutions, and more generally about living on Earth. Similarly, instead of thinking of the IPCC and its WGs as the only 'tool' in town – a Swiss army knife – one could think of developing different knowledge and assessment tools fit for particular purposes. This is especially the case now in a world that is more epistemically fragmented and ontologically complex than ever and moving toward a polycentric and nationally oriented policy terrain on climate change.

This could mean moving away from comprehensive assessments to more topically and geographically focused and integrated evaluations. This could be pursued by the IPCC, or by other national and local institutions. For example, the last decade has witnessed the emergence of local IPCCs to guide the implementation of climate change policies 'in the field' – the New York City Panel on Climate Change established in 2009 is a precursor in that regard. If the IPCC is to be continued, it could also write reports with other knowledge institutions –specialised among others in food, biodiversity, energy, trace, finance, human rights – or establishing collaborations with a wider range of stakeholders at different levels of governance. For example, the IPCC/IPBES workshop organised in June 2021 brought much needed information on the synergies and trade-offs between biodiversity protection and climate change mitigation and adaptation, which was reflected in the WGII AR6 report. The IPCC could also move away from centring on global climate projections or proposing ready-made solutions, to instead offer a more careful examination of 'inconvenient truths' – such as historical responsibilities, social and political (in)feasibilities, the underlying drivers of inaction, or the new forms of capitalist domination that the climate transition is creating. As many contributions show, however, the IPCC, in its current intergovernmental form, is not fit for this task.

One could also argue, more provocatively, that we need to hear less about the IPCC and its 'dire' or 'code red' assessments. This does not mean that expertise is not needed anymore, but that it should not be expected – as it is still often the case – to be the primary driver for climate attention and action. It is now the time to move the focus of attention to the political leaders and decision-makers, with all their contradictions and inconsistencies, and request of them to assume the difficult choices that are needed, rather than lean, even if rhetorically, on 'policy neutral' global knowledge to instruct their paths. Climate change is now much less a scientific problem than it is a political and cultural predicament.

The knowledge and arguments contained in *A Critical Assessment of the Intergovernmental Panel on Climate Change* are partial, contingent and contextual. This is true of all knowledge, including that constructed by the IPCC. Yet this book is so far the broadest and most comprehensive assessment of the IPCC as an institution. It offers a 'snapshot' of what an international group of social science researchers understands about it, shaped by the available literature and by the contributors' own situated experiences and judgements. It is a contribution to future debates about the IPCC – and about the role of science in society more generally – offered in good faith.

Notes

1 We want to thank in particular Clark Miller and Shin Asayama for suggesting and developing this metaphor.
2 We thank Shin Asayama for suggesting and developing this metaphor.

Glossary

Boundary objects are objects that inhabit several intersecting social worlds (e.g. science and politics) and satisfy the informational requirement of these different worlds. They are plastic enough to adapt to local needs and the constraints of the several parties employing them, yet robust enough to maintain a common identity across sites (Star and Griesemer, 1989: 393).

Boundary organisations exist at the frontier of the two relatively different social worlds of politics and science, but they have distinct lines of accountability to each. They involve the participation of actors from both sides of the boundary, as well as professionals who serve a mediating role (Guston, 2001: 401).

Boundary spaces are sites where the work of social ordering takes place in ongoing processes of negotiation, translation and accommodation (Mahony, 2013: 31).

Boundary work refers to the ideological style found in scientists' attempts to create a public image for science by contrasting it favourably to non-scientific intellectual or technical activities (Gieryn, 1983: 781)

Civic epistemology refers to the institutionalised practices by which members of a given society test, affirm and deploy knowledge claims used as a basis for making collective choices. (Jasanoff, 2011: 255)

Co-production is used to describe how the domains of nature, facts, objectivity, reason and policy cannot be separated from those of culture, values, subjectivity, emotion and politics (Jasanoff, 2004: 3).

Cosmopolitan knowledge refers to diversity in how communities know and experience climate change (Jasanoff, 2012).

Expert elicitation is a structured approach to systematically consult experts on uncertain issues. It is most often used to quantify ranges for poorly known parameters, but may also be useful to further develop qualitative issues such as definitions, assumptions or conceptual (causal) models (Knol et al., 2010).

Epistemic community refers to a network of professionals with recognised expertise and authoritative claims to policy-relevant knowledge in a particular issue area (Haas, 1992: 3).

Epistemic things are objects to be studied and worked on through the scientific process, which are characterised partly by the things not yet known and the questions they open up for study (Rheinberger, 1997).

Generative events have the potential to foster the disordering conditions in which reasoning is forced to 'slow down', creating opportunities to arouse 'a different awareness of the problems and situations that mobilise us' (Whatmore, 2009: 588).

Knowledge-ways are sets of knowledge practices – ways of making and dealing with knowledge and expertise –that become stabilised within particular institutional settings (Jasanoff, 2005).

Science–policy interfaces are relations between scientists and policy actors that enable exchanges and co-evolution of knowledge with the aim of enriching decision-making (based on Van den Hove, 2007: 807)

Truth spots are places that lend credibility to beliefs and claims about natural and social reality, about the past and future, and about identity and the transcendent (Gieryn, 2018: overview).

Visual indicates a representation perceived through sight, encompassing a wide range of publishable media (videos, photographs, maps, graphs etc.).

Weighted concepts helps to analyse the struggles that the appearance of new objects of knowledge generate, by situating such contestation within the field of political action that these objects have the potential to shape (Hughes and Vadrot, 2019: 18).

Bibliography

Adler, C. E. and Hirsch Hadorn, G. (2014). The IPCC and treatment of uncertainties: topics and sources of dissensus. *Wiley Interdisciplinary Reviews: Climate Change*, 5(5): 663–676.

Afsen, K. H. and Skodvin, T. (1998). The Intergovernmental Panel on Climate Change (IPCC) and Scientific Consensus: How Scientists Come to Say What They Say about Climate Change. CICERO Policy Note 1998:3, University of Oslo, ISSN: 0804-4511.

Agarwal, A., Kalpana, S. and Ravi, C. (1982). *State of India's Environment: A Citizen's Report*. New Delhi: Centre for Science and Environment.

Agarwal, A. and Narain, S. (1991). *Global Warming in an Unequal World*. New Delhi: Centre for Science and the Environment.

Agrawala, S. (1998a). Context and early origins of the Intergovernmental Panel on Climate Change. *Climatic Change*, 39(4): 605–620.

Agrawala, S. (1998b). Structural and process history of the Intergovernmental Panel on Climate Change. *Climatic Change*, 39(4): 621–642.

Agrawala, S., Broad, K. and Guston, D. H. (2001). Integrating climate forecasts and societal decision making: challenges to an emergent boundary organization. *Science, Technology, & Human Values*, 26(4): 454–477.

Ahmed, S. (2012). *On Being Included: Racism and Diversity in Institutional Life*. Durham, NC and London: Duke University Press.

Alcamo, J., Bouwman, A., Edmonds, J., et al. (1995). An evaluation of the IPCC IS92 emission scenarios. In: Houghton, J. T., et al. (eds.), *Climate Change 1994: Reports of Working Groups I and II of the Intergovernmental Panel on Climate Change, forming part of the IPCC Special Report to the first session of the Conference of the Parties to the UN Framework Convention on Climate Change*. Cambridge: Cambridge University Press.

Allan, J., Gutiérrez, M. and Bhandari, R. (2016). Summary of the 44th Session of the IPCC: 17–20 October 2016, *Earth Negotiations Bulletin*, 12 (677). International Institute for Sustainable Development – Reporting Services.

Anderson, B. (1991). *Imagined Communities: Reflections on the Origin and Spread of Nationalism*. New York: Verso Books.

Anderson, K. (2015). Duality in climate science. *Nature Geoscience*, 8: 898–900.

Anderson, K. and Jewell, J. (2019). Debating the bedrock of climate-change mitigation scenarios. *Nature*, 57: 348–349.

Anderson, K. and Peters, G. (2016). The trouble with negative emissions. *Science*, 354: 182–183.

Anon. (2011). Evolving the IPCC. *Nature Climate Change*, 1(8): 227.

Anon. (2018). Editorial: Science benefits from diversity. *Nature*, 558: 5.

Anon. (2021). Food science faces its 'IPCC' moment. *Nature*, 595: 332.

Asayama, S. (2021). Threshold, budget and deadline: beyond the discourse of climate scarcity and control. *Climatic Change*, 167(3): 33.

Asayama, S., Bellamy, R., Geden, O., Pearce, W. and Hulme, M. (2019). Why setting a climate deadline is dangerous. *Nature Climate Change*, 9(8): 570–572.

Asayama, S. and Ishii, A. (2014). Reconstruction of the boundary between climate science and politics: the IPCC in the Japanese mass media, 1988–2007. *Public Understanding of Science*, 23(2): 189–203.

Asdal, K. (2008). Enacting things through numbers: taking nature into account/ing. *Geoforum*, 39(1): 123–132.

Augé, M. (1995). *Non-Places: Introduction to an Anthropology of Supermodernity*. New York: Verso.

Aven, T. (2020). Climate change risk – What is it and how should it be expressed? *Journal of Risk Research*, 23(11): 1–18.

Aven, T. and Renn, O. (2015). An evaluation of the treatment of risk and uncertainties in the IPCC reports on climate change. *Risk Analysis*, 35(4): 701–712.

Ayers, J. M. and Huq, S. (2009). The value of linking mitigation and adaptation: a case study of Bangladesh. *Environmental Management*, 43(5): 753–764.

Aykut, S. C., Morena, E. and Foyer, J. (2021). 'Incantatory' governance: global climate politics' performative turn and its wider significance for global politics. *International Politics*, 58: 519–540.

Bacevic, J. (2022). Epistemic injustice and epistemic positioning: towards an intersectional political economy. *Current Sociology*. http://doi.org/10.1177/00113921211057609

Bäckstrand, K. (2015). Civic society. In: Pattberg, P. and Zelli, F. (eds.), *Encyclopedia of Global Environmental Governance and Politics*. Cheltenham: Edward Elgar Publishing.

Baker, M. (2015). Over half of psychology studies fail reproducibility test. *Nature*, 27 August. http://doi.org/10.1038/nature.2015.18248

Barkemeyer, R., Dessai, S., Monge-Sanz, B., Renzi, B. G., and Napolitano, G. (2016). Linguistic analysis of IPCC summaries for policymakers and associated coverage. *Nature Climate Change*, 6(3): 311–316.

Barry, J. (2021). Green republicanism and a 'Just Transition' from the tyranny of economic growth. *Critical Review of International Social and Political Philosophy*, 24(5): 725–742.

Barry, A., Born, G. and Weszkalnys, G. (2008). Logics of interdisciplinarity. *Economy and Society*, 37(1): 20–49.

Bazeley, P. (2003). Defining 'early career' in research. *Higher Education*, 45: 257–279.

Beatty, J. and Moore, A. (2010). Should we aim for consensus? *Episteme, A Journal of Social Epistemology*, 7(3): 198–214.

Beck, S. (2011a). Moving beyond the linear model of expertise? IPCC and the test of adaptation. *Regional Environmental Change*, (11): 297–306.

Beck, S. (2011b). Between tribalism and trust: the IPCC under the 'public microscope'. *Nature and Culture*, 7(2): 151–173.

Beck, S. (2012). The challenges of building cosmopolitan climate expertise: the case of Germany. *Wiley Interdisciplinary Reviews: Climate Change*, 3(1): 1–17.

Beck, S. and Forsyth, T. J. (2015). Co-production and democratizing global environmental expertise: The IPCC and adaptation to climate change. In: Hilgartner, S., Miller, C. A. and Hagendijk, R. (eds.), *Science and Democracy: Making Knowledge and Making Power in the Biosciences and Beyond*. New York: Routledge. pp. 113–132.

Beck, S. and Mahony, M. (2018a). The IPCC and the new map of science and politics. *Wiley Interdisciplinary Reviews: Climate Change*, 9(6): e547.

Beck, S. and Mahony, M. (2018b). The politics of anticipation: the IPCC and the negative emission technologies experience. *Global Sustainability*, 1: e8.

Beck, S. and Oomen, J. (2021). Imagining the corridor of climate mitigation – What is at stake in IPCC's politics of anticipation? *Environmental Science & Policy*, 123: 169–178.

Beck, S., Borie, M., Chilvers, J., et al. (2014). Towards a reflexive turn in the governance of global environmental expertise. The cases of the IPCC and the IPBES. *GAIA*, 23(2): 80–87.

Beck, S., Jasanoff, S., Stirling, A. and Polzin, C. (2021). The governance of sociotechnical transformations to sustainability. *Current Opinion in Environmental Sustainability*, 49: 143–152.

Beck, U., Giddens, A. and Lash, S. (1994). *Reflexive Modernization: Politics, Tradition and Aesthetics in the Modern Social Order*. Stanford, CA: Stanford University Press.

Begum, R. A., Lempert, R., Ali, E., et al. (2022). Point of departure and key concepts. In: Pörtner, H. O. et al. (eds.), *Climate Change 2022: Impacts, Adaptation, and Vulnerability*. Cambridge: Cambridge University Press. pp. 1–102.

Bell, M. L., Davis, D. L. and Fletcher, T. (2004). A retrospective assessment of mortality from the London smog episode of 1952: the role of influenza and pollution. *Environmental Health Perspectives*, 112(1): 6–8.

Berkes, F. (2018). *Sacred Ecology*. 4th ed. Abingdon: Routledge.

Bernstein, S. (2001). *The Compromise of Liberal Environmentalism*. New York: Columbia University Press.

Biermann, F. (2001). Big science, small impacts–in the South? The influence of global environmental assessments on expert communities in India. *Global Environmental Change*, 11(4): 297–309.

Biermann, F. (2011). New actors and mechanisms of global governance. In: Dryzek, J. S., Norgaard, R. B. and Schlosberg, D. (eds.), *The Oxford Handbook of Climate Change and Society*. Oxford: Oxford University Press. pp. 685–695.

Biermann, F. (2020). World environment organization. In: Morin, J. F. and Orsini, A. (eds.), *Essential Concepts of Global Environmental Governance*. Abingdon: Routledge. pp. 291–293.

Bjurström, A. and Polk, M. (2011). Physical and economic bias in climate change research: a scientometric study of IPCC Third Assessment Report. *Climatic Change*, 108(1): 1–22.

Bodansky, D. (2001). The history of the global climate change regime. In: Luterbacher, U. and Sprinz, D. F. (eds.), *International Relations and Global Climate Change*. Cambridge, MA: MIT Press. pp. 23–40.

Boehmer-Christiansen, S. (1994a). Global climate protection policy: the limits of scientific advice. Part 1. *Global Environmental Change*, 4: 140–159.

Boehmer-Christiansen, S. (1994b). Global climate protection policy: the limits of scientific advice. Part 2. *Global Environmental Change*, 4: 185–200.

Boehmer-Christiansen, S. (1995). Britain and the International Panel on Climate Change: the impact of scientific advice on global warming, Parts 1 and 2. *Environmental Politics*, 4(1): 1–18 and (2):175–196.

Boehmer-Christiansen, S. (1996). Political pressure in the formation of scientific consensus. *Energy and Environment*, 7: 365–376.

Boehmer-Christiansen, S. and Kellow, A. (2002). *International Environmental Policy. Interests and the Failure of the Kyoto Process*. Cheltenham: Edward Elgar.

Bolin, B. (1991). The Intergovernmental Panel on Climate Change. In: Jäger, J. and Ferguson, H. L. (eds.), *Climate Change: Science, Impacts, and Policy, Proceedings of the Second World Climate Conference*. Cambridge: Cambridge University Press.

Bolin, B. (2007). *A History of the Science and Politics of Climate Change: The Role of the Intergovernmental Panel on Climate Change*. Cambridge: Cambridge University Press.

Bony, S., Stevens, B., Held, I. H., et al. (2013). Carbon dioxide and climate: perspectives on a scientific assessment. In: Asrar, G. and Hurrell, J. (eds.), *Climate Science for Serving Society*. Dordrecht, Netherlands: Springer. pp. 391–414.

Borie, M., Gustrafsson, K. M., Obermeister, N., Turnhour, E. and Bridgewater, P. (2020). Institutionalising reflexivity? Transformative learning and the Intergovernmental science-policy Platform on Biodiversity and Ecosystem Services (IPBES). *Environmental Science & Policy*, 110: 71–76.

Borie, M., Mahony, M., Obermeister, N. and Hulme, M. (2021). Knowing like a global expert organization: comparative insights from the IPCC and IPBES. *Global Environmental Change*, 68: 102261.

Bounegru, L., De Pryck, K., Venturini, T. and Mauri, M. (2020). 'We only have 12 years': YouTube and the IPCC Report on Global Warming of 1.5oC. *First Monday*, 25(2). Available at: https://journals.uic.edu/ojs/index.php/fm/article/view/10112 (Accessed: 2 July 2020).

Boykoff, M. and Pearman, O. (2019). Now or never: how media coverage of the IPCC Special Report on 1.5°C shaped climate-action deadlines. *One Earth*, 1(3): 285–288.

Boykoff, M. T. and Yulsman, T. (2013). Political economy, media, and climate change: sinews of modern life. *Wiley Interdisciplinary Reviews: Climate Change*, 4(5): 359–371.

Broome, J. (2020). Philosophy in the IPCC. In: Brister, E. and Frodeman, R. (eds.), *Philosophy for the Real World*. London: Routledge. pp. 95–110.

Brown, H. and Green, M. (2017). Demonstrating development: meetings as management in Kenya's health sector. *Journal of the Royal Anthropological Institute*, 23(S1): 45–62.

Brown, H., Reed, A. and Yarrow, T. (2017). Introduction: towards an ethnography of meeting. *Journal of the Royal Anthropological Institute*, 23(S1): 10–26.

Brown, M. B. (2009). *Science in Democracy: Expertise, Institutions and Representation*. Cambridge, MA: MIT Press.

Bruce, J. P., Lee, H. and Haites, E. F. (eds.) (1996). *Climate Change 1995: Economic and Social Dimensions of Climate Change–Contribution of Working Group III to the Second Assessment Report of the Intergovernmental Panel on Climate Change*. Cambridge: Cambridge University Press.

Bruine de Bruin, W., Rabinovich, L., Weber, K., Babboni, M., Dean, M. and Ignon, L. (2021). Public understanding of climate change terminology. *Climatic Change*, 167(3–4): 37.

Brysse, K., Oreskes, N., O'Reilly, J. and Oppenheimer, M. (2013). Climate change prediction: erring on the side of least drama? *Global Environmental Change*, 23(1): 327–337.

Callaghan, M., Schleussner, C.-F., Nath, S., et al. (2021). Machine-learning-based evidence and attribution mapping of 100,000 climate impact studies. *Nature Climate Change*, 11: 966–972.

Campbell, L. M., Corson, C., Gray, N. J., MacDonald, K. I. and Brosius, J. P. (2014). Studying global environmental meetings to understand global environmental governance. *Global Environmental Politics*, 14(3): 1–20.

Carey, M., James, L. C. and Fuller, H. A. (2014). A new social contract for the IPCC. *Nature Climate Change*, 4: 1038–1039.

Carraro, C., Edenhofer, O., Flachsland, C., Kolstad, C., Stavins, R. and Stowe, R. (2015). The IPCC at a crossroads: opportunities for reform. *Science*, 350 (6256): 34–35.

Carton, W., Asiyanbi, A., Beck, S., Buck, H. and Lund, J. (2020). Negative emissions and the long history of carbon removal. *Wiley Interdisciplinary Reviews: Climate Change.* 11(6): e671.

Casado, M., Gremion, G., Rosenbaum, P., et al. (2019). The benefits to climate science of including early career scientists as reviewers. *Geoscience Communication*, 3: 89–97.

Caseldine, C. J., Turney, C., and Long, A. J. (2010). IPCC and palaeoclimate: an evolving story? *Journal of Quaternry Science*, 25(1): 1–4.

Cash, D., Clark, W., Alcock, F., Dickson, N., Eckley, M. and Jäger, J. (2002). *Salience, Credibility, Legitimacy and Boundaries: Linking Research, Assessment and Decision Making.* WP RWP02–046, Faculty Research Working Papers Series, John F Kennedy School of Government, Harvard University, Cambridge, MA.

Castells, M. (2018). *Rupture: The Crisis of Liberal Democracy.* Hoboken, NJ: John Wiley & Sons.

Castree, N., Bellamy, R. and Osaka, S. (2021). The future of global environmental assessments: making a case for fundamental change. *The Anthropocene Review*, 8(1): 56–82.

Chan, G., Carraro, C., Edenhofer, O., Kolstad, C. and Stavins, R. (2016). Reforming the IPCC's Assessment of Climate Change Economics. *Climate Change Economics*, 7(1): 1–16.

Chen, D., Rojas, M., Samset, B. H., et al. (2021). Framing, context, and methods. In: Masson-Delmotte, V., Zhai, P., Pirani, A., et al. (eds.), *Climate Change 2021: The Physical Science Basis. Contribution of Working Group I to the Sixth Assessment Report of the Intergovernmental Panel on Climate Change.* Cambridge: Cambridge University Press.

Chubin, D. E. and Hackett, E. J. (1990). *Peerless Science: Peer Review and U.S. Science Policy.* Albany: State University of New York Press.

Clarke, L., Jiang K., Akimoto, M., et al. (2014). Assessing transformation pathways. In: Edenhofer, O., Pichs-Madrugada, R., Sokona, Y., et al. (eds.), *Climate Change 2014: Mitigation of Climate Change. Contribution of Working Group III to the Fifth Assessment Report of the Intergovernmental Panel on Climate Change.* Cambridge and New York: Cambridge University Press. pp. 413–510.

Clark, W. C., Mitchell, R. B. and Cash, D. W. (2006). Evaluating the influence of global environmental assessments. In: Mitchell, R. B., Clark, W. C., Cash, W. and Dickson, N. (eds.), *Global Environmental Assessments: Information and Influence.* Cambridge, MA: MIT Press. pp. 1–28.

Cointe, B., Cassen, C. and Nadaï, A. (2019). Organising policy-relevant knowledge for climate action: Integrated Assessment Modelling, the IPCC, and the emergence of a collective expertise on socioeconomic emission scenarios. *Science and Technology Studies*, 32(4): 36–57.

Cointe, B., Ravon, P.-A. and Guérin, E. (2011). *2°C: The History of a Policy-Science Nexus.* 19/11. Paris: IDDRI.

Compagnon, D. and Bernstein, S. (2017). Nondemarcated spaces of knowledge-informed policy making. *Review of Policy Research*, 34(6): 812–826.

Corbera, E., Calvet-Mir, L., Hughes, H. and Paterson, M. (2016). Patterns of authorship in the IPCC Working Group III report. *Nature Climate Change*, 6: 94–99.

Corner, A. and Groves, C. (2014). Breaking the climate change communication deadlock. *Nature Climate Change*, 4(9): 743–745.

Craggs, R. and Mahony, M. (2014). The geographies of the conference: knowledge, performance and protest. *Geography Compass*, 8(6): 414–430.

Cresswell, T. (2004). *Place: A Short Introduction*. Oxford: Blackwell.

Curry, J. A. and Webster, P. J. (2013). Climate change: no consensus on consensus. *CAB Reviews*, 8(001): 1–9.

Dahan-Dalmedico, A. (2008). Climate expertise: between scientific credibility and geopolitical imperatives. *Interdisciplinary Science Reviews*, 33(1): 71–81.

Dahan-Dalmedico, A. (2010). Putting the Earth System in a numerical box? The evolution from climate modeling toward climate change. *Studies in History and Philosophy of Modern Physics*, 41(3): 282–292.

Dahl, T. and Fløttum, K. (2017). Verbal-visual harmony or dissonance? A news values analysis of multimodal news texts on climate change. *Discourse, Context & Media*, 20: 124–131.

Dairon, E. and Badache, F. (2021). Understanding international organizations' headquarters as ecosystems: the case of Geneva. *Global Policy*, 12(Sup.7): 24–33.

Dauvergne, P. (2021). Global governance and the Anthropocene: explaining the escalating global crisis. In: Weiss, T. G. and Wilkinson, R. (eds.), *Global Governance Futures*. London: Routledge.

David-Chavez, D. M. and Gavin, M. C. (2018). A global assessment of Indigenous community engagement in climate research. *Environmental Research Letters*, 13(123005).

De Pryck, K. (2018). *Expertise under Controversy: The Case of the Intergovernmental Panel on Climate Change (IPCC)*. PhD Dissertation, Institut d'études politiques de Paris and Université de Genève.

De Pryck, K. (2021a). Intergovernmental expert consensus in the making: the case of the summary for policy makers of the IPCC 2014 Synthesis Report. *Global Environmental Politics*, 21(1): 108–129.

De Pryck, K. (2021b). Controversial practices: tracing the proceduralization of the IPCC in time and space. *Global Policy*, 12(Sup.7): 80–89.

De Pryck, K. and Wanneau, K. (2017). (Anti)-boundary work in global environmental change research and assessment. *Environmental Science & Policy*, 77: 203–210.

Death, C. (2011). Summit theatre: exemplary governmentality and environmental diplomacy in Johannesburg and Copenhagen. *Environmental Politics*, 20(1): 1–19.

Delvenne, P. and Parotte, C. (2019). Breaking the myth of neutrality: technology assessment has politics, technology assessment as politics. *Technological Forecasting and Social Change*, 139: 64–72.

Demeritt, D. (2001). The construction of global warming and the politics of science. *Annals of the Association of American Geographers*, 91(2): 307–337.

Demeritt, D. and Rothman, D. (1999). Figuring the costs of climate change: an assessment and critique. *Environment and Planning A*, 31(3): 389–408.

Devès, M. H., Lang, M., Bourrelier, P.-H. and Valérian, F. (2017). Why the IPCC should evolve in response to the UNFCCC bottom-up strategy adopted in Paris? An opinion from the French Association for Disaster Risk Reduction. *Environmental Science & Policy*, 78(Supplement C): 142–148.

Díaz, S., Settele, J., Brondizio, E. S., et al. (2019). Pervasive human-driven decline of life on earth points to the need for transformative change. *Science*, 366: 1327.

Díaz-Reviriego, I., Turnhout, E. and Beck, S. (2019). Participation and inclusiveness in the Intergovernmental Science–Policy Platform on Biodiversity and Ecosystem Services. *Nature Sustainability*, 2: 457–464.

Doyle, J. (2011). *Mediating Climate Change*. Abingdon: Routledge.

Draper, D. (1995). Assessment and propagation of model uncertainty. *Journal of the Royal Statistical Society. Series B: Statistical Methodology*, 57: 45–97.

Duarte, T. (2019). O painel brasileiro de mudanças climáticas na interface entre ciência e políticas públicas: identidades, geopolítica e concepções epistemológicas. *Sociologias, 21:* 76–101.

Dudman, K. and de Wit, S. (2021). An IPCC that listens: introducing reciprocity to climate change communication. *Climatic Change*, 168(1–2): 2.

Dunlap, R. E. and McCright, A. M. (2011). Organized climate change denial. In: Dryzek, J. S., Norgaard, R. B. and Schlosberg, D. (eds.), *The Oxford Handbook of Climate Change and Society*. Oxford: Oxford University Press. pp. 144–160.

Dupuy, J. P. (2012). The precautionary principle and enlightened doomsaying. *Revue de Métaphysique et de Morale*, (4): 577–592.

Dryzek, J. S. (2012). *Foundations and Frontiers of Deliberative Governance*. Oxford: Oxford University Press.

ECOSOC and Permanent Forum on Indigenous Issues (2007). *Report of the Secretariat on Indigenous Traditional Knowledge*. Available at: www.ncbi.nlm.nih.gov/pubmed/20845205 (Accessed: 12 February 2022).

ECOSOC and Permanent Forum on Indigenous Issues (2013a). *Study on How the Knowledge, History and Contemporary Social Circumstances of Indigenous Peoples are Embedded in the Curricula of Education Systems*. Available at: https://digitallibrary.un.org/record/746773?ln=en (Accessed: 12 February 2022).

ECOSOC and Permanent Forum on Indigenous Issues (2013b). *Study on Resilience, Traditional Knowledge and Capacity-Building for Pastoralist Communities in Africa*. http://doi.org/10.1093/oxfordhb/9780199560103.003.0007

ECOSOC and Permanent Forum on Indigenous Issues (2014). *Study to Examine Challenges in the African Region to Protecting Traditional Knowledge, Genetic Resources and Folklore*. http://doi.org/10.1093/oxfordhb/9780199560103.003.0007.

ECOSOC and Permanent Forum on Indigenous Issues (2015). *Study on the Treatment of Traditional Knowledge in the Framework of the United Nations Declaration on the Rights of Indigenous Peoples and the Post-2015 Development Agenda*. UN Digital Library. Available at: https://digitallibrary.un.org/record/788550?ln=en (Accessed: 12 February 2022).

Edenhofer, O. (2011). Different views ensure IPCC balance. *Nature Climate Change*, 1: 229–230.

Edenhofer, O. and Kowarsch, M. (2015). Cartography of pathways: a new model for environmental policy assessments. *Environmental Science & Policy*, 51: 56–64.

Edwards, P. N. (1999). Global climate science, uncertainty and politics: data-laden models, models-filtered data. *Science as Culture*, 8(4): 437–472.

Edwards, P. N. (2010). *A Vast Machine: Computer Models, Climate Data and the Politics of Global Warming*. Cambridge, MA: MIT Press.

Edwards, P. N. and Schneider, S. H. (1997). IPCC 1995 Report: Broad consensus or 'scientific cleansing'? *Ecofables/Ecoscience, 1:* 3–9.

Edwards, P. N. and Schneider, S. H. (2001). Self-governance and peer review in science-for-policy: The case of the IPCC Second Assessment Report. In: Miller, C. A. and Edwards, P. N. (eds.), *Changing the Atmosphere: Expert Knowledge and Environmental Governance*. Cambridge, MA: MIT Press. pp. 219–246.

Ekwurzel, B., Frumhoff, P. C. and McCarthy, J. J. (2011). Climate uncertainties and their discontents: increasing the impact of assessments on public understanding of climate risks and choices. *Climatic Change*, 108(4): 791.

El-Hinnawi, E. (2011). The intergovernmental panel on climate change and developing countries. *The Environmentalist*, 31(3): 197–199.

Elzinga, A. (1996). Shaping worldwide consensus: the orchestration of global change research. In: Elzinga, A. and Landström, C. (eds.), *Internationalism and Science*. London: Taylor Graham. pp. 223–255.

ENB [Earth Negotiations Bulletin] (2021). Summary of the 54th Session of the Intergovernmental Panel on Climate Change and the 14th Session of Working Group I: 26 July–6 August 2021. *IISD*, 12(781): 1–27.

ERC [European Research Council] (2021). *Starting Grant*. Available at: https://erc.europa .eu/funding/starting-grants (Accessed: 16 December 2021).

ETC Group (2017). *Re: Conflicts of Interest of Authors on the IPCC Special Report on the Impacts of Global Warming of 1.5°C Above Pre-industrial Levels*. Available at: www .etcgroup.org/files/files/ipcc_conflict_of_interest_release_051217.pdf (Accessed: 25 January 2022).

European Union (2021). 2050 Long-Term Strategy. Available at: https://ec.europa.eu/ clima/eu-action/climate-strategies-targets/2050-long-term-strategy_en (Accessed: 12 February 2022).

Ezrahi, Y. (1990). *The Descent of Icarus: Science and the Transformation of Contemporary Democracy*. Cambridge, MA: Harvard University Press.

Ezrahi, Y. (2012). *Imagined Democracies: Necessary Political Fictions*. Cambridge: Cambridge University Press.

Fankhauser, S. and Tol, R. S. J. (1998). The value of human life in global warming impacts – a comment. *Mitigation and Adaptation Strategies for Global Change*, 3: 87–88.

Farrell, A., VanDeveer, S. D. and Jäger, J. (2001). Environmental assessments: four under-appreciated elements of design. *Global Environmental Change*, (11): 311–333.

Fearnside, P. M. (1998). The value of human life in global warming impacts. *Mitigation and Adaptation Strategies for Global Change*, 3: 83–85.

Feder, T. (1996). Attacks on IPCC report heat controversy over global warming. *Physics Today*, 49(8): 55–57.

Field, C. B. and Barros, V. R. (2015). Added value from IPCC approval sessions. *Science*, 350(6256): 36.

Fink, L. (2020). *A Fundamental Reshaping of Finance*. Black Rock. Available at: www .blackrock.com/corporate/investor-relations/2020-larry-fink-ceo-letter (Accessed: 12 February 2022).

Fiol, C. M. and Lyles, M. A. (1985). Organizational learning. *Academy of Management Review*, 10: 803–813.

Fischer, F. (2019). Knowledge politics and post-truth in climate denial: on the social construction of alternative facts. *Critical Policy Studies*, 13(2): 133–152.

Fløttum, K., Gasper, D. and St. Clair, A. L. (2016). Synthesizing a policy-relevant perspective from the three IPCC 'worlds' – a comparison of topics and frames in the SPMs of the Fifth Assessment Report. *Global Environmental Change*, 38: 118–129.

Fogel, C. (2005). Biotic carbon sequestration and the Kyoto protocol: the construction of global knowledge by the intergovernmental panel on climate change. *International Environmental Agreements: Politics, Law and Economics*, 5(2): 191–210.

Ford, J. D., Cameron, L., Rubis, J., et al. (2016). Including indigenous knowledge and experience in IPCC assessment reports. *Nature Climate Change*, 6: 349–353.

Ford, J. D., Vanderbilt, W. and Berrang-Ford, L. (2012). Authorship in IPCC AR5 and its implications for content: climate change and Indigenous populations in WGII. *Climatic Change*, 113: 201–213.

Forest Peoples Programme et al. (2020). *Local Biodiversity Outlooks 2: The contributions of indigenous peoples and local communities to the implementation of the Strategic Plan for Biodiversity 2011–2020 and to renewing nature and cultures. A compliment to the fifth edition of the Global Biodiv.* Moreton-in-Marsh, UK: Forest Peoples Programme. Available at: www.localbiodiversityoutlooks.net (Accessed: 12 February 2022).

Foucault, M. (1991). Governmentality. In: Burchell, G., Gordon, C. and Miller, P. (eds.), *The Foucault Effect: Studies in Governmentality*. Chicago, IL: University of Chicago Press.

Franz, W. E. (1998). Science, skeptics and non-state actors in the greenhouse. *ENRP Discussion Paper E-98-18*. Kennedy School of Government, Harvard University. Available at: www.belfercenter.org/sites/default/files/files/publication/Science%20Skeptics%20and%20Non-State%20Actors%20in%20the%20Greenhouse%20-%20E-98-18.pdf (Accessed: 19 January 2022).

Freedman, A. (2019). Climate scientists refute 12-year deadline to curb global warming. *Axios*. Available at: www.axios.com/climate-change-scientists-comment-ocasio-cortez-12-year-deadline-c4ba1f99-bc76-42ac-8b93-e4eaa926938d.html (Accessed: 15 March 2019).

Fry, I. (2002). Twists and turns in the jungle: exploring the evolution of land use, land–use change and forestry decisions within the Kyoto Protocol. *Review of European Community and International Environmental Law*, 11(2): 159–168.

Fuglesteved, J., Guivarch, C., Jones, C., et al. (2021). The SSP scenarios as used in Working Group I. Cross-Chapter Box 1.4. In: Masson-Delmotte, V., Zhai, P., Pirani, A., et al. (eds.), *Climate Change 2021: The Physical Science Basis. Contribution of Working Group I to the Sixth Assessment Report of the Intergovernmental Panel on Climate Change*. Cambridge: Cambridge University Press.

Fuller, S. (2002). *Social Epistemology*. 2nd ed. Bloomington: Indiana University Press.

Funtowicz, S. O. and Ravetz, J. R. (1990). *Uncertainty and Quality in Science for Policy*. Amsterdam: Kluwer Academic Publishers.

Funtowicz, S. O. and Ravetz, J. R. (1993). Science for the post-normal age. *Futures*, 25(7): 739–755.

Futhazar, G. (2016). From Climate to Biodiversity – Procedural transcriptions and innovations within IPBES in the light of IPCC practices. In: Hrabanski, M. and Pesche, D. (eds.), *The Intergovernmental Platform on Biodiversity and Ecosystem Services (IPBES). Meeting the Challenge of Biodiversity Conservation and Governance*. London: Routledge. pp. 102–118.

Garard, J. and Kowarsch, M. (2017). If at first you don't succeed: evaluating stakeholder engagement in global environmental assessments. *Environmental Science & Policy*, 77: 235–243.

Garb, Y., Pulver, S. and VanDeveer, S. D. (2008). Scenarios in society, society in scenarios: toward a social scientific analysis of storyline-driven environmental modelling. *Environmental Research Letters*, 3(4): 045015.

Garnett, S. T., Burgess, N. D. and Fa. J. E., et al. (2018). A spatial overview of the global importance of Indigenous lands for conservation. *Nature Sustainability*, 1(7): 369–374.

Gates, W., Boyle, J. S., Covey, C., et al. (1999). An overview of the results of the Atmospheric Model Intercomparison Project (AMIP 1). *Bulletin of the American Meteorological Society,* 80(1): 29–56.

Gaulkin, T. (2021). Why the bad news in IPCC reports is good news for visual learners. *Bulletin of the Atomic Scientists.* Available at: https://thebulletin.org/2021/08/why-the-bad-news-in-the-ipcc-report-is-good-news-for-visual-learners/ (Accessed: 20 August 2021).

Gay-Antaki, M. (2021). Stories from the IPCC: an essay on climate science in fourteen questions. *Global Environmental Change,* 71: 102384.

Gay-Antaki, M. and Liverman, D. (2018). Climate for women in climate science: women scientists and the Intergovernmental Panel on Climate Change. *Proceedings of the National Academy of Sciences of the United States of America,* 115(9): 2060–2065.

Geden, O. (2015). Policy: climate advisers must maintain integrity. *Nature,* 521(7550): 27–28.

Ghaleigh, N. S. (2016). Science and climate change law – The role of the IPCC in international decision-making. In: Gray, K. R., Tarasofsky, R., and Carlarne, C. (eds.), *The Oxford Handbook of International Climate Change Law.* Oxford: Oxford University Press. pp. 56–71.

Gieryn, T. F. (1995). Boundaries of science. In: Jasanoff, S., Markle, G. E., Peterson, J. C. and Pinhch, T. (eds.), *Handbook of Science and Technology Studies.* Thousand Oaks, CA: Sage Publications. pp. 393–443.

Gieryn, T. F. (1999). *Cultural Boundaries of Science: Credibility on the Line.* Chicago, IL: University of Chicago Press.

Gieryn, T. F. (2002). What buildings do. *Theory and Society,* 31(1): 35–74.

Gieryn, T. F. (2018). *Truth-Spots: How Places Make People Believe.* Chicago, IL: The University of Chicago Press.

Gilbert, M. (2002). Belief and acceptance as features of groups. *Protosociology,* 16: 35–69.

Gills, B. and Morgan, J. (2020). Global climate emergency: after COP24, climate science, urgency, and the threat to humanity. *Globalizations,* 17(6): 885–902.

Girod, B., Wiek, A., Mieg, H. and Hulme, M. (2009). The evolution of the IPCC's emissions scenarios. *Environmental Science & Policy,* 12: 103–118.

Godal, O. (2003). The IPCC's assessment of multidisciplinary issues: the case of greenhouse gas indices. *Climatic Change,* 58(3): 243–249.

Goeminne, G. (2013). Does the climate need consensus? The politics of climate change revisited. *Symploke,* 20(1–2): 147–161.

Grundmann, R. (2006). Ozone and climate: scientific consensus and leadership. *Science, Technology, & Human Values,* 31(1): 73–101.

Guardian (2010a). US Embassy cables: US lobbied Rajendra Pachauri to help them block appointment of Iranian scientist. *Guardian,* 6.12.2010. Available at: www.guardian .co.uk/world/us-embassy-cables-documents/168194 (Accessed: 7 February 2022).

Guardian (2010b). US Embassy cables: Norway supports US plan to block election of Iranian climate scientist. *Guardian,* 6.12.2010. Available at: www.guardian.co.uk/ world/us-embassy-cables-documents/166258 (Accessed: 7 February 2022).

Guardian (2010c). US Embassy cables: Brazil considers US plan to block election of Iranian climate scientist. *Guardian,* 6.12.2010. Available at: www.guardian.co.uk/ world/us-embassy-cables-documents/166298 (Accessed: 7 February 2022).

Guillemot, H. (2010). Connections between climate simulations and observation in climate computer modeling. Scientist's practices and 'bottom-up epistemology' lessons. *Studies in History and Philosophy of Modern Physics,* 41: 242–252.

Guillemot, H. (2017). The necessary and inaccessible 1.5° objective: A turning point in the relations between climate science and politics? In: Aykut, S. C., Foyer, J. and Morena, E. (eds.), *Globalising the Climate: COP21 and the Climatisation of Global Debates*. Abingdon: Routledge. pp. 39–56.

Gulizia, C., Langendijk, G., Huang-Lachmann, J.-T., et al. (2019). Towards a more integrated role for early career researchers in the IPCC process. *Climate Change*, 159: 75–85.

Gustafsson, K. M. (2018). Producing expertise. The Intergovernmental Science-Policy Platform on Biodiversity & Ecosystem Services' socialisation of young scholars. *Journal of Integrative Environmental Sciences*, 15(1): 21–39.

Gustafsson, K. M. (2021). Expert organizations' institutional understanding of expertise and responsibility for the creation of the next generation of experts: comparing IPCC and IPBES. *Ecosystems and People*, 17(1): 47–56.

Gustafsson, K. M. and Berg, M. (2020). Early-career scientists in the Intergovernmental Panel on Climate Change. A moderate or radical path towards a deliberative future? *Environmental Sociology*, 6(3): 242–253.

Gustafsson, K. M., Berg, M., Lidskog, R. and Löfmarck, E. (2019). Intersectional boundary work in socializing new experts. The case of IPBES. *Ecosystems and People*, 15(1): 181–191.

Gustafsson, K. M., Diaz-Reviriego, I. and Turnhout, E. (2020). Building capacity for the science-policy interface on biodiversity and ecosystem services: activities, fellows, outcomes, and neglected capacity building needs. *Earth System Governance*, 4(100050): 1–10.

Gustafsson, K. M. and Lidskog, R. (2018a). Organizing international experts: IPBES's efforts to gain epistemic authority. *Environmental Sociology*, 4(4): 445–456.

Gustafsson, K. M. and Lidskog, R. (2018b). Boundary organizations and environmental governance: performance, institutional design, and conceptual development. *Climate Risk Management*, 19: 1–11.

Guston, D. H. (2001). Boundary organizations in environmental policy and science: an introduction. *Science Technology & Human Values*, 26(4): 399–408.

Guston, D. H. (2006). On consensus and voting in science: from Asilomar to the National Toxicology Program. In: Frickel, S. and Moore, K. (eds.), *The New Political Sociology of Science: Institutions, Networks and Power*. Madison: The University of Wisconsin Press. pp. 378–404.

Guterres, A. (2021). Secretary-General calls latest IPCC climate report 'Code red for humanity', stressing 'irrefutable' evidence of human influence. Available at: www .un.org/press/en/2021/sgsm20847.doc.htm (Accessed: 7 February 2022).

Gutiérrez, M., Johnson, S., Kulovesi, K., Muñoz, M. and Schipper, L. (2007). *Summary of the 9th Session of IPCC Working Group III and 26th Session of the IPCC: 30 April– 4 May 2007*, *Earth Negotiations Bulletin*, (321), International Institute for Sustainable Development – Reporting Services.

Gutiérrez, M., Kosolapova, E., Kulovesi, K. and Yamineva, Y. (2012). *Summary of the 35th Session of the IPCC: 6–9 June 2012*, *Earth Negotiations Bulletin*, 12 (547), International Institute for Sustainable Development – Reporting Services.

Haas, P. M. (1992). Epistemic communities and international-policy coordination – Introduction. *International Organization*, 46: 1–35.

Haas, P. M. (2004). When does power listen to truth? A constructivist approach to the policy process. *Journal of European Public Policy*, 11: 569–592.

Haas, P. M. (2017). The epistemic authority of solution-oriented global environmental assessments. *Environmental Science & Policy*, 77: 221–224.

Haas, P. M. and McCabe, C. (2001). Amplifiers or dampeners: international institutions and social learning in the management of global environmental risks. In: The Social Learning Group (eds.), *Learning to Manage Global Environmental Risks: A Comparative History of Social Responses to Climate Change, Ozone Depletion and Acid Rain.* Cambridge, MA: MIT Press. pp. 323–348.

Haas, P. M. and Stevens, C. (2011). Organized science, usable knowledge, and multilateral environmental governance. In: Lidskog, R. and Sundqvist, G. (eds.), *Governing the Air: The Dynamics of Science, Policy, and Citizen Interaction.* Cambridge, MA: MIT Press. pp. 125–162.

Haikola, S., Hansson, A. and Fridahl, M. (2019). Map-makers and navigators of politicised terrain: expert understandings of epistemological uncertainty in integrated assessment modelling of bioenergy with carbon capture and storage. *Futures*, 114: 102472.

Hajer, M. A. (2012). A media storm in the world risk society: enacting scientific authority in the IPCC controversy (2009–10). *Critical Policy Studies*, 6(4): 452–464.

Hansen, J. E. (2007). Scientific reticence and sea level rise. *Environmental Research Letters*, 2: 024002.

Hansson, A., Anshelm, J., Fridal, M., and Haikola, S. (2021). Boundary work and interpretations in the IPCC review process of the role of bioenergy with carbon capture and storage (BECCS) in limiting global warming to 1.5°C. *Frontiers in Climate*, 3: 643224.

Haraway, D. (1988). Situated knowledges: the science question in feminism and the privilege of partial perspective. *Feminist Studies*, 14(3): 575–599.

Harold, J., Lorenzoni, I., Shipley, T. F. and Coventry, K. R. (2016). Cognitive and psychological science insights to improve climate change data visualization. *Nature Climate Change*, 6(12): 1080–1089.

Harold, J., Lorenzoni, I., Shipley, T. F. and Coventry, K. R. (2020). Communication of IPCC visuals: IPCC authors' views and assessments of visual complexity. *Climatic Change*, 158: 255–270.

Harper, K. C. (2003). Research from the boundary layer: civilian leadership, military funding and the development of Numerical Weather Prediction (1946–55). *Social Studies of Science*, 33(5): 667–696.

Haunschild, R., Bornmann, L. and Marx, W. (2016). Climate change research in view of bibliometrics. *PLoS One*, 11(7): e0160393.

Hausfather, Z. and Peters, G. (2020). Emissions – the 'business as usual' story is misleading. *Nature*, 577: 618–620.

Havstad, J. C. and Brown, M. J. (2017). Neutrality, relevance, prescription, and the IPCC. *Public Affairs Quarterly*, 31(4): 303–324.

Hays, S. P. (1999). *Conservation and the Gospel of Efficiency: The Progressive Conservation Movement, 1890–1920.* No. 40. Pittsburgh, PA: University of Pittsburgh Press.

Hecht, A. D. and Tirpak, D. (1995). Framework agreement on climate change: a scientific and policy history. *Climatic Change*, (29): 371–402.

Hermansen, E. A. T., Lahn, B., Sundqvist, G. and Øye, E. (2021). Post-Paris policy relevance: lessons from the IPCC SR15 process. *Climatic Change*, 169(7): 1–18.

Hewitson, B., Waagsaether, K., Wohland, J., Kloppers, K. and Kara, T. (2017). Climate information websites: an evolving landscape. *Wiley Interdisciplinary Reviews: Climate Change*, 8: e470.

Heymann, M. (2010). The evolution of climate ideas and knowledge. *Wiley Interdisciplinary Reviews: Climate Change*, 1(4): 581–597.

Heymann, M. and Hundebol, N. R. (2017). From heuristic to predictive. Making climate models into political instruments. In: Heymann, M., Gramelsberger, G. and Mahony, M. (eds.), *Culture of Prediction in Atmospheric and Climate Science. Epistemic and Cultural Shifts in Computer-Based Modelling and Simulation.* Abingdon: Routledge. pp. 120–136.

Hill, R., Adem, Ç., Alangui, W. V., et al. (2020). Working with indigenous, local and scientific knowledge in assessments of nature and nature's linkages with people. *Current Opinion in Environmental Sustainability,* 43: 8–20.

Hiramatsu, A., Mimura, N. and Sumi, A. (2008). A mapping of global warming research based on IPCC AR4. *Sustainability Science,* 3(2): 201–213.

Ho-Lem, C., Zerriffi, H. and Kandlikar, M. (2011). Who participates in the Intergovernmental Panel on Climate Change and why: a quantitative assessment of the national representation of authors in the Intergovernmental Panel on Climate Change. *Global Environmental Change,* 21(4): 1308–1317.

Hoppe, I. and Rödder, S. (2019). Speaking with one voice for climate science – climate researchers' opinion on the consensus policy of the IPCC. *Journal of Science Communication,* 18(03): a04.

Hoppe, R. (1999). Policy analysis, science and politics: from 'speaking truth to power' to 'making sense together'. *Science and Public Policy,* 26: 201–210.

Hoppe, R., Wesselink, A. and Cairns, R. (2013). Lost in the problem: the role of boundary organisations in the governance of climate change. *Wiley Interdisciplinary Reviews: Climate Change,* 4: 283–300.

Houghton, J. T. (2007). An overview of the intergovernmental panel on climate change (IPCC) and its process of science assessment. In: Hester, R. E. and Harrison, R. M. (eds.), *Global Environmental Change.* London: Royal Society of Chemistry. pp. 1–20.

Houghton, J. T. (2008). Madrid 1995: Diagnosing climate change. *Nature,* 455(7214): 737–738.

House of Commons (2010). *The Disclosure of Climate Data from the Climatic Research Unit at the University of East Anglia.* London: Science and Technology Committee. Available at: https://publications.parliament.uk/pa/cm200910/cmselect/cmsctech/387/38703.htm

Hughes, H. R. (2012). *Practices of Power and Knowledge in the Intergovernmental Panel on Climate Change (IPCC).* Unpublished PhD thesis. Department of International Politics: Aberystwyth University, Wales.

Hughes, H. R. (2015). Bourdieu and the IPCC's symbolic power. *Global Environmental Politics,* 15: 85–104.

Hughes, H. R. and Paterson, M. (2017). Narrowing the climate field: the symbolic power of authors in the IPCC's assessment of mitigation. *Review of Policy Research,* 34(6): 744–766.

Hughes, H. R. and Vadrot, A. B. M. (2019). IPBES and the struggle over biocultural diversity. *Global Environmental Politics,* 19(2): 14–37.

Hulme, M. (2009). *Why We Disagree about Climate Change: Understanding Controversy, Inaction and Opportunity.* Cambridge: Cambridge University Press.

Hulme, M. (2010). Problems with making and governing global kinds of knowledge. *Global Environmental Change,* 20(4): 558–564.

Hulme, M. (2011a). Reducing the future to climate: a story of climate determinism and reductionism. *Osiris,* 26(1): 245–266.

Hulme, M. (2011b). Meet the humanities. *Nature Climate Change,* 1(7): 177–179.

Hulme, M. (2013). Lessons from the IPCC: do scientific assessments need to be consensual to be authoritative? In: Doubleday, R. and Wilsdon, J. (eds.), *Future Directions for Scientific Advice in Whitehall.* Cambridge: Centre for Science and Policy. pp. 142–147.

Hulme, M. (2016). 1.5 °C and climate research after the Paris Agreement. *Nature Climate Change,* 6(3): 222–224.

Hulme, M. (2018). 'Gaps' in climate change knowledge: Do they exist? Can they be filled? *Environmental Humanities,* 10(1): 330–337.

Hulme, M. (2019). Climate emergency politics is dangerous. *Issues in Science and Technology,* 36(1): 23–25.

Hulme, M., Lidskog, R., White, J. M. and Standring, A. (2020). Social scientific knowledge in times of crisis: what climate change can learn from coronavirus (and vice versa)? *Wiley Interdisciplinary Reviews: Climate Change,* 11: e656.

Hulme, M. and Mahony, M. (2010). Climate change: what do we know about the IPCC? *Progress in Physical Geography,* 34(5): 705–718.

Hulme, M., Zorita, E., Stocker T. F., Price, J., and Christy J. R. (2010). IPCC: cherish it, tweak it or scrap it? *Nature,* (463): 730–732.

IAC [InterAcademy Council] (2010). *Climate Change Assessments: Review of the Processes and Procedures of the IPCC.* Amsterdam, Netherlands. Available at: https://archive.ipcc.ch/pdf/IAC_report/IAC%20Report.pdf (Accessed: 15 January 2022).

IAMC (2017). IAMC Website, Scenario Working Group presentation. Available at: https://web.archive.org/web/20160819202205/http://www.globalchange.umd.edu/iamc/scientific-working-groups/scenarios/ (Accessed: 8 February 2022).

IEA [International Energy Agency] (2021). *World Energy Outlook 2021.* www.iea.org/reports/world-energy-outlook-2021

IISD (2014). Summary of the 10th Session of Working Group II of the Intergovernmental Panel on Climate Change (IPCC) and Thirty-Eighth Session of the IPCC: 25-29 March 2014. *Earth Negotiations Bulletin,* 12(596): 1–20.

Inuit Circumpolar Council (2013). *Application of Indigenous Knowledge in the Arctic Council.* Available at: https://iccalaska.org/wp-icc/wp-content/uploads/2016/03/Application-of-IK-in-the-Arctic-Council.pdf (Accessed: 8 February 2022).

Inuit Circumpolar Council (2021). *Ethical and Equitable Engagement Synthesis Report.* Available at: www.inuitcircumpolar.com/project/icc-ethical-and-equitable-engagement-synthesis-report/ (Accessed: 8 February 2022).

Inuit Tapiriit Kanatami (2018). *National Inuit Strategy on Research.* Ottawa. Available at: www.itk.ca (Accessed: 11 August 2020).

IPCC (1988). *Report of the First Session of the WMO/UNEP IPCC, 9-11 November 1988.* Geneva.

IPCC (1990a). *Climate Change: The IPCC Scientific Assessment.* Houghton, J. T., Jenkins, G. J. and Ephraums, J. J. (eds.). Cambridge: Cambridge University Press.

IPCC (1990b). *Climate Change: The IPCC Response Strategies.* Cambridge: Cambridge University Press.

IPCC (1991). IPCC-7. *Report of the 5th Session of the WMO/UNEP Intergovernmental Panel on Climate Change, (Geneva, 13–15 March 1991).* pp. 22–23.

IPCC (1996). *Climate Change 1995 – The Science of Climate Change: Contribution of Working Group I to the Second Assessment Report of the Intergovernmental Panel on Climate Change.* Houghton, J. T., Meiro Filho, L. G., Callendar, B. A., et al. (eds.). Cambridge: Cambridge University Press.

IPCC (2003). Proposal for handling emissions scenarios related issues in AR4. Annex 5 in: *Report of the 21st Session of the IPCC (Vienna, 3 and 6–7 November 2003).*

IPCC (2005). *Guidance Notes for Lead Authors of the IPCC Fourth Assessment Report on Addressing Uncertainties.* Geneva: IPCC. Available at: www.ipcc.ch/site/assets/uploads/2018/02/ar4-uncertaintyguidancenote-1.pdf (Access 8 February 2022).

IPCC (2006a). *Policy and Process for Admitting Observer Organizations* (adopted in 2006 and last amended in 2012). Geneva: IPCC. Available at: www.ipcc.ch/site/assets/uploads/2018/09/ipcc-principles-observer-org-1.pdf (Accessed: 25 January 2022).

IPCC (2006b). Further work of the IPCC on emission scenarios. Annex 4 in: *Report of the 25th Session of the IPCC (Port Louis, Mauritius, 26-28 April 2006).* Available at: www.ipcc.ch/meeting-doc/25th-session-of-the-ipcc/

IPCC (2009a). *Use of Funds from The Nobel Peace Prize.* IPCC-XXX/Doc.8 in: *Report of the 30th Session of the IPCC.* Antalya, Turkey, 21–23 April 2009. Geneva: IPCC.

IPCC (2009b). Improving Participation of Developing/EIT Countries in the IPCC: Summary and Recommendations. IPCC-XXXI/Doc.11 in: *Report of the 31st Session of the IPCC.* Geneva: IPCC. Available at: www.ipcc.ch/meeting-doc/ipcc-31-and-plenary-sessions-of-the-three-ipcc-working-groups/ (Accessed: 8 February 2022).

IPCC (2009c). *Report of the 30th Session of the IPCC (Antalya, Turkey, 21–23 April 2009),* Geneva: IPCC. Available at: www.ipcc.ch/site/assets/uploads/2018/05/final_report_30.pdf (Accessed: 25 January 2022).

IPCC (2011). *Decisions Taken with Respect to the Review of IPCC Processes and Procedures Communications Strategy (Report of the 33rd Session of the IPCC, 10–13 May 2011, Abu Dhabi).* Geneva: IPCC. Available at: www.ipcc.ch/site/assets/uploads/2018/03/doc13_p33_review_tg_proposal_communications_strategy.pdf (Accessed: 30 July 2021).

IPCC (2012a). Progress Report and Planning for the Next Round of the Scholarship Programme. IPCC-XXXV/Doc. 8 in: *Report of the 35th Session of the IPCC. Geneva, Switzerland, June 6-9, 2012.* Geneva: IPCC.

IPCC (2012b). *Workshop Report of the IPCC Workshop on Socio-economic Scenarios.* IPCC Working Group III Technical Support Unit, Potsdam Institute for Climate Impact and Research, Potsdam Germany. Available at: www.ipcc.ch/publication/ipcc-workshop-on-socio-economic-scenarios/ (Accessed: 8 February 2022).

IPCC (2013a). *Procedures for the Preparation, Review, Acceptance, Adoption, Approval and Publication of IPCC Reports.* Appendix A to the Principles Governing IPCC Work. Last amended 2013. Geneva: IPCC. Available at: www.ipcc.ch/site/assets/uploads/2018/09/ipcc-principles-appendix-a-final.pdf (Accessed: 6 February 2022).

IPCC (2013b). *About the IPCC: Organization.* (Updated). Geneva: IPCC. Available at: www.ipcc.ch/organization/organization.shtml#.UcLdOvnqmSo   (Accessed: 8 February 2022).

IPCC (2014a). *Climate Change 2014: Mitigation of Climate Change. Contribution of Working Group III to the Fifth Assessment Report of the Intergovernmental Panel on Climate Change.* Edenhofer, O., Pichs-Madrugada, R., Sokona, Y., et al. (eds.). Cambridge: Cambridge University Press.

IPCC (2014b). *Climate Change 2014: Synthesis Report. Contribution of Working Groups I, II and III to the Fifth Assessment Report of the Intergovernmental Panel on Climate Change.* Pachauri, R. K. and Meyer, L. A. (eds.). Geneva: IPCC. www.ipcc.ch/report/ar5/syr/

IPCC (2015a). Assessing Transformation Pathways. Chapter 6 in: *Climate Change 2014: Mitigation of Climate Change. Contribution of Working Group III to the Fifth Assessment Report of the Intergovernmental Panel on Climate Change.* Edenhofer,

O., Pichs-Madrugada, R., Sokona, Y., et al. (eds.). Cambridge: Cambridge University Press. pp. 413–510. Available at: http://doi.org/10.1017/CBO9781107415416 (Accessed: 30 December 2020).

IPCC (2015b). IPCC Scholarship Programme. IPCC-XLII/INF. 10 in *Report of the 42nd Session of the IPCC.* Dubrovnik, Croatia, 5–8 October 2015. Geneva: IPCC.

IPCC (2016a). IPCC Scholarship Programme. IPCC-XLIV/Doc. 10 in *Report of the 44th Session of the IPCC.* Bangkok, Thailand, 17–20 October 2016. Geneva: IPCC.

IPCC (2016b). *Meeting Report of the Intergovernmental Panel on Climate Change Expert Meeting on Communication.* Lynn, J., Araya, M., Christophersen, Ø., et al. (eds.). Geneva: IPCC/WMO.

IPCC (2016c). *Review of the IPCC Communication Strategy.* IPCC-XLIV/Doc.6. 44th Session of the IPCC, Bangkok, Thailand. Available at: www.ipcc.ch/apps/event manager/documents/40/200920160710-Doc.6_ReviewComsStrat.pdf (Accessed: 12 February 2022).

IPCC (2016d). *Expert Meeting on the Future of the Task Group on Data and Scenario Support for Impacts and Climate Analysis (TGICA).* Shongwe, M., Tall, A., Wratt, D., et al. (eds.). WMO. Geneva: Switzerland. Available at: https://archive.ipcc.ch/ pdf/supporting-material/EMR_TGICA_Future.pdf (Accessed: 6 November 2021).

IPCC (2017a). *Report of the 46th Session of the IPCC.* Montreal, Canada, 6–10 September, 2017. Geneva: IPCC. Available at: www.ipcc.ch/meeting-doc/ipcc-46/ (Accessed: 22 February 2022).

IPCC (2017b). *Meeting Report of the Intergovernmental Panel on Climate Change Expert Meeting on Mitigation, Sustainability and Climate Stabilization Scenarios.* London: IPCC Working Group III Technical Support Unit, Imperial College London.

IPCC (2017c). *Working Group I Contribution to the IPCC Sixth Assessment Report (AR6) Background information.* IPCC Working Group I – 13th Session. Montreal, 7–8 September 2017. Available at: www.ipcc.ch/site/assets/uploads/2018/04/ 040820170312-WGI_inf1_background_information.pdf (Accessed: 6 November 2021).

IPCC (2017d). *Chapter Outline of the Working Group II Contribution to the IPCC Sixth Assessment Report (AR6).* Decision. As Adopted by the Panel at the 46th Session of the IPCC. Montreal, Canada, 6–10 September 2017. Available at: www.ipcc.ch/site/ assets/uploads/2018/03/AR6_WGII_outlines_P46.pdf (Accessed: 6 November 2021).

IPCC (2018a). *Global Warming of 1.5 C. An IPCC Special Report on the Impacts of Global Warming of 1.5 C above Pre-Industrial Levels and Related Global Greenhouse Gas Emission Pathways.* Masson-Delmotte, V., Zhai, P., Pörtner, H.-O., et al. (eds.). Geneva: IPCC. Available at: www.ipcc.ch/sr15/ (Accessed: 12 February 2022).

IPCC (2018b). *IPCC Factsheet: How Does the IPCC Select its Authors?* Geneva: IPCC. Available at: www.ipcc.ch/site/assets/uploads/2018/02/FS_select_authors.pdf (Accessed: 29 October 2021).

IPCC (2018c). *Report of the 48th Session of the IPCC.* Incheon, Republic of Korea, 1–5 October 2018. Geneva: IPCC. Available at: www.ipcc.ch/site/assets/uploads/2018/ 12/final_report_p48.pdf (Accessed: 1 March 2022).

IPCC (2018d). *Report of the 47th Session of the IPCC.* Paris, France, 13–16 March 2018. Geneva: IPCC. Available at: www.ipcc.ch/event/47th-session-of-the-ipcc/ (Accessed: 8 February 2022).

IPCC (2018e). *Proposed Terms of Reference for the Task Group on the Organization of the Future Work of the IPCC in Light of the Global Stocktake.* Geneva: IPCC. Available at: https://archive.ipcc.ch/organization/gst.shtml (Accessed: 25 January 2022).

IPCC (2018f). *Report by the Ad Hoc Task Force on the Future of the Task Group on Data and Scenario Support for Impact and Climate Analysis*. Prepared for: Forty-Seventh Session of the IPCC, Paris, France, 13–16 March 2018. IPCC-XLVII/Doc. 9. Available at: https://archive.ipcc.ch/apps/eventmanager/documents/49/020320180441-Doc.%209-ATF-TGICA.pdf (Accessed: 6 November 2021).

IPCC (2018g). *Expert Meeting of the Intergovernmental Panel on Climate Change on Assessing Climate Information for Regions*. Moufouma-Okia, W., Masson-Delmotte, V., Pörtner, H.-O., et al. (eds.), IPCC Working Group I Technical Support Unit, Université Paris Saclay, Saint Aubin: France. Available at: https://archive.ipcc.ch/pdf/supporting-material/AR6_WGI_EM_Regions.pdf (Accessed: 6 November 2021).

IPCC (2019a). Information for participants. In: *Report of the 50th Session of the IPCC. Geneva, Switzerland WMO headquarters August 2-6, 2019*. Geneva: IPCC. Available at: www.ipcc.ch/site/assets/uploads/2019/06/IPCC-50.-INF-NOTE-Geneva_V5.pdf (Accessed: 15 January 2022).

IPCC (2019b). *Report from the Task Group on Gender*. Geneva: IPCC. Available at: www.ipcc.ch/site/assets/uploads/2019/01/110520190810-Doc.-10-Rev.1TG-Gender.pdf (Accessed: 29 October 2021).

IPCC (2019c). *Report of the 49th Session of the IPCC*. Kyoto, Japan, 8–12 May 2019. Geneva: IPCC.

IPCC (2019d). IPCC Scholarship Programme. IPCC-XLIX/Doc. 9, Rev.1 In: *Report of the 49th Session of the IPCC*. Kyoto, Japan, 8–12 May 2019. Geneva: IPCC.

IPCC (2019e). Progress report of the task group on the organization of the future work of the IPCC in light of the global stocktake. IPCC-XLIX/INF. 6, Agenda Item: 6.2 in: *Report of the 49th Session of the IPCC*. Geneva: IPCC. Available at: www.ipcc.ch/site/assets/uploads/2019/01/100420191037-INF6Stocktake.pdf (Accessed: 25 January 2022).

IPCC (2019f). Technical Summary. In: Pörtner, H. O., Roberts, D. C., Masson-Delmotte, V., et al., *IPCC Special Report on the Ocean and Cryosphere in a Changing Climate*. Cambridge: Cambridge University Press.

IPCC (2019g). *Climate Change and Land: An IPCC Special Report on Climate Change, Desertification, Land Degradation, Sustainable Land Management, Food Security, and Greenhouse Gas Fluxes in Terrestrial Ecosystems*. Shukla, P. R., Skea, J., Calvo Buendia, E., et al. (eds.). Cambridge: Cambridge University Press.

IPCC (2020a). *What Is an Expert Reviewer of IPCC Reports?* Geneva: IPCC. Available at: www.ipcc.ch/2020/12/04/what-is-an-expert-reviewer-of-ipcc-reports/ (Accessed: 5 January 2022).

IPCC (2020b). *The IPCC's First Virtual Lead Author Meeting: An Evaluation by the Technical Support Unit of Working Group III of the Intergovernmental Panel on Climate Change*. Available at: www.ipcc.ch/site/assets/uploads/2020/07/IPCC-WG-III-TSU-Report-Evaluating_the_IPCCs_first_Virtual_Lead_Author_Meeting.pdf (Accessed: 15 January 2022).

IPCC (2021a). *Climate Change 2021: The Physical Science Basis. Contribution of Working Group I to the Sixth Assessment Report of the Intergovernmental Panel on Climate Change*. Masson-Delmotte, V., Zhai, P., Pirani, A., et al. (eds.). Cambridge: Cambridge University Press.

IPCC (2021b). *About the IPCC*. Geneva: IPCC. Available at: www.ipcc.ch/about/ (Accessed: 22 June 2021).

IPCC (2021c). *About the Scholarship Programme*. Geneva: IPCC. Available at: www.ipcc.ch/about/scholarship/ (Accessed: 30 December 2021).

IPCC (2021d). *IPCC WGI Interactive Atlas*. Geneva: IPCC. Available at: https://inter active-atlas.ipcc.ch/ (Accessed: 8 February 2022).

IPCC (2021e). *Review of the IPCC Communications Strategy*. IPCC-LIII(bis)/INF. 12 in: *Report of the 53rd Session of the IPCC*. Electronic Session, 22–26 March 2021. Geneva: IPCC. Available at: www.ipcc.ch/meeting-doc/ipcc-53-bis/ (Accessed: 8 February 2022).

IPCC (2021f). IPCC Communications Strategy Update. IPCC-LIII(bis)/INF. 13 in: *Report of the 53rd Session of the IPCC*. Electronic Session, 22–26 March 2021. Geneva: IPCC. Available at: www.ipcc.ch/meeting-doc/ipcc-53-bis/ (Accessed: 8 February 2022).

IPCC (2022). Summary for Policymakers. In: Pörtner, H. O., et al. (eds.), *Climate Change 2022: Impacts, Adaptation, and Vulnerability*. Cambridge: Cambridge University Press. pp. 1–35.

IPCC (n.d.(a)). *How Does the IPCC Work?* Geneva: IPCC. Available at: https://archive .ipcc.ch/organization/organization_structure.shtml (Accessed: 15 January 2022).

IPCC (n.d.(b)). *IPCC Focal Points*. Geneva: IPCC. Available at: www.ipcc.ch/apps/con tact/interface/focalpoints.php (Accessed: 19 January 2022).

Jabbour, J. and Flachsland, C. (2017). 40 years of global environmental assessments: a retrospective analysis. *Environmental Science & Policy*, 77: 193–202.

Janzwood, S. (2020). Confident, likely, or both? The implementation of the uncertainty language framework in IPCC Special Reports. *Climatic Change*, 162(3): 1655–1675.

Jasanoff, S. (1987). Contested boundaries in policy-relevant science. *Social Studies of Science*, 17: 195–230.

Jasanoff, S. (1990). *The Fifth Branch: Science Advisers as Policymakers*. Cambridge, MA: Harvard University Press.

Jasanoff, S. (ed.) (2004). *States of Knowledge: Co-production of Science and the Social Order*. London: Routledge.

Jasanoff, S. (2005). *Designs on Nature: Science and Democracy in Europe and the United States*. Princeton, NJ: Princeton University Press.

Jasanoff, S. (2010a). Testing time for climate science. *Science*, 328(5979): 695–696.

Jasanoff, S. (2010b). A new climate for society. *Theory, Culture & Society*, 27(2–3): 233–253.

Jasanoff, S. (2011a). Constitutional moments in governing science and technology. *Science and Engineering Ethics*, 17: 621–638. https://doi.org/10.1007/s11948-011-9302-2.

Jasanoff, S. (2011b). Cosmopolitan knowledge: climate science and global civic epistemol- ogy. In: Dryzek, J., Norgaard, R. B. and Schlosberg, D. (eds.), *Oxford Handbook of Climate Change and Society*. Oxford: Oxford University Press. pp. 129–143.

Jasanoff, S. (2019). Controversy studies. In: Ritzer, G. and Rojek, C. (eds.), *The Blackwell Encyclopedia of Sociology*. Oxford: Blackwell Publishing.

Jasanoff, S. and Kim, S.-H. (eds.) (2015). *Dreamscapes of Modernity: Sociotechnical Imaginaries and the Fabrication of Power*. Chicago, IL: University of Chicago Press.

Johnson, J. T., Howitt, R., Cajete, G., et al. (2016). Weaving Indigenous and sustainability sciences to diversify our methods. *Sustainability Science*, 11: 1–11.

Jomisko, R. L. (2013). Harry's code: an interview with Harry Collins. *Nordic Journal of Science and Technology Studies*, 1(1): 25–29.

Jordan, A., Huitema, D., Van Asselt, H. and Forster, J. (eds.) (2018). *Governing Climate Change: Polycentricity in Action?* Cambridge: Cambridge University Press.

Kanerva, J. and Krizsán, A. (2021). Discouraging climate action through implicit argumen- tation: an analysis of linguistic polyphony in the Summary for Policymakers by the Intergovernmental Panel on Climate Change. *Discourse & Communication*, 15(6): 609–628.

Kear, M. (2016). The new prometheans: technological optimism in climate change mitigation modelling. *Environmental Values*, 25(1): 7–28.

Keohane, R. O. (2015). The global politics of climate change: challenge for political science. PS*: Political Science & Politics*, 48(1): 19–26.

Keppo, I., Butnar, I., Bauer, N., et al. (2021). Exploring the possibility space: taking stock of the diverse capabilities and gaps in integrated assessment models. *Environmental Research Letters*, 16: 053006.

Knol, A. B., Slottje, P., van der Sluijs, J. P., et al. (2010). The use of expert elicitation in environmental health impact assessment: a seven step procedure. *Environmental Health*, 9(19):1–16.

Knorr Cetina, K. (1999). *Epistemic Cultures: How the Science Makes Knowledge.* Cambridge: Harvard University Press.

Knutti, R., Masson, D. and Gettelman, A. (2013). Climate model genealogy: generation CMIP5 and how we got there. *Geophysical Research Letters*, 40(6): 1194–1199.

Knutti, R., Rogelj, J., Sedláček, J. and Fischer, E. M. (2016). A scientific critique of the two-degree climate change target. *Nature Geoscience*, 9(1): 13–18.

Kouw, M. and Petersen, A. (2018). Diplomacy in action: Latourian politics and the Intergovernmental Panel on Climate Change. *Science and Technology Studies*, 31(1): 52–68.

Kovach, M. (2009). *Indigenous Methodologies: Characteristics, Conversations and Contexts.* Toronto: University of Toronto Press.

Kowarsch, M., Garardm, J., Riousset, P., et al. (2016). Scientific assessments to facilitate deliberative policy learning. *Palgrave Communications*, 2: 16092.

Kowarsch, M. and Jabbour, J. (2017). Solution-oriented global environmental assessments: opportunities and challenges. *Environmental Science & Policy*, 77: 187–192.

Kowarsch, M., Jabbour, J., Flaschland, C., et al. (2017). A road map for global environmental assessments. *Nature Climate Change*, 7(6): 379–382.

Kunelius, R., Eide, E., Tegelberg, M. and Yagodin, D. (eds.) (2017). *Media and Global Climate Knowledge: Journalism and the IPCC.* New York: Palgrave.

Kuramochi, T., Roelfsema, M., Hasu, A., et al. (2020). Beyond national climate action: the impact of region, city, and business commitments on global greenhouse gas emissions. *Climate Policy*, 20(3): 275–291.

Lahn, B. (2018). In the light of equity and science: scientific expertise and climate justice after Paris. *International Environmental Agreements: Politics, Law and Economics*, 18: 29–43.

Lahn, B. (2021). Changing climate change: the carbon budget and the modifying-work of the IPCC. *Social Studies of Science*, 51(1): 3–27.

Lahn, B. and Sundqvist, G. (2017). Science as a 'fixed point'? Quantification and boundary objects in international climate politics. *Environmental Science & Policy*, 67: 8–15.

Lahsen, M. (1999). The detection and attribution of conspiracies: the controversy over Chapter 8. Chapter 5 in: Marcus, G. E. (ed.), *Paranoia within Reason: A Casebook on Conspiracy as Explanation.* Chicago: University of Chicago Press. pp. 111–136.

Lahsen, M. (2009). A science–policy interface in the global south: the politics of carbon sinks and science in Brazil. *Climatic Change*, 97(3): 339–372.

Lahsen, M. (2016). Trust through participation? Problems of knowledge in climate decision making. In: Pettinger, M. E. (ed.), *The Social Construction of Climate Change: Power, Knowledge, Norms, Discourses.* Abingdon: Routledge. pp. 197–220.

Lahsen, M., Couto, G. D. and Lorenzoni, I. (2020). When climate change is not blamed: the politics of disaster attribution in international perspective. *Climatic Change*, 158: 213–233.

Laidler, G. J., Hirose, T., Kapfer, M., Ikummaq, T., Joamie, E., and Elee, P. (2011). Evaluating the Floe Edge Service: how well can SAR imagery address Inuit community concerns around sea ice change and travel safety? *The Canadian Geographer / Le Géographe Canadien*, 55(1): 91–107.

Latour, B. (1993). *We Have Never Been Modern*. New York: Harvester/Wheatsheaf.

Latour, B. and Woolgar, S. (1979). *Laboratory Life*. Princeton: Princeton University Press.

Lawler, A. (2002). Pachauri defeats Watson in new chapter for global panel. *Science*, 296 (5568): 632.

Leclerc, O. (2009). Les règles de production des énoncés au sein du Groupe d'experts intergouvernemental sur l'évolution du climat. In: R. Encinas de Muñagorri (ed.), *Expertise et Gouvernance du Changement Climatique*. Paris: LGDJ. pp. 59–92.

Lee, H. (2015). Turning the focus to solutions. *Science*, 350: 1007.

Leggett, J., Pepper, W. J. and Wart, R. J. (1992). Emissions scenarios for IPCC: an update. In: Houghton, J. T., Callander, B. A. and Varney, S. K. (eds.), *Climate Change 1992. The Supplementary Report to the IPCC Scientific Assessment*. Cambridge: Cambridge University Press.

Lenhard, J. and Winsberg, E. (2010). Holism, entrenchment, and the future of climate model pluralism. *Studies in History and Philosophy of Science Part B: Studies in History and Philosophy of Modern Physics*, 41(3): 253–262.

Lidskog, R. and Sundqvist, G. (2015). When does science matter? International relations meets science and technology studies. *Global Environmental Politics*. 15(1): 1–20.

Lim, M., Lynch, A. J., Fernandez-Llamazares, A., et al. (2017). Early-career experts essential for planetary sustainability. *Current Opinion Environmental Sustainability*, 29: 151e157.

Limoges, C. (1993). Expert knowledge and decision-making in controversy contexts. *Public Understanding of Science*, 2: 417–426.

Linnér, B.-O. and Wibeck, V. (2019). *Sustainability Transformations: Agents and Drivers Across Societies*. Cambridge: Cambridge University Press.

Liverman, D., von Hedemann, N., Nying'uro, P., et al. (2022). Survey of gender bias in the IPCC. *Nature*, 602: 30–32.

Livingstone, D. (2003). *Putting Science in Its Place: Geographies of Scientific Knowledge*. Chicago: The University of Chicago Press.

Livingston J. E., Lövbrand, E. and Alkan Olsson, J. (2018). From climates multiple to climate singular: maintaining policy-relevance in the IPCC synthesis report. *Environmental Science & Policy*, 90: 83–90.

Livingston, J. E. and Rummukainen, M. (2020). Taking science by surprise: the knowledge politics of the IPCC special report on 1.5 degrees. *Environmental Science & Policy*, 112: 10–16.

Loreau, M., Oteng-Yeboah, A., Orroyo, M. T. K., et al. (2006). Diversity without representation. *Nature*, 442(7100): 245–246.

Lövbrand, E. (2004). Bridging political expectations and scientific limitations in climate risk management – on the uncertain effects of international carbon sink policies. *Climatic Change*, 67(2–3): 449–460.

Lövbrand, E. (2009). Revisiting the politics of expertise in light of the Kyoto negotiations on land use change and forestry. *Forest Policy and Economics*, 11(5–6): 404–412.

Lövbrand, E., Beck, S., Chilvers, J., et al. (2015). Who speaks for the future of Earth? How critical social science can extend the conversation on the Anthropocene. *Global Environmental Change*, 32: 211–218.

Low, S. and Schäfer, S. (2020). Is bio-energy carbon capture and storage (BECCS) feasible? The contested authority of integrated assessment modeling. *Energy Research and Social Science*, 60: 101326.

Lunde, L. (1991). *Science or Politics in the Global Greenhouse? The Development Towards Scientific Consensus on Climate Change*. Lysaker: Fridtjof Nansen Institute.

Lynas, M. (2011). Conflicted roles over renewables. *Nature Climate Change*, 1(8): 228–229.

Lynn, J. and Peeva, N. (2021). Communications in the IPCC's Sixth Assessment Report cycle. *Climatic Change*, 169: 18.

Maas, T. Y., Montana, J., van der Hel, S., et al. (2021). Effectively empowering: a different look at bolstering the effectiveness of global environmental assessments. *Environmental Science & Policy*, 123: 210–219.

Mach, K. J. and Field, C. B. (2017). Toward the next generation of assessment. *Annual Review of Environment and Resources*, 42: 569–597.

Mach, K. J., Mastrandrea, M. D., Freeman, P. T., et al. (2017). Unleashing expert judgment in assessment. *Global Environmental Change*, 44: 1–14.

MacKenzie, D. A. (2006). *An Engine, Not a Camera: How Financial Models Shape Markets*. Cambridge, MA: MIT Press.

MacKenzie, D. (2009). Making things the same: gases, emission rights and the politics of carbon markets. *Accounting, Organizations and Society*, 34(3–4): 440–455.

Mahony, M. (2013). Boundary spaces: science, politics and the epistemic geographies of climate change in Copenhagen, 2009. *Geoforum*, 49: 29–39.

Mahony, M. (2014a). The IPCC and the geographies of credibility. *History of Meteorology*, 6: 95–112.

Mahony, M. (2014b). The predictive state: science, territory and the future of the Indian climate. *Social Studies of Science*, 44(1): 109–133.

Mahony, M. (2015). Climate change and the geographies of objectivity: the case of the IPCC's burning embers diagram. *Transactions of the Institute of British Geographers*, 40: 153–167.

Mahony, M. and Hulme, M. (2018). Epistemic geographies of climate change: science, space and politics. *Progress in Human Geography*, 42(3): 395–424.

Maldonado, J., Bennett, T. M. B., Chief, K., et al. (2016). Engagement with indigenous peoples and honoring traditional knowledge systems. *Climatic Change*, 135: 111–126.

Malone, E. L. and Rayner, S. (2001). Role of the research standpoint in integrating global-scale and local-scale research. *Climate Research*, 19(2): 173–178.

Manning, M. R., Petit, M., Easterling, D., et al. (2004). *IPCC Workshop on Describing Scientific Uncertainties in Climate Change to Support Analysis of Risk and of Options*. Geneva: IPCC. Available at: https://archive.ipcc.ch/pdf/supporting-material/ipcc-workshop-2004-may.pdf (Accessed: 12 February 2022).

Marres, N. (2018). Why we can't have our facts back. *Engaging Science, Technology, and Society*, 4: 423–443.

Martin, B. (2014). *The Controversy Manual*. Sparsnäs: Irene Publishing.

Martinez, J. (2020). The great smog of London. *Encyclopaedia Britannica*. Available at: www.britannica.com/event/Great-Smog-of-London (Accessed: 16 June 2021).

Masood, E. and Ochert, A. (1995). UN climate change report turns up the heat. *Nature*, 378: 119.

Mastrandrea, M. D., Field, C. B., Stocker, T. F., et al. (2010). *Guidance Note for Lead Authors of the IPCC Fifth Assessment Report on Consistent Treatment of Uncertainties*. Geneva: IPCC. Available at: www.ipcc.ch/site/assets/uploads/2017/08/AR5_Uncertainty_Guidance_Note.pdf (Accessed: 12 February 2022).

Mastrandrea, M. D. and Mach, K. J. (2011). Treatment of uncertainties in IPCC Assessment Reports: past approaches and considerations for the Fifth Assessment Report. *Climatic Change*, 108(4): 659–673.

Mastrandrea, M. D., Mach, K. J., Plattner, G. K., et al. (2011). The IPCC AR5 guidance note on consistent treatment of uncertainties: a common approach across the working groups. *Climatic Change*, 108(4): 675–691.

McConnell, F. (2019). Rethinking the geographies of diplomacy. *Diplomatica*, 1: 46–55.

McCright, A. M. and Dunlap, R. E. (2010). Anti-reflexivity the American conservative movement's success in undermining climate science and policy. *Theory Culture & Society*, 27: 100–133.

McIntyre, S. and McKitrick, R. (2005). The M&M critique of the MBH98 Northern Hemisphere climate index: update and implications. *Energy & Environment*, 16(1): 69–100.

McMahon, R., Stauffacher, M. and Knutti, R. (2015). The unseen uncertainties in climate change: reviewing comprehension of an IPCC scenario graph. *Climatic Change*, 133(2): 141–154.

McMahon, R., Stauffacher, M. and Knutti, R. (2016). The scientific veneer of IPCC visuals, *Climatic Change*, 138 (3–4): 369–381.

Medin, D. L. and Lee, C. D. (2012). Presidential column: diversity makes better science. *APS*. Association for Psychological Science. Available at: www .psychologicalscience.org/index.php/publications/observer/2012/may-june-12/diver sity-makes-better-science.html (Accessed: 29 October 2021).

Merton, R. K. (1948). The self-fulfilling prophecy. *The Antioch Review*, 8(2): 193–210.

Miguel, J., Mahony, M., and Monteiro, M (2019). A 'geopolítica infraestrutural' do conhecimento climático: o Modelo Brasileiro do Sistema Terrestre e a divisão Norte-Sul do conhecimento. *Sociologias*, 21: 44–75.

Miller, B. (2013). When is a consensus knowledge-based? Distinguishing shared knowledge from mere agreement. *Synthese*, 190(7): 1293–1316.

Miller, C. A. (2001a). Scientific internationalism in American foreign policy: The case of meteorology. In: Miller, C. A. and Edwards, P. N. (eds.), *Changing the Atmosphere: Expert Knowledge and Environmental Governance*. Cambridge, MA: MIT Press. pp. 167–218.

Miller, C. A. (2001b). Hybrid management: boundary organizations, science policy, and environmental governance in the climate regime. *Science, Technology, & Human Values*, 4(26): 478–500.

Miller, C. A. (2004). Climate science and the making of a global political order. In: Jasanoff, S. (ed.), *States of Knowledge: The Co-production of Science and Social Order*. London: Routledge. pp. 46–66.

Miller, C. A. (2008). Civic epistemologies: constituting knowledge and order in political communities. *Sociology Compass*, 2(6): 1896–1919.

Miller, C. A. (2009). Epistemic constitutionalism in international governance: the case of climate change. In: Heazle, M., Griffiths, M. and Conley, T. (eds.), *Foreign Policy Challenges in the 21st Century*. Cheltenham: Edward Elgar. pp. 141–163.

Miller, C. A. (2015a). Globalizing security: science and the transformation of contemporary political imagination. In: Jasanoff, S. and Kim, S. H. (eds.), *Dreamscapes of Modernity*. Chicago: University of Chicago Press. pp. 277–299.

Miller, C. A. (2015b). Knowledge and democracy: the epistemics of self-governance. In: Hilgartner, S., Miller, C. and Hagendijk, R. (eds.), *Science and Democracy*. London: Routledge. pp. 216–237.

Miller, C. A. and Edwards, P. N. (eds.) (2001). *Changing the Atmosphere: Expert Knowledge and Environmental Governance*. Cambridge, MA: MIT Press.

Miller, C. A. and Muñoz-Erickson, T. A. (2018). *Designing Knowledge*. Tempe: Consortium for Science, Policy & Outcomes.

Minx, J. C., Callaghan, M., Lamb, W. F., Garard, J., and Edenhofer, O. (2017). Learning about climate change solutions in the IPCC and beyond. *Environmental Science & Policy*, 77: 252–259.

Monteiro, M., Seixas, S., and Vieira, S. (2014). The politics of Amazonian deforestation: environmental policy and climate change knowledge. *Wiley Interdisciplinary Reviews: Climate Change*, 5: 689–701.

Moore, A. (2017). *Critical Elitism*. Cambridge: Cambridge University Press.

Moran, G. (1998). *Silencing Scientists and Scholars in Other Fields: Power, Paradigm Controls, Peer Review, and Scholarly Communication*. Greenwich, CT: Ablex Publishing.

Morelli, A., Johansen, T. G., Pidcock, R., et al. (2021). Co-designing engaging and accessible data visualisations: a case study of the IPCC reports. *Climatic Change*, 168: 26.

Morseletto, P., Biermann, F. and Pattberg, P. (2017). Governing by targets: reductio ad unum and evolution of the two-degree climate target. *International Environmental Agreements: Politics, Law and Economics*, 17(5): 655–676.

Moss, R. H. (1995). The IPCC: policy relevant not driven: scientific assessment. *Global Environmental Change*, 5: 171–174.

Moss, R. H., Babiker, M., Brinkman, S., et al. (2008). *Towards New Scenarios for Analysis of Emissions, Climate Change, Impacts, and Response Strategies*. Geneva: IPCC.

Moss, R. H., Edmonds, J. A., Hibbard, K. A., et al. (2010). The next generation of scenarios for climate change research and assessment. *Nature*, 463(7282): 747–756.

Moss, R. H. and Schneider, S. (2000). Uncertainties. In: Pachauri, R., Taniguchi, T. and Tanaka, K. (eds.), *Guidance Papers on the Cross Cutting Issues of the Third Assessment Report of the IPCC*. Geneva: IPCC. pp. 33–52.

Najam, A., Rahman, A. A., Huq, S., and Sokona, Y. (2003). Integrating sustainable development into the Fourth Assessment Report of the Intergovernmental Panel on Climate Change. *Climate Policy*, 3(S1): S9–S17.

Nakicenovic, N., Alcamo, J., Davis, G., et al. (2000). *Special Report on Emissions Scenarios*. Cambridge: Cambridge University Press.

Nalau, J., Becken, S., Schliephack, J., et al. (2018). The role of indigenous and traditional knowledge in ecosystem-based adaptation: a review of the literature and case studies from the Pacific Islands. *Weather, Climate, and Society*, 10(4): 851–865.

National Grid (2021). *Future Energy Scenarios 2021*. London. Available at: www .nationalgrideso.com/document/202851/download (Accessed: 21 July 2021).

Nerlich, N. and Jaspal, R. (2014). Images of extreme weather: symbolising human responses to climate change. *Science as Culture*, 23(2): 253–276.

Newell, P. (2006). *Climate for Change: Non-state Actors and the Global Politics of the Greenhouse*. Cambridge: Cambridge University Press.

Nightingale, A. J., Eriksen, S., Taylor, M., et al. (2020). Beyond technical fixes: climate solutions and the great derangement. *Climate and Development*, 12(4): 343–352.

Nocke, T. (2014). Images for data analysis: the role of visualisation in climate research processes. In: Schneider, B. and Nocke, T. (eds.), *Image Politics of Climate Change: Visualizations, Imaginations, Documentations*. New York: Columbia University Press. pp. 54–77.

Nordlund, G. (2008). Futures research and the IPCC assessment study on the effects of climate change. *Futures*, 40(10): 873–876.

NRC [National Research Council] (1979). *Carbon Dioxide and Climate: A Scientific Assessment*. Washington, DC: National Academy Press. https://doi.org/10.17226/12181.

OAS [Organization of American States] (2016). *American Declaration on the Rights of Indigenous Peoples*. Washington, DC: Organisation of American States.

O'Brien, K. (2012). Global environmental change II: from adaptation to deliberative transformation. *Progress in Human Geography*, 36(5): 667–676.

O'Neill, B. C., Carter, T., Ebi, K., et al. (2020). Achievements and needs for the climate change scenario framework. *Nature Climate Change*, 10(12): 1074–1084.

O'Neill, B. C., Kriegler, E., Riahi, K., et al. (2014). A new scenario framework for climate change research: the concept of shared socioeconomic pathways. *Climatic Change*, 122: 387–400.

O'Neill, B. C., Oppenheimer, M., Warren, R., et al. (2017). IPCC reasons for concern regarding climate change risks. *Nature Climate Change*, 7(1): 28–37.

O'Neill, B. C., Tebaldi, C., van Vuuren, D. P., et al. (2016). The Scenario Model Intercomparison Project (ScenarioMIP) for CMIP6. *Geoscientific Model Development*, 9: 3461–3482.

O'Neill, S. J., Hulme, M., Turnpenny, J. and Screen J. A. (2010). Disciplines, geography, and gender in the framing of climate change. *Bulletin of the American Meteorological Society*, 91(8): 997–1002.

O'Neill, S. J., Williams, H., Kurz, T., et al. (2015). Dominant frames in legacy and social media coverage of the IPCC Fifth Assessment Report. *Nature Climate Change*, 5: 380–385.

O'Reilly, J. (2015). Glacial dramas: typos, projections, and peer review in the Fourth Assessment of the Intergovernmental Panel on Climate Change. In: Barnes, J. and Dove, M. (eds.), *Climate Cultures*. New Haven, CT: Yale University Press. pp. 107–126.

O'Reilly, J., Brysse, K., Oppenheimer, M. and Oreskes, N. (2011). Characterizing uncertainty in expert assessments: ozone depletion and the West Antarctic ice sheet. *Wiley Interdisciplinary Reviews: Climate Change*. 2: 728–743.

O'Reilly, J., Oreskes, N. and Oppenheimer, M. (2012). The rapid disintegration of projections: the West Antarctic Ice Sheet and the IPCC. *Social Studies of Science*, 42(5): 709–731.

Obermeister, N. (2017). From dichotomy to duality: addressing interdisciplinary epistemological barriers to inclusive knowledge governance in global environmental assessments. *Environmental Science & Policy*, 68: 80–86.

Oppenheimer, M., O'Neill, B. C., Webster, M. and Agrawala, S. (2007). The limits of consensus. *Science*, 317: 1505–1506.

Oppenheimer, M., Oreskes, N., Jamieson, D., et al. (2019). *Discerning Experts: The Practices of Scientific Assessment for Environmental Policy*. Chicago, IL: University of Chicago Press.

Oppenheimer, M. and Petsonk, A. (2005). Article 2 of the UNFCCC: Historical origins, recent interpretations. *Climatic Change*, 73(3): 195–226.

Oreskes, N. (2004). The scientific consensus on climate change. *Science*, 306: 1686.

Oreskes, N. (2019). *Why Trust Science?* Princeton, NJ: Princeton University Press.

Oreskes, N. and Conway, E. M. (2010). *Merchants of Doubt: How a Handful of Scientists Obscured the Truth on Issues from Tobacco Smoke to Global Warming*. New York: Bloomsbury Press.

Oreskes, N., Shrader-Frechette, K. and Belitz, K. (1994). Verification, validation, and confirmation of numerical models in the earth sciences. *Science*, 263: 641–646.

Ostrom, E. (2009). *A Polycentric Approach for Coping with Climate Change*. World Bank Policy Research Working Paper 5095. Washington, DC: World Bank.

Ourbak, T. and Tubiana, L. (2017). Changing the game: The Paris Agreement and the role of scientific communities. *Climate Policy*, 17(7): 819–824.

Pachauri, R. K. (2009). Statement of Dr. R. K. Pachauri. 22 September. Available at: https://archive.ipcc.ch/pdf/presentations/rkp-statement-unccs-09.pdf (Accessed: 19 February 2022).

Pachauri, R. K., Taniguchi, T., and Tanaka, K. (eds.) (2000). *Guidance Papers on the Cross Cutting Issues of the Third Assessment Report of the IPCC*. Geneva: IPCC. Available at: www.ipcc.ch/publication/guidance-papers-on-the-cross-cutting-issues-of-the-third-assessment-report-of-the-ipcc/ (Accessed: 12 February 2022).

Packalen, M. and Bhattacharya, J. (2015). *Age and the Trying Out of New Ideas*. National Bureau of Economic Research Working Paper No. 20920. Cambridge, MA.

Paglia, E. and Parker, C. (2021). The Intergovernmental Panel on Climate Change: guardian of climate science. In: Boin, A., Fahy, L. A., and 't Hart, P. (eds.), *Guardians of Public Value*. London: Cham, Palgrave Macmillan. pp. 295–321.

Pallett, H. and Chilvers, J. (2013). A decade of learning about publics, participation, and climate change: institutionalising reflexivity? *Environment and Planning A*, 45: 1162–1183.

Palmer, J., Owens, S. and Doubleday, R. (2019). Perfecting the 'elevator pitch'? Expert advice as locally-situated boundary work. *Science and Public Policy*, 46(2): 244–253.

Parsons, M., Fisher, K. and Nalau, J. (2016). Alternative approaches to co-design: insights from indigenous/academic research collaborations. *Current Opinion in Environmental Sustainability*, 20: 99–105.

Paterson, M., (1996). *Global Warming and Global Politics*. London/New York: Routledge.

Patt, A. (2007). Assessing model-based and conflict-based uncertainty. *Global Environmental Change*, 17(1): 37–46.

Patt, A. and Dessai, S. (2005). Communicating uncertainty: lessons learned and suggestions for climate change assessment. *Comptes Rendus Geoscience*, 337(4): 425–441.

PBL [Netherlands Environmental Assessment Agency] (2010). *Assessing an IPCC Assessment. An Analysis of Statements on Projected Regional Impacts in the 2007 Report*. The Hague: Netherlands Environmental Assessment Agency.

Pearce, D. (1996). Climate confusion. *Environment and Planning A*, 28(1): 8–10.

Pearce, D. (1997). Economists and climate change. *Environment and Planning A*, 29(1): 1–4.

Pearce, W., Grundmann, R., Hulme, M., Raman, S., Kershaw, E. H. and Tsouvalis, J. (2017a). Beyond counting climate consensus. *Environmental Communication*, 11(6): 723–730.

Pearce, W., Grundmann, R., Hulme, M., Raman, S., Hadley Kershaw, E. and Tsouvalis, J. (2017b). A reply to Cook and Oreskes on climate science consensus messaging. *Environmental Communication*, 11(6): 736–739.

Pearce, W., Mahony, M. and Raman, S. (2018). Science advice for global challenges: learning from trade-offs in the IPCC. *Environmental Science & Policy*, 80: 125–131.

Petersen, A. C. (2000). Philosophy of climate science. *Bulletin of the American Meteorological Society*, 81(2): 265–271.

Petersen, A. C. ([2006] 2012). *Simulating Nature: A Philosophical Study of Computer-Simulation Uncertainties and Their Role in Climate Science and Policy Advice*, 2nd ed. Boca Raton, FL: CRC Press.

Petersen, A. C. (2007). Is het Watt of watt? Dagboek: Achter de schermen van de Parijse klimaatconferentie [Is it Watt or watt? Diary: Behind the scenes of the climate conference in Paris], about the IPCC Plenary of Working Group I (29 January–1

Bibliography 299

February 2007) in the Dutch weekly news magazine *Vrij Nederland*, 10 February 2007, pp. 20–21. [In Dutch]

Petersen, A. C. (2011). Climate simulation, uncertainty, and policy advice – the case of the IPCC. In: Gramelsberger, G. and Feichter, J. (eds.), *Climate Change and Policy*. Berlin: Springer. pp. 91–111.

Petersen, A. C., Blackstock, J. B., and Morisetti, N. (2015). New leadership for a user-friendly IPCC. *Nature Climate Change*, 5: 909–911.

Pielke, R., Jr. (2018). Opening up the climate policy envelope. *Issues in Science and Technology*, 34(4): 33–40.

Pielke, R., Jr. (2002). Policy, politics and perspective. *Nature*, 416: 367–368.

Pielke, R., Jr. and Ritchie, J. (2021). Distorting the view of our climate future: the misuse and abuse of climate pathways and scenarios. *Energy Research and Social Science*, 72: 101890.

Pinch, T. (2015). Scientific controversies. In: Wright, J. D. (ed.), *International Encyclopedia of the Social & Behavioral Sciences*. Second Edi. Amsterdam: Elsevier. pp. 281–286.

Poortvliet, P. M., Niles, M. T., Veraart, J. A., Werners, S. E., Korporaal, F. C. and Mulder, B. C. (2020). Communicating climate change risk: a content analysis of IPCC's Summary for Policymakers. *Sustainability*, 12(12): 4861.

Porter, J. R., Challinor, A. J., Henriksen, C. B., Howden, S. M., Martre, P. and Smith, P. (2019). Invited review: Intergovernmental Panel on Climate Change, agriculture, and food – a case of shifting cultivation and history. *Global Change Biology*, 25(8): 2518–2529.

Porter, T. M. (1995). *Trust in Numbers: The Pursuit of Objectivity in Science and Public Life*. Princeton, NJ: Princeton University Press.

Pörtner, H. O., Scholes, R. J., Agard, J., et al. (2021). *IPBES-IPCC Co-Sponsored Workshop Report on Biodiversity and Climate Change*. IPBES and IPCC. http://doi.org/10.5281/zenodo.4782538.

Provost, G. (2019). Rigorous and relevant: applying lessons from the history of IPCC Special Reports to the Post-Paris Agreement world. *Harvard Environmental Law Review*, (43): 507–546.

Raman, S. and Pearce, W. (2020). Learning the lessons of Climategate: a cosmopolitan moment in the public life of climate science. *Wiley Interdisciplinary Reviews: Climate Change*, 11, e672.

Randalls, S. (2010). History of the 2° C climate target. *Wiley Interdisciplinary Reviews: Climate Change*, 1(4): 598–605.

Rayner, S. and Malone, E. L. (eds.) (1998). *Human Choice and Climate Change*, 4 Vols. Columbus, OH: Battelle Press.

Reisinger, A., Howden, H., Vera, C., et al. (2020). *The Concept of Risk in the IPCC Sixth Assessment Report: A Summary of Cross-Working Group Discussions*. Geneva: IPCC. Available at: www.ipcc.ch/event/guidance-note-concept-of-risk-in-the-6ar-cross-wg-discussions/ (Accessed: 11 February 2022).

Rescher, N. (1993). *Pluralism: Against the Demand for Consensus*. Oxford: Oxford University Press.

Rheinberger, H.-J. (1997). *Toward a History of Epistemic Things: Synthesizing Proteins in the Test Tube*. Stanford: Stanford University Press.

Riousset, P., Flachsland, C. and Kowarsch, M. (2017). Global environmental assessments: impact mechanisms. *Environmental Science & Policy*, 77: 260–267.

Ripple, W. J., Wolf, C., Newsome, T. M., et al. (2021). World scientists' warning of a climate emergency 2021. *BioScience*, 71(9): 894–898.

Rivera-Ferre, M. G. (2020). From agriculture to food systems in the IPCC. *Global Change Biology*, 26(5): 2731–2733.

Robertson, S. (2021). Transparency, trust, and integrated assessment models: an ethical consideration for the Intergovernmental Panel on Climate Change. *Wiley Interdisciplinary Reviews: Climate Change*, 12(1): e679.

Rodhe, H. (2013). Bert Bolin (1925–2007) – a world leading climate scientist and science organiser. *Tellus B: Chemical and Physical Meteorology*, 65(1): 20583.

Rothstein, H., Borraz, O. and Huber, M. (2012). Risk and the limits of governance: exploring varied patterns of risk-based governance across Europe. *Regulation & Governance*, 7: 215–235.

Rowe, E. (2012). International science, domestic politics: Russian reception of international climate-change assessments. *Environment and Planning D: Society and Space*, 30: 711–726.

Rueschemeyer, D. and Skocpol, T. (eds.) (1996). *States, Social Knowledge, and the Origins of Modern Social Policies*. Princeton, NJ: Princeton University Press.

Ruffini, P.-B. (2017). *Science and Diplomacy*. New York: Springer International Publishing.

Sanford, M., Painter, J., Yasseri, T. and Lorimer, J. (2021). Controversy around climate change reports: a case study of Twitter responses to the 2019 IPCC report on land. *Climatic Change*, 167(3–4): 1–25.

Sarewitz, D. (2004). How science makes environmental controversies worse. *Environmental Science & Policy*, 7: 385–403.

Sarewitz, D. (2011). Does climate change knowledge really matter? *Wiley Interdisciplinary Reviews: Climate Change,* 2(4): 475–481.

Savo, V., Lepofsky, D., Benner, J., et al. (2016). Observations of climate change among subsistence-oriented communities around the world. *Nature Climate Change*, 6: 462–473.

Sawatzky, A., Cunsolo, A., Jones-Bitton, A., et al. (2020). 'The best scientists are the people that's out there': Inuit-led integrated environment and health monitoring to respond to climate change in the Circumpolar North. *Climatic Change*, 160(1): 45–66.

Schellnhuber, H. (1999). Earth system' analysis and the second Copernican revolution. *Nature*, 402: C19–C23.

Schipper, E. L. F., Dubash, N. K. and Mulugetta, Y. (2021). Climate change research and the search for solutions: Rethinking interdisciplinarity. *Climatic Change*, 168(3): 18.

Schneider, S. H. (1991). Report on reports: three reports of the Intergovernmental Panel on Climate Change. *Environment: Science and Policy for Sustainable Development*, 33(1): 25–30.

Schön, D. and Argyris, C. (1996). *Organizational Learning II: Theory, Method and Practice*. Reading, MA: Addison Wesley.

Schulte-Uebbing, L., Hansen, G., Macaspac Hernández, A. and Winter, M. (2015). Chapter scientists in the IPCC AR5 – experiences and lessons learned. *Current Opinion Environmental Sustainability,* 14: 250–256.

Scott, J. C. (1995). *Seeing Like a State: How Certain Schemes to Improve the Human Condition Have Failed*. Hartford, CT: Yale University Press.

Sénit, C.-A., Biermann, F. and Kalfagianni, A. (2017). The representativeness of global deliberation: a critical assessment of civil society consultations for sustainable development. *Global Policy*, 8: 62–72.

Shackley, S. (1997). The IPCC: consensual knowledge and global politics. *Global Environmental Change*, 7: 77–79.

Shackley, S., Risbey, J., Stone, P. and Wynne, B. (1999). Adjusting to policy expectations in climate change modeling: an interdisciplinary study of flux adjustments in coupled atmosphere-ocean general circulation models. *Climatic Change*, 43: 413–454.

Shackley, S. and Skodvin, T. (1995). IPCC gazing and the interpretative social sciences. *Global Environmental Change*, 5(3): 175–180.

Shackley, S. and Wynne, B. (1996). Representing uncertainty in global climate change science and policy: boundary-ordering devices and authority. *Science, Technology, and Human Values*, 21(3): 275–302.

Shackley, S. and Wynne, B. (1997). Global warming potentials: ambiguity or precision as an aid to policy? *Climate Research*, 8(2): 89–106.

Shapin, S. (1998). Placing the view from nowhere: historical and sociological problems in the location of science placing. *Transactions of the Institute of British Geographers*, 23(1): 5–12.

Shapin, S. (2010). *Never Pure: Historical Studies of Science as If It Was Produced by People with Bodies, Situated in Time, Space, Culture and Society, and Struggling for Credibility and Authority.* Baltimore, MA: The John Hopkins University Press.

Shaw, A. (2005). *Policy Relevant Scientific Information: The Co-Production of Objectivity and Relevance in the IPCC.* Berkeley, CA: Breslauer Symposium, University of California International and Area Studies.

Shaw, A. and Robinson, J. (2004). Relevant but not prescriptive? Science policy models within the IPCC. *Philosophy Today*, 48: 106–117.

Shaw, C. (2013). Choosing a dangerous limit for climate change: public representations of the decision-making process. *Global Environmental Change*, 23(2): 563–571.

Shukla, J., Hagedorn, R., Miller, M., et al. (2009). Strategies: revolution in climate prediction is both necessary and possible: a declaration at the World Modelling Summit for climate prediction. *Bulletin of the American Meteorological Society*, 90: 175–178.

Siebenhüner, B. (2002). How do scientific assessments learn? Part 1. Conceptual framework and case study of the IPCC. *Environmental Science & Policy*, 5(5): 411–420.

Siebenhüner, B. (2003). The changing role of nation states in international environmental assessments – the case of the IPCC. *Global Environmental Change*, 13(2): 113–123.

Siebenhüner, B. (2014). Changing demands at the science–policy interface: organizational learning in the IPCC. In: Hey, E., Raulus, H., Arts, K. and Ambrus, M. (eds.), *The Role of 'Experts' in International and European Decision-Making Processes: Advisors, Decision Makers or Irrelevant Actors?* Cambridge: Cambridge University Press. pp. 126–147.

Silberzahn, R., Uhlmann, E. L., Martin, D. P., et al. (2018). Many analysts, one data set: making transparent how variations in analytic choices affect results. *Advances in Methods and Practices in Psychological Science*, 1: 337–356.

Simpson, N. P., Mach, K. J., Constable, A., et al. (2021). A framework for complex climate change risk assessment. *One Earth*, 4(4): 489–501.

Skea, J., Shukla, P., Al Khourdajie, A. and McCollum, D. (2021). Intergovernmental Panel on Climate Change: transparency and integrated assessment modelling. *Wiley Interdisciplinary Reviews: Climate Change*, e727.

Skodvin, T. (2000a). Revised rules of procedure for the IPCC process. *Climatic Change*, 46(4): 409–415.

Skodvin, T. (2000b). *Structure and Agent in the Scientific Diplomacy of Climate Change: An Empirical Case Study of Science-Policy Interaction in the Intergovernmental Panel on Climate Change.* Dordrecht: Kluwer Academic Publishers.

Skrydstrup, M. (2013). Tricked or troubled natures? How to make sense of 'Climategate'. *Environmental Science & Policy*, 28: 92–99.

Smallman, M. (2016). Public understanding of science in turbulent times III: deficit to dialogue, champions to critics. *Public Understanding of Science*, 25(2): 186–197.

Smith, H. A. and Sharp, K. (2012). Indigenous climate knowledges. *Wiley Interdisciplinary Reviews: Climate Change*, 3(5): 467–476.

Social Learning Group (2001). *Learning to Manage Global Environmental Risks*. 2 vols. Cambridge, MA: MIT Press.

Søgaard Jørgensen, P., Evoh, C. J., Gerhardinger, L. C., et al. (2019). Building urgent intergenerational bridges: assessing early career researcher integration in global sustainability initiatives. *Current Opinion Environmental Sustainability*, 39: 153–159.

Spier, R. (2002). The history of the peer-review process. *Trends in Biotechnology*, 20(8): 357–358.

Standring, A. and Lidskog, R. (2021). (How) Does diversity still matter for the IPCC? instrumental, substantive and co-productive logics of diversity in global environmental assessments. *Climate*, 9(6): 99.

Star, S. L. (2010). This is not a boundary object: reflections on the origin of a concept. *Science, Technology, & Human Values*, 35(5): 601–617.

Star, S. L. and Griesemer, J. R. (1989). Institutional ecology, 'translations' and boundary objects: amateurs and professionals in Berkeley's Museum of Vertebrate Zoology, 1907–39. *Social Studies of Science*, 19(3): 387–420.

Stavins, R. (2014). Is the IPCC government approval process broken? 24 April. Available at: www.huffpost.com/entry/is-the-ipcc-government-ap_b_5223421 (Accessed: 19 February 2022).

Stengers, I. (2005). The cosmopolitical proposal. In: Latour, B. and Weibel, P. (eds.), *Making Things Public*. Cambridge, MA: MIT Press. pp. 994–1003.

Stern, P. and Dietz, T. (2015). IPCC: social scientists are ready. *Nature,* 521: 161.

Stirling, A. (2010). Keep it complex. *Nature*, 468: 1029–1031.

Stocker, T. F. and Plattner, G. K. (2016). Making use of the IPCC's powerful communication tool. *Nature Climate Change*, 6(7): 637–638.

Stouffer, R., Eyring, V., Meehl, G. A., et al. (2017). CMIP 5 scientific gaps and recommendations for CMIP 6. *Bulletin of the American Meteorological Society*, 98(1): 95–105.

Sundqvist, G., Bohlin, I., Hermansen, E. and Yearley, S. (2015). Formalization and separation: a systematic basis for interpreting approaches to summarizing science for climate policy. *Social Studies of Science*, 3(45): 416–440.

Sundqvist, G., Gasper, D., Lera St. Clair, A., et al. (2018). One-world or two?: science-policy interactions in the climate field. *Critical Policy Studies*, 12(4): 448–468.

Swart, R., Bernstein, L., Ha-Duong, M. and Petersen, A., (2009). Agreeing to disagree: uncertainty management in assessing climate change, impacts and responses by the IPCC. *Climatic Change*, 92(1): 1–29.

Tàbara, J. D., St. Clair, A. L. and Hermansen, E. A. T. (2017). Transforming communication and knowledge production processes to address high-end climate change. *Environmental Science & Policy*, 70: 31–37.

Tallberg, J., Sommerer, T., Squatrito, T. and Jönsson, C. (2013). *The Opening Up of International Organizations: Transnational Access in Global Governance*. Cambridge: Cambridge University Press.

Teng, F. and Wang, P. (2021). The evolution of climate governance in China: drivers, features, and effectiveness. *Environmental Politics*, 30(Sup.): 141–161.

Tengö, M., Brondizio, E. S., Elmqvist, T., Malmer, P. and Spierenburg, M. (2014). Connecting diverse knowledge systems for enhanced ecosystem governance: the multiple evidence base approach. *Ambio*, 43: 579–591.

Teso-Alonso, M.-G., Morales-Corral, E. and Gaitán-Moya, J.-A. (2021). The climate emergency in the Spanish media and the 'Decalogue of recommendations for reporting on climate change'. *Communication & Society*, 34(2): 107–123.

Tirpak, D. and Vellinga, P. (1990). Emissions scenarios. In: IPCC, *Climate Change: The IPCC Response Strategies*. Cambridge: Cambridge University Press.

Tollefson, J. (2010). Climate science: an erosion of trust? *Nature News*, 466: 24–26.

Touzé-Peiffer, L., Barberousse, A. and Le Treut, H. (2020). The Coupled Model Intercomparison Project: history, uses, and structural effects on climate research. *Wiley Interdisciplinary Reviews: Climate Change*, 11(4): e648.

Trench, B. (2008). Towards an analytical framework of science communication models. In: Cheng, D., Claessens, M., Gascoigne, T., Metcalfe, J., Schiele, B. and Shi, S. (eds.), *Communicating Science in Social Contexts*. Netherlands: Springer. pp. 119–135.

Turnhout, E., Dewulf, A. and Hulme, M. (2016). What does policy-relevant global environmental knowledge do? The cases of climate and biodiversity. *Current Opinion in Environmental Sustainability*, 18: 65–72.

UN (2007). *UNDRIP United Nations General Assembly Declaration of the Rights of Indigenous Peoples, A/RES/61/295*. Available at: www.un.org/esa/socdev/unpfii/documents/DRIPS_en.pdf (Accessed: 2 March 2022).

UNDP (2020). *People's Climate Vote: Results*. www.undp.org/publications/peoples-climate-vote#modal-publication-download

UNEP (2021). *Why Private Sector Engagement Matters*. Available at: www.unep.org/about-un-environment/private-sector-engagement/why-private-sector-engagement-matters (Accessed: 15 January 2022).

UNFCCC (2015). *Adoption of the Paris Agreement. United Nations Framework Convention on Climate Change*. Conference of the Parties (COP) twenty-first session. FCCC/CP/2015/L.9/Rev.1

Vadrot, A. B. M. (2017). Knowledge, international relations and the structure–agency debate: towards the concept of 'epistemic selectivities'. *Innovation: The European Journal of Social Science Research*, 30(1): 61–72.

van Bavel, B. (2021). Indigenous knowledges in the IPCC assessment process: time for a reboot. Chapter 4 in: *Diversifying Knowledge(s) to Advance Climate-Health Responses Locally and Globally*. Unpublished PhD thesis, University of Leeds, UK.

van Beek, L., Hajer, M., Pelzer, P., van Vuuren, D. and Cassen, C. (2020a). Anticipating futures through models: The rise of Integrated Assessment Modelling in the climate science–policy interface since 1970. *Global Environmental Change*, 65: 102191.

van Beek, L., Metze, T., Kunseler, E., Huitzing, H., de Blois, F. and Wardekker, A. (2020b). Environmental visualizations: framing and reframing between science, policy and society. *Environmental Science & Policy*, 114: 497–505.

van den Hove, S. (2007). A rationale for science-policy interfaces. *Futures*, 39(7): 807–826.

van der Hel, S. and Biermann, F. (2017). The authority of science in sustainability governance: a structured comparison of six science institutions engaged with the Sustainable Development Goals. *Environmental Science & Policy*, 77: 211–220.

van der Sluijs, J., van Eijndhoven, J., Shackley, S. and Wynne, B. (1998). Anchoring devices in science for policy: the case of consensus around the climate sensitivity. *Social Studies of Science*, 28(2): 291–323.

van der Veer, L., Visser, H., Petersen, A. and Janssen, P. (2014). Innovating the IPCC review process – the potential of young talent. *Climatic Change*, 125: 137–148.

Vardy, M., Oppenheimer, M., Dubash, N. K., O'Reilly, J. and Jamieson, D. (2017). The Intergovernmental Panel on Climate Change: challenges and opportunities. *The Annual Review of Environment and Resources*, 42: 55–75.

Vasileiadou, E., Heimeriks, G. and Petersen, A. C. (2011). Exploring the impact of the IPCC Assessment Reports on science. *Environmental Science & Policy*, 14(8): 1052–1061.

Vaughan, C. (2016). *An Institutional Analysis of the IPCC Task Group on Data and Scenario Support for Impacts and Climate Analysis (TGICA)*. A working paper of the Climate Services Partnership CSP 20160101. Available at: www.climate-services.org/wp-con tent/uploads/2016/04/Vaughan-TGICA-Institutional-Analysis-Jan-15-2016_final.pdf (Accessed: 3 September 2021).

Venturini, T. (2010). Diving in magma: how to explore controversies with actor-network theory. *Public Understanding of Science,* 19(3): 258–273.

Venturini, T. and Munck, A. (2021). *Controversy Mapping: A Field Guide*. Cambridge: Polity.

Venturini, T., De Pryck, K. and Ackland, R. (2022). Bridging in network organisations: the case of the Intergovernmental Panel on Climate Change (IPCC). *Social Networks*. https://doi.org/10.1016/j.socnet.2022.01.015

Verheggen, B., Strengers, B., Cook, J., et al. (2014). Scientists' views about attribution of global warming. *Environmental Science & Technology*, 48: 8963–8971.

Victor, D. G., Gerlagh, R. and Baiocchi, G. (2014). Getting serious about categorizing countries. *Science*, 345(6192): 34–36.

Victor, D. G. (2015). Embed the social sciences in climate policy. *Nature*, 520: 27–29.

Viner, D. and Howarth, C. (2014). Practitioners' work and evidence in IPCC reports. *Nature Climate Change*, 4: 848–850.

von Bernstorff, J. (2021). New Responses to the legitimacy crisis of international institutions: the role of 'civil society' and the rise of the principle of participation of 'the most affected' in international institutional law. *European Journal of International Law*, 32: 125–157.

Voosen, P. (2020). Europe builds 'digital twin' of Earth to hone climate forecasts. *Science*, 370: 16–17.

Walsh, L. (2010). Before climategate: visual strategies to integrate ethos across the 'is/ ought' divide in the IPCC's Climate Change 2007: Summary for Policy Makers. *Poroi*, 6(2): 33–61.

Walsh, L. (2015). The visual rhetoric of climate change. *Wiley Interdisciplinary Reviews: Climate Change*, 6(4): 361–368.

Wang, Z., Altenburger, R., Backhaus, T., et al. (2021). We need a global science-policy body on chemicals and waste. *Science*, 371: 774–776.

Wardekker, A. and Lorenz, S. (2019). The visual framing of climate change impacts and adaptation in the IPCC assessment reports. *Climatic Change*, 156: 273–292.

Watson, R. T. (2005). Turning science into policy: challenges and experiences from the science–policy interface. *Philosophical Transactions of the Royal Society B: Biological Sciences*, 360(1454): 471–477.

Weart, S. R. (2008). *The Discovery of Global Warming: Revised and Expanded Edition*. Cambridge, MA: Harvard University Press.

Weart, S. R. (2021). *The Discovery of Global Warming: International Cooperation*. Available at: https://history.aip.org/climate/internat.htm (Accessed: 14 August 2021).

Weyant, J., Azar, C., Kainuma, M., et al. (2009). *Report of 2.6 versus 2.9 Watts/m² RCP Evaluation Panel*. Integrated Assessment Modelling Consortium, 2009. Available as IPCC-XXX/INF.6.

Whatmore, S. J. (2009). Mapping knowledge controversies: science, democracy and the redistribution of expertise. *Progress in Human Geography*, 33(5): 587–598.

Whyte, K. (2018). What do Indigenous knowledges do for Indigenous peoples? In: Nelson, M. K. and Shilling, D. (eds.), *Keepers of the Green World: Traditional Ecological Knowledge and Sustainability*. Cambridge: Cambridge University Press. pp. 57–82.

Wible, B. (2014). IPCC lessons from Berlin: Did the 'Summary for Policymakers' become a summary by policy-makers? *Science*, 345(6192):34.

Wilhere, G. (2021). A Paris-like agreement for biodiversity needs IPCC-like science. *Global Ecology and Conservation*, 28: e01617.

Wilkinson, M. D., Dumontier, M., Aalbersberg, A., et al. (2016). The FAIR guiding principles for scientific data management and stewardship. *Scientific Data*, 3: 160018.

Wimsatt, W. K. and Beardsley, M. C. (1946). The intentional fallacy. *The Sewanee Review*, 54(3): 468–488.

World Meteorological Organization (WMO) (2021). *The WMO Building / Conference Centre*. Available at: https://public.wmo.int/en/resources/wmo-building-conference-centre (Accessed: 15 January 2022).

Wynne, B. (1984). The institutional context of science, models, and policy: the IIASA energy study. *Policy Sciences*, 17: 277–320.

Wynne, B. (1993). Public uptake of science: a case for institutional reflexivity. *Public Understanding of Science*, 2: 321–337.

Xue, W., Hine, D., Marks, A., Phillips, W. and Zhao, S. (2016). Cultural worldviews and climate change: a view from China. *Asian Journal of Social Psychology*, 19: 134–144.

Yamineva, Y. (2017). Lessons from the Intergovernmental Panel on Climate Change on inclusiveness across geographies and stakeholders. *Environmental Science & Policy*, 77: 244–251.

Yarrow, T. (2017). Where knowledge meets: heritage expertise at the intersection of people, perspective, and place. *Journal of the Royal Anthropological Institute*, 23(S1): 95–109.

Yearley, S. (2009). Sociology and climate change after Kyoto: what roles for social science in understanding climate change? *Current Sociology*, 57(3): 389–405.

Yona, L,. Cashore, B. and Bradford, M. A. (2022). Factors influencing the development and implementation of national greenhouse gas inventory methodologies. *Policy Design and Practice*. http://doi.org/10.1080/25741292.2021.2020967

Zillman, J. W. (2007). Some observations on the IPCC assessment process 1988–2007. *Energy and Environment*, 18: 869–892.

Zillman, J. W. (2009). A history of climate activities. *WMO Bulletin*, 58(3): 141–150.

Zommers, Z., Marbaix, P., Fischlin, P., et al. (2020). Burning embers: towards more transparent and robust climate-change risk assessments. *Nature Reviews Earth & Environment*, 1: 516–529.

Zorita, E. (2019). The climate of the past millennium and online public engagement in a scientific debate. *Wiley Interdisciplinary Reviews: Climate Change*, 10(5): e590.

Index

Note:

Material in Figures or Tables is indicated with *italic* page locators; material in boxes with **bold** type and references to footnotes carry the suffix 'n'.